HOLLYWOOD PARK

HOLLYWOOD

PARK

A MEMOIR

MIKEL JOLLETT

CELADON
BOOKS
—
NEW YORK

This is a work of nonfiction. In a few cases with minor characters, several different people have been combined into one individual. Also, some names and/or identifying details have been changed to protect the privacy of certain individuals.

HOLLYWOOD PARK. Copyright © 2020 by Mikel Jollett. All rights reserved. Printed in the United States of America. For information, address Celadon Books, a Division of Macmillan Publishers, 120 Broadway, New York, NY 10271.

www.celadonbooks.com

Endpaper photo courtesy of author

Designed by Jonathan Bennett

Library of Congress Cataloging-in-Publication Data

Names: Jollett, Mikel, author.
Title: Hollywood Park : a memoir / Mikel Jollett.
Description: First edition. | New York : Celadon Books, 2020.
Identifiers: LCCN 2020002685 | ISBN 9781250621566 (hardcover) |
    ISBN 9781250621542 (ebook)
Subjects: LCSH: Jollett, Mikel—Childhood and youth. | Rock
    musicians—United States—Biography. | Synanon (Foundation)
Classification: LCC ML420.J7394 A3 2020 | DDC 782.42166092 [B]—dc23
LC record available at https://lccn.loc.gov/2020002685

Our books may be purchased in bulk for promotional, educational, or business use. Please contact your local bookseller or the Macmillan Corporate and Premium Sales Department at 1-800-221-7945, extension 5442, or by email at MacmillanSpecialMarkets@macmillan.com.

First Edition: May 2020

10 9 8 7 6 5 4 3 2 1

For Poppy and Lou

ESCAPE

Some things you forget. Other things you never do. But . . . places, places are still there. If a house burns down, it's gone, but the place—the picture of it—stays, and not just in my rememory, but out there, in the world. What I remember is a picture floating around out there outside my head. I mean, even if I don't think it, even if I die, the picture of what I did, or knew, or saw is still out there. Right in the place where it happened.

–TONI MORRISON, BELOVED

ANCIENT CITIES
TO THE EAST

W e were never young. We were just too afraid of ourselves. No one told us who we were or what we were or where all our parents went. They would arrive like ghosts, visiting us for a morning, an afternoon. They would sit with us or walk around the grounds, to laugh or cry or toss us in the air while we screamed. Then they'd disappear again, for weeks, for months, for years, leaving us alone with our memories and dreams, our questions and confusion, the wide-open places where we were free to run like wild horses in the night.

It happened all at once, my brother and I sitting naked in the bath, playing with our toy boats, listening to the music and the sound of muffled voices from the next room. We are swaddled in red and green wool blankets and readied for sleep: story time, pajamas, the rubbing of tired eyes. Goodnight canyon. Goodnight mountain. Goodnight building. Goodnight stars. Crayons are put away, cubbies cleaned, teeth brushed. I drift to sleep and am rattled awake, surprised to see my mother's face with her shaved head, her hazel-green eyes, her round Dutch cheeks and crooked yellow coffee-stained teeth, "Hi, Goo. Wake up. We have to leave. It's not safe here."

I've been told this woman's name is "Mom." That's what I'm told to call her. I know the word is supposed to have some kind of special meaning. She comes to visit me. She's sadder than the others. She wears overalls and squeezes me, talks about how she misses me, her eyes forever darting around the room like a nervous bird. My eyes are filled with sleep, my head heavy. "But I'm tired."

Bonnie and Clubby are the other women. They're with me every day. They're funny. They talk in strange voices and always have a game to play or a slice of apple or crackers and juice. They call me "Son." Pronounced "Suuuuuun" in a low baritone on account of my deep voice, round belly and overbite that makes my top lip stick out in a funny way. They always say they could just "eat my face." They're big and soft, like warm pillows I can fall into. Clubby talks in a strange way that doesn't use any *r*'s. "Well, waddya think, kid? You gonna get in yo jammies o' wut?" She says it's because she's from a place called New Yoke. Which is far away from California.

The woman I'm told to call "Mom" cries when she comes to visit. She reads me a book or we walk around the compound, the big golden field, or I sit in her lap as she sings songs with words I don't understand—"Fair-a, jhock-a, fair-a jhock-a, door may voo, door may voo." She combs my hair, tells me she misses me. "Don't be sad, Mom," I tell her. I tell her that most of all. "Don't be so sad all the time." She stares at me when I eat like she's trying to memorize something, like she's about to say something but decides not to.

"I love you, Goo. My little boy." Tears in her eyes fall on the bib of her clean blue overalls. Everyone wears overalls here. I have three pairs. Then she disappears again and I find Clubby and Bonnie and we laugh and build things out of Popsicle sticks or play hide-and-seek with the other kids until bath time, then song time, singing:

There's a land that I see where the children are free . . .

Then bedtime when there are stories of dragons and castles and baby birds and moons that talk to children and children who talk to cats and blue butterflies that talk to lions. Then they say goodnight to me, to Cassidy, to Guy, to Dmitri—my best buddy—then Noah.

When I wake up, when all the other kids are still sleeping, Mom shakes me and says, "We have to go, we have to go now. You have to be quiet, honey."

I tell her I need some water. She has a look I've never seen as I feel my chest sink into itself like there's something sharp and hot at the bottom of my throat. "What about Clubby and Bonnie?"

"Shhh . . . We can write to them, I promise." She picks me up. The other kids are fast asleep. There's a soft yellow light coming from the doorway of the bathroom with the low toilet next to the craft tables. Debbie, who watches over us at night, stands next to the woman I am told to call Mom. She looks scared. My brother Tony is in the doorway, already dressed, his arms crossed. His head is shaved just like mine.

"Where are we going, Mom?" My throat is dry and I feel a blankness spreading from my stomach, up over my chest, going out over my arms and legs to my fingers and toes.

"To the car, to go see Grandma and Grandpa."

A car? I don't understand. I've seen cars driving in and out of the long driveway at the front of the building but I've never been in one. They look so big and fast. I wonder if it will feel like flying. When Dad comes to visit, he rides a loud, two-wheel car called a moto-cycle. He leans back on the seat with his hands on the handlebars which makes it look exactly like he's floating on air.

The world is as big as the playground, the field, the forest on the far side of the road and this room where I sleep with Dmitri and Cassidy after song time, as big as Clubby and Bonnie with their funny voices and tomato soup and toast.

The woman I'm told to call Mom is looking for my shoes. Debbie goes to the cubby closet and opens the door to the cubby where I keep my overalls, underwear, socks and the baseball Dad gave me signed by Steve Garvey, who is a professional baseball player. Dad likes baseball, I think. I have a bag where I keep my toothbrush and a yellow plastic comb that's too big for my shaved head. I have marbles and chalk and the pictures I drew with Bonnie on construction paper. I don't have any toys. None that are mine anyway. All the kids have to share our toys and no one can even keep a bike if someone brings you one.

Debbie puts my things in a paper bag and hands them to Mom. We start for the door. "Wait, Mom. No one will know where I am when they wake up."

"It's okay sweetie."

"Shut up dummy!" Tony says.

"Shhhhhh!!" Mom pulls him to her hip.

"But why do we have to leeeeeave?"

She lets out a deep breath, puts me on the ground, gathers us like a mother hen.

She squints, holding her eyes closed tight, her hands over her forehead, then opens them and looks at me, grabbing my hands in hers. She reaches for Tony but he turns away. "Listen, I know you don't understand, but we have to leave right now and we can't let anyone find out, okay? So I need you guys to be quiet. We're going on an adventure."

Her eyes move wildly from me to my brother, back to me. "You can sleep in the car. And when you wake up, you'll be at Grandma and Grandpa's house and we'll all have Dutch rolls and cheese."

There's no reasoning with her. I try to imagine what the house looks like. I've never left the School, which is what everyone calls this place. I wonder if it's got a big door. Mom once told me they had lots of music boxes, that Grandma was crazy for small boxes that play music when you open them.

I look at Tony's face for clues but he's got his chin pressed against the door frame, holding the paper bag with his stuff in it. My head feels woozy as my eyes fall on the buttons of Debbie's blue overalls. She's nice but she's new. I miss Clubby because she used to be with us at night and would hold me when I had a bad dream and call me Suuuuuun. She would tell me we were safe here, all of us here in Synanon, living together, a great big family, a tribe of humans who love each other and love the world and love the little babies most of all.

Debbie whispers something to Mom. Tony is mad. I'm told he's my brother. I see him on the playground but he never plays with the other kids. He sits by himself. I sit by him sometimes but I don't think he likes me because he pushes me and tells me to leave him alone. He's three years older and twice my size. People say we look like each other but I don't see it.

Mom picks us up. She seems so much like a giant bird. Like she swooped down from the sky and got us. I want to tell her not to worry, that I can fly too. I'm strong enough and sometimes when I'm dreaming, my ears get big—big enough to be like wings—and I can fly anywhere I want. I just flap them and soar way up into the sky. I tell myself, *Remember, you have to remember this when you wake up. You can fly.* And I'm remembering now because I just woke up. I want to tell her but there's no time. She beats her wings and we take flight over the school, the playground, the yard, the field, the buildings, the entire Synanon compound where we played games and ate and sang and slept. Where we heard the adults screaming through the speakers of the Wire, the in-house radio, with its crackle and hiss letting us hear the sounds of people laughing, people crying, people yelling, people dancing, a jazz band playing music. The Punk Squad, the mean teenagers with their cursing and cuffed jeans getting punched in the face if they ever talk back. Every week one of them runs away and everybody gets so mad. The sound of Chuck, the Old Man, the leader, talking about things we don't understand. He says he loves us but he's always so angry. And the bird, we are told to call her "Mom," flapping furiously, eyes locked on some faraway point as she clutches her chicks and we fly up over Tomales Bay with its streams draining into the Pacific Ocean, the giant redwoods on the hillside, the big waves crashing against the rocks on the coast, slowly breaking them into tiny pieces, fracturing them, pulling them apart—until they're soft to the touch, portable and broken, easy to walk on, to place into a small plastic bag for a tourist visiting with sunburned ankles from some ancient city to the east.

CHAPTER 2

THE BIG ROAD

There's a brown car waiting in the parking lot at the front of the compound. The driveway looks different at night. I've seen stars before, when Bonnie and Clubby would take us outside to lie on our backs and look up at the sky. Bonnie and I have chosen a star for me. It's easy to find, hanging over the pine trees at the edge of the field. But I don't see it. I wonder where it's gone. I want to point at it and name it and say hello. All I can hear is the shuffling of our feet, a soft cooing from the woods and the rumble of the engine in the parking lot. The air smells damp, like concrete and pine needles, a big cloud of steam bursting from behind the long brown sedan. There's a man sitting in the front seat with a short blond mustache that goes halfway across his upper lip.

I can't believe my luck that I get to ride in a car. "Is that your car, Mom? Who's that man?"

"That's your grandfather." She opens the rear door and helps us in.

"Hi-dee do," says Grandpa Frank. I see his eyes in the little mirror. He looks like an older, short, mannish version of Mom. Same round cheeks which I'm later told are something called "Dutch." Mom has told me stories about him, that he was on the Olympic team for Dutch but that he couldn't go because they canceled the Olympics because of the war. Mom says Grandpa has the strongest hands in the world because he was a gymnast, that he was in two different armies for two different countries, America and Dutch. She told me he was far away fighting the Germans when she was born and that Grandma Frieda sent him a picture of her.

She showed it to me once: it was a round-cheeked baby girl sitting on a chair in a white apron, a bonnet on her head. "Daddy carried this on his ship. Carried it in his pocket." He would look at the picture, crouched in a hole in the ground when the Germans would drop bombs on him and his friends in a place called the Bulge where there was a big battle and awful things happened but Grandpa won't talk about it because it was so terrible. All he'd ever say is that he would look at the picture and whisper, "Gerredina. Daddy loves you."

"Hi Dad." Mom climbs into the front seat. She looks around, scanning the parking lot, the woods, the driveway that leads to the Big Road.

"Where are we going?" Tony says.

Grandpa Frank is frozen in his seat, staring straight ahead, hands on the steering wheel. Mom turns around.

"We're leaving, honey."

"Will we be back by lunch?"

"No. I'm sorry. We won't."

"But Noah has my baseball card!" Tony yells, stomping his foot.

"I'll get you some new cards," Grandpa says.

It's strange to hear a man speak. We're so used to the women. His voice is deep and certain. The men don't come to the School very often and when they do, we stare at them like wild beasts from our storybooks. They have beards or mustaches, big muscles and leather boots. Some are bald with hair on their arms, necks and chests. They're so tall and when they play with us, they throw us in the air to show us how much stronger they are. It's fun to be small next to something so big.

"Okay," Tony mumbles. I can tell he's just as stunned as me. We aren't used to the men.

Mom closes her eyes and puts her hands over her ears. She rubs her temples. She looks exactly like Noah when he got stuck in the big tree behind the School.

"Are we going to live with Grandma and Grandpa?"

"For a little while, yes. But then we'll probably live somewhere else."

"But what about Bonnie and Clubby?" I ask. "And Dmitri? Will I see them? Are they leaving too? Are they coming with us?"

"I don't know if they're leaving. I hope so. We can write to them."

"What does that mean?" I can write letters. I know my alphabet as well as Dmitri and we read books together, at bedtime, and sometimes during the day. But I don't understand why writing matters, what the letters on a piece of paper have to do with sitting on Bonnie's lap naming stars or playing with Clubby and being called Suuuuuun.

"You're just gonna have to trust me, honey. We have to go now."

The ride down the driveway is bumpy. I'm amazed as I'm pushed back into the seat. I look back at the School. The rear window looks like a giant movie. I think about my friends asleep in their cots, the time I woke up in the middle of the night to find Dmitri talking with his eyes closed. I got out of my cot and put my ear right up next to his mouth to hear what he was saying, but it was just pieces of words. "He's dreaming," Clubby whispered. I looked over my shoulder and saw her smiling face, the deep-set eyes with heavy black circles, the short clipped hair, the massive shoulders protruding up in swells from beneath the straps of her overalls. "Sometimes when people are dreaming, they talk and sometimes they don't."

"Will he hear me if I talk to him?"

"Nah, he can't hear you. He's not really there. He's somewhere in his head. That's what a dream is. When you imagine you're somewhere you've never been while you're sleeping."

The stars are moving so quickly behind the Synanon compound as we turn onto the highway. The Big Road! Wow! I try to flap my ears so I can fly back. I want to hug Bonnie and sit next to Dmitri's cot to see if he's dreaming right now. Maybe we both are. Maybe this is his dream. How can you tell?

My brother sits on the other side of the backseat. He keeps pushing down on his knuckles with his cheek until they pop. Our brown paper bags are stacked between us.

I feel a pull toward the playground and the yard, a tug like a string stretched to a breaking point. I want to crawl into Bonnie's lap, to sleep. But the highway—there are other cars on it going so fast they look like blurs, like the wings of a hummingbird. The green signs go by overhead with names of places on them: San Francisco, Los Angeles, Oakland, Sacramento. It feels exactly like flying in my dreams, like my arms stretched behind me, legs tucked and I'm leaping, higher and higher until I'm up above all of it, looking down. And there, from that perch above the clouds, I see a stone wall that rises to a gray tower. I can just walk across the cloud and let myself in. When I close my eyes, I see all the people from Synanon: crying and dancing and laughing and screaming and riding swings and eating macaroni and cheese. Bonnie, Clubby, Dmitri, Cassidy, Guy, Noah. And Dad. I close my eyes hard to see Dad, but I can't. He's blurry like the cars on the highway. So I open them and see Mom hunched over in the front seat, her round Dutch cheeks covered in tears and my brother with his mouth tight and his fists clenched, staring out the window at the strange cars and highway signs.

MOM WAS RIGHT about the music boxes. Grandma and Grandpa's house is filled with them. There is one in the bedroom that has a picture of a blue windmill and one in the living room made of old wood. They play pretty songs when you open them. There's another in the kitchen where we eat Dutch cheese and rolls. In the living room there's something called a grandfather clock. There are some small clocks sitting on shelves, some are made of crystal, some of metal, one is made from a green stone and has a white face with no numbers. That one's my favorite.

In Synanon we had tables and chairs and poster board and a big swing set and dishes made of plastic. We ate and made crafts at short wooden tables. This house is filled with paintings and furniture that's been carved to look like waves or flowers or faces or buildings. There's an old fisherman in a ratty hat staring down at the dining room table, a cat made of glass that prowls on the shelf in the living room. There's a painting on tiles of little rivers that go right through a city in Dutch. The couch is creamy white with little green flowers and stuffed thicker than any pillows I've ever seen. I wonder if a king lives here since Grandpa's golden chair looks like a throne.

I like Grandpa Frank because he talks to us and whenever we leave to go somewhere, he gives us a "smack on the fanny," which means a hard hit on the butt. He's funny about it, lining us up one by one. It's true that his hands are very strong. He lets me grab his fingers and squeeze as hard as I can while he laughs.

He's always making little jokes with us. We'll say, "What are we doing today, Grandpa?"

And he'll say, "Today, we are going to the dump."

We'll laugh and say, "No we're not! We're gonna play!" Because we know he's going to take us to collect golf balls in his golf cart or to see his boat, the little white one he keeps at the dock.

Grandma will lean in and say, "Stop teasing the boys, Frank."

"Jokes! It's important to laugh, you know."

Grandma is skinny with blue-white hair and small teeth so that you can barely see them when she smiles, if she smiles. Her face is bunched up, like she's hiding something, something that escapes little by little through the day as she sits in her favorite chair in a thin blue robe across from Grandpa, drinking from a tall cup filled with ice and "Dutch." That's what she calls it: "Frank, dear, will you refill my Dutch?" Grandpa gets up from his throne and walks over to a small counter where he pours an orangish-brown liquid from a crystal bottle into the tall glass. It smells like sweet gasoline. She drinks the Dutch all day long every day and as she gets sleepier, her meanness leaves her like air from a balloon so that by the time dinnertime comes, she wants us to come sit by her. She smiles with her little teeth and says, "Hi schweety, are you happy here? Would you like a piece of candy?"

Mom says Grandma's family lived in America before she moved to Dutch. Her dad was a coal miner and their family did something called quaking, which made them Quakers, so Grandma couldn't do fun stuff like dance or play cards. One day she moved to New York to become a nurse which is where she met Grandpa who took her back to Dutch.

The mornings are worse for her. She says, "I have such a headache. Frank, dear, will you bring me my pills?" She shuffles her feet when she walks like she's afraid to take steps too big while Grandpa Frank gets her pills or her slippers or her breakfast or another sweating glass of Dutch delivered at eleven fifteen A.M. sharp.

Mom is gone in the afternoons when Tony and I play outside on the grass. Grandpa sits on his chair and calls out, "A dit dit dit . . . Watch out for the bees." I don't know if this is Dutch or if it's just how grandpas talk because I've never known another grandpa. They were in our storybooks with their white hair and bent backs. They have something to do with the moms and the dads. They seem permanent, like the trees. Grandpa tells us we have to be nice to Mom. She's been through so much.

Grandma says at least she "finally got away from that awful place and good riddance to that drug addict ex-husband of hers."

I know she's talking about Dad but in Synanon everyone was a drug addict so I don't understand why she's so mad about it. Anyway we never used the words "drug addict." We would just say someone was a Dope Fiend. People said this with pride and I'm pretty sure that's what we are and if someone were to ask us whether we are white or black or Dutch or Italian, I'm not really sure but I know we're all Dope Fiends because that's all anyone ever talks about.

Tony draws monsters. I draw superheroes. Tony draws big battle scenes with tanks and soldiers and explosions, beasts with horns and big teeth that drip blood. They hold axes and clubs and guns in their claws. My superheroes fly through the air trying to kill the monsters. It's never clear who wins. Grandpa says we should draw something nice for Mom so I draw a picture of her with long hair because even though it's shaved all the way to the scalp and everybody stares at her when we go to Goodwill, she says it used to be long and pretty and that's the way she likes to see herself in pictures. Plus she says men like long hair and she wants to be pretty for a man and no man wants a single mom with a bald head.

Mom gets an album and shows me photos from when she was growing up in Holland. She shows me the house where they lived. She says she grew up speaking Dutch which sounds like if you speak with peanut butter and crackers in your mouth. She didn't come to the United States until she was fourteen and there was no one to speak Dutch with anymore so she spoke English or she didn't speak at all.

She tells me there were bomb craters all around the neighborhood that she used to play in. They were like giant tears in the earth, like a piece of the earth had been scooped out. There was a war and Grandpa fought in it and that's when she was born and afterward she lived in a big house but there was still rubble everywhere and those giant holes in the ground right in the middle of where everybody lived.

I ask her if she ever saw the bombs go off. She says it was all over by then but that craters from a war are a good place for a kid to go and hide.

CHAPTER 3

C–U–L–T

No one ever tells us we escaped from a cult. No one uses that word, except Grandma. Everyone else calls it Synanon or sometimes they say it was a "commune." And everyone says it was great, "before it went bad." That's how they put it. Like it was milk that went sour.

When Mom argues with Grandma in the living room, she says that it saved our lives. She'll put her hands up and say, "Where was I supposed to go?"

Grandma says, "You could've come home! I knew it was a mistake sending you to Berkeley." Mom doesn't know what to do when people get mad at her. It's like she's missing the piece of the brain made for yelling so instead she crumples up like a piece of paper and buries her head under pillows. She tells us how important Berkeley was. How she went off to college when she was only fifteen because she was so smart and she met all kinds of new people there and she learned how to change the world by sitting down in different places so they could beat Thatasshole Reagan.

She marched and she sat and she sang and they got hit with tears gas because they needed to stop a war (it was in a place called Vietnam) and have Civil Rights but Thatasshole Reagan didn't want those things so he sent soldiers to launch tears gas at them which made them cry. They sat on the street with their arms locked and the soldiers on horses came straight at them and they weren't sure if they were going to die but that's what you have to do if you want to change the world.

Mom always says, "Synanon was mild compared to Berkeley." Berkeley was the center of the world, she says. And the government was killing young men "to defend a lie." I don't know what the lie was but I bet she was scared. She says the bodies of those young boys were *hidden*. Like we're supposed to forget they died at all. I don't know who these boys are or how old they were or if we're next. And I'm proud of Mom for trying to stop it and protect the boys like us, even though Thatasshole Reagan threw tears gas at her (which might explain why she cries so much, it's the gas).

I wonder about the bodies. Where did they hide them? Could I stumble on one in the bushes outside Grandma and Grandpa's house? Are people sad?

Mom says that Synanon was going to change the world, before it went bad. Synanon was going to be the new way people lived, all together, being honest and free and not taking drugs. She says people needed a new way to live because the old way wasn't working anymore and she was proud to be part of it, this new group of people who were going to change the world.

It all sounds great when she tells it but did they have to make it so the kids were alone so much?

"Synanon was *mild*?" Grandma gets so mad when Mom says that. "They took your kids, Gerry, and put them in that, that *place*." She spits the word out like a piece of meat caught in her small teeth.

"Synanon had a good school." The School is where they put the kids when they took us from our parents. It's where we all lived from the time we were six months old. Since Chuck, the Old Man, said that Dope Fiends would just mess up their kids anyway, we were all put in a building together to become children of the universe. You had to listen to Chuck. We had Demonstrators who were like teachers and classes and songs and I was lucky because I had a Bonnie. She would hug me every day and sing songs with me and call me "Suuuuuun" and ask me what I want for a snack.

Most of the other kids didn't have a Bonnie though and some never even saw their moms or their dads. They just never came to visit. Dmitri said he doesn't remember his mom's face. She was somewhere else. He didn't know where his dad was. The Demonstrators say we don't need our parents because we have each other. But we don't like sharing our toys and

I didn't know who to talk to when I woke up with a bad dream or fell off the monkey bars.

The older kids say that in the World Outside Synanon kids live with their parents and their parents take care of them. They hug you and kiss you and talk to you and pick you up. And it's the same ones every day. They take you places and those are all your people and the whole group is something called a "family."

All the kids in Synanon wish they had one of those.

Even if the mom or the dad was a Dope Fiend or busy trying to change the world. At least you weren't alone.

Some of the kids were very sad. Tony used to sit alone at the edge of the playground all day. He would turn away when one of the Demonstrators tried to hug him. He doesn't trust the adults and he doesn't play with other kids that much. When Mom came to visit, she would say he's just like that and he needs to learn how to "deal with his anger." But maybe it's because someone did bad things to him. That happened sometimes. The kids would get hit really hard or locked in a closet and there was no mom or dad to tell because they lived somewhere else and you couldn't even remember their faces.

Maybe it's just because he was alone so much. He's almost seven and I don't think Mom knows what it's like to be alone for almost seven years.

Mom says it was "a good school."

"It was an orphanage!" Grandma screams. "That's what you call a place where strangers raise your kids!" Grandma says that Mom doesn't even know who put us to bed or who woke us up or who taught us to read. She says we were sitting ducks. (We did play Duck Duck Goose a lot.) "You made them orphans, Gerry!" Grandma will point at us from her chair as we pretend not to listen. She has less control by the late afternoon, after her third or fourth glass of Dutch.

Mom doesn't hear her. She's good at not hearing people. If we tell her we're hungry, she'll say, "No you're not. You ate earlier." If one of us says, "I'm sad," she tells us it's not true, that we're happy now because we're with her.

It's strange for someone to tell you your own feelings but maybe she knows better than we do.

She never says, "Why are you sad?" or "It'll be okay." It's like we're not allowed to be sad. We're not allowed to be anything but what she tells us. She won't hit us or scream. She'll just wrap herself up in a ball on the couch and let her face go all blank. She'll say, "It's not my fault," as she rocks her knees on the bed. She shakes her head and stares or she starts to cry until one of us tells her it'll be okay, that we're not sad, Mom, we were just kidding. We're happy now because we are with her. Then she'll wipe her tears and tell us she missed us every day.

Sometimes when we talk to her, she just stares at the ceiling with her hands on her chest and her face goes blank like she isn't there at all. Grandpa says she's sad but Grandma calls it the "deep-russian." Tony will shake her shoulder or flash his hand in front of her face. We're not sure what to do because we don't know her very well. We only know her from the visits. And if she has the "deep-russian" then we know it's our job to get her out of it because who else is going to do it?

We know she hates Thatasshole Reagan because she and Grandma argue about it. They argue about everything. Mom says, "Reagan is a fascist, Mother." Or, "If Thatasshole wins the presidency, we won't have a thing in the world." When Mom says this, Grandma stares at her like something is ticking inside her, something turning and turning alone in her head like the crushed ice at the bottom of her glass.

"He was governor. You kids didn't stop anything. It was a big tantrum. A tantrum with slogans and songs and drugs. Why couldn't you just stay at Mills College? Why did you have to leave for Berkeley?"

Mom laughs when Grandma says that because everyone knows you couldn't use drugs in Synanon. That was the whole point. She tells her that the people in Synanon were starting a better world. Then she'll say, "I hated Mills, Mother. All those future Stepford wives learning how to be obedient little cogs in the machine of commerce."

"At least they got to lead normal lives. You go off and join some cult."

There's that word again. C-U-L-T. I know my letters because everyone at Synanon knows their letters, even the little kids. My favorite one is O. I like to imagine there's a whole world on the other side of it, a quiet place you can go to take a nap if you can just make yourself small enough to fit through the middle.

"C-U-L-T" is an ugly word. It looks like the C is spitting the U right at the L. The T is standing still with its arms out, trying to keep its distance from the other letters. They don't seem like four letters that want to be in the same word together. Maybe that's why everyone looks so mad when they say it.

"Well, I wish I hadn't given them my babies," Mom whispers. She looks at us. She always tells us Dad would've died without Synanon because he was such a Dope Fiend that he ended up in prison and he needed to go to Synanon and live there and play the Game so he could be out of prison and clean from drugs and not die.

Grandpa cooks dinner in the kitchen and Grandma is in her stuffed green chair in a robe, the glass of Dutch on the tray next to her.

"I liked Jimmy. Everyone did. He was funny." When Dad visited us on his moto-cycle, you could hear the noise from the engine echoing off the hills and fields. We'd stop whatever we were doing and run to the front of the School because we knew it was him and he was a Tribe Leader, which meant he was really important in Synanon. Even Chuck respected him because nobody was tougher than Dad. He managed the gas station on Pico where the auto mechanics worked back before he moved to Tomales Bay because everyone said he knew a lot about cars, and people. He'd get off the bike and turn off the engine and we'd run up to him and he'd scoop us up.

We felt safe with Dad even though Grandma says mean things about him. "I know he quit the heroin, but I'll never understand how you could marry someone who just got out of prison."

Tony says Dad went to Synanon after an overdose, which is when you take too many drugs and your body goes to sleep. Some friends just dropped him on the front porch one day. Chuck, the Old Man, let him in and Dad spent a week on the couch shivering and throwing up into a bucket. That's how the heroin gets out of your body, through all the puke.

Mom gives Grandma a sharp look then points at us.

"How could you trust a man like that?"

Grandma is cooking rice with chicken that she learned to make for Grandpa when he was in a place called "Indianezia." It's my favorite. He'll stay in the kitchen looking after it while Mom and Grandma argue. Grandpa says that after he got home from the war, he had a company that took boats from Dutch to a place called Indianezia so that people in Dutch could have things from there. The house is filled with masks and little statues of smiling women in pointy gold hats, wooden men with bones through their noses that he brought back from Indianezia. They had a big house in Dutch where Mom and her sister Pam, who is something called an aunt, and her brother Jon, who is something called an uncle (those are things that happen in "families"), all lived with him and Grandma. They even had a maid who lived there with her husband and they took care of the babies a lot of the time. Mom says that's who raised her, the nanny, because Grandpa had his boats and Grandma had her Dutch.

Maybe that's why she put us in the School, because she didn't think parents were supposed to raise their kids.

This was before they moved to America when Mom was fourteen years old so she and Jon and Pam could go to good American colleges like Stanford.

When Uncle Jon comes to visit, you can hear him for miles. He drives a big, loud moto-cycle like Dad. He doesn't look like the Synanon people with their shaved heads because he's got a long beard and long blond hair. Mom says he came to visit us in Synanon once and just sat in the back thinking all the people were weird. He's nice to us, making jokes like Grandpa does.

Aunt Pam visits too with her kids who are something called cousins (there sure are a lot of titles to keep track of when you have something called a family). Their names are Marci and Paul and they play with us on the floor or draw at the table. Uncle Jon gave us another cousin named Heidi. Cousins are good because they're like friends who look like you. Aunt Pam has Dutch cheeks like Mom and a warm laugh and she'll hug us and tell us she missed us when we were "in that place." Mom will give her a look and everyone gets quiet.

Mom says our dad "wasn't so bad," and Grandma gets so angry. "He was a criminal! And a junkie! And he left you for a tramp." I pretend to look away. "A good man would've stayed. A good man would've gotten you out of that horrible place!"

Mom says that she and Dad are "friends" now and that they both "love us very much." I'm not sure what a tramp is but since everyone lived together in Synanon, Mom had to walk downstairs the day after Dad left while I was still in her belly and Dad was sitting in the big common room with the tramp on his lap. Mom says she knew then that she had to be strong for me because it was her job to guard me because I was a special life that had to be born into the world.

Tony says Dad was thinking with his ding-a-ling.

"All I ever wanted was a man to take care of me. Just a normal man."

"Then why'd you marry a drug addict?" Grandma looks at Mom who holds a pillow on her lap, staring at the blank white walls. "I don't know what you expect your father and I to do but at some point you need to learn that the world isn't just some fantasyland. All the crazies and weirdos and here you are with no husband, no money, two kids and a shaved head. You look like a mental patient."

Grandma doesn't know that you have to be nice to Mom or she'll go into the deep-russian.

"Who's hungry?" Grandpa yells.

"Do you think that's why we moved to California? So you could end up like this?"

Mom sits still on the couch like she's trying to solve a problem in her head. "I just wanted to see you. We'll leave soon."

"And what are you going to do with them?" She lifts her palm toward the dining room table where Grandpa put the steaming-hot bowls of spicy chicken and rice. "You know the crazies are looking for you and you can't hide those kids forever."

CHAPTER 4

BLOOD ON THE DRIVEWAY

The apartment in East Oakland is on the second floor of a building that looks like a giant spaceship. There are blue stairways that look like jets and huge pipes on the roof that look like a nose pointing toward space. It's our new home. It sits on a corner across from a gas station and a hamburger stand with an electric sign saying, "Oscar's Char Broiled ¼ lb. Burgers." Tony says there's nothing better than a cheeseburger and fries but how would he know? We've never been to a restaurant.

There's no furniture in the apartment when we move in so we take our clothes out of the brown grocery bags and make neat piles in the living room for a couch. Tony stacks the jackets for a bed and I make a table from our shoes so we can kick our feet up. It's better than regular furniture because we can use our imaginations and make the pile into any shape we want.

When we lie down to stare at the ceiling, Mom sets up her record player. It's a small plastic suitcase that unfolds into little speakers and a turntable. All she has to do is plug it in and suddenly the empty room is filled with voices and instruments, all the people she carries with her in her record collection: Joan Baez and Bob Dylan, Duke Ellington, Miles Davis, Tchaikovsky and Beethoven, small white 45s of the Beatles and the Doors.

The record player is always on in the spaceship because it feels less empty that way.

She makes us chicken soup on a hot plate since there's no stove and pours it into white plastic cups which she says saves us time because it means we don't have to do dishes like other people. The shoe table won't hold the soup and crackers so we sit on the floor, leaning back against the wall to listen to Joan Baez.

When she sings, her voice fills the room like she's hanging over us, high and silky, a sad angel who makes us feel like we are swimming in a sea of Joan Baezes, surrounded by her voice. It gets in your ears and fills your head, surrounding it, bouncing off the clothing and the shoe table, the T-shirts and socks and underwear that make up the bed. There's a long window on the front wall. We can hear the cars outside and someone yelling as they walk down the street while we blow on our cups of soup. Mom says it's good that we are "with the people now and not holed up in some guarded fortress like Nixon."

We are the only four people on earth. Tony, me, Mom, and Joan Baez. Her voice echoes off the tinny walls of our spaceship:

> There is a house in New Orleans
> They call the Rising Sun
> And it has been the ruin of many a poor girl
> And me, oh God, I'm one.

Mom says Synanon was like a giant circle, bigger than anything and leaving feels like she's outside of it, outside of herself which is also the circle. She doesn't know who the person inside her head is without it. The space feels so small with only her.

She tells us about the Synanon band, the dancing they did every night after the Game. Everyone would gather in a big room and dance, letting their bodies shake and shiver and jump and flap. "We knew how to have a good time. No doubt about that," she says, shaking her head and looking out the window at the flashing sign for Oscar's Burgers. "And your father was a great dancer." She says they danced all night. That it was special to dance with friends and they were in love and free from the eyes of the world. That was the good part about it. The music.

We drift to sleep. When I wake up, Mom is snoring on her back with Tony on one side and me on the other. It's strange to be in a new place. The silence. The darkness. The strange voices from the sidewalk. *Where are Dmitri and Bonnie and Clubby? Are they in the circle? Am I outside the circle now?*

Mom tells us that things are different here in the World Outside Synanon. That the World Outside Synanon has different rules than Synanon did. We can let our hair grow and we can own bikes and kids live with their moms and dads. There's no Game, which was a big circle where everyone would sit and yell at each other. Everyone in Synanon had to play it. It started as something only Dope Fiends did so that new Dope Fiends could learn from old Dope Fiends, because it's hard for Dope Fiends to hear anything unless someone is yelling at them. At first it was something called Group Therapy but then it changed when the Old Man decided it needed to be more extreme. That's when all the yelling happened.

People liked it for some reason so when all the Squares moved in, the people like Mom who didn't do drugs but wanted to live in Synanon so they could change the world, they played it too. You could be mean in the Game. You could say anything. You could call someone an "asshole" or a "bastard" or a "piece of shit." You could accuse them of doing bad things, say all the ways they were lying and running and hiding. You could say the worst things about them. But then when it was over, you had to be nice. You had to smile and hug the person you just called a piece of shit. They had to hug you back and pretend they weren't mad and wait until the next Game to call you an asshole.

In the Game everyone was equal but Mom says that "some people were more equal than others," because everyone knew you couldn't say bad things about Chuck or the other leaders, even if they were mean, even if they made you get divorced and shaved your head and took your kids away.

That's what made it a C-U-L-T.

Everything in the World Outside Synanon is so much bigger than everything used to be. That's what I think when we go for a drive to San Jose. There are cars in the streets and huge buildings and buses filled with people all staring ahead, not talking to each other. The noise comes from machines. Jackhammers and lawn mowers, air conditioners and diesel engines shooting black smoke in the air. There's so much movement. So many people. *Why don't they talk to each other?*

We go to Oscar's for lunch and Tony wants a whole cheeseburger. Mom says he'll never finish it so we have to share one instead. It comes with a basket of hot, salty yellow French fries the size of our fingers that we cover in ketchup. When Mom cuts the Oscar burger in half, red juice and mustard squirt into the basket and Tony and I lift our halves to toast them like princes. I think this must be how rich people live with cheeseburgers for lunch whenever you want. Tony says Dad took him for burgers before but I don't believe him because he eats his whole half, licks the salty juice off his hands then licks the waxy paper from the bottom of the basket.

We cross a huge bridge made of metal and concrete and see the water stretched out in all directions, the factories on the shoreline behind us, Alcatraz prison in the middle of the bay surrounded by boats. *Everything is so big! What could have made it all? How could you think of everything at once?*

It feels like something created by giants. Like they walked the earth and put a building here, a bridge there, kicking a tunnel into the mountain with their giant shoes.

It's late by the time we get back from dinner at Grandma and Grandpa's house in San Jose and when we get to the top of the stairs of the spaceship, the apartment door is wide open. Mom pulls Tony and me toward the railing. "Hello?" She leans forward squeezing my hand. "Is someone there?" We wait outside while she goes through the door.

Tony says maybe Dad came to visit so we look for his moto-cycle in the parking lot on the other side of the railing but we don't see it anywhere.

We hear Mom's voice coming from the inside of the apartment, "Oh, dear . . . For heaven's sake . . . Well, shit."

We go inside and find her sitting in the middle of the floor. Our stuff is everywhere, the bags turned over, the clothing and records spread out on the cream carpets.

"I don't get it," Mom says. "What could we possibly have that somebody would want to steal?"

We wait outside for the police and when they arrive, they nod at us as they walk by with their flashlights darting around the room, bursting through the big window in the front of the spaceship.

One of the two cops asks Mom questions from the doorway while she sits on the floor with her back against the wall. He's got a brown mustache and a real live gun in a black holster on his waist. He wants to know if we had any valuables. Any jewelry or a TV set or credit cards?

Mom looks embarrassed as she shakes her head.

"We had a record player," Tony says. It must be worth something since it's what filled up the empty room.

Mom kneels down. We sift through the thrift-store jeans and socks, placing them in a big pile in the center of the room. Bob Dylan has a boot mark right through his leather jacket. Some of the other records are under clothes or thrown against the wall. The record player is gone.

The cop asks if it was valuable. Mom shakes her head and tells him it was just an old plastic thing.

THERE'S A PICTURE of Dad we keep in a small golden frame on the windowsill at the front of the apartment. He's stretched out on his back smiling with his shaved head, sideburns, and big black mustache. I take it down sometimes to stare at it, trying to imagine where he is and what he's doing. When I see my face in the mirror, I don't see him. People say sons look like their fathers but I have corn-silk hair and big funny teeth, a pug nose and Dutch cheeks like Mom. Dad has black hair and a big Italian nose. There's a darkness around his eyes, his skin deep brown, the color of caramel and there's something to the smile, something like a flash of light, the feeling that he's already laughing at the joke he wants to tell you.

Mom said he left Synanon too, that it's just too crazy now that they're splitting up marriages and forcing all the men to have vast-ectomies. Since the Old Man's wife died, he decided no one should be married. So hundreds of couples had to get divorced. It was for the good of the world, he said. So they had a big meeting and decided everyone would get a new partner and one day everyone found out who their new husband or wife was, even if it was someone they didn't know that well. Mom says that some people thought that was nuts and that's when a lot of people started to leave. Because only a C-U-L-T would do a crazy thing like that.

This made the Old Man angry so he started a group that had guns and boots and trained how to fight and these men started beating people up who were trying to leave. They called them "splittees," the people who tried to leave. "Dirty fucking splittees."

Dad left too. He's living with another woman and her daughter some-where near Los Angeles now.

Phil is the only man we know. He's a friend of Mom's from Synanon. He parks his van in the long driveway next to the spaceship. He knocks on the door every few days so he can come inside to use our shower. He just left too and is still getting used to the World Outside Synanon. His orange VW camper van looks like a giant pumpkin. He'll bow his head when he walks through the doorway, holding his towel and toothbrush in his hand, his shoulders hunched, the wire glasses, the soft voice asking about the soap. He stays for dinner sometimes before heading back out to the van where he sleeps at night.

His ex-wife is still in Synanon and so is his daughter, Darla. Mom says Phil wants Darla to live with him but Synanon won't allow it so Phil went to a judge to prove Synanon is not a good place for a child to live. I hear them talking when I stay up late with the door open because the bedroom is too dark. He says he's scared, that he got a visit from two men, two of the Old Man's crew, who told him to "back off the legal stuff" or there could be trouble. He was about to sub-peena the Old Man, which is when you make someone go and face a judge. He thought if the judge knew about the School, how the babies are taken away from their parents like an orphanage, he would let him have his daughter back. But he's scared of the men because everyone knows they're beating people up. He doesn't know what to do. He wants to see his daughter.

I wonder if Dad feels this way. If he looks at pictures of me the way I look at pictures of him or if he's too busy on his moto-cycle in his new place with his new woman in Los Angeles.

Darla comes for dinner with Phil and we all eat Oscar's Burgers because it's a celebration since he hasn't seen her for so long. Darla is my age and looks more like a porcelain doll than a kid. She has creamy-white skin and black hair cut straight across her eyebrows. She smiles with crooked teeth and eats her fries as she sits in Phil's lap. After dinner she and I play with the Legos from the big bag that we got at the Goodwill on University Avenue. She says her mom is the prettiest in the whole world and I say my dad is the coolest in the world and Phil and Mom say, "Hey, what about us?"

WHEN WE MOVE to the house on Spaulding Avenue in Berkeley, Phil moves in with us. He brings his orange VW van, following us as we drive in the old white Vega with wooden doors that Grandpa bought us for eight hundred dollars. It's packed with pots and pans and clothes that we got at the Salvation Army.

The street looks like a tunnel beneath the branches of the big trees that line the sidewalk. There are leaves on the ground everywhere, over the pavement, the gutters, forming a brown-and-yellow blanket on the lawns and driveways. Mom says we'll have our very own house where we'll live with Phil and even Darla sometimes and we won't hear the neighbors through the walls or have to walk up the big stairs of the spaceship with our bags of food from the food bank where we have to wait in the long line for bags of flour and sugar and milk and the orange rubbery cheese that's good for noodles or grilled cheese sandwiches.

It's a brown house with a big porch with nine concrete steps and a long driveway running down the side. There are two bedrooms and a bathroom, a real kitchen, a living room, even a tree in the backyard covered in white flowers. We run inside and call dibs on the bigger bedroom which Phil says we were going to have anyway since the three of us have to share it.

I like Phil and I wonder if this is what dads are like. He doesn't hug me, but sometimes he puts his hand on my shoulder and squeezes it and I feel a warmth in my chest like a hug and it's good. I know he's not my dad but I like that he lives with us because it's safer with more people.

Is this what it means to have a family?

When he gets home, he lifts Darla up in his skinny arms and she clings to him like a little monkey. I think how lucky she is to be with her dad. I don't even mind when Mrs. Morris thinks he's my father. She lives next door with her two kids. "You should tell your dad it's garbage day," she says to me from the porch next door. I don't know what to say because my dad is in the golden picture frame, in a house in another city with other people, so I don't say anything.

Phil walks out and says he already knows it's garbage day. He puts his hand on my shoulders and squeezes them and I feel the warmth because I know he doesn't mind if she thinks he's my dad even though I already have a dad. It means I don't need to explain to her that he's gone and we're sad about it.

A pretend family is better than no family. It's better than being at a school that's really an orphanage where you wake up and there's no one to talk to.

Mom says single mothers have it the hardest in the world and Mrs. Morris is a single mother and we don't understand how hard it is and it's not her fault we were in the school like an orphanage even though she sent us there and we shouldn't make her feel bad about it because Dad would've died without that place and all she ever wanted was a man to take care of her and we're not sad now, we're happy because we can be a family even though we know it's just pretend.

She lies down on the bed and her face goes blank and we know she has the deep-russian so I rub her back and tell her I'm not sad.

When it rains, Phil sweeps the water from the yellow floor in the kitchen because it seeps in from the back porch beneath the door. There's a drainpipe with a hole that splashes water like a faucet that gets into the house and makes a little lake on the kitchen floor. It's nice to be in a house though. He even turns the garage at the end of the long driveway into a playroom for Darla and me. It's got a concrete floor and high wooden shelves where he puts the toys.

Darla and I play in there all day. There's a big rug from Goodwill on the floor so it isn't so cold even though we have to wear sweaters when the chill comes.

Mom says everyone in Synanon went crazy. They think we belong to them. They think we are their kids, not hers. Darla and I have to stay in the garage because Mom says they might try to find us and take us back. I guess it's safer in there but it gets old just sitting on the concrete all day. I know she's scared for us. I think the men who spoke to Phil scared her too.

Some days we can hear the ice cream truck on the street, the slam of screen doors and the kids from next door pedaling their bikes trying to chase after it. We hear them playing freeze tag or hopscotch or drawing pictures on the sidewalk with chalk. We listen to them talk, trying to re-member which is which. They're lucky since they get to go outside. "That's Sarah. She's the tall one with the curly hair and freckles. She lives in the green house with the flower bushes out front. I think she got a new bike."

"Na-ah. That's Molly. Sarah's her sister with the brown hair."

Tony never plays with us. He's either drawing his monsters or looking at baseball cards or reading the stack of *Mad* magazines from the Salvation Army. "I need a new Mike Schmidt. The corner is bent on this one." Mom is gone during the day because she has to work on her Vestigation into the people Synanon is trying to hurt. She interviews people who were beaten up or yelled at or scared and puts it all into a book that she's going to give to the government. Phil is home sometimes but he is busy trying to stop the nuclear plant called Diablo Canyon because nuclear plants kill people.

Tony says Mom doesn't care what happens to us, that she took us from Synanon because she didn't like Dad. She tries to hug him at night but he crosses his arms and turns away. He tells me stories about Dad carrying a sawed-off shotgun for ten years inside his trench coat, how when he was in prison everyone was afraid of him because he has a black belt in karate and a loud voice when he's mad. "Dad was in charge of a lot of people in Synanon and that's why Mom doesn't like him," he says. "Even Chuck listens to Dad because everyone knows he was the toughest guy there." I try to picture Dad but there's only the blurry image of the jeans and the moto-cycle, the face in the gold frame.

"Dad was in prison for years but it didn't bother him because he knew how to take it. He and Uncle Pete would fight anybody and it didn't matter how many there were." I don't know if the stories Tony tells me are true or not but I wish he didn't know more about Dad than me. He talks like he lived with him every day even though I would see him sitting alone on the playground in Synanon. He would jump up off the ground with a great big smile when Dad came to visit us. "You'll see, Dad's going to take us out of here. You won't need to worry about nothing because everyone's afraid of Dad." That sounds good because we're tired of being in the garage all day hiding from the bad men.

Sometimes Tony goes out onto the street even though he's not supposed to. He doesn't care. Mom gets tired of fighting him so she lets him since he screams, "I hate you!" and she gets the look that goes on forever.

Tony is down the street and I am playing on the front porch and Mom is drinking coffee in the dining room under the yellow chandelier with her friend who has yellow teeth like Mom and big curly brown hair. Darla is gone with her mom and even though Tony gets to play on the street, I still have to stay on the front porch.

Phil pulls into the driveway in his orange van. He gets out and when he reaches in for the groceries, I see two men walk up behind him. The men have something on their faces, something like masks the color of skin that push their noses flat against their faces. Even in the masks you can tell they both have shaved heads which means they're from Synanon.

They're holding skinny black clubs that look like little baseball bats. One carries his low in his hand and the other taps his softly on the ground as they walk up behind Phil. At first I think maybe they're playing a joke on him because I've heard people play dress up on Halloween even though we never did it in Synanon. Why else would they have those masks over their faces? Why else would they hide behind the orange camper van where Phil can't see them?

Phil looks up at me and smiles when he gets out. Before I can say anything, one of the men runs up behind and hits him over the head. Phil falls onto the ground. It's weird how he falls, like a stack of Lincoln Logs that's been tipped over. His body folds into a weird shape with his legs sticking out under him.

I jump back and look around the doorway to see if anyone else saw it. I don't know if I'm supposed to scream or run or yell but I don't want the men to see me. The second man hits Phil's legs, which seem to bounce around like rubber. One of his gray sneakers flies off. Phil puts his head between his arms with his face down and starts to scream.

His voice echoes into the street. It's so quiet and all I can hear is "Heeeeeelp! Heeeeeelp!"

The men are saying something. I can't make the words out but you can tell they're angry. I close my eyes hard and hear the clubs hit Phil's body between the screams. It sounds like something hitting meat. When I open my eyes and look around the column on the porch, Phil is looking straight at me from between his arms.

He looks sad, almost like he's saying sorry. There's blood on his forehead and a weird bend in his legs and I want to tell him there's nothing for him to be sorry about.

I think as long as I stay still, I am invisible. I can disappear. *How do I make myself smaller? Can I flap my ears and fly now? Will they see me?*

Some of the kids from the block are watching from across the street. I see Tony standing there with them in a red sweatshirt from Goodwill. I wonder why nobody does anything. Phil goes quiet and one of the men puts his club on his shoulder and looks at them. "Do any of you know where Tony and Mikel are?" The words come out muffled through the mask which pushes his nose down in a funny way.

I see Tony freeze as the kids look from face to face, shaking their heads slowly, some staring at the men, some staring at the ground. I wonder if Tony can become invisible too. I close my eyes and try to give him the power. *Don't breathe. Don't do anything.*

"Anyone?!"

Nobody says a word. They probably don't know our names.

Mrs. Morris comes running out to her porch, her brown hair big and wild. She tells the men she called the cops so they better leave. The men look around like they have all day then slowly turn to walk up the block. Mom and her friend run out to the porch. Soon an ambulance comes and takes Phil away while we all watch. He looks so skinny and helpless when they put him in the back.

After the ambulance leaves, Mom takes us back to Grandma and Grandpa's house in San Jose. Grandpa lets us in, whispering because it's late. "I made the bed up for you and the boys. You can stay as long as you want."

Mom puts us down and grabs onto him, burying her head in his shoulder, "I didn't know, Dad. I didn't know."

"Shhh, shhh," he pats her on the back lightly. "You're okay now. That's okay. That's my girl." She puts us to bed but I can't sleep because I keep picturing the men in the masks. Every noise I hear outside, every creak of the house, every time my brother turns over in his sleep—I wonder if it's the men with the clubs, if they followed us here and we're next. I picture Phil on the ground, the way he fell over all at once.

Why were they so mad? What did we do wrong? Is Tony right about Mom? Is she angry at Dad for divorcing her so she stole us so he can't see us? Are they mad at us for leaving?

When I wake up in the morning, the sheets are cold and wet and I know I've done a bad thing. I know Mom is sad and Grandpa always tells me she's been through so much. I don't want to get in trouble so I wait until Tony and Mom go to the living room and take the pee-soaked sheet to the garbage in the back outside the glass door. I know there's a fresh sheet in the closet so I put it on the fold-out bed as quietly as I can before going to the kitchen for Dutch cheese and rolls.

We know the stories of the other people who left Synanon and the bad things that happened to them. We hear Mom talking about them all the time. One man was bitten by a rattlesnake that someone left in his mailbox. He nearly died from the bite. One man came home to find his dog hanging from a tree. Tony says he heard a story that the teenagers, the Punk Squad who were given to Synanon by the courts so they could get clean off drugs, were beaten by the Synanon people. They kept trying to escape but they couldn't get away fast enough because they were so far from any cities or towns up in the Tomales Bay compound. Chuck bought a thousand rifles. He's training the men he calls the Imperial Marines to defend Synanon at all costs. They look like soldiers with their shaved heads and big boots and matching denim overalls. There's a trial from Mom's Vestigation and that's when the tapes come out, the tapes of the Old Man saying crazy things. He wants legs broken and ears cut off and put into jars. He wants a revolution.

Phil is in a coma for a month. He has a cracked skull and broken bones and something called men-in-ji-tis in his head. We don't visit because Mom is afraid the men from Synanon are watching.

I tell her, "I'm scared of the men, Mom."

She says, "No you're not. You're happy because you're with your mother now." I keep trying to tell her I'm afraid and I'm having nightmares but she won't listen. It's like the words don't exist once I say them.

She says, "You're fine." Then she says, "This has been really hard on me. You know it's not easy to lose your husband and then also have to worry about losing your kids."

I don't know what to do because I feel something close up inside me, like a gasp that echoes up from a well. Like if she can't hear my words then maybe they don't exist and I can just hide up in the room in the clouds by myself. I tell myself again and again, *You're not scared. You're happy now. You're not scared. You're happy now.* So I try to pretend and I smile at her and I give her a hug because she's been through so much and I know it's my job.

And when we do talk about it, Mom says how difficult it was for her and I say yeah, that must have been hard because they looked so mean with those masks on.

She says, "But you weren't even there."

I have to remind her that I watched it from the porch, that Phil and I locked eyes, that the men asked for me and Tony, that Tony was with the kids across the street, that he was scared too.

I wonder if she's right. If what's real is the World of Synanon or the World According to Mom, which are different things. And they exist outside the castle in the clouds, the place where I'm safe behind the thick stone walls.

I don't know if the fear is real or if I can just pretend to not feel it, to lock it up like in a bottle and put it on a shelf and, just like Mom, pretend it isn't there.

She says, "Oh," and I watch as her face fills with worry, like she's left the stove on somewhere, like there's something she can't quite remember. She stares at the wall with her fist over her mouth, the way she does when she gets the look from the deep-russian.

"Right. Right. Well. This has all been very hard on me."

I don't have the words for the thing inside me, the blank white like ice at the bottom of my throat. I want her to tell it to me, to see it and help me name it. Do feelings exist if no one sees them? Did I imagine it? The feeling of not knowing, of wondering what is real, bounces around inside my chest. I don't know what I'm supposed to call it. I don't know what I'm supposed to tell people about Phil, about Synanon, about Dad, about Mom, about the fear and the sadness and the fact that I don't know if it's real because Mom won't see it.

"Mom? Mom?"

"Yes, Goo."

"Are we safe here?"

"I think so."

"Because I'm scared."

"No you're not. You're happy to be with your mother and away from that place that kept us apart."

"But Phil almost died."

She shakes her head. "This has been such a hard time on me. This too? On top of everything else?" She looks away and I am alone in the room again. After a minute she stares at me, "What, sweetie? What was it? But how would you know what happened? You weren't even there."

For months my dreams are of men in masks and broken bones, blood on the driveway and running away as fast as I can. I wake up to wet sheets and when Mom finds them, she tells me I need to stop wetting the bed like a little boy even though I never wet the bed before the bad men came. I try to replay the moment, what I could've done differently, how I should've fought them or made Mom move us or screamed to make them stop. Mom is small, fluttering around the big shoulders of the men, dodging the skinny clubs as they swing at my brother and me. There is no place that is safe from their reach, nowhere to go to get far enough away. They're under the couch. They're in the closet. And Dad, he is somewhere else, somewhere vague and fuzzy on his moto-cycle, riding down a highway, a blur, a glimpse of something I can't quite see as I sit alone in that room in that house in the city where my mother went to change the world.

OREGON

"Where are the people?" resumed the little prince at last. "It's lonely in the desert."

"It is lonely when you're among people, too," said the snake.

—ANTOINE DE SAINT-EXUPÉRY, *THE LITTLE PRINCE*

CHAPTER 5

HE'S GOT THE WHOLE WORLD IN HIS HANDS

The mountains between Oregon and California are the largest things I've ever seen. They jut out in rocky peaks all around us as we drive north in the dirty white Chevy Vega with the wooden doors. Something about it seems like the work of giants. The valley is a giant footprint, the lake is a giant handprint, the river was made by dragging something heavy and sharp across the land. I wonder how a boulder perched on a cliff over the freeway got there. I wonder if the boulder will fall as the Vega wheezes up the steep hill, if after thousands of years of watching and waiting, a simple gust of wind might be enough to send it tumbling down the hill to crush us or block the road so no one can ever follow.

I am in the backseat, eating a piece of beef jerky packed by Grandpa. No one knows where we are. Mom has made sure of that.

There are pine trees that rise up over the forest like spearheads jutting out of the earth. At one point, Mom says that we are about to cross the California border into Oregon and I'm glad the mountains are so tall because maybe it means it'll be harder for anyone to get to us.

Mom keeps saying how much better Oregon will be. How safe it is. How clean. That you can breathe there because there are fewer people and cars and less smog and trees everywhere. She tells us she has a new job at the state mental hospital in Salem, that we'll have enough money for food and clothes and a place to live because "everything in Oregon costs less than California so you don't have to kill yourself just to eat and pay the rent."

Her new job is helping men getting out of prison to not do drugs. She's an expert at that since that's what happened to Dad.

She knows all about addiction which is a disease you get in the brain and also in the heart. Whole families get it too and you don't just get over it by stopping the drugs. Everyone in the family has it whether they are the ones using the drugs or not. You have to have a higher power and go to meetings and say prayers and admit you're powerless. Mom knows this because that's all anyone talked about in Synanon and even before that she read so many books at Berkeley.

I don't understand how I could have a disease when I'm only five years old. Also we weren't part of a family at the School like an orphanage and the smell of Grandma's Dutch makes me sick to my stomach.

I don't think Dad needed any of this. He's tough and everyone in Synanon said how funny he was and how much he helped them. "Your dad is one funny sumbitch," people were always saying. "And he saved my ass. No one's seen more life than your dad and so you couldn't bullshit with him. You can't con a con man."

Mom gets sad if we talk about Dad and you can't talk to her when her face goes blank and her eyes go far away and she's in the deep-russian.

I think maybe sadness runs in families too and since we're in the same family, we feel her sadness too. We share it like our Dutch cheeks and corn-silk hair. We know that Dad is somewhere else in the world and I wonder if he's laughing right now or helping someone not be a Dope Fiend or riding his motorcycle on a different highway while we're here in this car in the mountains with Mom going to some place called Oregon.

I remember how I used to sit in Bonnie's lap during story time every night. I know she wasn't a mom because everyone told me a mom is someone who gives you birth and she didn't do that. Also Mom tells me I will always be hers and that's what a mom is. But still I miss Bonnie because she used to hug me and play little games and take me out on days when she wasn't even working in the School. She worked the Cube, which meant she worked for a week then was off for a week, and she'd even come in on her days off to take me hiking or read me a story before bed.

Bonnie says she wanted to be a teacher but then when she got to Synanon they told her they had a school and she knew that's where she belonged, with the kids. Everyone had different jobs. Dad ran the auto shop.

Some people cooked food, some cleaned up, some even sold things like pens and cups to businesses with their name printed right on the pen.

I was in the Orange Room with all the other little kids and Tony was in the Green Room with the bigger kids and Bonnie is always there in my memory. I can't remember a time she wasn't sitting by me in the Commons, where we ate lunch, or playing hot hands with me on the playground. Is that a mom? Someone who you can't ever remember not loving you?

When the parents came to visit, someone would always say, "Here come the Headsuckers. Be careful you don't give those kids pointy heads!" We didn't know what that meant, but one day Clubby told me not to listen because it was just Chuck being mean and it's good for parents to want to hug and kiss their kids even if Chuck thinks it's bad.

Mom says Chuck wanted to make "a new type of person who didn't need parents and could just rely on themselves," and that's why we couldn't see our parents, so we could become these new people. I don't feel new. I think we're just normal and I miss Bonnie and I don't want to have to hide on the other side of these mountains.

Mom has one friend in Salem, a woman who helped her get the job helping prisoners not be Dope Fiends. The woman is the only person in the world who knows where we are. That way we're safe. Mom says when we get there, we'll make new friends too and that life is going to be different in Oregon. It's going to be the Three Musketeers—Mom and Tony and me—versus the whole world. We are going to be happy now and she deserves it after what she's been through. Synanon just went crazy when they started to force the men to have those vast-ectomies and started beating everyone up so she decided to leave and even though Phil got beaten up and even though we're hiding in this car hundreds of miles away, it's easy to imagine because anything seems possible when you're up in the mountains surrounded by trees and rivers and endless skies so we start singing songs:

> *He's got the whole world in his hands,*
> *He's got the whole world in his hands.*

I picture two hands as big as mountains cradling the world like a bowl with everything in it: all the plants and animals and trees and people and buildings with giant ghostlike fingers stretching around it. Tony and I name the things we see out the window, placing them in the song, singing at the top of our lungs:

He's got the mountains and the trees in his hands,
He's got the mountains and the trees in his hands,
He's got the mountains and the trees in his hands,
He's got the whole world in his hands.
He's got a broken-down truck in his hands,
He's got a broken-down truck in his hands,
He's got a broken-down truck in his hands,
He's got the whole world in his hands.

And it feels like maybe Oregon will be something new, something better. We're all singing and Grandpa made us lunches to eat: ham sandwiches with cheese and mustard on rolls with beef jerky. It's salty and sweet and I even get an Orange Crush soda which I've never had, because we aren't allowed to eat sugar. Mom says sugar is a drug and it'll kill you just the same as alcohol, which is why no one in Synanon was allowed to eat sugar so we usually have water or milk or an apple or yogurt for a treat but since it's not every day that you move to a whole new state, she lets us drink the Orange Crush.

The window is down and I'm drinking pop and we're all doing a silly dance where we move our shoulders up and down and back and forth in our seats there in the mountains that separate Oregon from the bad men and the bad things in Berkeley. Then Tony sings,

He's got the mommies and the daddies in his hands,
He's got the mommies and the daddies in his hands.

Mom stops singing and stares out the window with her hands gripping the steering wheel. She stays silent for a long time. I give Tony a punch on the shoulder from the seat behind him. "What?! I was just singing."

"I know you were, sweetie," Mom says. "It's all right." Tony turns around and gives me the look he gives when he wants me to know he's going to get me later, which he always does, pinning me to the ground with his knees and pounding on my chest while I scream.

"Why are you crying, Mom?"

She puts her elbow on the ledge of the window and leans her head into her hand. A big green sign on the side of the highway says, "Welcome to Oregon."

"Are you sad?"

"No, honey, I'm happy we're moving to a new place where we can be together and it'll be clean and we can breathe."

"I'm sad," I say. "I miss the School and Bonnie and Dmitri and macaroni and cheese."

She says, "No you don't." She tells me I'm happy we're moving. It wasn't safe there so we left and we're all together now and I'm happy I can be somewhere safe and clean where a person can breathe. She says I'll make friends and they'll be good plus I get to be with my mom now.

I remember that a "Mom" is supposed to be a special thing, that's what I was told one time she came to visit us in the School: "This is your mom. She would've been your parent if you weren't a child of the universe. You belong to her." She tells me I'm her son and she wanted kids so she wouldn't be alone anymore and now she has us and it is a son's job to take care of his mother.

"I'm so glad we're all together," she says from the front seat. She reaches a hand back toward me with a palm open for me to hold. I put my hand in hers and she closes her fingers around it. The hand feels bigger than I am, bigger than the car, the road, the mountains and the sky.

AFTER DRIVING ALL day, stopping only at a diner where Tony and I got our own hamburgers even though I didn't finish mine, just as the sky is turning a dark blue, we see a sign on the side of the highway that reads, "Salem, Oregon, Population 89,233."

It's been raining since we left the mountains. It rains as we drive through town. The heater in the Vega puts out a lukewarm, gassy air that smells like stale oil and burned rubber as we listen to the steady *thwup thwup* of the wipers on the windshield. The gray streets are filled with old cars and overgrown bushes, leaning fences, collapsing porches, mobile homes, gravel alleys overrun with weeds and blackberry bushes twisting between the power lines, storefronts, donut shops, hunting supplies, churches, wooded parks and a strange smell that stings the nostrils we later find out comes from a mushroom cannery on the edge of town.

Every few blocks there is a house with boarded-up windows and overgrown lawns, some covered in black streaks from fires that burned the houses which were left to rot. Everywhere are trees, pine trees with pointy green needles, some taller than buildings with branches fanning out in all directions. It looks like a place that was built by trees and conquered by people.

We pass a white marble building with a giant golden man on top holding a big golden ax, a cape slung over his shoulder. The man stands legs apart, looking off into the distance. I wonder if this man saved the people from the trees or the trees from the people. I wonder if the giant golden lumberjack will protect us from the bad men. If they'll see him and be scared of the giant ax so they'll leave us alone.

I picture him stepping down from his marble perch and picking up our car in his big hands, carrying us on his back across the rivers and lakes, over the mountains and valleys and highways, back to Tomales Bay where we can sing songs and play games with the other kids while he stands guard if the bad men come with their masks and clubs.

The houses are farther apart on the edge of town so it feels more like we're driving through a forest. Fields of green grass and bushes run right up against the black rain-slicked street as we cross a small bridge over a stream and come to a sign that says, "Battle Creek Lodges," our new home.

The building looks like a big green gingerbread house with a curved roof. There's a crisp quiet even in the light rain when we get out of the car, the feeling of being hidden among mountains.

Tony yells, "Deer!" pointing toward the field. We see it, hunched and cautious, taller than we are with its antlers bobbing over the tall weeds. Mom takes a deep breath, closing her eyes as if to savor the air while Tony and I carry the cardboard boxes of Goodwill dishes and hand-me-down clothes into the apartment. It's got an electric wall heater, an actual kitchen with a stove, and a stained mattress turned sideways on the floor of the bedroom where we fall facedown to sleep. It seems as good a place as any to hide.

In the morning, the sun is out and there is steam rising from all the puddles in the parking lot. We see squirrels, chipmunks, even a prairie dog in his hole as Tony and I walk through the tall grass field next to the gingerbread building looking for sticks and rocks to throw. It reminds me of the fields next to the compound in Tomales Bay, except wetter and colder. The Battle Creek runs beneath the road and every now and then a car breaks the silence as we watch it speed away, wondering when the world got so quiet.

"I bet we could go fishing in there if we wanted to," Tony says. We've never fished, only seen the flow of water as it disappeared into a two-foot concrete pipe in Oakland, a dirty river of paper trash and cigarette butts. "I think all we need are earthworms and maybe a string or something."

We walk back to the apartment to hunt for supplies as the sun falls behind a cloud and the air gets thick with mist. It starts to rain. It rains all morning. First in a cloud that springs up like fog, then in sheets that pound the concrete as we watch from the front window. Finally it settles into a steady rhythm, the sound of water falling off the roof, flowing in the gutters, the drip drip drip around the windows, raining all afternoon as we wait for it to stop in the front room with our Legos and crayons. We hear it falling outside the bedroom window when we go to sleep, wondering when it will break so we can explore the field, to get lost in the grove of trees like the golden pioneer on the marble building downtown.

Mom gets us raincoats and rubber galoshes from Goodwill and we promise her we'll stay dry when we go outside in the dark afternoon. The water runs along the highway in a stream, muddy with whitecaps. We see the shadow of a river rat the size of a small cat in the creek below our feet where we hoped to fish. The water gets in our socks, our shoes, our skin, our pores and we soon realize that the sun was a dirty trick and we are destined to be wet.

"Maybe it'll just rain forever," Tony says.

CHAPTER 6

THE COWBOYS WHO LEFT

Tony starts school and Mom starts her job at the state mental hospital. I go to day care at an apartment two buildings over run by a mean woman with black hair pulled back on her head and a hairy mole on her top lip. Tony joins me there after school. We sit with the other kids and watch *The Electric Company*. We're not used to the TV or the other kids who scream at it when the letters come on: "*E! F!*" We already know our letters because all the kids at the School knew their letters. At the end of the day we watch *Bonanza* which is the best show because of all the outlaws and heroes and cowboys, all those men on their horses.

We don't like the mean woman who runs the day care because she lets her kids make fun of us for the holes in our shoes and jeans. Her daughter, who is about my age, says, "Your sneakers are talking to me," because the rubber on the front comes apart when I walk. When we play hide-and-seek, she says, "You two should hide in the trash. No one would even notice." The other kids laugh at us or they keep their distance.

The mean woman says it's not right to make fun of people less fortunate than you. "But for the grace of God go you, honey." She shakes a finger with a hand on her hip. But her daughter doesn't get in trouble. Not really. None of them do. And I don't think the woman likes me because I don't understand the way she talks to all the children like they are babies.

When I say, "I'd prefer not to do crafts. Is there another activity?"

She says, "What's wrong with you? You talk like you're thirty, ha-ha!" And dumps the box of matchsticks on the floor in front of me.

Mom is gone nights when she goes to meetings at a place called Al-Anon. She says it helps her to understand what happened to her. She's always telling us how she just needs to cope, needs time to "figure out answers to the questions life keeps posing to her." There's a poster on the wall of the apartment that reads,

> God grant me the Serenity
> To accept the things I cannot change,
> The courage to change the things I can,
> And the wisdom to know the difference.

It's written in curvy white letters over a picture of a wave crashing against a rock. I see her saying the words to herself. Her lips move with her eyes closed as she leans against the wall and says the prayer, waiting for the water to boil for the noodles.

Mom is lonely. We know that because she tells us, "Your dad already has someone else. He was the love of my life." Then she disappears in her mind for a while. Her eyes get glossy as she blinks, shakes her head and says, "You look more like him every day."

I hear her talking on the phone when she comes home at night, when she thinks we're asleep. Just bits and pieces: "Well, he seems nice, but I think he hates his ex-wife . . . A beard? I guess I don't mind a beard . . . Jesus, Diane, I don't know. Is he a good man?"

I know that she's what you call a "single mother" and I know she wants to stop being one which is why she is growing her hair out.

The mean woman at the day care has a husband who comes home at the end of the day in work boots covered in sawdust. He stomps right into the bedroom and the woman who ignores us, who lets her kids tease us, who yells for us to clean up or come inside for a snack with her deep husky voice, just flattens her hair and brings him a beer from the fridge, saying that she's sorry she forgot to put it in the icebox earlier. She's one person with us and another with him and it seems like a magic trick, this power that he has over her. I wonder if Mom was like that with Dad or anyone because she's always alone.

When Christmas Eve comes and Mom makes hot apple cider in a big pot with cinnamon sticks, the smell fills the apartment. We have a small tree we decorated with construction paper and the antique glass bulbs Mom got from Grandma and Grandpa. She says it's going to be a great Christmas, that it's us against the world, the Three Musketeers.

A man knocks on our door and Tony and I run to answer it. He has a clipboard and a tie. He says, "Hi. Can I speak to the man of the house?"

We look at each other.

"Is your father home?"

"No. But our mom is." She pushes us inside and talks to the man who is trying to get her to sign something and I wonder, *Are we the men of the house? Is Mom? I didn't know we needed one.*

The men on *Bonanza* look out for the women, defending their honor, picking up their handkerchiefs when they drop them, like cowboys are supposed to do. Little Joe sits on a golden green hilltop next to a lake with Alice. He told his brothers he's going to ask her to marry him. *Who are these men?* They have something we don't. They seem rare, like wild dogs or birds you capture and put in a cage, something fleeting and hard to spot.

One night Mom walks out of the bathroom with makeup on her face. Her eyes bright, red powder on her big Dutch cheeks. She's even put lipstick on. Her straight brown hair has started to grow out. It falls down almost to her shoulders. She parts it in the middle, pulling the long bangs back behind her ears. She's wearing a gold necklace and gold earrings with red stones, a long flowery green-and-white skirt and a red blouse. Instead of her usual leather sandals, she's wearing green shoes.

She does a turn. "Well, how do I look?"

Every kid knows the answer to that question.

She says she's going to meet a friend. She hugs us and smiles and tells us to be nice to the girls someday. Even the quiet ones. This is her constant plea to us. "Make sure you ask the quiet ones to dance, okay? They want to dance too." She makes us promise her. It sounds nice, all this dancing with different people.

The men seem like cowboys to me, like the ones on TV. There's no talk of sharing or "serenity" or makeup or brushing your teeth or the "questions life poses." They have big boots and guns and horses and cigarettes. They walk into town with their hats pushed forward, an unlit match hanging from their teeth. The women say, "Don't leave. Please.

Stay." Or they say, "Get out! Just get out, you no good rascal!" So you wonder which one you're going to be. Because she is standing in the doorway in her makeup and fancy clothes and you know how much she just wants someone who will stay, with his beard or his mustache, his cowboy boots and his horse lassoed to the front porch. And the thing that he can promise her is the thing we can't as we pretend to be the men of the house, with no gun and no horse, like fighting lions with a stick, lighting an enormous fire we hope someone will see so he'll ride here and find this anxious, tired and lonely woman standing in the doorway with her gold earrings on.

"You look really pretty Mom."

WHEN SPRING COMES, it's still raining. Mom says the apartment is too small for a "family" and we need to live closer to a real school so she found us a house at the bottom of a hill, between the graveyard and the state mental hospital. She says it'll take her thirty years to pay for it but damn it, the Three Musketeers will have our own house. Mom's job at the state hospital is secure at least as long as Thatasshole Reagan "doesn't shut it down to build more bombs." When we drive by, the hospital grounds are huge, with cream-painted buildings covered in safety-glass windows behind high fences topped with barbed wire and endless green fields going all the way out to D Street. It's impressive. Tony says *One Flew Over the Cuckoo's Nest* was filmed there which makes us feel important.

The day we move in, Mom rents a U-Haul truck and mentions that her friend Paul is going to help us. She leaves us alone at the apartment at Battle Creek and when she comes back there is a big white-and-red van parked next to her Vega. Behind the wheel is a man with thick glasses, a mess of thinning hair on his head and a thick bushy black beard that goes all the way down his neck. He looks exactly like a hairy human turtle.

When he gets out, we see that he is hardly taller than Mom. He's wearing a black velvet striped collared shirt and baggy jeans that sag at the butt. "The damn thing keeps sticking. I don't think it knows its job. I tried to reason with it. It didn't listen." He cracks a smile at Mom who smiles back with her crooked yellow teeth.

"Hey guys, this is my friend Paul." Tony and I look at him then at each other. I know he knows and he knows I know that we're both thinking the same thing: this guy is funny looking.

Mom's new friend Paul cocks his head sideways to look at us. "Looks like we got a lot of work to do. Which one of you is older?"

"I am," Tony says.

"Okay, good, good. Maybe you can drive the van." Tony smiles despite himself. "I can't make heads or tails of that thing. You guys got any orange juice?" He walks right into the kitchen and opens the fridge. He says there's milk but it needs Hershey's syrup to make it chocolate.

"We're not allowed to have sugar," we say in unison.

"Are you Mikel?" He kneels down next to me. His wrists and knuckles are covered in dark strands of black hair like a Labrador. He talks fast and makes lots of jokes. "Are these your Legos? How many do you have? Do you have the ones where you can make a spaceship? Those are my favorite."

He sits with me a while and we build Lego stuff while Tony asks him about baseball. "I'm more of a Pete Rose man. If Reggie Jackson's so great, why's he always striking out?"

"But he hits a lot of home runs too."

"Yeah, true, true. You seem to know a lot about baseball. I'll bet you're pretty good."

Tony blushes. "I'm okay. I want to be a pitcher."

"That's the best position there is! That or shortstop, as long as you're not stuck in right field."

Paul is the exact opposite of Reggie Jackson, short and balding, hairy, messy. But he doesn't seem to care what we think of him which is good because most adults try to get us to think they're smarter than us.

After we pack the van, we pile into the Vega and follow it through the rain down D Street to our new house. It's still raining as we get out of the car. The air smells of damp plants, wet gravel and chimney smoke. My feet are cold because of the crappy heater in the Vega. None of it feels real, the green house that stands like a giant A. There are two yellow-brown trees on either side of a gravel walk that leads to six stairs and a porch and a house, a real house, with a redbrick chimney on the side. The odd hairy man carries boxes inside to the big living room with its painted-over fireplace, the kitchen with room for a table, the stairs that lead down to a basement underground where Tony and I get our own room. I can't believe we get a whole building to ourselves.

There is a room at the end of the hallway downstairs that feels like a cave where a mother wolf would go to raise her pups. It's dry, and warmer than the other rooms. Mom calls it a den which is exactly what wolves call it. In the corner of the den there is a black wood-burning stove next to a stack of wood and newspapers.

Paul opens the hatch at the front of the iron stove and builds a fire with some wood he brought.

I'm surprised by how good he is with the wood and the matches, how he's fearless of splinters or brick dust on his jeans as he kneels on the ground. It's strange how this short oddball of a man knows his way around the objects of the real world.

Paul disappears with the U-Haul once we unload all the boxes and returns in a black Chevy mini-truck with a camper shell and an orange stripe down the side. He walks around and opens the rear gate and out jumps a brown-and-white dog with floppy ears and a tiny nub of a tail the size of a fist. "This is Pepper," he says. Pepper's tail jerks back and forth as she licks our hands and runs around the yard to pee.

We go to A&W, where Mom lets me order a whole hamburger for my-self and a root beer float the size of my head.

She tells us there's a Little League nearby at a place called Parrish Field and a school down the street called Englewood Elementary. It has a great big field in front and a park behind it right in the middle of a little forest. She says that's where we'll go to school. Plus there's a bunch of kids on the street for us to play with.

"Doesn't sound too bad," Paul says, dipping his fries five at a time into a lake of ketchup on his plate.

"Do you play baseball?" Tony asks.

"A little. But I'm more into fishing and hiking and camping and stuff."

"Paul's a woodsman," Mom says in her dreamy way.

"What in the hell is that?"

Paul crooks his head toward Tony. "Don't know, really. I guess it means I like trees."

"Trees are boring."

"That's what I like about them." Paul speaks quietly, a little smile around his lips like he knows the punch line to a joke but he's not telling. I like him. I can tell Tony does too.

After dinner we drive back to the house and unpack the boxes of dishes and towels and clothes. Soon Paul says he has to go home and he gathers Pepper with a leash and grabs Mom by the waist and kisses her, right there in the living room in front of us. He stops at the door and gives us a weird little wave and walks out.

There is a silence in the house after he leaves, an emptiness that echoes off the furniture and boxes without Pepper running from person to person, without Paul's big turtle childlike movements. I want him to come back, to maybe just lean in the doorway while I fall asleep on the floor.

WE PLAY THREE Flies Up in the street after school with the other kids from the block. We play Smear the Queer in the field in front of Englewood Elementary School. We play Butts Up with a tennis ball inside the covered basketball court next to the baseball diamond. We play street football, dodgeball, kickball, baseball, freeze tag and guns. We race our bikes down the hill to see who is faster, who is stronger, who is tougher, who has the balls to climb the fence and get on the roof of the school, who races their bike against the cars and who waits at the corner for the cars to drive by. There are never any girls and there aren't any men.

Derek is the bucktoothed boy who lives at the top of the street. When he falls off his bike and skins his knee, he screams all the way home. A large woman in a white T-shirt and shorts comes out onto the porch and kneels down. He jumps into her arms. She says, "Are you okay, my little man? Show Mommy where the boo-boo is. Can you do that?" He nods his head, his eyes full of tears. She kisses the skin above the wound and says to wait while she gets a Band-Aid.

Derek sits quietly sniffling while Tony and I watch, in awe.

Why is she talking to him like he's a baby? Why is he crying like one? It's strange, like a dog howling at a siren, something that happens without thinking. The child cries. The mother comforts him. It doesn't make any sense.

The woman we call Mom taught us to cook hot dogs and eggs on the electric stove so if we get hungry we can feed ourselves because the most important thing for a kid to learn is independence. She tells us she saved us from Synanon and that she had kids because she was lonely and that a boy's job is to take care of his mother. If we skin our knees, we know how to clean the wound, how to put hydrogen peroxide on it to make sure it doesn't get infected.

Derek's mom returns with a chocolate cookie. She hands him the cookie and places a Band-Aid tenderly over the raw skin. "There. Like new." She hugs him close and he leans his head against her cheek. I don't understand any of it.

The woman we call Mom cries some nights and I lean against her and I say, "It's okay, Mom. One day at a time."

And she says, "How do you talk like that when you are just a kid?" But all I do is repeat the words written in wooden letters on the wall in the kitchen. It seems to make her happy to think of me this way, like I am older or wiser or bigger than her.

Those nights I just go blank, like I could tie every bad thing inside me to a balloon and let it float up into the sky, disappearing beyond the clouds. And I think nothing can ever get to me because my secret is I'm different and nothing bad will ever happen to me. I can fly if I really want to and we don't need the things other kids need because we're special. We were alone in the School like an orphanage and we know how to take care of ourselves even if it means taking care of Mom too.

Derek's mom says we're like wild dogs running through the street.

We don't know if that's true because we don't know if anything is true like space travel or Martians or the tooth fairy or Reaganomics. It's all part of some big dusty book that we're too young to read. The rules are so different in the World Outside Synanon. The answers come in pieces, bit by bit as we explore the neighborhood around the house on Breys Avenue: bullets explode if you hit them with a hammer, there is no Santa Claus, do not cry in front of other boys, cats land on their feet no matter how close to the ground they are when you drop them, dog food tastes bad, don't say what you're thinking, kids can buy cigarettes from vending machines, gasoline will burn on water, candy bars can be stolen, Mom has read over a thousand books, a Labrador can beat a German shepherd in a fight, parents are supposed to protect you, bullies are mean, we're bad at baseball, we're good at reading, we're latchkey kids, we're poor, we're special, we're smart, we're different, we're alone.

WHEN I'M IN the tub, I let the warm water fill up all the way to the top edge and fall under, holding my breath and listening to my heartbeat. When I come up for air, Mom is sitting there, her hips pressed against the white plastic of the bathtub in her blue jeans, her now long hair falling past her shoulders, her hand extended for me to hold.

I feel a crowding, like my body is not my own. I want to tell her to leave but I don't have the words, the words can barely form in my mind, like the connection between my brain and the place where words are made runs through her.

The woman I'm told to call Mom is saying something but I let the water cover my ears to drown the words. Her hand closes around mine and all that's left is a blankness, as white as the walls of the tub. I know she thinks this is a close moment. "Hey, I'm your mom. Don't I have the right to sit here with my son?" she says. And I know it's my job. *Let's hold hands and chat, honey.* There's nothing I can say to her. It feels like I have been taken from somewhere warm to somewhere cold and this new place has a new bargain like we are bad if we don't act how she imagines little boys are supposed to act.

After all, she did us a favor and it is now our job to repay her. We are close and "close" means whatever she needs it to mean, whatever she thinks it means, even the days she lies in bed for hours with the deep-russian, even on the days she's crying in a heap on the floor, she knows what's real and I don't because even then she tells me, "You're going to grow up and do something great, something that will change the world." So it feels like a ladder I must climb up into the clouds to get away from this emptiness, to be somewhere warm. Except every time I climb it, when I get to the top, there's nothing there but quiet and cold and another ladder to climb.

Another night she calls me into the bedroom and she is lying facedown on the bed with her pants pulled down to the top of her behind. Next to her is a small jar that smells like peppermint and a slim white plastic object the shape of a rocket. "My back hurts, sweetie. Take some of that ointment and put it on my back." I grab the jar because I know it is my job to do whatever she asks because she is the reason I was born and so I rub the sticky ointment on her back. She grabs the little white plastic rocket and twists the bottom and it starts to make a buzzing sound. She hands it to me, "Now hold this on the skin." It shakes in my hand, making my fingers go numb as I place it on her back. I don't know why her back hurts or why this helps. And I don't know why I feel like I want to jump out of my head, like I am not a person at all but a ghost or a tool like a fork or the pliers Paul leaves under the sink. I am two inches tall of empty invisible nothing.

Whenever she asks me to do things like this, I don't know how to tell her I don't want to because it's like the idea doesn't exist in her mind. I'll say, "Do I have to?" Then she gets mad or worse, she turns in on herself with her mouth all scrunched up like she's about to cry and I know I'm being an Ungrateful Son.

When I tell Tony about it, he says the white thing is called a vibrator and I'm too young to know what it's for. "It's for her back," I say. He gives me the look he gives me to tell me I'm a dumb little kid and the next time Mom asks me to hold it on her back I tell her I don't want to. She tells me to stop being such an Ungrateful Son so I hold the tiny rocket on her back and feel myself slip through the ceiling to a space behind a wall fifty feet thick. From this place I can decide to be whatever I need to be for the world. I can be the Good Son who will act precisely as I am expected to act. I can disappear.

I'm just too small next to this mountain of *reasons*.

Because the reasons are endless and I know every one by heart: that we are a close "family" now that we left Synanon together and I am her special smart boy who will take care of her and make sure she's not lonely and it's my job to grow up to be special enough to explain to the world all the sacrifices she made for me, to dance with the quiet ones whether I want to or not, to be the cowboy who never leaves, to be her revenge on the cowboys who did.

CHAPTER 7

WALKING THROUGH YANKEE STADIUM WITH BABE RUTH

And then on the morning of my sixth birthday, just days after Mount St. Helens erupted, spewing fire, mud and ash over the entire Pacific Northwest, ash that traveled through the air and landed in the gutters in front of our house on Breys Avenue, ash that we collected solemnly in small jars and placed in secret spots for safekeeping, there is Dad, sitting quietly on the edge of my bed with his hands in his lap. I rub my eyes to get a good look. That curly black hair, that thick gold necklace, the faded jeans, the brown café leather jacket, the cowboy boots, the deep laugh lines around his hazel-green eyes as he smiles with that tan, weathered face that looks like it's been dragged behind a truck for a thousand miles.

"Hey, dude. Happy birthday." I jump up and throw my arms around his neck. He smells like Old Spice and skin lotion. *Dad. Da. Pop. Poppy.* I don't understand. *How does a blur come to life? How did he find us here in our hiding spot on the other side of the mountains? Did he ride his motorcycle?* It's too fantastic to imagine.

Tony wakes up in the bed across from mine. "Dad!" He jumps up and throws his arms around him, burying his face in his shoulder.

I can hear Tony cry and I don't know why but I start to cry too and then the three of us just sit there, two blond heads buried into the broad shoulders of our dark Italian father. A blur come to life in jeans on my bed.

He says, "I missed you guys."

"How did you get here?"

"I flew on a plane."

"Why?"

"I came for Mick's birthday."

"Just for the day?"

"Yep."

"But isn't that really far?"

"Not so far."

"When are you leaving?"

"Later tonight, but your mom and I talked. You guys are going to come stay with me next summer in Los Angeles."

"Really?! The whole summer?!"

I stare at his face trying to memorize it, to give sharp outlines to the blur in my head. Eyes, brownish green. Hair, black, curly. Mustache, thick and bushy, covering all the space between his mouth and his nose. Crow's-feet. Lines on his forehead. It seems the sun is shining on him, even in the dark room in the basement.

We have breakfast with Mom then he takes us to the field in front of the school to play baseball. He has us stand in the outfield with our gloves as he hits balls to us to practice fielding. He tells us to crouch, to keep our knees bent and our bodies low with our gloves centered between our legs. We chase down grounders and line drives. We kneel afterward at home plate and he says we're going to get pizza for lunch. We walk the two blocks back to the house on Breys Avenue.

Some of the other kids are tossing a football in the street as we walk up with our dad. He's tall, in his orange-brown cowboy boots with the big heels, hairy with olive skin so different from my white hairless arms, my overbite which makes my mouth stick out in a funny way like the apes in *Planet of the Apes*. It feels like walking with a trophy, with a tank, like walking through Yankee Stadium with Babe Ruth. I want to scream, "Hey everyone, this is my dad you little shits! He's only here for the day. He flew from Los Angeles where he lives, though he could've ridden his motorcycle over the mountains if he wanted to."

The boys are silent as we walk by. That's the power of a dad, I think. Your own private pit bull, your own private genie, your own private Zeus.

He takes us to Shakey's where he lets us order two bottomless Cokes and an extra-large pepperoni pizza. I can't help but stare at him as we walk to the booth to sit down, to take note of the dip of his walk which has the slightest rhythm to it, almost like a dance, his hand swinging just a little lower than it needs to, the smallest bounce between strides. He comes up behind me at the table, puts his hand on my shoulder and pats me on the chest. There's a closeness to it. I think, *I am a son. I have a father.*

I memorize the walk, trying to get the rhythm down. It doesn't quite work without the boots. His speech has a music to it. "Let's get you boys some pizza. If I don't eat soon, we're gonna have ourselves a fuckin' *problem.*" He's not afraid to swear in front of us, like we're in on something, just us boys. And he swears so poetically, so effortlessly. "Those goddamn Padres suck shit this year. They only got like two bats on the whole damn team." "That shitbird Reagan couldn't find his ass with his own hands." "It's a good truck but the fuckin' carburetor is busted again."

The fuckin' carburetor. I repeat the words under my breath, practicing for emphasis. The trick is to roll the word "fuckin'" out like it's nothing, like you don't even care about it, like it's just a short detour on the way to the word "carburetor." *Oh, did I say "fuck"? I didn't even realize.* I don't even know what a carburetor is but when Dad says that word between bites of pepperoni pizza, when he shakes his head, I shake mine too as if to say, "Yeah Dad, no fuckin' shit. It must be the fuckin' carburetor. That's your problem right there."

I repeat the phrase in my head, trying to imagine ways I can work it into my daily speech. "Well, Derek, see the problem with your bike is the fuckin' carburetor." And "Ah well, Mom, I hate to say it but the reason the oven won't turn on is the fuckin' carburetor."

"And don't even get me started on Thatasshole Reagan," he says, pulling a stringy piece of pizza from his mouth. "I tell you what, if your mom loses her job, it'll be because of Thatasshole Reagan. Thatasshole will say anything to get elected." He's been called Thatasshole so many times by so many people I don't even know his first name. When I heard the name "Ronald" Reagan on TV, I figured Thatasshole must have a brother who's running for president.

When we get to talking, Dad says that Synanon wasn't so bad. Tony and I are on our third glass of sugary-sweet soda. I've mixed Mountain Dew, Sprite and Orange Crush with it to make what we call a Suicide. I don't want to go anywhere. I wonder if we could live right here in this red booth next to the big window at the Shakey's on Market Street drinking pop and listening to Dad talk. "Synanon was a great place, before it went bad. We used to say we were in the people business. We did one thing: we took people who had problems and we turned them around so they were a better person."

"So why'd you leave?"

"Well, after so long, Chuck started to buy his own bullshit. Waddya gonna do?" He puts his hands out, raising his shoulders.

"Did you really carry a gun, Dad? Before Synanon? Like a real shotgun?" Tony has told me these stories, about the drugs and the fights and the crime and Chino state prison. He collects them. We both do. And we know this is a rare moment, alone with Dad with our pop and bellies full of pizza.

"Oh, sure. I had to."

"But couldn't people see it?"

"No, I used to wear a long brown trench coat to hide it. I didn't really use it but you never know. Having a gun pointed at your head is a lousy way to spend a Saturday night."

"What did you do? Did you rob houses or steal cars? Was it like organized crime?"

"More like *dis*-organized crime. We wrote bad checks and stole credit card numbers. We ran some drugs. We were too high to be very organized about it." He lets out a cackle and looks me in the eye, a joke we share, just us guys.

"Weren't you scared in prison?"

"Not really. It wasn't so bad. The trick is to make everyone think you're crazy. That way they leave you alone. If someone walked up to me trying to give me a ration of shit, I would just start screaming at the top of my lungs. After a while, people got the point, you know?"

He tells us this like it's information we might find useful someday.

"And never take no shit from the guards. 'Cause they'll try to make you feel like you're nothing. You can't let anybody treat you that way. Especially those sonsabitches.

"I had a number. They give everyone a number. Mine was A-73581. When they lined you up, they would call you by your number instead of your name. And I would say, 'Fuck you, I have a name, asshole. Call me by my name.' I got to be such a pain in the ass they didn't want to deal with me because it made them look bad if they didn't react. So they'd say, 'I'm gonna lock you in solitary.' I'd say, 'Big deal. I'm *locked up*. Right? How many times you gonna lock me up?'"

There's a rhythm to the stories, a pace, like he's told them a thousand times. He's not embarrassed or ashamed. It's more like this is what he knows and he's not going to pretend to know other things. He knows about prison and he knows about cars. He knows about drugs and he knows about Dope Fiends. He knows about baseball, horse racing and those fuckin' carburetors.

He stays for dinner that night and he's gone by the time I wake up the next morning. I carry the day with me in the back of my head, repeating the things he said over and over again. I focus on what he looked like, the way he smelled, whispering, *That fuckin' carburetor. How many times you gonna lock me up?* The way his blue jeans fell over the top of his boots, the small green dot of tattoo on the middle knuckle of his left hand. How he said, "We'll go to the beach and I'll teach you to bodysurf. It's easy," when he came to my room before bed that night. He slipped a twenty-dollar bill into my hand with a smile. "Here. It's good to have a little cash in your pocket." Then he gave me a kiss on the cheek and I felt the roughness of his thick mustache on the corner of my mouth. He walked out and I felt a pull on my chest as he went, like something stretching to its limit. He paused at the doorway maybe because he felt it too. This stretching. This thing like we're supposed to stick together.

"I'm gonna take you to Hollywood Park when you come to L.A. You can bet the ponies with me. There's nothing like a day at the races. You'll see."

CHAPTER 8
FATHER FIGURES

Paul is at the house all the time. He comes on Friday night for dinner and he's still there when we wake up on Saturday morning. He eats cereal in his underwear and watches cartoons with us. We get three channels, 2, 4 and 8. Every Saturday morning we switch between *Looney Tunes, Super Friends* and *Fat Albert*. Paul sits right down on the floor with us in his torn underwear. We both like him because he doesn't suddenly change the channel or start talking about Reagan.

Mom stays in bed on Saturday mornings reading books. She's got hundreds of them, stacked on a shelf against the wall. She's always saying, "TV will rot your brain." She gives us books about animals and books about trees and books about people who live in the ice and snow. Sometimes I read the books and sometimes I just pretend to. Tony doesn't even bother pretending. "What I need is an aluminum bat," he says, when she gives him a book about baseball. Every now and then she shouts, "Paul!" and he disappears into the bedroom.

After a while Paul stops going home. He brings more and more stuff over to the house, his camping gear, his fishing poles, his clothes.

One night Mom says we're having a Big Talk which we know is a big deal because the only other time we've ever had one was when Tony and I started a fire in the woodstove when no one else was home. We were spanked. Bare ass, with paddles. Which was something she always said she was against and it hurt her more than it hurt us.

She says Paul is going to be living with us from now on and how do we feel about that? Tony says he doesn't care and that Mom should do whatever she wants. It's not like it matters to her what he thinks anyway. She says that's not true and that she cares a lot about what he thinks. So he says he thinks it's cold here and it rains all the time so why can't we live back in California where it was sunny and everyone didn't think we were weird? Mom says there's nothing she can do about that, we can't afford to live in California plus she has her job at the state mental hospital and doesn't Tony like his Little League team? Tony says it's okay but he needs cleats. Everyone else on the team has baseball cleats and he has to play in his bubble gum shoes with no tread from Goodwill. Also, why does he have to share a room with his shithead little brother who's always saying little shithead things?

I tell him to shut up and Mom says don't call your little brother names and he says why not, he's a sneaky little son of a bitch and it's not fair that he has to live with me and that he doesn't have real baseball cleats. Mom says, go to your room if you're going to talk like that so Tony gets up and stomps his feet on the floor as he walks through the kitchen and down the stairs to our room where he slams the door.

"He's such a dick."

"Don't talk like that. What do you think about Paul coming to live with us?"

I say I like him, that he's nice to us and he makes her happy. I say this because I know it's what I'm supposed to say even though I'd probably say it anyway because Paul slips us candy when Mom isn't looking and when he's around I don't have to hold the white plastic rocket on her back.

Mom says Paul is going to be my father figure now and that all boys need a father figure. I want to tell her I already have a dad and just because he's in Los Angeles doesn't mean he's not my father figure but I know she doesn't want to hear it. She says I need a role model that I see every day. All the books say so. I'll understand it someday when I read books like she does. It's basic Child Psychology.

Sometimes I think Tony is right to be mad. Maybe I should be too but he's better at it and I don't know how to disagree with Mom. He does it all the time. Maybe it's because he was older when he left Synanon so he didn't really know her until he was almost seven. I had a Bonnie who was like a mom and I don't think he had anyone because he never says anything good about it. Mom thinks maybe something bad happened to him there. That might be true but I want to tell her being alone is bad enough already. It's bad enough to wake up with no one to talk to and I don't know why she always forgets that's how it was for us.

It's hard to feel loved when you are alone. Tony was alone for almost seven years.

He's sadder than I am. I know that. But sometimes he forgets how much he hates me and he's almost nice. He throws rocks with me in the alley and helps me light my Luke Skywalker action figure on fire with the gasoline from the gas can. He likes that. I love him, mostly because we're brothers and we look alike and I know we have to stick together. At least that's what people say.

Paul never says anything about being a father figure. His face turns red and he goes quiet when Mom says it. He pretends his hunting knife needs sharpening and stands over the sink with the blade and a flat stone. He says, "Don't force it" or "Let it alone, Gerry."

She says, "But you're going to be their role model." Paul doesn't seem to be convinced. I think he knows we already have a dad.

Paul sits with us before bed while Mom reads upstairs about Child Psychology. He reads Tony's comics and listens to Michael Jackson with us on the tape recorder that Dad gave me when he came to visit. He says, "Did you have a good day?" And even if I say Derek and I got in a fight, he won't cut me off and tell me how I need to be a better person. He listens then says, "Next time you should just tell him he can't ride your bike without asking" and "He's your buddy, so you got to try to be nice to him."

He says now that he's living here, he wants to be an "open book" and I can ask him any questions I want. So I do.

"Why are you home all the time? Don't you have a job?"

"I had one. I was training to be an EMT, which is someone who drives around in an ambulance and helps people who are hurt."

"Are you still an EMT?"

"Well, I lost my job."

"So how'd you meet our mom?"

"Through the program. She's in Al-Anon and I'm in AA and we know some of the same people."

"You're in AA? Doesn't that mean you're an alcoholic?"

"A recovering alcoholic. That's what we say."

"When was the last time you drank?"

"Two years ago."

"What did you drink?"

"Didn't matter. The point was to get drunk."

"Why?"

"Because then I could forget about everything."

"Why'd you want to do that?"

"I don't know. I guess I didn't like myself very much."

"Why not?"

"This just doesn't end with you, does it, kid?"

"You said I could ask whatever I wanted."

"Fair enough. At first I didn't like myself because I wanted to be a doctor but I wasn't smart enough so I drank to feel better. Then after a while I didn't like myself because I drank so much. So I drank to forget that too."

"That doesn't sound fun."

"It wasn't. It's a disease, you know. Like polio or cancer."

"Is it contagious?"

"No. But it runs in families."

"Isn't that the same thing?"

"Not really. But it progresses like a disease does. It gets worse and worse as time goes on. Eventually, it got to the point where I didn't even go to bars. I'd just get a bottle and go park my truck somewhere in the woods. I'd wake up and wonder where I was. That's when I knew I had a problem and I went to AA."

"Do you like AA?"

"It beats drinking alone in the woods."

"What do you do at AA?"

"We talk about when we drank and how bad it was and we help each other work the twelve steps."

"What are the twelve steps?"

"They're a bunch of things that you do that make it so you don't feel like you need to drink anymore."

"Did you do all twelve?"

"I did them all in one weekend."

"Is that fast?"

"Yeah. That's not really how you're supposed to do it. So then I went back and did them over six months or so."

"Did you feel better?"

"I did, actually. I felt lighter. Like I didn't need to forget so much because I liked myself more. I can't believe I'm telling all this to a little kid. You sound like you're thirty, ha-ha!"

"Do you love my mom?"

"Yes I do."

"Are you going to marry her?"

"I don't know."

"Can we watch cartoons now?"

"Sure."

He takes us fishing down on the banks of the Willamette River beneath the West Salem bridge. He has a green tackle box full of lures and we go to a bait shop to buy earthworms and bright pink garlic marshmallows for the rainbow trout. He teaches us how to curl the worm around the hook so it goes through the body in three different places, how to cast the line out and reel it in slowly, careful not to hit anyone standing behind us, how it's important to release the line at just the right point to get the most distance. Tony catches a trout. We put it on a metal line attached to a rock in the river that goes through the mouth of the fish and back out through the gills. He teaches us to skin it, right there on a flat rock on the shore of the Willamette with a fillet knife that he uses to cut open the belly and take out all the guts. Then he cuts the head off, splitting it into two halves right down the middle. We take it home and Paul fries it up with garlic and butter and salt and we wish we could eat fried fish every night.

When Tony and I start school at Englewood Elementary three blocks away, Paul is there to pack our lunches in the morning and even walks with us to the front gate. I've never been to school before so when I see the huge yellow building in front of the baseball diamond, it seems like a spaceship. I think maybe I'm going on a journey somewhere. I know I'm supposed to go inside because that's where all the other kids are going, into the spaceship to be launched into space.

There are so many kids in my class and they are all different shapes and sizes. Timothy Manning, who seems mean with his dirty face, making fun of everyone from the back row. There's a girl who wears dirty clothes like

Tony and me, but she smells like pee. This is good, I think because even though our clothes have holes in them, at least we don't smell. There's a boy with smooth, well-trimmed black hair and tight designer jeans with white stitching that says Jordache across the pocket and a pretty blond girl in a dotted blue dress. She looks like a doll, something I'm not allowed to be near in my dirty pants and stained red ski vest from the Salvation Army.

On the first day the teacher gives everyone number lines that are supposed to teach us how to add. One plus one then three plus two. You take your pencil down the line to mark the answer. But I already know how to add and subtract and multiply and I don't understand why the other kids can't do it too. I watch them struggle and wonder what I'm missing. The teacher gives me a workbook for second graders that has pictures of birds inside circles and I have to say how many are in the circle and how many are outside it and how many there are total and again I don't understand why we would have to write something so silly.

When I give her the workbook back, she reads it and after a little while she tells me we should go visit the third-grade teacher. So we go across the hall to the third-grade class during nap time and the teacher there gives me a workbook. She shows me how I'm supposed to follow directions and put my name in the upper-right-hand corner on each page, so I do. Then she says do I understand and I say yes and they both watch me read the workbook which is all about blocks and numbers and shapes and making change for a dollar.

One day the vice-principal comes into the classroom and talks to my teacher who calls me up to the front of class. We sit down in the corner and he says, "Have you ever been to school before?" And I say no because I don't think the Synanon School counts since it was like an orphanage and nobody talks about it. So he says, "Do you do schoolwork at home?" I say no because maybe that's cheating, to talk about all the books Mom gives me. I don't want to get in trouble and these kids are all bigger than me and they've been to school before and my brother is in fourth grade and he's always putting me in headlocks and breaking my stuff.

The vice-principal says they need to talk to my mom about it but maybe I'd be "more comfortable" in a different class. He says he called her at work but she was busy and I say, "Well yeah, she's got a lot of prisoners to deal with," and he gives me a funny look.

When I tell Mom all about the workbooks and what the vice-principal said, she says she isn't surprised because all we ever did in Synanon was read and write and I'm the special life that she had to protect and bring into the world so I could change it someday.

She skipped two grades in school when she moved to the United States from Dutch but she hated it because everyone was older than her and no one spoke Dutch and it was hard to have friends.

When the vice-principal takes me out of class, he puts me at a desk in his office and says he wants me to do a test. After the test I get to go outside for recess. All the boys climb on the monkey bars and play tag in the field and I'm thinking about the test and about the story I read about a poor couple who couldn't buy Christmas gifts for each other so the woman sold her hair to buy a watch chain for her husband. But the husband sold his watch to buy a brush for his wife's hair so neither of them can really use the gifts that they were given. The gift is a waste. The test asks you to give an example of ironing but I just write down that it's funny that they tried to help each other by giving away the thing they love the most and at the end they realize they don't really need possessions anyway as long as they have each other which is what Mom is always telling us when we want her to buy us a new *Star Wars* action figure.

I'm walking through the field and a big group of kids run by and one of them nearly runs into me so Timothy Manning runs up and says, "What's wrong with you?"

"Nothing. I was just thinking."

"You're in the way, dummy. We're playing freeze tag." He's got straight black hair and he stands over me with his shoulders back and his fists at his side even though he's skinny and maybe half the size of my brother who I have to fight all the time. There's no Demonstrator, which is what they called teachers in the Synanon School. When you had a problem with another kid, you were supposed to tell everyone your feelings so that you could learn to be a new kind of person who doesn't need parents. But that seems like a terrible idea when a boy is standing over you with a bunch of kids with dirty faces and balled-up fists. The bell rings and that means recess is over and we all have to go back inside.

"I didn't see you."

"Yeah, no shit. Mikel. What kind of sissy name is that? Mikel Pick-ell. Mikel Pick-ell!" he yells as he walks away. I know Timothy Manning doesn't like me but I don't know why. Maybe it's because I'm too short or because my pants have holes or because my teeth stick out like the apes from *Planet of the Apes*. I wonder if this is what school will always be like.

Mom comes to the school at the end of the day and I go to the office instead of going out to play and the vice-principal tells her that the test I took says I should skip to at least third grade, maybe fourth. Has she thought about putting me in private school? She says public school is just fine thank you very much and that we couldn't afford private school anyway and she doesn't want to "in-doctor-nate" her kids with a bunch of religious bullcrap. She says she skipped two grades and went off to college when she was only fifteen and it wasn't good for her because of Child Psychology so I should just stay in first grade with other kids my own age even if that means the work is easy. He says that I won't be challenged and that could lead to behavioral problems. He's going to put me in the Talented and Gifted Program, which means I get to go on field trips sometimes but it still won't be the appropriate challenge. She says she's not going to mess me up by putting me with a bunch of kids who are older than me.

The vice-principal sees that you can't argue with her once she's made up her mind about Her Values so I stay in the first grade.

CHAPTER 9

THE RABBITS

Paul walks back and forth with a tape measure and a pencil, marking places on the wood inside the barn in the backyard against the alley. He says it's time that he "contribute," and since we're always eating hot dogs and noodles, we need healthier food so he's going to start raising rabbits for us to eat for dinner. Mom says rabbits are the most efficient way to turn vegetables into meat.

I've only ever seen rabbits on TV like Bugs Bunny or the jackrabbits that used to run through the fields behind the School in Synanon. Tony says, so we're just going to eat rabbit now? Like, bunnies? And Mom says yeah what's wrong with that? He says because they're pets not food. She says we won't be treating them like pets and food is food and we can't afford meat from the store and he can't grow up eating only noodles and government cheese from the food bank.

"It'll be good, you'll see. Rabbit tastes like chicken."

"Who's going to kill them?"

"We are. It's easy."

Tony says they're basically just big rats and Mom says no they're a good source of lean protein. Doesn't he want strong muscles to play baseball with?

"Why does everything we do have to be so weird?" he says. "Why can't we just be like normal people and eat normal things?" Mom says that normal people eat rabbit and Tony says no they don't, they eat hamburgers and chicken and ice cream after dinner.

"Why do you have to make everything so difficult?" But he says that she's the one who makes everything difficult and he hates it here and wishes he lived in Los Angeles with Dad. Mom starts to cry because she doesn't know how to get mad. It's like the anger rises up in her then turns into tears the second it gets to her eyes.

She says, "I tried to have a normal life. That's all I wanted. Just a husband and kids and a normal family that loved each other. But then they took my babies from me and everyone went crazy so what was I supposed to do? What do you want me to do, Toe?"

Tony is quiet because nobody has an answer to that question.

He goes to his room and Paul goes outside. I tell Mom that he's always angry about something. She reaches her hand out for me to hold, her face buried in her elbow as I sit next to her in the wolf den. If I could open up my chest at that moment, there would be nothing but a blank shield inside, a barrier, rigid and sealed, from which nothing escapes, into which nothing is absorbed. It starts at the bottom of my throat and runs all the way to my knees. I hide behind it. I hold it up over me. I feel it there when I swallow, when I breathe. There are no tears because tears come from the heart and the heart is beneath the shield. There's no anger either or sadness, just a feeling that I have to figure out the right thing to say.

"Rabbit sounds like it could be good. Progress not perfection." I picture chasing rabbits around the yard, the fall and crack of an ax, the way it must get stuck in your teeth when you eat it.

"Who made you such an old soul?" she says. I shift my weight. She likes to say this but all I ever do is repeat the things I hear the adults say. I think I know what "progress not perfection" means. I've read it on the little pamphlets for Al-Anon Mom leaves around the house. But I also know that to her it means something different, something more. I like the power this gives me, to be thought of as an adult or a wise man, someone to be relied upon in a crisis, someone who's stronger than all of them and can't be shaken. And I believe it. After all, I can do anything.

But then sometimes I forget and I get mad. I want to run away. I'm scared and I'm sad. I have nowhere to put it. I don't know the words so I just repeat the ones I read in the AA pamphlets.

"It'll be okay, Mom. Remember to let go and let God."

"One day at a time."

"Progress not perfection."

THE FIRST TIME Paul slaughters the rabbits, we are at school. When we come home, there is a white plastic bucket full of guts in the backyard next to the tree covered in powdery lye. The smell of blood and fur is thick in the air. The rabbit carcasses are stacked on top of each other on a table, bound for the freezer downstairs. The gray-brown pelts are piled neatly on the gravel path leading to the barn. The ground beneath the tree is red with blood. He's placed the heads in a plastic bag in the alley behind the barn. You can follow the smell of it, to open the bag and see tiny white maggots crawling over their eyes.

Tony picks up Paul's hunting knife with its carved bone handle and thick six-inch blade and cleans it off with the hose. We both like the knife. Paul lets us hold it sometimes. It's bigger than my forearm, heavy, like a sword, the curved blade rounding to a point at the tip. We hold it sideways in front of our faces and imagine we are David Carradine in *Kung Fu* walking alone through the Chinese desert.

Paul hands each of us a shovel to work on the piles of rabbit droppings under the empty cages in the barn. "Rabbit shit is the cleanest of all shits," he says. "It makes for great fertilizer. You could practically eat it." The small, round black pellets of manure have an earthy smell. We shovel it into a wheelbarrow then carry the bucket to a pile next to the shed where Paul keeps his tools. "We're going to start composting. From now on anything plant or animal doesn't go in the trash. It goes here."

The compost heap grows in the weeks afterward as we add eggshells and rabbit bones, apple cores and lemon peels. Paul rents a tiller and tears up the ground next to the house so that the grass and weeds turn to mulch. He boxes in four large gardens with wooden boards and Mom plants tomatoes, squash, cucumbers, carrots, cabbage, lettuce and even strawberries. Saturdays are for pulling weeds and once the vegetables begin to grow, she avoids store-bought produce if she can.

After the first slaughter, we eat rabbit most nights. Tony considers this a kind of torture and is in constant protest just like Mom was in Berkeley under Reagan. He squirms in his chair. He crosses his arms. He stares at his plate. He says, "This piece looks bad. What if I just eat the potatoes?" Or he says, "I think rabbit can make you sick. We studied it in school today."

Mom makes baked rabbit and lemon rabbit. She makes stir-fry rabbit with peppers and onions and "rabbit surprise," which is leftover baked rabbit that has been cut up and put into a casserole dish. Sometimes Mom fries up a rabbit kidney in a pan or a veiny rabbit heart the size of a plum. The organs struggle and spit, dancing around the hot frying pan like they're still alive, filling the house with the gamy smell of hot blood. Mom will lift the kidney whole with a fork and plop it in her mouth without even salting it. It's amazing to watch her eat something so disgusting. It seems to us like a kind of sorcery.

When Mom dares to serve rabbit liver as an entrée, Tony refuses to eat at all. He just stares at his plate and shakes his head.

Mom says, "There's good nutrition in that liver."

"I'm not eating this. It's disgusting."

Mom crosses her arms and says, "You can't get up until you eat your liver." There's a silence in the kitchen as the words ring out. I look down at the slab of tough, unseasoned meat on my plate and poke it with a fork. Eventually I take a bite. It tastes exactly the way rabbit manure smells.

Tony doesn't budge. He sits all through dinner, then after dinner when I take a bath, all through *The Greatest American Hero* and teeth brushing. I walk into the kitchen to check on him, "Maybe just eat a little." But he shakes his head and lays it into the crook of his elbow at the table.

Just before bedtime, when the lights are off and I am in bed wondering who is going to win the standoff, whether Tony is simply going to start a new life there in the kitchen next to his uneaten plate of liver, maybe pitch a tent beneath the table or set up his sleeping bag next to his chair, I hear Mom walk in and say, "Okay, you can get up. I don't know what to do with you. But you're going to bed without supper." Tony runs downstairs and jumps into the bed next to me, pulling the covers over his head.

"Why didn't you just eat some of it? Just to make her happy?"

"That's not my job."

On a Saturday morning Mom announces that she is going to make a pot of rabbit stew using only vegetables from our garden. She has a kind of hypnotized look in her eyes, a dreaminess as she slices the zucchini and tomatoes and tosses them into the big metal pot that we see on Christmas when she makes warm apple cider with cinnamon sticks. She adds onions and celery and potatoes and bits of rabbit. The pot boils all afternoon, filling the house with an earthy aroma that gets in our clothes and hair. When dinner comes, she stands at the pot proudly and says, "See, we can be self-sufficient if we want to. No money from the government or a corporation, just people living off their own labor."

I offer her my bowl because I'm certain we're about to hear a lecture about Nixon. He was impeached just after I was born. The events are always connected in my head since they've been described to me that way so many times. "Well, you were born right when they got Thatbastard Nixon so I knew we were on to something." It's not clear exactly where the stew fits into the story but I know "living off our own labor" is a way to "stick it to the man" who is always "stepping on the little guy" and that eating rabbit stew is my patriotic duty.

After dinner, the big pot goes into the fridge where it sits overnight and, as Mom puts it, "steeps." Like the special cheese in the drawer that we're not allowed to eat, the philosophy is that rabbit stew gets better "as it ages." So, on night two of rabbit stew, we sit down to eat a thicker version of the soup we ate the night before. The carrots have begun to lose their shape and bits of rabbit meat have separated into long strings. The celery is still mostly intact and there is still the occasional potato.

By night three, there is a palpable resentment in the air. Mom spoons the thick stew into our bowls. Paul wants to support Mom's project to "live off the grid" and as a rule does not complain when she cooks. But after two reheatings and three days in the fridge, the stew has become something more like a slop. It is still possible to distinguish solids from liquids but it is no longer possible to distinguish solids from each other. Potatoes and carrots and celery and rabbit clump together in a mushy gel the consistency of thickened snot. We lift the stew into the air with spoons and let it drip slowly back into our bowls.

By day four of rabbit stew, it is not entirely clear if what is left in the big pot is technically food. A grayish brown mass sits in the center. Chewy bits of caked stew, blackened from four nights of reheating on the stove, have fallen off the sides and are only distinguishable from the clumps of vegetable by their shape, which is flat, like little squares of tomatoey skin. Mom serves the stew in silence. Tony and I stare at our bowls, trying to remember brighter days. Even Paul taps the goop with his spoon, testing it cautiously, like it might jump. He looks up at Mom, who says, "What? It's better now. It's absorbed the spices."

Tony takes a bite, twisting his mouth in disgust as his face loses color. "I don't feel good. Can I have something else?"

"No you cannot. Eat your dinner. This is good nourishment."

I watch him lift his spoon slowly to his mouth with an unsteady hand. He sniffs at it, throws his head back like he's been punched, and throws up right into his stew bowl.

We freeze. I think maybe he's faking it and I'm mad that I didn't think of it first. But as he pulls his mouth away, covered in red and orange spit, chunks of vegetable on his chin, it's clear he waged the most effective nonviolent protest yet. If this isn't passive resistance, I don't know what is.

I expect Mom to scoop the puke out of his mouth and put it back into the pot because at this point what would be the difference?

Paul says, "Jesus, Tony," as he wipes his face with a hand towel. They go into the bathroom to clean up. Mom stands silently next to her pot of homegrown rabbit stew, defeated and alone with her thoughts.

I wonder if this is how Nixon felt.

When they walk back in, Paul says, "Maybe we should go out to eat tonight."

I don't say a word.

Mom says, "But what'll we do with all this stew?"

WHEN SLAUGHTERING TIME comes around again, Mom decides it's time we learn about the "cycle of life" so that we can understand our food comes from somewhere besides the grocery store. Paul sits us down in the backyard early on a Saturday morning and tells us, "This isn't a game, so I need you guys to take it seriously. I can teach you but only if you respect it. Don't go fartin' around with the knife or the lye or the club."

He gets the black metal rod down from the loft in the barn where he keeps his rifle and ties a string around a branch from the tree in front of the shed. "This is where we hang the rabbits, to drain the blood." He takes a scooper from a bucket of white powder and shakes it down the trunk of the big tree next to the toolshed. "This is lye. Don't touch this stuff. It's there to make sure none of the blood or guts turn to rot on the tree."

We go into the barn where the litters of three-month-old bunnies are waiting in their cages. They aren't quite as big as the breeders, the mama bunnies and papa bunnies we've named Peter and Princess, the huge brown floppy-eared bunny we've named Fred who sits around his cage all day. But they aren't small either. We've been careful not to name the young ones since Mom says you can't be friends with your food.

Paul opens a cage and picks up one of the adolescent gray bunnies by the loose skin around its neck. It kicks and flails. He's careful to keep the sharp claws away from his face, holding it out with a stiff arm as we follow him outside.

He kneels down and pins the rabbit to the gravel with his left hand, picking up the black iron club with his right. "The important thing is to hit him hard on his head. You want to knock him out so he doesn't suffer. Not two hits. Not three. One hard smack across the back of the skull." He lifts the pipe and brings it down hard. There's a crushing sound as metal hits bone. Bunny eyes shoot back in their sockets, bunny legs kick straight out. Paul holds it up and carries it to the tree while it squirms. "He's knocked out. That's just nerves leaving the body."

I can't help but think of Phil in the driveway and the bad men from Synanon.

We grab another from the barn. He holds it down by its neck on the gravel path and says, "Remember you've got to hit him hard. That's the humane thing to do. Hitting him softly only means he suffers more." He hands me the iron rod. "Go ahead."

I feel the weight of it. The club is heavier than I expected it to be, not quite as heavy as a baseball bat, but smaller, denser, so that as I take practice swings, the end falls much faster than I expect and I have trouble with my aim. I squeeze tight and hit the bunny on the head. It kicks and squirms. "No!" Paul yells in my ear. "You got to hit it hard. Now you just hurt him. Swing again!"

There's a trickle of blood coming from the rabbit's nose as it struggles under his hand. "Now! Hit him! Hard!" I swing the club again, feeling it ricochet back when it hits the skull. The bunny lets out an awful wheezing sound as its left eye bugs out and falls halfway from its socket. It's still kicking and trembling, a small bright red pool forms under its head. Little spots of blood dot the gravel. "Goddamn it! Give me the goddamn club!" He takes it from my hand and smashes it over the rabbit's skull with a loud crack that seems to echo off the barn and the house, down the alley and up into the sky. The bunny falls limp.

"That's why you gotta hit 'em hard."

"I tried. I was just afraid to hurt it."

"You've got to kill it on the first hit. That's the whole point."

He ties the rabbit's foot to the string on the tree as it flops and twitches against the trunk. He walks over to the table he's set up and picks up the big hunting knife, carrying it low, blade down, below his waist. He grabs the ears and cuts off the head, sawing through the neck. Thick dark red blood flows out in streams over the powdery white lye.

He throws the head in a bucket. "You have to let all the blood get out before you do anything else." We wait in silence while the blood drains.

Paul breaks each of the rabbit's legs "to make it easier to remove the skin." He makes an incision just below the point where the string has been tied around the rabbit foot. He cuts and pulls, cuts and pulls, removing the fur in one big piece, slicing away stubborn bits of creamy white skin. When the pelt is halfway down, he puts down the knife and gives it a hard pull, removing it all at once. What's left is a small rabbit carcass dangling from a tree. At this point it looks more like the meat we see on our plates every night than the bunnies that hop around in their cages.

By the time we get to the tenth rabbit, I get the hang of it. How to hold it down by the neck, even saying "shhhh" to calm it before bringing that club down as hard as I can with all my strength and determination to not make him suffer, to crack the life out of it on the back of its skull in one swing.

We cut off the heads, remove the skin and empty the guts, careful to cut out the little green gall sac that hangs inside the rib cage. "That's the nasty stuff," Paul says. "Got to be careful not to puncture the sac. Could ruin the meat."

When we're done, we put the carcasses into small bags and take them down to the freezer in the basement. "How about some cocoa?" Paul says. "But not that sugar-free shit your mom buys. I got the good stuff." He gets a chair and climbs up to reach the cabinet above the sink, moving aside the purple cold medicine and a box of gauze. "My stash," he says with a wink. We have cocoa and he gives us each a five-dollar bill. "Good job today. Now you guys know how to slaughter. It's basically the same with all animals. In theory you could field dress a moose."

I drink my cocoa and try not to think about the bunnies, about the queasiness in my stomach, how I didn't want to hurt them, how doing so meant that I had to imagine it as a game and not the thunderclap of life as it ends and I watch their little bunny souls fly up into the sky.

CHAPTER 10
SUUUUUUN

There is a crackle of static from the plastic yellow phone when my brother hands it to me in the living room. We have a ritual when Dad calls from Los Angeles. The ritual is we fight over who gets to talk to him first and Tony wins. I don't mind. He's nice to me when he's talking to Dad and Mom lets us stay up past bedtime since she's always telling us children need a father figure even if it's a drug addict ex-con who left her for a tramp.

Dad says he's looking forward to seeing us in L.A. in the summer and that we can go to the beach and he'll take us to Disneyland and how does that sound? It sounds like another world to me and I'm not sure if he's even serious and if he were to say, "Just joking. Ha-ha," I would say, "Good one, Dad."

"I have someone here who wants to talk to you."

"Me? Who?"

"Hold on."

I hear the shuffle of movement through the tinny speaker and then a familiar voice that seems to speak in song. "Hello? Is this the Mouseketeer, Mr. Mikel himself, writer of stories, drawer of pictures? Is this really and truly the one and only Suuuuuun?"

"Bonnie?"

"Who else calls you Suuuuuun, silly?"

"But. What?" I can't find the words. It's been years and yet her voice is so familiar, like the sound of birds in a tree. She sings a silly little song,

"Mouse-kateer, Mouse-kateer, we can't wait 'til you get here." There's something ancient, a memory, like everything from Synanon before the move, before the bad men with their clubs in Berkeley who made us come here to hide in the rain.

"But what are you doing there with my dad?"

She says he just showed up one day. She opened the door and he was standing on her doorstep in his socks with his boots in his hand. "That was three months ago. He won't leave. I can't get rid of him so we shacked up."

"Shacked up?"

"Yep. That dad of yours is one crazy guy. He can't wait to see you next week. Every night he wakes me up and says, 'Are they here yet? Are they here yet?'"

The warmth in her voice seems out of place in Salem, Oregon. She says, "Okay, Suuuuuun, I love you."

"I love you too."

It's different from how those words are spoken in the house on Breys Avenue, which is like a question I'm supposed to know the answer to. These words are more like when your feet are cold from cleaning the rabbit barn in the rain so you come inside and put them next to the woodstove to watch the water steam off your shoes. I thought maybe I dreamed her up but there she is on the other end of that phone, "shacked up" with my dad somewhere near the ocean on the other side of the mountains a million miles away.

I PROMISED MYSELF I would memorize the details of Dad better this time. How he looks, how he talks, the way he walks. I go through the checklist in my head. Curly black hair like an Afro. Mustache. Tan neck. The boots. The jeans. The lines on his face around his eyes when he smiles. That cackle. The slight dip and the swing of the arms as he turns on the heel of his boot. When we land at the airport in Los Angeles, I see him standing next to Bonnie at the end of the hallway. He's got a goofy smile and she's decked out in a long purple dress, hanging on his arm with her curly dark brown hair. I can't even walk the last twenty feet so I run and throw my arms around his neck as he lifts me up and says, "Hey, dude. You're here. You're actually here."

Bonnie squeezes me. "Suuuuuun! Did they let you fly the plane?! I heard they let you do that sometimes."

Their apartment in Playa del Rey is only blocks from the ocean. On the way home from the airport, Bonnie takes us down a highway where you can see the waves and the sand, the big oil tankers parked offshore and the people playing in the surf. The apartment is on a sunny street at the back of a courtyard with a redbrick wall under a huge purple tree called a jacaranda that Dad says sounds like a kind of snake.

There's ice cream in the fridge and big bottles of soda pop, string cheese and crackers, potato chips, frozen dinners, Popsicles, burritos and fruit. We can't believe our luck. We've never seen so much food. Tony asks Dad if we can really have string cheese anytime we want. He gives him a strange look. "Sure. Of course. If you're hungry, eat." We fill our bellies with Fruit Roll-Ups and bags of Fritos, microwave *taquitos* and celery with peanut butter and raisins.

At night we sit with Dad while he watches the Dodgers, smoking his Marlboro Lights and drinking a six-pack of white Budweiser cans. Nobody seems to care that he drinks in the house, or that he drinks at all. He doesn't seem any different after the sixth beer than he did after the first. He just talks louder, yelling at the TV, "Dodger blue, my ass. These bozos play like a junior high rec team."

"Dodger blue, my ass!" we yell in unison.

I know Mom would say that once an addict always an addict and therefore Dad shouldn't be drinking and she may be right but it just doesn't feel bad. Maybe because he's in the house. Maybe because it's just beer, not heroin. Maybe it's as simple as he doesn't leave.

He likes to talk about sports, about people I know nothing about. "Kareem was un-guardable last year. Un-*guard*-able. The release on that skyhook is like nine feet in the air. Watchu gonna do, climb a fuckin' ladder?" I make a mental note of phrases so I can repeat them later to the kids back in Salem. *Kareem Abdul-Jabbar. Un-guardable. Fuckin' ladder.*

We hang all over him, grabbing on to his neck and pulling on his arms. "You got to do some push-ups, kid." He picks us up, tying us into pretzels as we try to wrestle him to the ground.

He sends us for cigarettes at the Dales Jr. Market down the street. "Here, tell the guy they're for your dad. Marlboro Lights, in the hard box."

He gives Tony five bucks. He never asks for change so we spend it on Starburst and Hershey bars, asking for quarters for the *Donkey Kong Jr.* next to the door where we play doubles.

We sleep in the living room on the fold-out couch. It's never completely dark because of the huge window bringing the moonlight and electric lights from the courtyard.

He takes us to his shop where he's the manager, overseeing the mechanics like he did in Synanon, the team of Goodyear Tire salesmen. The place is called Foogerts, in the center of the city on a busy intersection. There's a showroom with walls stacked floor to ceiling with tires. Next to it is a hydraulic lift where they put the cars when they change the tires with noisy air guns pulling off the lug nuts with one squeeze of a trigger. One of his mechanics says, "Hey, Jimmy! You see that shit on lift two?"

Dad says, "Yeah, fucking Fiats, man. Too many hoses and wires. How do you drive a thing like that? Those I-talian engineers." He looks at us with a wink. "The Italians take too many lunch breaks. They made shitty tanks too. The old lady used to say if it wasn't for Fiat, Mussolini would've stayed in power and Italy wouldn't have switched sides. Bad Italian engineers are the reason we don't speak German."

At night I drift into the bedroom where Bonnie is reading Stephen King or Danielle Steel. I sit by her side or sometimes I curl into the bend of her knee as she lies sideways. We call this my "favorite spot." She says, "So, Suuuuuun, you bored with baseball? You got a girlfriend in that school of yours yet or what?"

We lie on our backs looking up at the ceiling, discussing school or how mean Tony is or her family or Dad or our mom. She's horrified by the rabbits. "So you have to cut their heads off? That's terrible." I tell her it's not so bad and you got to eat anyway.

She tells me about her job where she does phone sales and what it was like in Synanon when they made her get divorced from her husband, Eddie, who she loved. She seems so confused by it. She wanted to stay married but Eddie believed in the "Synanon system." "We got to trust it," he said. "We came this far."

The Old Man said that the marriages had to end and that was that. Either people got divorced or they left.

"I didn't know what to say. This was my husband telling me he was going off to be with another woman." All the couples were paired with other people by the Old Man and Eddie liked the woman he was paired with, Emily Durst. "She was pretty, I guess," Bonnie says, wiping her nose with her hand. She was paired with Lenny Dickenson who was short with bad breath. She wanted to leave but stay married. But Eddie wanted to stay which meant divorce. "So we got divorced and here I am." She lets out a bitter laugh.

She looks at me. "I can't believe I'm telling all this to a little kid. What are you, thirty? Ha-ha!"

Whenever I ask her about the School and how the Old Man wanted us to be new, special kinds of people, she says, "That was his bullshit. To me, you were just a baby. And you know, you don't plan to fall in love, you just do. I had a special bond with you. It's weird how that happens. Someone puts a kid in your life and next thing you know you're like a . . ." She pauses and looks at me.

"Like a mom," I say. She hugs me and tells me I was always special to her even though Chuck wanted us to be the new kinds of people who aren't children of their parents but children of the universe which if you think about it just means we were no one's children.

"What two-year-old is independent?" she says. "You were a little baby. You all were."

Bonnie's parents are Grandma Juliette and Grandpa Nat. That's what they tell us to call them from the first time we visit them at their house in the center of the city, just off Fairfax and Wilshire Boulevard. Grandma Juliette is a tiny woman with an electric smile in red lipstick and red boots whose face shakes as she opens the door and says, "Look at the *punim* on this one!" She squeezes me tight. She is in the doorway next to her golf clubs in the house where Bonnie grew up. She and Grandpa Nat bought the house in 1956 after a trip to California from Brooklyn, when she sat in a sunlit garden and thought, *We're never going back.*

Grandpa Nat is in the living room watching golf. He lights up when he sees us. "Bonita!" he says and stands up to give Bonnie a hug, singing, "Bonita . . . Chiquita . . . banana." He turns to Dad and says, "Hey, Jimmy, so good to see you," leaning in to give him a wet kiss on the lips. "You taking care of my girl?" He's tan and handsome with a broad face and piercing blue eyes, wearing a golf shirt and white shorts that show off legs strong from years of golf and handball. He and Dad like each other. There seems to be an understanding they share. *Life is hard, let's enjoy what we have.*

Bonnie told me that Grandpa Nat's family came from a place called Pole-land "before the war," the one Grandpa Frank fought in for Dutch and America. They left aunts and uncles and cousins there. They were all killed by a very bad man named Hitler. Some of them got out before the war but others could not be convinced to leave so they ended up losing their homes, then working in camps then put in trains then in furnaces. Grandpa says there were six million of them who died because of the bad man, Hitler. It's too big of a number to think about all at once. I try to imagine, like the bunnies, the sound made by six million claps of thunder rising up into the clouds leaving a tear in the sky so big it could be seen from anywhere on earth.

It's great to have a new grandpa and a new grandma, these funny and kind people who treat me like a grandson. I wish I could have all the aunts and uncles and cousins I could've had if it weren't for that crazy man Hitler who hated Grandpa Nat and his family so much.

Grandma Juliette is my favorite. She doesn't care if I hear dirty jokes. If someone says, "Mom, where is the fuckin' ice? I've been looking all over for it," she puts her hands over my ears and says, "Don't you ever say the word 'ice' in front of my grandson."

Bonnie's sister Nancy is a large woman with brown hair who moves exactly like a little girl in a woman's body. She is a singer with a high voice that she says is a "soprano." Jeannie is Bonnie's other sister. She's short and funny and just joined the Police Academy because she's going to become a cop. Even though she's so small, I can see why because there's something tough about her. When someone teases her, she doesn't give an inch.

They have another sister named Joey who died when she was only nineteen years old. Her eyes turned yellow and they took her to the doctor and three weeks later she was dead from something called hepatitis. They cried and cried and Bonnie says it taught them that family is precious and you should enjoy it while you can and make it bigger if you can and I feel so lucky to suddenly have more family.

Bonnie says she doesn't believe in God. Neither does Grandma or

Grandpa. She says religions get carried away. People believe too hard and start to "buy their own bullshit." She says it's been the cause of more death and suffering than any other force on earth. Her eyes get small and she pounds her fist and I wonder if she's mad about Synanon or God, Chuck Dederich or Hitler. They seem to be fused together in her mind as examples of what happens when people believe in something too much.

All I know is that we lived in the School like an orphanage and Grandpa Nat lost all those people he loved and maybe it's okay to believe in things as long as it doesn't mean people have to be alone or dead.

WHILE DAD AND Bonnie are at work, we go to summer camp which takes us to the beach or the zoo or a park where we drink from giant coolers of red fruit punch. Sometimes we play baseball. A coach comes and teaches us to field grounders and get under fly balls, how to bunt and slide and lead off from first base so that the pitcher can't throw you out. Dad picks us up at the end of the day and takes us to Toes Beach at sunset where we bounce in the waves, riding up onto his shoulders as he throws us into the surf. The water is cold when you first go in but Dad tells us to just run at it and dive, to let the cold hit you all at once so you can forget about it. We cling to him as he heads deeper into the ocean until our feet can't touch the bottom. We use him as a home base, swimming away into the deep water, then swimming back to hold on. He seems to know that's what he's there for, piling us into his truck even if he's dog tired after twelve hours on his feet in the middle of a six-day workweek.

Toes is not the best beach in the world. It's nothing like those tanning spots for teenagers in Manhattan Beach that we drive by, or the surfing coves in Malibu that you see in magazines, nothing like the long stretches of spotless sand from all the movies about California. No tourist would visit here. There are enormous red-and-white smokestacks spitting black clouds of pollution into the air from the oil refinery to the south. Just to the north is the mouth of Ballona Creek, which is where all the storm drains from the city empty into the ocean with their cigarette butts and dog shit. The 747s taking off from the runway at LAX seem close enough to touch as they fill the sky with a rumble, casting massive dark shadows over the sand. But we don't care. It doesn't matter. We care about the taste of salt in our mouths, the white foam in our hair, the soft waves as they pour over us and Dad, shirtless and tan in the sun, standing still like an anchor in the water.

Afterward we go to Might-T-Mart to get raspberry frozen yogurt which we eat in the car before we get home so Bonnie doesn't know and we can still have ice cream after dinner. "It'll be our secret," Dad says with a wink.

There's a nook in front of the big window where the sun hits a patch on the ground and you can sleep in it on lazy afternoons if you don't feel like doing anything. Bonnie will put Linda Ronstadt on the stereo and move around the apartment singing in one of her night robes.

You can sing. You can not sing.

You can sleep. You can not sleep.

You can eat. You can not eat.

They ask me how I'm doing and how I'm feeling and what I want for dinner, where I want to go this weekend. It feels like exhaling after holding your breath for so long. Like I've been crouched in a flinch, the way you tense up before getting socked in the face, and I can finally let my guard down. We both get tan. Fatter. We fight less. We eat more. We lie with eyes closed in the sun thinking of precisely nothing.

Some nights the music fills the place and there's nothing to do but dance. Bonnie puts Michael Jackson on and *Thriller* booms through the little apartment. Let's put on a show! So we go into the back bedroom and work out a dance routine.

It's close to midnight, and something evil's lurking in the dark . . .

We coordinate jumping jacks and push-ups, rolling on the floor in unison, high-fiving when we get up, moonwalking away from each other then spinning back together to grab our elbows and drop to our knees for the big finale. When we are ready, we go out into the living room and Bonnie drops the needle next to Michael Jackson's head as he lies there in his white suit. We stand with arms stretched downward and eyes closed as Vincent Price's voice comes out of the speakers until the moment the beat kicks in and we launch into our steps, dancing around the living room, moving in unison, our long blond corn-silk hair, our deeply tanned, ice-cream-fat tummies hanging out as we jump and spin and Bonnie sways her hips in her blue silk robe and Dad pumps his knees and fist in rhythm from his perch on the couch.

We dance, thinking only of the music, the steps we've memorized, the fullness in our chests as we leap across the carpet with wild abandon in nothing but our matching tighty-whities.

AT THE END of the summer, Dad takes us to Hollywood Park. Bonnie says he goes almost every Sunday when we are in Oregon. He has a bunch of phrases he likes to say, things he picked up from horse racing. "I'd rather be lucky than good." Or "Nothing like a day at the races. You got the world by the ass." Or "Favorites usually lose." This one is like a slogan to him, the kind of thing you'd put on a poster if he was famous: Jim Jollett . . . *favorites usually lose.*

Dad is a fan of the underdog. That's what he says. I think maybe it's because he thought he'd be dead by now. Between the heroin and the prison and the disorganized crime, he can't believe his luck that he's "still kicking." He says he feels lucky he gets to live in an apartment with Bonnie, work six days a week in an auto shop and take us to the beach or the track on Sundays.

Sometimes he comes home from Hollywood Park and hands us each twenty bucks. "I caught a horse," is all he'll say with a wink. We can't believe our luck. But he says not to be too happy, if the horse had lost, he'd be taking twenty bucks from us but he never does.

He says he's going to teach us how to bet, that he'll "stake" us, which means if we win, we get to keep the money but if we lose then we don't have to pay him.

The grandstand is enormous, rising like a spaceship from the sea of blacktop of the parking lot. Dad is chatty as we walk from the car to the gates, he keeps his hands on my shoulders, the heat from the asphalt warming our feet, the smell of hot dirt and car exhaust and the distant sound of a bugle filling the air. "Okay, we'll get some food. We gotta have some lunch. Then we'll lay some bets." He's got a pen in his mouth and little reading glasses on the end of his nose as he pays our admission and we buy a racing form.

A few of the men recognize him when we walk in. They're studying racing forms in their old hats, visors. An enormous white man in an old blue windbreaker, his huge gut hanging out, yells, "Hey, Jimmy. Those your boys?"

Dad introduces us.

"Ehhh, Jimmy! Who you got in the fifth? I'm twelve ways into the Pick Six, but I ain't got a horse in the fifth." A skinny, older black man in a purple hat yells from the next table.

Dad looks his way and tells him his pick and then, turning to us, he says with pride, "These are my boys."

"You gonna teach them the fambly business?" The man laughs. I feel a swelling in my chest like a warm wave that washes over me with Dad's hands on my shoulders. I watch their faces as they look at him and me, comparing our sizes, looking for the resemblance. I wonder if it's hard to see.

To be a son, to have a father, to be out at the track, with the men all trying their luck. *Is this what the men do?*

Dad has reserved a box for us near the finish line, on the edge of the perfect dirt oval surrounding an infield of palm trees, hot dog carts, a playground and a small lagoon with white waterbirds swimming in it like a postcard. The smooth brown oval of dirt is a mile around, slightly wet and combed by three green tractors after every race. A man in a green jacket and top hat with khaki riding pants and knee-high boots lifts a long bugle to his mouth in front of the starting line:

buh buh buh bup buddah bup buddah bup bup bup bup buhhh
buh buddah bup buddahdah bup bup bup buddahdah buhhhhh

Dad once told us he came straight to the races the day he got out of prison. He just wanted to be outside and free for a day in the sun. He wore a new hat and came with his brother Pete. They had a few beers and laid some bets and he always remembered that moment of freedom.

He buys us two corned beef sandwiches, some chips, a drink and a chocolate ice cream. We take the food to our box where he opens a racing form and shows us how each page is a different race and each name is a different horse. He says the numbers say how likely it is a horse will win. So if a horse is five to one, that means you get five dollars for every one dollar you bet.

Tony says he already knew that because they studied fractions last year and I'll learn it in a few years too. Dad takes his pen and circles the odds.

"Five to one. Does that make sense." He does this a few times, with a few horses he bets. "So this one is eight to one. So how many dollars do I win for every dollar I bet?"

That's easy, I say. You win eight. It seems as good a way as any to learn fractions since I'm usually bored in school.

He lets us choose horses for the two-dollar bets he's going to place for us and gets us tickets we can hold when he goes to lay his bets from the wad of twenties in his wallet.

It's impossible not to scream during a horse race. The horses march like royalty to the white starting gate. Everyone goes quiet once the last horse is in place. The bell goes off and you hear "and away they go" through the tinny speakers. You watch as they tear down the far straightaway into the final turn, and then your horse jumps forward, right to the front of the pack. You scream, "Go, Seven! C'mon, baby!" Because your dad is next to you and he's screaming it too since you bet the same horse. You can't help it. The queen of England would scream at that moment. It's instinct. All animals understand speed. So number seven crosses the finish line and you go to the window with your dad's hand on your shoulder and you hand the man your ticket and suddenly like magic your two dollars has become ten dollars and at that moment the future seems different. Like anything is possible. There's just the crowd and the track and the horses and your dad picking you up and squeezing you and telling you it's good to have some luck. "You and me, kid, we got the world by the ass."

CHAPTER 11

BINGE

When we get back to Oregon, Mom takes one look at me and says, "Wow, you got fat!" She pats my tummy, the one Bonnie calls my "cute little boy belly," since it sticks out from beneath my cutoff shirt.

I suck in my gut since I know I've done a bad thing.

"We're gonna need to put you on a diet unless you want everyone thinking you're fat." When we get back to the house, back to the moldy bread and four-day-old rabbit, she says we don't need snacks in the house since it'll be unhealthy for us to eat too much.

When we go out to the grocery store, she points at a woman and says, "See that lady right there with the tight top? She's too fat to wear something that tight. She shouldn't do that in public." She's always saying things like that. "Some women don't understand how to dress. Aren't they embarrassed? Jeez."

I know she knows more about these things than I do but Bonnie is a big woman and we all call her bubby because she's chubby but cute and she says women should dress however they want and we're beautiful boys, exactly the way we are.

It's strange because Mom says that Grandma always told her that she and her sister were fat and that she didn't like it so I wonder why she does it too. My aunt Pam doesn't look fat to me and when we go to visit Grandma and Grandpa in San Jose, she's there with my cousins. She watches us while we play with those kind eyes of hers, like she wants to protect us. When one of her kids cries, she rushes over and hugs them and tells them it's okay and I wonder why Mom doesn't do stuff like that.

Aunt Pam had a husband but they got divorced and now she works two jobs to put herself through school full-time studying computers at college, all while taking care of a two-year-old and a five-year-old. She seems like some kind of superhero to me.

Uncle Jon got married and when he gets to the house in San Jose, he has his pretty wife, Andy, with him and their two little boys (they are also called cousins) named Logan and Bryce and their older sister, Heidi, who was from Uncle Jon's first marriage. Uncle Jon still has the beard and the long hair and he seems like the coolest guy because he and Andy built a whole house in the mountains for their family to live in. He seems like Grandpa, like they have the strongest hands in the world.

Grandma takes more pills now because since her car accident she is in a lot of pain. It's hard for her to walk and she always tells us, "Don't ever get old. It's no fun." She was driving her GTO (which everyone says she liked to drive fast even though she wasn't driving fast on the day of the accident) and a car hit her head-on and crushed her spine. She didn't want to do the exercises or surgeries that were supposed to help her so now she drinks Dutch all day in her chair and takes pills and seems to sink into the chair more and more as the day goes on.

Everyone is sad because the doctors told Grandpa that he has cancer in his bones but he won't talk about it and always says, "I'm fine, I'm fine," and that his job is to "take care of Mother." Mom says he was always like that because Grandma had nervous breakdowns when they were still living in Dutch and Grandpa always took care of her. His family wanted him to marry someone better than the daughter of a coal miner. His mother died and his father remarried within three months and Grandpa Frank was so angry about it he stopped talking to them and devoted himself to Grandma and that's the kind of thing that also can happen in something called a family.

WHEN I GET back to school, I wonder if the other second graders think I got fat too so I remember to always suck in my gut because it's bad to be fat. At lunch I eat only half my sandwich because I don't want people to stare at me even though it makes me dizzy and it was good in California to just be able to eat when we were hungry.

By the winter, Paul disappears. We come home from school one day at the end of fall and Paul's truck is gone. There is no trace of him in the house or the backyard where we find him most afternoons, tending to the rabbits or doing chores in the garden. We go down the street to play and when I come home at dusk, Mom is sitting at the kitchen table with her hands in her lap. "Have you seen Paul?" We don't say it but we know where he is. A kind of silence falls over the house. We all retreat to our corners knowing not to name the thing we see in our minds.

Mom wakes me early the next morning. It froze overnight which means the rabbit water is frozen in the barn and must be replaced. I take a flashlight outside and one by one remove the water dishes from the cages, listening to the thump of feet on wire as the rabbits scurry in the dark. I fill a pitcher with hot water and walk back and forth between the kitchen sink and the rabbit barn to melt the ice. The sun rises as I feed them, putting pellets in each of the fifty cages with a plastic scoop from the feed bag. The sky has turned a kind of orangish blue in the crisp morning air. When I go inside, Mom and Tony are still sleeping so I pour a bowl of cereal and pack my lunch for school.

When I get home, Paul is still gone. Mom is sitting on the couch. She says, "I have to get back to the hospital. I'm taking you guys to the Boys Club. I'll pick you up after work."

Tony and I sit on the edge of the basketball court at the Salem Boys Club while the other boys play basketball or go upstairs to race the electric cars on the big track in the loft. We keep to ourselves, playing War silently with one of the huge combined decks from the toy bin as if scared that if we open our mouths, our secret will come flying out.

Mom picks us up at six. We eat dinner quietly, the sound of forks on plates drowning out the thoughts in our heads: that we have been left again. We are alone and it is winter and we are cold. We've run out of firewood for the iron stove in the basement that heats the house. A cold snap comes in and we forget to leave the water running so the pipes freeze and there is no water for baths, no tap from the sink. We watch our breath as it comes out in white puffs, lying under a pile of blankets in our room in the basement with socks on our hands and winter ski hats on our heads.

Eventually, Mom orders a cord of wood and asks Tony to split it into kindling with a maul and hatchet.

Once the wood has been chopped and the house warmed up, I find Mom lying on the floor next to the woodstove, sobbing. She says Paul called. He was drunk and told her he thought he deserved a "prettier" woman. He didn't want to act like he was married anymore, he was too broken, he wanted to leave Oregon and go be a forest ranger in Washington State. "It's just the disease talking, Mom," I say as she lies there in a ball with her face in the carpet.

She looks up, an awful expression of helplessness on her face. "How do you know how to talk like that?" I shrug. I'm only repeating something I've heard her say a hundred times. I don't really know what it means.

Mom has the blank look on her face like the one she says the men in the state mental hospital get. She can say only two or three sentences at a time before her voice trails off and she loses concentration and you can see her go into the deep-russian.

She goes to Al-Anon meetings at night "to cope." Each morning I get up at five to tend to the rabbits in the dark then watch the sun rise before school.

Paul is gone a month. We come home from school and he's in the living room sitting next to Mom. His hair is wet and combed, his beard trimmed, revealing a nose that looks like a red lightbulb and a patchy pink face that deserves a beard. He's wearing clean clothes. It's clear they've been crying. He stands up and puts his arms out. We hug him and he says he's sorry, that he is going to get help and get better. We can't help but cry because he is back and we know that's what we're supposed to do in this scene, that's what the script says in all the stories we've heard about broken families where the alcoholic comes home filled with tears and regret. But mostly we are relieved because we know there will be food tonight and the house won't freeze.

CHAPTER 12

F-A-M-I-L-Y

"Hi, I'm Frank. I'm an alcoholic."

"Hi, Frank!"

I am swaddled in a wool blanket sitting at the edge of a big circle of fifty people around an enormous campfire. Above us is a canopy of pine trees, beyond that a clear night sky filled with a thousand dots of light. Tony is sitting on the dirt ground whittling a stick with a pocketknife. Everyone here is an alcoholic, I'm told, who's trying to go through "recovery." When Paul returned, we spent the winter being told that it was time that we all started acting like a "family."

It's a strange word. F-A-M-I-L-Y. It's big and comforting and each letter is different. Just look at it. The *F* is for father right there at the front. The *M* for mother is in the middle, connecting all the others. It's a long word but usually people say it in one breath, like "famly" as if the *I* doesn't matter. Without the *F* it's just an "ambly," a thing that ambles around from place to place. Without the *M* it's just a "Fably," which is a story about something that does not exist. For months after Paul got back, that word was all we heard. It was time to "act like a famly," to learn to "talk like a famly," to eat together "like famlies do." The word seems to me like a cave, something big and simple you can walk inside to get away from a storm called loneliness.

Frank's got a big nose that erupts from his face over his red cheeks. On his head is a fishing cap covered in lures, like the ones Paul showed us on our trips to the Willamette under the West Salem bridge. His big belly sticks out from under his buttoned overalls and blue flannel shirt.

This is Frank's fire. He lit it by placing a roll of black toilet paper, soaked in motor oil, beneath a structure of kindling and logs. It burned slowly for thirty minutes as the dry kindling caught and smoke poured out of the wet, mossy wood. "Me and Barb been comin' up here to Detroit Lake for twenty years now, sittin' round these fires, listening to old drunks talk about forgiveness and serenity."

Barb is his wife. She's a very kind, large woman with short brown hair who sits next to him nodding and smiling. She looks like she's been inflated with air, her thighs bursting, fighting against the blue denim of her jeans as she sits in a fold-up chair with her hands clasped in her lap.

Mom told me that Barb was a popular speaker in Al-Anon, that she traveled as far away as Eugene and McMinnville to "tell her story." When I asked her about what she meant by story, Mom said, "Everybody has a story in AA and Al-Anon. You know, what you went through with the disease and how it ruined your life before you found the program and admitted you were powerless and your life was in the hands of a higher power." I asked her what a higher power was and she said, "Like God." The point is to have a personal relationship, a "conscious contact," with him. I asked who him is? Jesus? Does he sit in a chair? Does he have a beard? She said some people say Jesus, some say nature and some say it's just "knowing the universe is bigger than all of us." I didn't know what she meant. I heard about how people go to church and that's where God is but we've never been to one except to get the government cheese. We knew some of the stories about him and at that point I know there's a God because whenever something good happens I look up at the sky and say thanks. I can feel that I'm talking to something real whether it's Jesus or a guy with a beard or just an enormous blue sky stretching out beyond anything.

"We used to come up here and fish for the weekend on the Santiam, me and my buddies from the navy. I don't know if we ever caught anything, because the whole point was to get as drunk as we could." There is a howl of laughter, led by Leslie McCarthy, who everyone calls Les, with his huge muttonchops and red suspenders where he hooks his thumbs when he speaks. His wife Diane sits by his side and laughs with him. Mom says it's good I met Les because I need male role models, ones that know how to talk about their feelings not just ride motorcycles or watch sports. It's basic Child Psychology.

Frank's voice sounds like a tire on gravel, like the Vega as it goes up the driveway at the house, low and patchy. It's like listening to a mountain talk. "We drank in the war too. One for courage, we would say. So I figured if one brought courage, what would four bring? How about seven?" More howls of laughter. "It got to the point where I hardly even got up unless I'd already finished a fifth of whiskey. Any drunk here could probably do goddamn brain surgery if he had a drink first." Somber faces, reflecting the orange warmth of the fire, smile and nod as they stare into the past. "You can do anything when you're drunk. You're the smartest person who ever lived and anyone who don't agree is a son of a bitch for sayin' so. Damn it if I couldn't have flown a B-25 over Tokyo and ended the whole goddamn war if I'd just had the money for the whiskey." The laughter floats in the air with the smoke as the circle closes in. It starts to feel like we are physically connected, all of us through the story that AA calls a "share."

I close my eyes and listen to the gravelly voice.

"Somehow I made it through the war without killing myself." He spits on the ground and wipes his face. He takes a pack of red-and-white Lucky Strikes out of the front bib of his overalls and lights one while he talks, the smoke falling out of his nose and mouth like a leaky chimney. "I honestly don't know how I did it. And when I came back, well, the world didn't make much sense. Found myself married, had Frank junior." He pauses, gathering himself. "All this was more reason to drink. If I was happy 'cause I was home with the baby, I would drink to celebrate. If I was upset, I had to drink to feel better. And if I was deep in the national forest, I would drink to pass the time."

My feet are warm and I like these stories. The alcoholics are better storytellers than the women in Al-Anon, which is mostly for wives. It's all fights in the street, calling Child Protective Services, divorces, phone calls from bars on birthdays, all the ways a man can mess up.

Mom says to me, "You see? That's why you can't ever drink."

But those men. The husbands. I wondered about them. All these old guys sitting around with battle scars and cigarettes talking about run-ins with cops and speeding down highways and fights in jail and war, hunting, tractors driven while drunk that ran into houses, boats capsized, guns fired, faraway homes filled with wives and children waiting for them, begging for them to come back. I wonder if I'm going to grow up to be one of them.

"People talk about rock bottom," Frank says. There's a shift in the circle, a tightening. "I don't even know what that is really. I once heard someone say, 'Rock bottom is when you drank up all the life in you, when you look down and the only thing you see is death.' Well, I wake up one morning alone in the house. My truck is in the driveway, the door is still open, my head is split in two, my face covered in filth 'cause I'd been throwin' up all night drinking that rotgut I kept in the shed. And I knew. Right then I didn't think, I damn well knew if I didn't stop drinkin', I would die. Every drunk knows he's got a problem, but the drink is his God and his mistress so he thinks, aw shit, I'll figure it out because you can't betray your God and mistress. Gotta have that flask. But then, sitting there alone in my house, I knew it was time. So I cleaned myself up and called my buddy Don, who said he'd been to a couple meetings in something called AA, and the next thing I knew I was sitting in the basement of the Catholic church listening to drunk after drunk tell story after story that coulda been straight from my own life.

"They gave me a book. The big book by Bill W. and I was determined, so I read it, read it all in one weekend with a jug of bourbon." A low rumble of laughter. "Showed up at the Monday night meeting and Don said, 'Frank, you drunk right now? 'Cause you can't bullshit a bullshitter.' I said yeah. So he gave me a cup of coffee and sat me in the back. After the meeting was over, he said, 'You got to break some habits.' So he said he'd take me to ninety meetings in ninety days and that's what we did.

"I got sober and got a new wife. Chose right this time." He grabs onto Barb's thick fingers. "And now we come up here and I ain't got a need to drink. Turns out, I like fishing. I like the cool water and the way the wind sounds when it picks up a gust in the trees. That's called serenity, I guess. I made my peace with it. I look around this fire and I know these faces: Joe and Les, this new guy Paul and his woman, Gerry. Gerry, we gonna have to get you a little less coffee, I think." Everyone laughs. Mom blushes, beaming. "But I'm glad I'm here with you and not somewhere drinkin'. I ain't got a mistress no more, but I got a God, a higher power, and he's in control now and it's better that way 'cause he knows what he's doing better 'n I do. I'm not saying everything is perfect. We all know we got our struggles." Heads nod, a low murmur of agreement. "But I got this woman, got Frank junior here, got a bucket a fish I caught and we fried some up to eat, got these trees, this fire, all of you, and I didn't drink today. That's all." He goes silent and we listen to the crack of the fire. Sparks fly up and disappear into the night sky.

"Thanks, Frank," Les says.

"Thanks, Frank," comes a chorus of quiet voices.

I feel warm there in the circle because everyone is happy to be together and sitting here is better than sitting at home eating rabbit for dinner. Everyone is so glad to be sober and it seems to me that alcohol must be the worst thing in the world since there are so many stories about it. All the kids left to freeze, all the women crying in the dark. There's a strange magic to the word since it's said constantly as the root of all evil as in "Well, in those days, we were *drinking*, so we didn't give a shit." People say, "It's good you guys are here so you can learn not to ever *drink*," as if we're getting a flu shot. And I wonder why everyone needs to drink so bad in the first place.

I think about the kids in all the stories, sitting alone in a truck shivering while their dads drink in a bar, left alone after school, on birthdays, Christmas, children hiding bottles from their parents, doctor's appointments missed, and I wonder if we are those children. Tony and me.

Everyone is so certain it's a "family disease" and we all have it whether we want to admit it or not. And so far I was born in Synanon and sent to the School because my dad did drugs and now we go to AA because my stepdad drinks. Grandma can hardly get out of bed without her Dutch so I can't help but wonder: Am I next? Which will I grow up to be? Because it seems like my choices are limited to being the one who leaves to use drugs or the one who stays home and cries about it. And that's no choice at all.

At the end of the meeting we all stand up in a circle and recite,

> *Our father who art in heaven*
> *Hallowed be thy name*
> *Thy kingdom come*
> *Thy will be done*
> *On Earth as it is in heaven*
> *Give us this day, our daily bread*
> *And forgive us our trespasses*
> *As we forgive those who trespass against us*

Lead us not into temptation
But deliver us from evil
For thine is the kingdom and the power and the glory forever.
Keep comin' back, it works!

There's a short silence and I'm proud of myself because I memorized the words to the Lord's Prayer from a pamphlet in the backseat on the drive up to the mountains. It was comforting to think about heaven and bread, to pretend we were one of those families who went to church on Sundays instead of three people who'd escaped from a C-U-L-T or a commune that went bad like old milk who met up with a drunk who raises rabbits. I didn't know what the words meant except I knew alcohol was the temptation because everyone knew that. And I wished I had more daily bread because we were usually out of bread.

I like the power of knowing the words themselves, as if knowing the prayer is a kind of shield that protects me. If I only know the words, that means I know God and I know how to bring him to life in his judgment and forgiveness, his kingdom which is bigger than everything. This God is more vivid than the vague and mysterious "higher power" I am always hearing about in meetings, the silent blue sky that goes on forever. And even though I didn't know him very well, I knew God was on my side because otherwise what was the point?

After the meeting Mom asks me if I liked listening to the stories and if I understood now that alcoholism is a family disease that affects everyone and I say I liked Frank's story the best because he's funny and talks like a mountain. Tony says, can we roast marshmallows now?

Everyone hugs each other, just walks around the fire finding a new person to squeeze. I get a hug from Paul first and a few of the other women. Les McCarthy walks up to me and says, "I guess they're letting you stay up tonight!" He picks me up and squeezes my chest hard. "It's good you're here with your mom." He puts me down and he tells Paul they're going to have a poker game later. "Nickel ante, sound good? We just play for fun." Paul says he doesn't know poker very well but he'll come. Tony is already in the car getting the marshmallows that we were told we could roast on the fire after the meeting.

Mom lets me stay up with the men for the poker game. I sit next to Paul at a table with Frank and Les and a few others. Frank smokes his short Lucky Strikes with no filters and says, "Let's play draw this time. One-eyed jacks and suicide kings wild." Or, "This one's Omaha, like Hold 'Em but with more chances to screw it up." I memorize the phrases knowing the kids on Breys Avenue will be impressed. Paul shows me his cards and makes bets with the small plastic chips in front of him. I study the men. They seem like buffalo to me. Proud and quiet, hairy and enormous. There's no small talk. When Mom has Diane over, they gab and gab and sometimes they'll play gin rummy but the game isn't as important as the talking, the sharing of feelings and thoughts and secret stories. The men burp and eat chips. They smoke and scratch chins. They say, "I got the aces this time, gentlemen," in a low rumble that sounds like a bowling ball rolling down a sidewalk. "Aw shit, I missed my straight." Cards are slammed down onto the table. "Who's got the old lady? I know one of you two chumps is holding trips." They don't mind explaining the game to me. Paul even lets me ante when Frank says, "Ante up, Seven-Stud Black Mariah with deuces wild."

The words are part of it. The way they're spat. There's power in them, like the Lord's Prayer. And like the prayer, they bring something to life. I think about those suicide kings. *Why did they kill themselves? Who took over the kingdom after they died? What happened to their queens? What about their sons, those one-eyed jacks? How did they lose their eyes? Did it have something to do with their dads who committed suicide? Did they drink too much? Is that the point of the game?* It's all so quick and violent, the phrases spat without effort. "I got the flush to the ace, so unless you're holding a boat, you better ship 'em," and "Sheeit, I think you're bluffing, but I ain't got the hand to call you down, pardner."

I fall asleep in the kids' tent next to Tony in my sleeping bag, repeating the phrases. "I got the aces, pardner. You better ship 'em . . . Well, shit, I missed my king . . . Okay, who's got the bitch?"

The AA campouts become a fixture in our world. Once a month we pack up Paul's truck with gear and head to Detroit Lake along the Santiam River or the Deschutes National Forest where the ground is red everywhere you look. We go to Beverly Beach where we camp right in the sand and spend mornings running down the Oregon coast next to the huge rocks that guard the coastline like kneeling giants, looking for seashells, racing Pepper down the shore, dodging the waves as they break against the sand. We got a new puppy from Pepper's litter that winter and named it Mork after Robin Williams's alien in the TV show *Mork & Mindy*. We call him "Mork the dork." He is a yappy black Lab mix, and when we take him to the coast, he jumps in the water then runs out away from the crashing waves up into our laps then tears off to search for crabs and starfish. Afterward, Tony and I pile into the back of Paul's camper-shell truck with all the gear for the ride back to Salem. We fall asleep on the mattress in the truck bed somewhere in the winding highways of the coastal Cascade Mountains—a big pile of sand and salt, dirt, seaweed, kelp, pillows and wet dog.

We are happier in nature. All of us. We take long walks through the woods, stopping to smell the scent of pine in the air, the distant snow-capped peak of Mount Washington or Three Sisters reminding us we are small and young. Paul teaches us to light campfires, to create pockets of air for the fire to lick the wood, to keep our faces away from the flames and blow on the bursting red coals when we want the fire to grow. We eat lunches of hot dogs and baked beans, roasted potatoes that we wrap in tinfoil and throw into the smoldering coals. We sleep hard at night, getting up to pee outside the tent, worried about bears, wondering at the stars and silence except for a nearby stream or the dull hoot of an owl. We wake up at dawn, toasty in our sleeping bags as we eat cereal or scrambled eggs and bacon that Paul fried up over the morning fire.

Out in the woods we are able to crawl into that word: F-A-M-I-L-Y. To let it provide shelter like the blue tarp we hang from the branches over the tents on rainy weekends. Perhaps it's that we're too busy to fight or because we can forget about the house on Breys Avenue or the fact that in Synanon we were alone and didn't even know what an F-A-M-I-L-Y was.

In a campground, everyone is cold, everyone sleeps in a tent and wears dirty clothes, so we're not ashamed. Maybe it's because Paul is so capable with his gear, his endless knowledge of trees, tents, tarps, fires, fishing and outdoor cooking. Mom is calmed by this. We all are. At the AA meetings, people say you can feel God when you walk through the woods, that he's everywhere: in the fallen logs and bird nests, in the beehives, the grass, the meadows and trees, an unseen force that surrounds you, connecting you to other living things, reminding you that you're part of something.

Maybe that's family too.

CHAPTER 13

HOW TO ESCAPE A MEXICAN PRISON

D ad drives with his middle fingers sticking out, rocking the steering wheel back and forth like he's flipping off every car on the freeway. We are heading south toward San Diego. He does this, he says, "for the assholes. So they know they're assholes." He yells at the cars that cut him off or tailgate or switch lanes without a signal or break too fast or cruise steadily in the blind spot of Bonnie's silver Honda Prelude. He says, "Learn to drive!" over the music from the radio while Bonnie sits next to him in the front seat. She reminds him that none of the other cars can hear him so they don't even know what he's saying. Dad shakes his head, "They know they're assholes. They know."

The 405 freeway stretches out in front of us, twelve lanes of white concrete and cars, the busiest stretch of freeway in the world. We pass through fields of flame-capped smokestacks, storage tanks like massive white aspirin pills, pipes, catwalks, scaffolding, and industrial lighting, the refinery wasteland of Carson with its factories and fast-food joints. We're on our way to see Dad's family: Grandma Mary, the saint, and our uncles Donny, Pete and Wes. Tony and I are in the backseat with Egg McMuffin sandwiches. We don't care where we're going because we can't believe we get hash browns and orange juice from McDonald's which Mom says is an evil corporation that's trying to destroy America from the inside by making everyone fat.

Dad likes to tell old stories when he drives, as if the point of the trip isn't the destination but the long journey in the car, the education we receive on family history, a kind of classroom where we sing, listen to music and eat junk food while we talk. He's got a slight smile on his face. "He likes having his boys around," Bonnie always tells us.

"All the true badasses are either dead or in prison." Dad is telling us about his brother Pete, who has a black belt in karate and does tai chi every morning. He was once an instructor in hand-to-hand combat for the Mexican *federales* who worked with Bruce Lee.

"Pete wasn't scared of nobody. I once saw him take on a whole carful of guys by himself." Pete did time too, four years in Folsom State Prison. When I ask what he got busted for, Dad laughs and says his usual line: disorganized crime.

Grandma Mary was born in San Francisco but then settled in the Little Italy area of San Diego in 1917. She worked as a hotel maid and raised four boys in a small house in East San Diego. She'd met Howard, my grandfather, but he only "stuck around" long enough to give her three wild boys "before he split." She eventually met Don, her second husband, who gave her a fourth wild boy, my uncle Donny. Things calmed down. But it was too late for the boys. "We went a little crazy," Dad says. He tells us that "a lot of I-talians" (pronounced "eye-talyuns") got houses in the area so the neighborhood was filled with "dagos" walking around with spit curls in big seersucker suits. Dad had some crazy clothes: baggy pink suits with huge shoulder pads and a long wallet chain. He looks out over the asphalt and overpasses. "We needed money, so what else could we do? We ran numbers, smuggled drugs, stole some cars. You know, your basic nonsense."

Dad wants us to know our heritage. Tony and I are sponges. It makes me feel important, like a prophecy that must be fulfilled. As if there is danger in our very blood. We pepper him with questions: "Did you ever shoot anyone? Where did you get the checks? How much money was it? Wasn't Donny in Vietnam? Was he part of it?"

"I never shot no one. But I been shot at a bunch of times. It was never that much money, just enough to get by. We weren't very good crooks." Pete was the oldest and the first to do time, mostly in the work camps like Viejas, the honor camps where you sweat in the sun laying asphalt all day. Dad is the comedian, who did his time in Chino state prison and also got in some trouble in Mexico. Wes was the only one who never went to prison. He became a schoolteacher and took care of Grandma Mary, moving her into his house when she could no longer work. Donny was the baby, "a real sweet kid before Vietnam fucked him all up." Something happened to him there. Dad says they never knew what. But it was probably drugs.

Dad wrote Donny letters from jail while he was in Vietnam but he never heard back. He says that he got into drinking and had some wild nights in Saigon. On the day he was shipped back, he got into trouble because on his way to a transport plane something moved in his giant duffel bag. The MPs got suspicious and stopped him right there on the tarmac. When they opened it, there was a small Vietnamese woman inside. At least that's the story.

"Stop exaggerating," Bonnie says, smiling.

"Hey, I'm just trying to let these guys know where they come from. They got the gene. They need to *know*."

Dad's father, who he never really knew very well, owned a used-car lot down on Broadway in Lemon Grove. It was a small corner business with a garage where the boys worked sometimes, fixing up old cars just enough to get them "off the lot." When they were off the clock, they built engines and put them into cars they raced to Tijuana and back. "Some of those vehicles were lowered so low you could push a pack of cigarettes down the street with the front bumper. That was the style, man." I try to picture Dad's curly-'froed head with a spit curl, his broad shoulders in an oversize suit with a wallet chain but it's something from another world, like a character he played in a movie once that disappeared when the credits rolled.

The house in San Diego is overflowing with people. Pete is tall and thin, handsome with dark tan skin and a slender mustache like one of those actors from black-and-white movies we see on TV where everyone carries a sword. Donny has big muttonchops and a goatee and sleeveless flannel showing off his big arms. He shows up with Rose, his quiet Mexican wife and our cousins Cindy, who is about my age, and David, the baby. Donny looks powerful in his Padres baseball cap, a lazy cigarette hanging on the edge of his lips when he talks. He's the loudest one in the group. He grabs me by the shoulders when I walk in and says, "Hey, bud. Your dad finally got you down here to hang out with your loco-ass family, eh? Bet you didn't know you had all this insane shit in your blood?" He pulls from a can of Budweiser, occasionally pouring a little into the mouth of the baby David who he holds in his arms. "The brew is good for the heart. Builds strength."

Wes is a large man who moves like a gentle bear. He's soft-spoken, unlike his brothers who wail and laugh and tease each other. Grandma Mary has white hair, deep wrinkles, and a big Italian nose. She practically shakes as she runs up to me to squeeze me. "Look at these boys, oh!" she says. She clasps her hands, smiles and says, "So handsome!" Grandma has a magnet of Saint Peter on her fridge and candles all around the house, each for a different saint who she talks to when she prays. "I know we're supposed to talk to a priest but I just talk to them anyway. I think they're listening." She's Catholic. Donny says that means we're Catholic too which is fine by me because all I ever knew was we were Dope Fiends or drunks. Catholic sounds much more respectable.

Great-Grandma Rossi is Grandma Mary's mom. She sits in a wooden rocking chair next to the sliding glass door which leads to a deck, an ancient, thin woman with sunken cheeks in a black dress and a black hat. She doesn't speak any English and keeps saying something in Italian that I don't understand: "Oddio! Mio bellissimo bambinos!" She pinches my cheeks hard and hands me a piece of licorice. Dad says she's ninety-seven years old and the "toughest old broad you're ever gonna meet."

They all love Bonnie. They hug her and say, "You hold on to this one, Jimmy. 'Cause if you don't, I'm taking her."

Grandma says, "You being good? This is a nice lady. You better be nice to her, Jimmy."

Dad laughs. "I'll keep her around for another week if she behaves." Bonnie shoots him a smile.

The adults order sandwiches from the Italian deli for lunch and we drink sugar sodas and eat salami and cheese with red sauce on torpedo buns.

"Your dad ever tell you we busted him out of a Mexican prison?" Pete asks me.

"Oh, don't start with that," Grandma says. "They don't need to know about that."

The men ignore her. "You boys. Always so *baaad*."

Pete cocks a thumb at Dad and says, "This smart guy right here was driving a car full of drugs across the border."

"It was my friend's car. I didn't know it had drugs in it."

"That's what he told the judge!" Donny yells. "That Mexican judge didn't even speak English and he knew bullshit when he heard it. Bullshit translates in any language. Bull-a-sheet-o!"

Dad shrugs his shoulders and says, "Well, it's true. I didn't know."

"Anyway, they stopped him at the border and found a pound of crank—or was it pills? Anyway a big bag of drugs—in the trunk. Sentenced him to five years. That's five years in a Mexican prison, which ain't nuthin' like these cushy cells they got at Chino or Folsom with people making wine in the sink and movie night every Saturday."

"You would know!" Donny hollers. "They got a Jollett wing up in Chino with the name carved above the door!"

Pete ignores him. "So that ain't easy time. The food alone. You can't eat it. The Mexicans don't give a shit what happens to you when you're locked up."

"It's true," Dad says. "There's a sewer running right down the middle of the cell. They give you a little army kit with a metal fork that's also a can opener and a small bowl with a chicken head in it. That's lunch. The rolls are made of flour and sawdust. You can see the black bugs baked right into 'em. But I never bothered with it, because my cell had a window onto the street, so you could give money to a kid and he'd go to the taco stand on the corner and bring you back something to eat. It wasn't so bad."

Pete continues, "So I was the karate instructor for the police and I was asking around trying to figure out who we could pay to get Jimmy out, because we knew he wouldn't last too long in there. We went and saw some *abogados*—those are lawyers—who told us to get used to it because there was no way they were going to release an American drug dealer caught at the Mexican border. So I told them, he's no drug dealer. He's just an idiot." Everyone laughs, including Dad. He doesn't care if he's the butt of the joke or the teller of the joke or the audience for the joke, as long as there's a joke.

"So one day," Dad says, "some guy came in and just opened my cell door and walked away. I didn't know why but after a few minutes I think well fuck it maybe he did it on purpose. When I get to the next door, the guard looks away and opens it. So I walk through that one too. I did this five or six times at five or six doors, not knowing if I'm about to be shot or what. Finally, I walked out to the street like it's nothing. I walked all the way to the American border. Just standing there in my dirty long green wool sweatshirt and a three-week beard, stinking from that cell. At first they didn't want to let me cross, until I spoke and they heard I was American. I said, 'Yeah, I just got out of jail.' So I borrowed a dime and called Pete and he and the old man came and picked me up."

"We paid off a Mexican federal judge," Pete says, his arm around Dad. "It cost twenty-five hundred dollars to bust this numskull out. We put him in a car and drove the hell back to San Diego."

"I haven't been back since. I think I'm still wanted."

Dad's life seems like a series of near misses. He was almost killed in a motorcycle accident when his bike fell over on its side speeding down the highway. He jumped up on it and skidded right across the U.S./Mexican border. He was almost killed by a collapsing VW van as it smashed into a bridge. When he realized what had happened, he climbed out of the car which had folded up like an accordion, walked home and called the cops to report it as stolen. He had guns put to his head but no one ever pulled the trigger. He was shot at and stabbed. There were endless bar fights. Endless trials and cops and social workers and always, in the background somewhere, one or another doe-eyed woman hoping he'd just do the right thing, for once. He seems like something from one of those old pirate movies we see on cable TV at the apartment in Playa del Rey, swashbuckling, daring, a twinkle in his eye, one step ahead of the blade until he was busted and stood before a judge trying to talk down his sentence.

Wes pronounces our name "JOLL-ette" like "wallet," even though Dad taught us to pronounce it "Joe-Lay." Wes says that's the way the old man said it and that's the way they "say it in the old country" and that we probably lost an *e* at Ellis Island or something and Dad started saying Joe-Lay because his first wife, Susan, who he married when he was sixteen years old in a shotgun wedding, liked the way it sounded. All we've ever known is Joe-Lay though, so that's what we say. Anyway, changing your name to impress a girl sounds exactly like Jollett behavior.

We have a half brother named Vince we've never met. Dad told us about him but since we've never seen him, he seems like one of those bits of folklore, one of those stories they tell. There's Dad riding on a fallen motorcycle as it skids across the Mexican border. There he is in a stalled plane at two thousand feet with Grandpa Howard trying to restart the engine. There he is with a son at sixteen years old who we don't even know. I wonder if he sees Dad differently, if he resents him for leaving, for all the birthdays he spent alone with a father in prison. It strikes me how a man can be all these things at once, in one lifetime: a prisoner, a drunk, a pirate, a fool filled with regret sitting alone in a dark cell, a pair of strong shoulders bouncing in the surf on a sunny day when you will live forever.

When we finally leave, when we are tucked into the backseat, having been educated, initiated into the world of Jollett men, Dad puts an Allman Brothers cassette in the tape deck of the Honda and begins to sing. He shakes his head, eyes squinted, pointing a finger in rhythm with the music. "You want to hear a smokin' guitar? Listen to 'em wail," he juts his face forward singing out into the freeway.

"You ever hear Fats Domino or the Big Bopper? Now *those* were songs." He teaches us the words to "Chantilly Lace," one line at a time, (she *had a pretty face and a ponytail hanging down*), making sure we get each syllable right. We practice until we can sing it perfectly, all three of us together, over and over again as we drive back from San Diego, knowing we are Jollett boys with danger in our genes, we are ramblin' men, born for the jailhouse and rock and roll, rebels and outlaws who ride motorcycles to outrun the cops while the women sit home worried and crying and we sing at the top of our lungs:

That wiggle in the walk, and a giggle in the talk,
Lord, make the world go round round round!

CHAPTER 14
PLAY BOY

On the front of the baseball cap is the word *P*L*A*Y*B*O*Y* spelled out in large black letters. It's as if it's yelling at you, somehow blinking like those signs you see on the side of the highway at night. "No Vacancy" or "Cocktails 'til Midnight." Tony got it from a bin at a swap meet we went to one afternoon the week before we left Los Angeles. Bonnie laughed when he put it on his head, standing there next to the bin in oversize green sunglasses, holding a Push Pop, which turned his lips orange in the sun. I think she thought it was a joke, "an eleven-year-old playboy, ha-ha," so she bought it for him. It's made of white cloth with a Velcro strap on the back. "Playboy" is a funny word. It's like a challenge. A boy need only choose: he is either a "play" boy or a "work" boy. So when Tony put it on for the flight and wore it through the airport and on the plane and the stewardess said, "Who's the little playboy in row twelve? Does the playboy want another Coke?" I felt as if he was simply announcing the choice he'd made. Play, it is.

When we land, we see Mom in the waiting area at the end of the jet bridge with her big crooked-tooth smile, her Birkenstock sandals. Her straight brown hair has grown long. I give her a hug and when she looks at Tony, she says, "Whoa, did you, uh, wear that on the plane?"

In the car on our way back to Salem from Portland International Airport she announces that Paul has decided to become a chimney sweep. It takes a minute to sink in since I don't really know what that is, only that it is in a category of jobs with "lion tamer" and "blimp pilot" that don't seem like things people do in real life. She says that it's a man who makes sure all the chimneys work, that it's a great career and there's lots of opportunity because of all the wood-burning stoves in town. "It's good he's going to contribute because we could sure use the money." She looks over at Tony, "So, um, that's a new hat. Where'd you get it?"

"At the swap meet."

"Do you know what it is?"

"Yeah it's a magazine."

"Do you know what's in the magazine?"

"Sure."

"And you're okay with that?" She peers at him and he goes quiet, ignoring her, looking over the bridges and trees, the view of the city as we cross the Willamette River.

When we get to the house on Breys Avenue, I tell Mom I want to play her a song by Jackson Browne. Dad gave me his cassette tape of *Running on Empty* which I listened to over and over again on the Walkman he bought me at the swap meet. Jackson Browne is his favorite which makes sense to me since he sings about the road, the diners and truckers and women you meet along the way and it reminds me of Dad out on his bike on the highway, the way I remembered him when he was a blur on a motorcycle. I put the tape into the deck and press play in the living room for her to hear and go downstairs to unpack my bag. I can hear Jackson Browne's voice filling up the house:

> *You take Sally and I'll take Sue*
> *There ain't no difference between the two*
> *Cocaine, runnin' all round my brain*

When the song ends, I come back upstairs and find Mom sitting on the floor with her legs tucked under her, one hand on the green shelf where we keep the stereo, crying. "These aren't my values," she whispers. "I didn't raise you to have these values."

"What values?"

"Drugs and *Playboy* magazine and just look at how fat you two got."

I feel bad because I did the bad thing again and ate too much food in

California and I'm confused because the song is about how drugs are bad. Jackson Browne is nearly dead as he sits in a room at the hospital and a doctor tells him it's "impossible" that he's only twenty-seven years old. "You look like you could be forty-five."

I tell her it reminds me of the AA meetings, the way everyone has a story, how they hit rock bottom before they get better.

"That's not the kind of story we tell. This glorifies drug culture."

"He's talking about how it will kill him."

"Oh, right, and he's so cool while he's doing it. You can hear him snorting the drugs and laughing! You don't hear about the families he's broken or the children he's left behind!"

"Jackson Browne? I didn't know he had kids."

"These aren't my values." She rocks herself back and forth, holding her knees. "I had kids so I could teach them *my* values."

Tony comes upstairs with the hat still on his head, the big block letters lighting up the living room. *P*L*A*Y*B*O*Y*.

"Why's she crying? Mom, why are you crying?"

"*Playboy?*" She looks at him. "You like *Playboy*? A magazine that treats women like sex objects? As if their only value is their sex appeal to men and once that's used up, once it's gone, they are tossed aside like trash."

"What are you talking about? It's just the naked human body. It's only natural."

"That's not natural." She points at the hat. "That's objectification. The photos in that magazine aren't of strong women. They're just bending over chairs and trying to look sexy. They may as well be show dogs. They might as well teach them to play fetch. What do you think women are?"

Tony shrugs his shoulders. "It's only a hat, Mom."

"I think you should take it off."

"No. It's my hat. I got it in Los Angeles. I want to wear it. You don't get to decide what I wear."

"I am your mother. This is my house. And you will not walk around in here with a hat that objectifies women. I'd like you to take it off."

"You can't make me. It's mine."

Mom stares at the ground as if looking into a deep pit. She whispers, "These aren't my values."

She gets up slowly and stands in the doorway. "Come here please." Tony walks up to her. She looks down at him. Tony grew all summer and though she is still bigger than he is, his eyes come up to her chin so that the *P*L*A*Y*B*O*Y* letters reflect in her eyes.

They stand like that for a moment, staring at each other. She looks more worried than angry like she's deep in thought. She says, "I'll get you a new hat. Will you please take it off?"

"No. I like *Playboy* and I don't see what the big deal is. Dad gets *Playboy* delivered to the apartment and Bonnie doesn't even care. It's just the human body."

"Your dad is an adult man and gets to make whatever decisions he wants. I learned that a long time ago. You are my son and you live in this house and I make the rules. If you don't take it off then you can't go to Little League."

Tony's eyes fill with the injustice. He shakes his head and says, "But it's mine. It's not yours. Why do I have to have *your* values?"

"Because you are my son."

"I wish I wasn't." He throws the hat on the ground and stomps on it, running to the front door where he turns and says, "You know, you're not always going to be bigger than me." He slams the door behind him. Through the front window I see him get on his bike and disappear up the street.

The stereo plays "The Load-Out." The song was written for the roadies who travel with the band to set up the stage every night. Dad always says it's a good life and an honest living, working for the band and taking it on the road. Mom takes a heavy breath, leaning against the door frame with her forehead on her hands. The *B*O*Y* of the crumpled hat stares up at her from the ground. She picks it up silently and walks out, leaving me alone in the living room with Jackson Browne, wondering if Mom is going to put me on another diet.

CHAPTER 15

THE SCAPEGOAT AND
THE SUPERCHILD

The beatings have gotten worse. It used to be mostly wet willies or flat tires or Indian burns, the kind of cruelty with a flashy name you could pass off as a joke. Tony would grab my head and say, "Noogie!" as he scrubbed his knuckle against my scalp until it was raw. The names themselves, "wedgie," "pantsing," "charley horse," seemed to justify the behavior, as if you could rename murder something like "knifey chests" and we'd all have a big laugh.

But it's gotten worse. Tony will pull my hair and tell me I'm such a "little mama's boy." He pins me down and puts his whole weight on my shoulders, letting a strand of thick spit dangle in a string from his mouth while I scream, "Get off!" He lets it nearly touch my face then sucks it back up into his mouth. Sometimes it's too late and the spit falls into my eye. He holds my hands down so I can't wipe it. I struggle to break free which only makes him madder. There are endless headlocks. Sometimes he simply trips me when I walk by. I'm not sure why he's angry but there's an old grudge hanging over it, something wounded in his voice as he pounds his finger on my chest with my arms pinned under his knees and says, "You're such a sneaky little kiss ass."

Mom says he's dealing with "a lot of anger" because he's not used to having an authority figure and that he's going to need to learn to deal with "his issues" soon or he'll end up going down the "path of addiction" just like his father did. She says this in front of him. She's always quoting some book or repeating some phrase that sounds like something from the group therapy she conducts with the prisoners at the Oregon State Hospital.

Tony will get mad and scream, "I'm not your fucking patient!"

But instead of screaming back, Mom will just say he needs to find a "more constructive" way to deal with his anger. This only makes him madder.

After he walks out, Mom will say it's a phase, that he's got too much of his father in him, that they are exactly alike. I know she's right because she knows our feelings better than we do, but it's weird because Dad is funny and nice to me. He never puts me in a headlock or spits in my face while I squirm.

THE BIKE ON the rack at Fred Meyer is a Huffy Pro Thunder with yellow mag wheels, blue rubber tires, and bright yellow handgrips. It's elevated five feet above the others, bathed in bright fluorescent light like a halo. It costs $150. I know we can't afford it, that we are not the kind of family where a boy gets a new bike every Christmas then rides over the trails behind the school in his brand-new Jordache jeans with the fancy white stitching on the back pocket like my friend Jesse. But when I see it on display at the store, an idea takes hold, the beauty of the thing, the way the space-age yellow paint lights it up beyond all imagining of lesser bikes, of rusty Goodwill Schwinns and my too-small red mini-Moto that makes my knees hit my elbows when I ride.

Tony sees me looking at it. "You wish."

When I bring it up with Mom, when I patiently explain my plan to save money to buy the $150 space-age dirt bike which is, after all, only seventy-five allowances, she offers me an extra dollar a week to clean the bathroom, sweep the stairs and mop the kitchen floor. Paul says he'll help me with the project, that I could mow lawns around the neighborhood or collect cans that he'll take to the recycling plant. It seems strange to me there would be money lying around like this, lawns to be mowed and cans in the garbage that could be money in a pocket. But it also seems like an impossibly large amount of money, like $150 isn't an amount of money that exists in the real world.

When school lets out, I go into the alley behind the house to look for cans. I find some old beer cans in a puddle next to the back of the barn. *Fifteen cents. Good. Only $149.85 to go.*

I go to the Plaid Pantry on Center Street and look around the dumpsters. There's an empty soda bottle sitting on the ground so I put it in the shopping bag I've tied around the frame of my mini-Moto. I open the lid to the dumpster and smell the sweet, rotting decay of old beer and sandwiches, milk cartons and used soda cups. I have to stand on a milk crate to look inside. The trash is in big black plastic bags. I look around before opening one because I know people will think I'm one of those Child Protective Services kids like the ones we see at the Boys Club who flinch when the basketball comes near them. I tear open a few bags. One has some bottles in it, so I put them into the shopping bag and move on. *Okay, that's a dollar.*

After a couple weeks I don't care who sees me. I don't care what they think. Sometimes it's fun to pretend to be homeless, to be wild like Timothy Manning and his friends, always covered in dirt and ready for a fight. I like the look of pity the old man from Plaid Pantry gives me when he finds me in the alley rooting through the dumpster. He says, "Listen, you can't go in there," like he's talking to an animal. I feel the urge to hiss or bare my fangs or scurry away on all fours.

I walk my mini-Moto around the neighborhood with a plastic bag tied around the frame, and when Derek sees me, he says, "You look like a bag lady! Ha-ha!" He chants, "Mick-ell, you smell, you smell like fuckin' hell!"

Paul says to ignore him because he's just a little shit anyway, and even though he's not supposed to tell me this because it's "anonymous," he says Derek's dad was in the program but disappeared and nobody's seen him for a long time.

When Christmas comes, I have seventy-five dollars of can, bottle, lawn, and chore money saved in a barrel-shaped piggy bank that Paul keeps at the top of the closet in their bedroom. Grandma and Grandpa send me a check for fifty dollars that's supposed to go to my college fund but Mom says we can put college off this year. Dad and Bonnie send me a check for another thirty-five with a note that says, "For the bike!"

Two days after Christmas, Paul takes me to Fred Meyer and we return at last with one yellow-and-blue Huffy Pro Thunder dirt bike in the back of his black mini-truck with the camper shell. I crawl into the back to wheel it out, careful not to scrape the new reflective pedals against the black metal truck bed. I bounce the rear tire lightly on the ground and pedal it up to the top of the hill on Breys Avenue to test it out, riding it down the block like a golden chariot. I feel the hot sweat on the back of my neck go cold in the crisp air as I fly down the street, the wind in my hair, the lightness of the frame, the feeling of escape, of freedom, an endlessness, no road too long, no destination too far. My world expands in front of me.

Tony is angry, standing arms folded on the porch when I get back. He says, "Why does he get a new bike?"

"He saved for it. He earned it. That's how it works." Paul closes the tailgate, replacing the blanket he keeps in the back just in case he needs a place to sleep.

"But why does he get one and I don't? I could've earned it too."

"You still can if you want."

"He's such a sneaky little shit. I do more chores than him. He doesn't deserve a bike."

I ignore him and pedal toward the school.

There is a circular concrete fountain the size of a swimming pool in the center of the wooded park behind Englewood Elementary. In the summer, on the weekends, the pipe that sticks up from the center shoots water ten feet in the air while kids gather under it to run and scream. Tony and I ran through it last year on a hot day, taking our shoes off to jump in. He was nicer then. We were on the same team. Now the fountain is empty and the park quiet, filled with the hush of wind through the needles on the big evergreens. Patches of sunlight cover the ground in yellow splotches as I ride down the dirt trail, jumping over the big knotty roots that cross it. I'm surrounded by the smell of pine and fresh mud. I ride back to the school.

I'm twisting through the hopscotch courts painted on the asphalt, in and out, over the three and around the five, when I see them. Timothy Manning and two older boys, both in dirty T-shirts, tossing a chewed-up green Nerf football in the center of the field. Timothy is skinny and small but carries himself like a much larger boy, his head high and his arms out. I heard he lives in a group home. Though they don't look related, there's a resemblance between him and the two boys as they toss the ball between them, a kind of low-hanging weariness to the jaw and the eyes, always a little dirt on the cheeks, alert like a pack of dogs.

They see me.

"Hey, man, nice bike!"

I pretend I can't hear them and study the hard plastic yellow mags on the front tire, which are so much sturdier than the metal spokes on my old red mini-bike.

"I said nice bike. Can I see it?" Timothy Manning walks straight toward me.

"I just got it. It's not broken in yet."

"I don't care. Let me see it. C'mon." He grabs the handlebars. I yank them away and take off toward the back of the big yellow school building. I can hear their footsteps behind me, trying to imagine it like a game of tag, like everyone's just messing around and I'm in on it. I cut through the rear parking lot and make a left into the breezeway between the school and the gym, thinking I can cut back through the park and get away but when I look up, the two boys block my exit in front of me. I stop.

"Don't be such a wimp. We just want to see your bike. You should learn to share." Timothy Manning walks up behind me, pushing me sideways on the concrete. I get up, holding my bike unsteadily as he grabs the seat. I don't know what to do.

Behind the shaggy black hair of the boy in the dirty purple shirt, I see Tony emerge suddenly in the sunlight of the breezeway. I can't believe he's here. There's a cosmic sense of timing to it. My big brother. The sixth grader. He's twice the size of Timothy Manning.

I scream, "That's my brother! Leave me alone!"

Tony has a strange look on his face. A kind of blankness as he walks, arms down as if in some kind of trance, right toward Timothy Manning and me.

"Oh, so you're the big brother? You here to stick up for this little bitch? We're supposed to be scared of you?"

Tony's face reveals nothing. He is calm. He walks in slow motion right up to Timothy Manning and says, "No, I hate that little shit." He picks up my yellow-and-blue Huffy Pro Thunder that I dug through trash to buy—seventy-five allowances, three thousand aluminum cans—and throws it into the brick wall of the gym. I watch as the handlebars break in half and the bike falls lamely on the red painted concrete. He walks away.

"Haaaaah ha aha ahah ha!" the boys scream. "Your brother hates you! Ha aha! What'd you think? He was gonna help? Whatcha gonna do? Cry? You gonna cry, you little *bitch*? You little *baby*."

There's a kind of cracking, something like a brittle bark that breaks in two while I stare at the bike on the ground and catch the back of my brother's long blond hair as he disappears behind the gym.

I don't understand it. I can't form words or thoughts. My busted bike. My brother who is not on my side. I push through the boys to the corner where I stare at the broken Huffy. After a moment, I feel a rock in my back. Then another. I don't move. I don't even mind the rocks. I feel their hands on me as they each push me and walk away. I can't take my eyes off the bike on the ground.

When were we together? Did I imagine that? Did I just imagine we survived something? That we came here to hide? He yells at Mom and she corrects him, telling him to control his temper. She uses those words she uses for the patients she treats at the mental hospital, those soon-to-be ex-con Dope Fiends from the state penitentiary in her "recovery" program. Terms like "borderline," "violent," "impulse control," and "attention deficit." She tells me about them because she tells me too much. She sees it in Tony. She tells me not to tell him but he knows. Of course he does. He sees it in her eyes. He is her science experiment, her personal psychology project. Like an animal in a cage, he's supposed to respond to "positive reinforcement" or the establishment of a "token economy" with "strict boundaries." He's supposed to learn to say the sentence "I'm sorry, Mom, you are right and I am wrong." When what he probably wants to say is, "Where were you? I was alone in that place for *seven years*." I know he thinks I am on her side because of it. Because of the lines I say, the ones she wants to hear about what kind of family we are, what kind of mother she is, the lines I know to repeat since watching Phil nearly die in the street knowing there are worse things and fearing those things more, to be like those family roles that children take on, the ones we read about in the Al-Anon literature for "children in families struggling with addiction" that she leaves around the house. I am the chosen child, the superchild, the one who can fly. Tony is the angry child, the scapegoat, the one who must sink.

But he sees it. He has to. He sees behind the curtain. He's the only one who does. And beyond the script is something else, the desire he has in this moment to destroy my new bike, my cherished and most prized possession, and in doing so, leave me to feel exactly as he does in the world. Alone.

I walk the broken bike home, wobbly and sobbing.

Paul is on the back porch tending to holes in the chicken wire that Pepper dug beneath the makeshift pen he built for her and Mork. He sees me. "What happened?"

I tell him the story. The park, the school, Timothy Manning and the boys from the group home, Tony, my broken bike. Paul is furious, dropping the hammer, spitting the nails in his teeth onto the ground. "He did *what*?"

We go into the kitchen, where Tony sits at the big table. Paul asks him if it's true.

"No. He broke it himself," Tony says. "'Cause he wanted me to get in trouble."

"Why would he do that?"

"Because he's a sneaky little shit. That's why." There is so much hatred in his eyes.

"I don't believe you," Paul says, trying to catch those angry eyes. "He spent months saving for that bike. He wouldn't just break it."

"Yes he would! That's how sneaky he is!"

"He's lying!" I scream.

"I know he is." Paul turns to Tony. "He's your *brother*, goddamn it! I just don't understand this. You are going to pay to have it fixed!"

"You can't make me! I won't do it! He made it all up!"

He runs down the stairs with a face full of tears and slams the door to our bedroom. Paul sits with me. He says we'll fix my bike, not to worry. It's just some light damage. I think of Tony and there is a split, a new idea of him emerges in my mind less like a teammate and more like an enemy or a force of nature, innately bad, like a sickness or the rot of an apple. When Mom gets home, she says she's sorry I have to deal with Tony's "impulse issues." I wince, even though I'm angry. Something feels wrong.

She takes away Tony's allowance and tells him she's going to give it to me until the bike is fixed. Tony says, "I don't care! Everyone here hates me! This is unfair! I hate all of you!" He refuses to do his chores. He sulks in his room. He never apologizes. He has made up his mind that this is a war and I am his enemy. But I'm just so sick of the noogies and headlocks, the spit in my eye, and if it's a war he wants, I decide I'm going to give him one.

CHAPTER 16

THE WAY OF ALL GREAT DRUNKS

On the day the crate of chimney sweep tools arrive, the air is crisp with a chill. As I walk down the street at dusk, Breys Avenue smells of burning wood. Fire means warmth and warmth means shelter which matters in a place with cold winters and two hundred days of rain every year. It's a good day to be a chimney sweep. A big white truck parks in front of our house and two men unload the wooden crate the size of a piano which Paul signs for. One by one he removes the tools and places them on the blue tarp: a black circular brush as big as a cat, a series of six-foot iron poles, steel wire brushes attached to a hemp rope, a wooden scraper, a wire-frame fan, a vacuum that looks like a rubber garbage can, and one black felt top hat. Paul puts the top hat on his head, covering his wild patchy black hair. "How do I look?"

"Like a bearded turtle going to a dance," Mom says.

"All those chimneys," Paul says. "Someone's gotta clean 'em." This is his contribution, one that allows him to keep tending to the rabbits, one that doesn't require him to leave the house for some "square nine to five" that he could never hold down because of "all the goddamn holes in the résumé."

Once they are set up with a call service and place an ad in the local Yellow Pages that reads "Stone Soup Chimney Sweeps" next to an outline of a man in a top hat hanging from a brick chimney, once Paul has read two books about the process and cleaned our chimney with Mom's help and we've heard for weeks about how this "new income" is going to "help out a lot around here," a call comes in for a job and we wave goodbye to Paul one Saturday morning after he packs the brushes, poles, vacuum and fan into the truck and drives away with that black top hat on. He's whistling as he climbs into the front seat. Mom says, "Isn't it amazing how you can still make a living with wood and fire in this age of jet planes and space travel?"

A few hours later he comes home covered in gray ash, a thick outline around his eyes from his goggles, his hands black from the grime, a noticeable slump in his shoulders. He describes to us a day of standing on a rooftop breathing in dust and scraping brick. "It couldn't have been that bad," Mom says. "Didn't it feel good to be out in the crisp air?"

"I was cold. Here." He hands her a check with a black thumbprint on it. "I'm going to wash up." He gets more jobs sweeping chimneys and each time he comes home covered in muck and ash. After a few weeks, he stops wearing the top hat when he goes out. "It makes me look stupid," he says. He stops watching cartoons with us, just washes up and takes a shower and says, "Well, that wasn't very fun."

When he leaves on a drinking binge again, when Mom comes home from work and there are three messages from the answering service from a woman on Thompson Avenue asking what happened to the man from Stone Soup Chimney Sweeps, when Mom's face goes white and she looks at us while cradling the receiver in her hand and asks, "Did Paul say where he was going," Tony says, "He didn't say anything, just packed up the truck and left." She puts the receiver down. We have cereal for dinner that night because she's too upset to cook. Tony declares that he's tired of rabbit and he doesn't care if we all die if that means we don't have to eat the disgusting little creatures anymore. Mom is too anxious to fight, which means that she's right on the edge of getting the depression.

The next morning I'm up at five again taking the frozen water bowls out of the barn, defrosting them with hot water in a pitcher from the kitchen sink, filling their food bowls with pellets from the fifty-pound feed bag at the back of the barn.

Paul parks his truck in front of the house a few nights later. We see him sitting there in the driver's seat, hunched over the steering wheel. Mom goes outside to talk to him while we wait in the living room. "He was drunk. I told him to go away until he is sober," she says when she comes back in. We tell her we don't care that he's drunk and it's better that he's home but she says kids shouldn't see adults "when they're using" because it might be bad for them. Tony says Dad drinks all the time and it's fine and Mom says, "Paul is an alcoholic so it's different. Your dad might be one too but he's a functional alcoholic." Tony says it doesn't matter if he can function or not, it's his house too so we should just let him sleep here since it's below freezing and all he has is his truck. Mom says the truck smells like puke because of the "Duck Pill" Paul takes to make him sick when he drinks as part of his recovery and she doesn't want us seeing him like that. We say we don't care. We just don't want him to freeze to death. She says that sometimes you have to practice "tough love" with people so they can reach "rock bottom" and go to AA. But Paul's already in AA, we say. And what if he dies? Mom says she's powerless over the disease and powerless over his actions. We say yeah but you could let him in the house so he has somewhere warm to sleep.

Every morning I take care of the rabbits and every night Mom checks the answering service to see if Paul took any of the chimney sweeping jobs. Every now and then he takes one. He probably does it drunk which Mom says is dangerous since he's up on rooftops but "at least he's work-ing" because otherwise the business will go under and they'll lose all the money they spent on the equipment. Without Paul's money from chimney sweeping, we're back to "stretching our food dollar," which means scrap-ing the dried-out peanut butter from the bottom of the gallon tub and nothing but bologna and bread with mustard and milk in our lunch pails and defrosted rabbit for dinner every night.

When I get home from school, I see Paul chopping wood with the big orange maul on the block next to the dog pen. He's wearing loose jeans and a dark blue velvet-collared shirt, his scraggly beard longer than usual. There is something off about the way he swings the maul, an unsteadiness that makes him stumble while he laughs to himself. He sees me and asks how school was. I stand a few feet back. He takes stock of his appearance, looking down at the maul swaying in his hands, the mess of his clothes, realizing the trouble he'll be in when he sobers up, laughing to himself in the way of all great drunks.

He is soft and fuzzy and odd and all I can think about is how he must've slept in the cold last night.

To be a drunk is to be a hero in a sad story.

"Can I have a hug?" he blurts out. I give him one, smelling the beer on his clothes, his body sweat and puke. "Thanks. I needed that. Are you guys okay?"

"Yeah, we're fine. Mom is sad."

"I know," he rubs the back of his head. "It's getting cold, so I thought I'd chop some wood for you."

"Thanks," I say, getting my bike from the back porch.

He pauses. "You know I love you right? I know you're not my kid but I love you."

"I know that," I say because it's true. "I love you too. I don't care if you're drunk."

He wipes his glasses with the front of his shirt, turns back toward the woodpile, places a knotty stump on it, lifts the maul above his head and brings it down with a thump. The wood goes flying, splintering in all directions. I get on my bike and take off for the afternoon.

He's gone when I get home and in his place Mom is inspecting the woodpile. "Did you do this?"

"No, Paul was here."

"I thought maybe he was. Was he drunk?"

"I think so. But he was nice. He can't help it, you know. He's sick."

"I know."

That night Paul is outside the house again, parked in his truck. The light from the streetlight falls on him and we can see him drinking from a brown paper bag. Mom goes outside and tells him he has to leave. We watch her stand next to the truck with her arms crossed in front of her. Paul gets out and hugs her and they stand there like that for a long time. His arms around her, her arms crossed. He says something then gets back in his truck. Exhaust smoke and steam fill the cold air as he starts the engine and drives away. Mom stands alone for a moment, staring at the ground, then comes back inside.

"It's bedtime," she says.

"It's only seven thirty."

"I mean for me." She goes into her room and closes the door behind her. I go to bed at nine thirty, but Tony stays up late watching *The A-Team*. I hear her get up and think she's about to yell at him for missing his bedtime but instead the footsteps go into the bathroom where the sink turns on. A few minutes later the footsteps retreat back to the bedroom. When I wake up, Tony is still in the living room, asleep on the couch with the TV on. The house is cold because there is no fire. The sun isn't up yet. I go outside with a flashlight to tend to the rabbits and when I come in, I turn on the stove and fry some eggs to eat with toast. I make a sandwich out of bologna, yellow mustard and wheat bread and put milk in my thermos. I knock on the door to see if Mom is okay. I can hear her crying in her room. "I'm fine, sweetie," she says through the door. "Just go to school."

It's silent outside from the frost and snow as I walk the three blocks to school. Everywhere are frozen windshields and slush-filled curbs, leafless trees shuddering in the wind. The quiet is broken by the crunch of my sneakers on the sidewalk and the swish of my arms against my brown ski jacket, the one with the corduroy shoulders and the tear in the side where the stuffing had fallen out which I'd patched up one morning with Elmer's glue and two pieces of black electrical tape.

WHEN PAUL SOBERS up, he asks Mom to marry him. There's no ring because he can't afford one even though Mom always says she wishes a good man would just "buy her a ring like my dad did for my mom," but there is a big wedding with a sugar-free lemon cheesecake. Mom buys us brand-new Lee jeans which we wear with matching white-collared shirts and brown-and-gray–striped clip-on ties. She has white ribbons and orange flowers in her hair as she walks down the aisle. Les McCarthy is there and so are Frank and Barb and Diane, all the people from the AA campouts. When he came back, Paul said, "I know I need to do better for this family and I will." And this time Mom hardly scolded him, probably because he asked her to marry him, which made up for his leaving.

After the wedding, when we are a family with a capital *F* for "father," legal and everything, Mom tells us that she loves Paul but if he leaves again, she's going to divorce him. We are still in our clip-on ties, eating leftover sugar-free lemon wedding cheesecake. She says he's a good man but he needs to be a better father to us. I know that Tony likes him too. We don't ever think of him as a father. He's more like another brother or maybe just someone who makes Mom easier to handle. When he's home, we have more money and fewer chores and she isn't locked in her room crying or lying on the floor next to the woodstove with that look that goes on forever.

At the wedding, Les McCarthy said to me, "Isn't it great your mom's getting married? She deserves happiness, don't you think?" I nodded and wondered why everyone always wanted us to be worried about her. I didn't tell him I was just glad that Paul was home so I didn't have to get up at five to deal with the rabbits and Tony wasn't as mean because Paul was bigger than he was and even though he never hit Tony, just being there made it less likely that Mom would fall into the depression or Tony would push me down the stairs when no one was looking.

CHAPTER 17

BROTHERS

Riding my bike on a crisp winter morning—the first sunny day in months after the endless rain ceased, the puddles steaming, the sun appearing like an embarrassed cousin from behind the gray-white clouds—weaving in and out of the cracks in the pavement under the canopy of trees on Eighteenth Street, inside left, outside right, bad luck to hit a crack, I suddenly hear a scream echo out through the neighborhood. There's something desperate about it, something sad, like a dog caught in the axle of a truck. I stop and park my like-new-again yellow-and-blue Huffy Pro Thunder against the curb to listen. Another scream. There's something familiar about it but I can't place it. I pedal toward the school to investigate out of instinct, the way a cat will lurch at a bird trapped behind glass.

I park my bike at the edge of the field at the school to see, there, in the middle of the baseball diamond, my brother lying sideways on the ground with his arms twisted in front of his chest and his long blond hair falling over a red tear-soaked face. His yellow-and-white uniform is covered in dirt, untucked in bunches around his stomach. Standing over him with one foot on his back is a tall, thin red-haired boy in a wool-collared brown leather jacket, smiling like a demon at the group of boys who've gathered to watch.

What is it about freckles that makes a boy so mean?

"Say another word!" he yells as he stands on my brother's back. "Anything. Just one word!"

"Stop it!" Tony cries.

The boy kicks him hard in the back. "What's wrong with you? Don't you understand English, motherfucker?"

Tony spots me and our eyes lock.

I walk up to the crowd of boys. I don't know any of them. "What's happening?"

"We were playing baseball and this kid started mouthing off to Brian saying he sucks at pitching. So then Brian got pissed and decided to kick his ass but the kid won't fight back. He's just lying there on the ground." I learn that Brian is Brian Medford and he is fourteen years old.

"Mick!" Tony screams. "Go get Paul! Hurry!"

"That's your brother? Hey, kid, c'mere." Brian Medford smiles at me like he's inviting me to a carnival game. "You got something to say? 'Cause if you do, I'm gonna make your brother pay."

"What do you mean?"

Brian Medford kicks Tony in the stomach. Tony makes a retching noise.

"I mean every time you talk, I'm going to hurt your brother."

"Every time?" He kicks him again.

Tony lets out an awful groan, part cry, part grunt, that sounds like "Ahh-ohh-urgh."

"Oh, so every time I speak you're gonna hurt him?" Brian Medford stomps a black Converse high-top right into Tony's ass.

"Yep."

A strange feeling comes over me as I realize the potential of the situation. Or maybe it's more like a feeling is lifted, the feeling of being under his thumb, or his weight, his spit, inside a headlock, watching him ruin another night where we could be sitting in the living room like a F-A-M-I-L-Y listening to Tchaikovsky. I smell the dirt of the field and feel the air on my neck and my arms begin to tingle.

"Anyway, as I was saying." Brian Medford kicks Tony in the side. It sounds like a mallet hitting a sack of meat. I circle over him. "*Star Wars* is a great movie. Some might say underrated, despite its great success." Brian Medford stomps on Tony's chest as he cries. I see his red face in the dirt, his eyes filled with tears, his mouth twisted in anguish and I feel a hatred for this too. For his weakness. For his inability to get up and fight back.

"Fuck you, you piece of shit!" Brian kicks him in the back of the head. "Yeah, mothafucker, what about now? You're not so fucking tough now are you?" Brian leans down and slaps him in the face in mockery, enjoying himself. "Who's the fucking pussy *now*?"

"Leave me alone! Stop!" Tony screams through tears, his face covered in dirt, his nose bloody, his hair twisted into patches of brown mud and green grass.

Brian Medford stands over him, a red-haired, freckled goblin smiling and cracking his knuckles. "Your little brother is one cold dude."

There is a tear in space and time, the laws of nature shifting. I've fallen through a hole into a place where I am the one with the power to hurt. I memorize his face all messed up in the dirt. I want to become something bigger than the land itself. *So this is what it's like to be the one with the power?* It's shocking to realize it's in me to be like him. I wonder if it's in him to be like me. If we didn't choose ourselves at all but just became what was required of us, like characters following a script.

He sobs under Brian Medford's shoe. He looks so sad. I try to focus on the anger, the revenge for my bike, but it's hard to look away from his face, not to wonder if this is what was behind the anger. Maybe he would like to be in my place. Maybe in a different life somewhere we would switch. Maybe I would be the bad son and he would be the good son. I can feel the cruelty of it, like the crack of the baton on the baby bunny's head, the clubs falling on Phil while he screams in the driveway. It makes me sick and sad. It mutes the colors of the world, turning yellow to gray and green to brown, extinguishing light and creating a dark place inside me.

I wish I could take my brother with me to somewhere new, where we could sit like other brothers do, those kids eating lunches of salami and cheese, peanut butter and jelly, and Frito-Lay potato chips, the feeling that you are protected, that there is enough for everyone, that a boy can close his eyes and sleep knowing someone is going to keep watch instead of the feeling we were both born with, that we know we are alone. Tony has it worse than I do, but I know how he feels because I feel it too. To have to study the faces of the adults, all the adults, who are always different, whose faces change constantly for mysterious reasons beyond our control or imagining, signifying danger or panic, fear or flight. *Which is it going to be tonight?*

"Okay, that's enough," I say. "Let's leave him alone."

"No," Brian Medford shakes his head. "It's not."

"He's not even moving. Just go home and we'll go home."

"No." He nudges Tony's whimpering head on the ground with his toe.

"I'm serious. Leave my brother alone!"

He kicks him again in the back and I feel something snap. "Leave him the fuck alone! That's my brother! Stop it!" The crowd of boys watching begin to whoop as I lower my head toward Brian Medford. Tony is a baby bunny. Tony is my puppy, Mork. Tony is Mom helpless on the floor of the den. Tony is Paul drunk and lonely, puking in the front of the truck. My big brother who likes pizza and macaroni and cheese, who dances around the apartment in L.A. with me in our matching tighty-whities.

I jump, running at Brian Medford with flailing arms. "Leave him alone! That's my brother! That's my brother!" He pushes me down and I get back up. My arms barely reach his chest. It's like trying to punch a giraffe. He pushes me hard and I fall down into the dirt next to Tony.

"You guys are crazy." He spits. He picks up a baseball glove from the ground and walks across the field to leave.

When he's a safe distance away, Tony gets up. He goes to the fence, crying, bloody. He grabs his bike and yells over his shoulder, "Someday somebody bigger than you is gonna kick your ass! You'll see!"

I follow him on my bike, trying to keep up. Sad for him and angry at myself. I know we are enemies, allies, traitors. Brothers.

Head down. Pedaling as hard as I can toward home, the spit still wet on my cheek, the brown dirt on his shoes flying off the pedals as we ride straight through the unlucky cracks on Eighteenth Street, I yell, "Someday you'll get yours! You'll see! You can't hurt him! That's my brother!"

CHAPTER 18
BULLETS

There is a gas can on the back porch meant for the lawn mower but since Paul doesn't check it, I use it to pour lines of gasoline from one side of the alley to the other, striking a match and standing back to watch the flame leap across the gravel and mud, dancing as it goes. I pretend I'm trying to learn about fire but mostly I just like to watch things burn. I burn small piles of dried grass, notebook paper, receipt paper, brown paper grocery bags, a Luke Skywalker action figure, part of an X-wing fighter, rabbit shit, dog shit, dog hair, cat hair, rubber bands, packs of matches, old T-shirts, old socks, fishing line and once, by accident, the yellow linoleum floor in the kitchen beneath the ledge of the oven door. In the course of my studies, I discover that rubber burns black with smoke that stinks up your clothes, that you can light a peanut on fire and hold it in your hand like a candle, that plastic melts like wax but hair curls up into a tiny ball like an electric snail as it sparks and sputters and stinks up the room, that a gas can, if emptied of all liquid gas and set with a match, will shoot a line of blue flame five feet into the air, big and hot enough to singe the eyebrows right off your face.

The box of bullets in the top drawer of Paul's desk reads, "Remington .22 Long Rifle." I know they're for the hunting rifle he keeps inside a zipped-up canvas bag in the loft of the barn. I take one out and hold it in my hand, feeling the weight of the smooth metal, scraping the circular lines around the bottom with my thumbnail. It looks harmless enough. I wonder if I can open it, if there is gunpowder inside and if so, how does it burn?

I take the bullet outside in the palm of my hand and I try crushing it with a pair of pliers but I don't have the strength to dent the metal so instead I place the bullet on the wooden stump Paul uses to cut the firewood. I pick up the blue hatchet from the woodpile and begin to whack at it. On the third hit, the hatchet handle kicks back in my grip and I hear a "Pow!" as the bullet explodes under me. I jump up and look around to see if anyone heard the explosion but there's nothing but the ghost of a thunderclap hanging in the air next to the toolshed.

"You fuckin' idiot," Tony says when I tell him about it. "Don't you understand the bullet went off? It could've gone into your stomach or your face and you'd be dead." He isn't alarmed, more like impressed. He gives me a punch in the shoulder.

I don't know why I like the fire so much, all I know is when something is burning, I feel like I made it happen and it feels good to have power over something, even if it sometimes gets out of control and almost burns the house down.

Derek steals Marlboro Reds from his mom when she's at work. She keeps cartons of them in the back of her closet in a white shopping bag. He takes a fresh box every few weeks and we go up into the loft in the barn to smoke, which is easy since Paul is gone and Mom is at work and no one goes into the rabbit barn except me.

Tony is also a Marlboro Reds man because they can be found all over in the cigarette machines at the trucker diners and sporting goods stores on Market Street, at Lancaster Mall next to the Orange Julius or in the movie theater lobby. All you need is a dollar fifty in quarters and if anyone says anything to you about being too young to smoke, you just say, "They're for my dad," and people nod and turn back to their pancakes and coffee.

Tony and I always share our cigarettes. It doesn't matter if it's the nasty Winstons I swipe from the Plaid Pantry next to the Hostess stand or the Marlboros Derek brings over or the unfiltered Camels Tony lifted from the door of his baseball coach's truck. It's an unwritten code to share them, to break rules together.

Derek comes over with some Reds and we climb up to the loft with a pack of matches and lean against the wall. We light our cigs as the sunlight filtering through the spotty roof of the barn creates small towers of white smoke in front of our faces.

"I like a good menthol after a meal," Tony says. He holds the cigarette casually between two fingers, a Red Vine in one hand. He takes a drag, then blows the smoke through the Red Vine. "It's just like a smoky mint."

"Yeah, menthols are good," I say, even though I've never had one. "But I don't understand why everyone doesn't just smoke 100s. Right? I mean they're bigger so you get more."

"Hundreds are for bitches and fags," Derek says. "I wouldn't be caught dead smoking one of those chick cigarettes."

"Absolutely."

"Oh, I know. I know. I was only joking."

CHAPTER 19
FAVORITES
USUALLY LOSE

Dad comes home to the apartment in Playa del Rey one quiet Saturday afternoon when we get to California for the summer and drops an envelope on the coffee table. It's thick and hits the wood with a smack.

He points at the envelope. "Open it."

Bonnie turns the volume down on the TV and leans forward, pushing open the flap with her long plastic nails. There's a flash of green.

Dad picks up the envelope and takes the money out. "I hit a horse."

"You what?"

"I hit the Pick Six at Del Mar. This is the payout."

"Honey!"

"Can I hold it?" Tony sits up.

Dad nods and Tony picks up the stack of hundred-dollar bills, licking his thumb like a Mafia accountant as he begins to count. "One, two, three . . ."

Bonnie puts her arms around Dad who says, "I knew the long shot was gonna win the sixth. That horse was due. The favorite scratched, so everybody bet the next horse down, but he wasn't shit on the grass. He's a front-runner. But it was a whole field of front-runners. So I says, 'I know that closer is gonna take this sumbitch.' Favorites usually lose, you know." He pauses. "Everybody needs a little luck."

"Twenty-six, twenty-seven, twenty-eight . . ."

"Everyone missed it, but guess who got it?" He points a thumb at his face. "I'm lucky, baby. Some guys got it."

"Aw, honey, you are lucky." She kisses him on the cheek.

"Forty, forty-one, forty-two. Wow." Even Tony is impressed. "That's forty-two hundred dollars."

"No point in going unless you can walk out owning the place," Dad says. "I knew I shoulda bet more."

I look at Dad. "Are we rich now?" I don't understand how much money this is. Can we buy a house or an island? Our own country?

"C'mon, let's get dinner. My treat. Anywhere you want to go." We decide on a big Mexican food meal so we go to the Red Onion and eat steak fajitas, shrimp, chips and guacamole, flan, and deep-fried strawberry ice cream.

When the check comes, Dad reaches into his wallet and drops a hundred-dollar bill on the tray. "Keep the change," he tells the waitress with a wink, even though it's only a forty-five-dollar meal.

"Honey!"

"What? We hit a horse. Got to spread the wealth around. Bad luck not to."

The waitress thanks him and comes back with a big plate of candies for us, hard white licorice and mints, and Bonnie gets up to use the restroom. When we're alone at the table with Dad, Tony says, "So when are you going to marry Bonnie?"

I look at him, excited. "Yeah. You're basically married anyway. What are you waiting for?"

We both know he can't tell if it's a game or if we're serious or if there's some kind of new magic brewing around our lives. Maybe catching that horse means anything is possible and happiness is as simple as choosing the right number on a ticket. You hit your long shot and you go home with a fat stack of bills in your pocket and take your boys out to a big dinner. That's the races.

"Maybe I will."

When she sits back down, there's a silence.

"What? What's the big secret? What I miss?"

"Nothing. Ask Dad. Dad . . ." We point at him.

Dad turns to her and says matter-of-factly, "What? I just think it's time."

"Time for what?" She's staring, smiling despite herself.

"You know, I mean, for us to get married." She looks at him, a charmed smile frozen on her face.

Tony holds up his Sprite like a champagne glass so I hold mine up too and Bonnie throws her head sideways into Dad and nobody knows if any of it is real. The horse and the money and the marriage proposal there in the Red Onion on Manchester Avenue.

When pressed, they say they're not sure people should even get married, it's just a "piece of paper" after all. What matters is how people treat each other. Anyway they've both been married before, a thing they talk about like sand castles they once built, destroyed by the tide. Bonnie was married to Eddie in Synanon when she was twenty. When Chuck's wife, Betty, died, the Old Man started talking about the impermanence of marriage and allegiance to the society, basically whatever needed saying so that everyone would have to go through what he went through by getting divorced. Some said they were relieved they didn't have to kill their husbands. So they split all the couples up and Bonnie left Synanon with a broken heart. She moved to the apartment in Playa del Rey to live in the aftermath of an idea so big it imploded under its own weight, leaving everyone to start new lives in the wreckage it left behind.

It left Bonnie wondering if marriage was a bigger idea or a smaller idea than a commune that tried to change the world before it went bad like sour milk. And now here she is, sitting across from this man and his two boys with salsa on their faces hoping their dad will marry her.

"We'll see," she says, red in the face, smiling as she grabs her purse and looks around for her makeup mirror.

MOM CALLS NEAR the end of the summer to tell us Paul has left on a binge again. She can't take it anymore and doesn't think "it's good for you guys" to see him that way. She explains this calmly, with a tone like a TV reporter delivering bad news about rain over the weekend.

She says she's sad that he's gone but she decided they have to get divorced. Her voice is very certain, detached, like she's talking about somebody else. "I have to let go of him. We'll talk more about it when you guys get back, but I just need you to know I'm okay and I'll be fine if I can find my way through this." She says she's been dealing with alcoholics and addicts her whole life and she can't be a victim anymore. "I'm gonna get better, I know it. I need your support, though."

Tony is silent. I say, "It's okay. I'm sorry, Mom." I say, "You've dealt with enough." My first thought is that without Mom, Paul will have nowhere to live. I picture him lying in a gutter passed out with a bottle inside a bag lying on his chest. I know he doesn't drink like this. He drinks in his truck in the woods. But in AA everyone talks about "functional drunks" who can have jobs and seem normal to outsiders and "gutter drunks" who can't handle anything and I know that Mom has just decided that Paul is officially a gutter drunk. I wonder if he's cold. I wonder if he's lonely. I wonder who's going to cut the wood and take care of the rabbits. Who is going to tell us jokes and take us fishing? I wonder if I'll ever see him again.

"He loves you guys and he's not a bad man, but he's just too sick."

I say, "I understand," and I say, "I love you, Mom," and I say, "I'm sorry this happened to you."

Bonnie looks worried. "Oh, honey, I'm so sorry. I know you love him. I hope your mom is all right. This is going to be hard on everyone, but maybe it's for the best?"

Dad says, "Well, that's too bad. Some guys never get it together and they end up drinking themselves to death. There's nothing you can do about it." He shakes his head. They both hug us and tell us they love us, that they are here to talk if we need anything. We go for frozen yogurt and when we get back we watch George Carlin and we laugh until we're red in the face.

It's so different how they see us. Mom is always trying to find a way to make us take care of her. Dad and Bonnie's first thought is always of us, how we might be sad, how it might be difficult *for us* that Paul is leaving. I know it's my job to take care of Mom and that all boys are supposed to take care of their mothers because that was the reason they were born. But it's nice to tell Bonnie I'm sad for Paul. Dad leans down and gives me a hug and says he liked Paul too and he seemed to be a good guy and he's sorry to see him go because it made it a little easier on everyone to have him around.

I like when he's gentle like this. The whole tough-guy exterior is gone in an instant and he seems more like a person trying to guide you through a storm. I remember that he did this for many people in Synanon. He saved their lives. People say he's a good man to talk to in a crisis. There's no judgment, even now, even of his ex-wife and our stepdad. There's just this quiet sense that he's seen it all, that it all can look pretty bad in the dark but starts to look better in the light and in any case he's not going anywhere. He sits with me, his arm draped around my shoulder. He tells me some jokes, repeating George Carlin's line about the words you can't say on TV. He pokes my ribs and messes up my hair and goes to the kitchen and comes back with an ice cream sandwich for us to split. We turn on the Dodger game and he's got a little half-cocked grin the whole time, making silly jokes about the players and umpires.

It's a new feeling. This thing that I feel when Dad gets like this. Like the wind has stopped blowing and I can hear. I feel quiet. Like nothing is required of me. There's no words I need to say and no problem I need to solve. I just sit with Dad and eat my ice cream sandwich as we listen to Vin Scully announce the batting order.

Bonnie and Tony disappear into the bedroom and close the door. You know it's a Big Talk because it ends with a hug when they walk out and Bonnie has a tear in her eye. She sits down next to me and says, "We've been discussing it and Tony thinks he should come live here in L.A. There's a junior high right down the street. I can drop him off in the morning and he can take the bus back. He's getting bigger and maybe your mom needs a break from him. Besides, teenage boys need their dads. What do you think?"

My first thought is, *Isn't that against the rules? I didn't know that was allowed.*

The second thought I have is about headlocks and Indian burns, getting pinned on my back while he pounds on my chest.

"I think it's a great idea!"

They look surprised. "Really?"

"Yeah!"

"You won't miss him?"

This feels like a trap. I know if I say no then it will turn into a talk about "brothers forgiving brothers" and how we're going to be best friends someday like Dad and Uncle Pete so we need to learn to get along. That all sounds distracting.

On the other hand, if I say yes, that might undermine the whole thing. I steal a glance at Tony who has an expression on his face that says something like *Don't you fuck this up for me you little son of a bitch.*

I choose the most diplomatic answer I can think of. "He's my brother. I want what's best for him."

They disappear to talk more in the bedroom and an hour later Bonnie announces Tony will come live in Los Angeles in the fall.

I can hear Dad's muffled voice wafting through the apartment when they call Mom. "Yeah, well, maybe it's for the best . . . He might just be too much for you to handle right now . . . I get it . . . No, we'd love to have him here." Bonnie is crying which means Mom is crying. Dad walks out into the living room and says to Tony, "Why don't you come talk to your mom?"

I hear Tony's voice between pauses from the other side of the open bedroom door: "Yeah, I really want to be here. It'll be fun . . . I'd rather go to a new school . . . I can join a new baseball team . . . We're only a few blocks from the beach . . . I know you love me, Mom."

I'm surprised she doesn't put up more of a fight.

When I go back to Oregon at the end of summer, I fly alone for the first time. And when Mom meets me at the gate, it's only her standing there. Paul is gone. She gives me a big hug and I try to smile, to act like I'm happy. But I can feel the weight of it. I know the depression is coming. It's as predictable as the rain in Salem. When we make the drive from the Portland airport back to the house on Breys Avenue, it's just the two of us and she talks the whole time about her feelings about leaving Paul, about how he's sick and it'll be better now and "it's just you and me against the world, kid," and I realize for the first time in my life that it's true.

CHAPTER 20

ROBERT SMITH IS
A FUCKING GOD

We have a new student. His name is Jake."

My fifth-grade teacher, Mrs. Wolfe, asks me to her desk and points to the back of the room where a giant, blond, pimply-faced kid in a T-shirt and green army pants sits awkwardly reading a Hardy Boys book. He's way too big for the tiny desk. His legs stretch out beneath him nearly to the back of the next chair. He ducked his head in the doorway when he walked in, his shoulders hunched, as if trying to disappear. He is six feet three inches tall and all of eleven years old. "He's a little shy, but he's real smart, so I thought maybe you could take him under your wing and show him around?"

"Sure."

My teacher says I'm not being challenged enough and that's why I get such bad grades even though it's the second time I've done fifth grade. I skipped fourth grade last year because it was determined I was in need of a "greater challenge," but then over the summer Mom changed her mind and decided that "no child should have to face age-inappropriate challenges" the way she did because they will be awkward and have no friends and "grow up to marry whatever alcoholic pays attention to them and that kind of thinking is what got her here, I mean you can't go around being a victim your whole life, at some point you've got to take charge and make changes for yourself." So now I'm in fifth grade again.

"Hey, man," I say and sit down at the empty desk next to the giant blond boy at the back of the room. "Where you from?"

"Nebraska."

"Where's that?"

"It's in the Midwest."

"What do you do there?"

"I don't know. There are a lot of farms. It's boring, but the Cornhuskers are there, so that's cool."

"What's a Cornhusker?"

"It's a football team. Everybody watches them play because they rule."

"Is that a good book?"

"It's okay. I've read most of them. At least it's not some Judy Blume bullshit."

"Bullshit." He tosses the word around like my dad talking about the Dodgers pitching staff. I know that this is a kind of test.

"Yeah, fuck that bullshit. There's a lot of fucking bullshit in this class. Fractions and cursive and other kinds of fuckin' bullshit like that." He smiles.

"Yeah. Do you guys play football here?"

"Every day at recess."

"Cool."

We talk about Michael Jackson and heavy metal, the Hardy Boys and fishing in the woods along the Santiam River. I take him to the football game at lunch, like he's my recruit, this six-foot-three, corn-fed, midwestern boy. He proves to be the best athlete on the field, moving swiftly among the child-size bodies trying to get around him or catch him or block his pass. It isn't just that's he's man-size. Even for a man, he'd be large. He's also just a nice guy. He makes jokes. He uses the power his size gives him to be generous, complimenting other players, saying, "Damn, bro, you run just like O.J. with that move," and "What can I say? The kid can flat out catch." His energy casts a friendly spell over the monkeys on the grass field in front of Englewood Elementary. As one of the smallest and least coordinated football players, I spend most of the time retrieving the football when it goes over the fence.

When the game is over and we walk back toward the big yellow school building, I expect him to move on to other friends, better football players, older kids. But instead he just sidles right up to me, my own personal giant, and says, "Damn, these guys don't know shit about football. You wanna come over after school?"

"THIS IS MIKEL. I met him at school." Jake's mom stands over a stove in yellow shorts and sandals frying something that spits grease on a range packed with dirty pots and coffee grinds. The house smells of two-day-old food and cat pee.

"Go find your sister. I think she's in the back. And I thought I told you to take out the trash. That fuckin' trash is taking over the house, damn it. Do some goddamn work for once! Mikel? What kinda name is that?"

"I don't know. Just one my parents gave me."

"You Russian?"

"No." I want to say I'm from "Dope Fiends" and was born in a C-U-L-T and raised in a school that's like an orphanage since that's the closest thing to the truth but I just give my stock answer. "It's like Miguel, but there's a *k*."

"Well, hi, Mick-ell. Are you staying for dinner? You gonna help my lazy-ass son with his chores?"

"Sure."

"When you're done with the trash, these goddamn dishes need doing. They been sitting here two fuckin' days already. You can wash while your friend dries them."

A little boy in a diaper watches us warily as he grasps onto her leg with his hand in his mouth.

"Jesus, Mom. Okay. I got it. C'mon." We go to the porch and grab the trash bags, then come back inside to wash the dishes. I quietly take note of the sugar in the house. Since we're not allowed to eat sugar because Mom says "it's a drug that'll kill you same as heroin," it has become my habit to catalog whatever sweets might be found in other houses. This one's pretty good: *One box of Froot Loops, some Fig Newton–type cookies, and what's this? Knockoff, generic Hostess chocolate donuts in the plastic sleeve?*

"Are you allowed to eat those?" I point at the chocolate donuts.

Jake stares at me. "What do you mean?"

"I mean, are those for you or your parents?"

Again, the look. "They're for everybody. You want a donut, man?"

"Sure. I mean if you're having one."

He grabs two donuts when we finish the dishes and leads me to his room in the attic. It's got a low ceiling, so he has to duck his giant head just to walk around in it. A queen-size bed fills up the middle of the room. On the makeshift shelves of milk crates and shipping pallets is a stereo and two speakers with a stack of vinyl records on top.

"You play hearts?"

"What's that?"

"It's a card game. You bid on tricks and the one who bids right at the end and gets the most tricks with hearts in them wins."

"No. Never heard of it."

"How about cribbage?"

"No."

"Gin rummy?"

"No."

"What do you do?"

"I don't know. Ride my bike and watch TV. Sometimes we smoke cigarettes behind the school." After the fights, as a kind of peace offering, Tony and I started smoking together. Now that he's in Los Angeles, I don't have anyone to smoke with.

"Oh. Well, you could smoke behind the fence in the alley. Nobody goes back there. But we don't have TV. We should go to your house next time."

"Hmm."

Jake puts a record on. It's got strange guitars that sound like they're underwater. He shows me the record cover. *Three Imaginary Boys* by the Cure. "Robert Smith is a fucking god," he says.

"Who?"

"The lead singer of the Cure. This guy." He points at a poster. It's a silhouette of a man with big wild hair and a guitar slung around him. Next to him are the words "Boys Don't Cry."

We listen to the weird guitars fill up the room, Robert Smith's strange warble floating over the band like some kind of wailing spirit. It's weird. But good weird. I like it, but I don't know why. Who are these imaginary boys?

We go into the kitchen to make noodles with canned tomato sauce, which we drown in butter, black pepper and the rubbery yellow government cheese that he must've gotten from the food bank. "This shit ain't bad in noodles, but you can't eat it straight." Jake laughs as he stirs the wedges into the pot. It's nice to have someone to joke with about government cheese.

We go back to his room. I tell him about Paul leaving and how we skin and eat rabbits for dinner and go to AA campouts and my brother who lives with my dad and Bonnie in L.A. He tells me he never knew his dad so I should feel lucky. All he knows is it was a man in Nebraska and how his mom was married to Craig and Craig has been in prison too. Sometimes Craig gets mad and threatens his mom but Jake gets in the middle so Craig screams at him. "He's a scary fuckin' dude when he's mad."

Craig is Alex and Ashley's dad, Jake's little brother and sister. Even though they have different fathers, he just wants to protect them and help them and you can tell he thinks it's his job. He says he found a little packet of white powder in the dresser once so he thinks Craig is still on drugs or holding them or selling them. "I'm not sure which to be honest but hey, at least when he's home, we got food in the house."

Jake says people come by the house looking for Craig, sometimes in the middle of the night. He answers the door in his white tank top and creased khakis then reaches into his pockets to get a baggy which he'll toss across the porch as he lights a cigarette. "Say what you will, the dude can sell and I'm not asking questions."

He tells me the Cure is the best band in the world because Robert Smith plays all the guitars and writes all the songs and they're not just about partying and whatever "bullshit Mötley Crüe or fuckin' Ratt songs are about." He says they're about real life, about how things get fucked-up but that it's okay to be fucked-up because at least you got other people who are fucked-up too. I nod and pretend to understand. We listen to three Cure records. I quietly decide to take down my Mötley Crüe poster as soon as possible.

He makes a tape of Cure songs for me on his stereo. I play it at night in bed on the Walkman Dad bought me. The songs are all so sad. He screams sometimes and he whispers sometimes and even the happy songs seem sad.

Yesterday I got so old I felt like I could die.

It feels good to feel bad. There's a relief like something I can't name, like something I can't talk about is finally being said. Mom tells us how happy we are and I know it's my job to pretend. If I tell her I'm sad, she just shakes her head and corrects me, telling me all the reasons I'm luckier than other kids. So I go to a place in my head where I can be alone. Listening to Robert Smith sing his happy songs about how sad he is feels like he's there too, like he has his Secret Place in his head where he goes and since he wrote a song about it, he's right here in my headphones, so we're in this Secret Place together. Me and Robert.

It's a place where we are allowed to be sad, instead of feeling like freaks of nature, us weirdos and orphans.

I pull my eyes out, hold my breath and wait until I shake.

Jake and I push our desks together in class so we can crack jokes about other kids or the crush he has on Miss Cork, the young blond PE teacher with the puffy bangs who Jake swears he's going to marry someday. We play football at lunch, and after school we go to his house to play cards and listen to records. Sometimes we shoot hoops and sometimes we get stuck watching Alex and Ashley while his mom goes shopping. She says she'll be right back but then disappears for five or six hours at a time, leaving us to figure out what to feed a couple of two-year-olds for dinner. When we go to Plaid Pantry, he buys something at the counter to distract the old man while I steal cigarettes from the Winston display. He doesn't smoke, but he seems to take a certain pride in the fact that I do, like it proves something about me, despite how small I am.

Everyone thinks he's older. Sometimes they think he's an adult so it's like having a special power because nobody messes with you when you're best friends with a giant and Jake is my first best friend and my best best friend in the world.

CHAPTER 21

THE GHOSTS THAT CROWD YOUR CASTLE IN THE SKY

Mom needs to start dating again. That's what she tells me. She needs to meet a good man and she can't be alone all the time. Paul still comes around to pick me up and take me places on weekends. Mom says, "It's important we have a relationship. After all, he was your first father figure." Paul doesn't seem to see it this way. I think he just likes taking me to Chuck E. Cheese or the water tubes out in Keizer. I think Mom gives him money but I prefer the trips when we don't spend any money, when we go fishing under the West Salem bridge or take long walks that turn into jogs and sprints in Minto-Brown Park. We decide I should be a runner since I love to run and that's usually a good start. We both like to see how far we can go before we have to cut through the fields and head back to the car from exhaustion. He takes me somewhere every weekend. We never had the money to go to these places as a F-A-M-I-L-Y, so it feels like the two of us are trying to make up for something. He's more distant now and he seems sad when he talks about the house on Breys Avenue. I can tell he misses us.

One Saturday, he doesn't show up. We are supposed to go down to the 4-H fair to check out the cows and the crafts. He thought it would be good for me to learn more about nature. Instead, he calls the next day to apologize. He says he had some work to do and couldn't make it, but Mom and I both know he's probably drinking again. He comes just once more, taking me to the school to play baseball but forgets a glove and a bat so all we have is one ball and one glove. He stands at home plate and throws grounders to me which I try to field and toss back to him. He's goofy about it, throwing the ball backward over his shoulder or throwing his glove in the air to knock it down when I throw it over his head.

When we get back to the house, when we say goodbye on the gravel path at the bottom of the six wooden stairs that lead up to the porch, he kneels down to give me a hug, his face right in mine, bushy and black and turtle-like. He has a tear in his eye that he wipes from behind his thick glasses while Mom stands over us. When he gets in his truck, the one Tony and I slept in on the way home from the Oregon coast, the one he drinks in alone and probably lives in now that he's "too sick to function," when he heads up Breys Avenue with his hand out of the window holding a wave to the street and turns right on D, Mom says he got sober just to come see me for the day.

I never see him again. The calls stop coming and so does his truck and later Mom tells me he's dead. He drank himself to death. There is no catch in her voice and no tears and no funeral to attend. It's not even a Big Talk. She says it matter-of-factly, like she's describing a tragedy that happened to people in another part of the world. A natural disaster that could not be avoided.

"How? What happened?"

"It's just something I heard," she says. "He was really sick."

The vagueness of the information, the sense that he is both alive and not alive, both a living father, a friend, a man in our house and someone who disappears to drink alone in the woods like some kind of sad ghost, always existed with him.

It seems there are ghosts everywhere. People who are both present and not present. They're real then gone until I see them in a dream, sitting up in bed in the dark thinking, *Did I imagine him? Where did he go?*

I can't stand the thought. *Did he die holding a bottle in his hand in the back of his truck? Or in a car crash? Is he lying frozen right now in a river-bed under a bridge somewhere in Portland? Did he miss me? Did he think we wanted him to leave?*

Did he even die at all? Why don't we ever talk about it?

But Mom never says a word about him and I don't know where to put all the things I know I'm not supposed to talk about anymore, the things I'm supposed to pretend never happened because they never happened in the World According to Mom. The list of things that don't exist is growing: there's the School, the bad men from Synanon with their clubs, the long depressions when she can't be moved from her bed, Dad and now Paul.

"It's just something I heard. He might just be drunk in a gutter somewhere. I don't know." That's all she ever tells me and now there is another ghost.

Our parents were like ghosts in Synanon, haunting us then disappearing again, leaving us to wonder what their connection to us was supposed to mean. *What is a mom and what is a dad and what is a family and if it's so special then why did you leave me?*

How long can you live with ghosts before deciding to become one? How long until the walls become clouds and the floor opens up like a clear blue sky and there's nowhere to go but your stone tower where you are the one who chooses who to haunt and how to haunt and when to haunt? You learn to act, to pretend, to inhabit different forms in your mind, different faces to the world, some of them terrifying, some charming, some cunning, some innocent, some a hundred feet tall, godlike and invincible, others tiny and frail, beseeching and ironic. Five, ten, ten thousand different ghosts of your creation, one for every person you meet, one for every occasion, so many that they crowd the hallways of your castle in the sky.

But somewhere within those imaginary walls, sitting alone in the dark above the clouds, you are aware that you are none of these things. Only sad.

CHAPTER 22

THE MEN
WHO LEAVE

Mom still goes to Al-Anon meetings even though Paul is gone. She tells me about an Al-Anon conference where there is a dance and she stood against the wall watching the men, noticing that she was attracted to the loners, the ones standing off by themselves, leaning against the wall. I wonder why she thinks this is something I need to know.

The twelve steps in Al-Anon are basically the same twelve steps as Alcoholics Anonymous. It's not clear why but it's something like once you build a ladder to the moon, you don't ask questions about why it works. You just climb it. There's a philosophy: don't look down and don't question. Which was the precise philosophy of Synanon before it went bad.

Step four is "Made a searching and fearless moral inventory of ourselves." Maybe that's what Mom is doing leaning against that wall at that dance and maybe that's why she tells me because I'm supposed to be following the steps too, taking inventory and admitting the nature of my wrongs to people.

When I say I miss Paul, she says, "It was really hard for me to let him go. All of this has been very difficult for me. Sitting at home waiting and wondering if he's going to come back is not easy stuff, kid. It was hard but it's better that he's gone and you guys were never that close anyway." I tell her about Minto-Brown Park and fishing and the long walks and watching cartoons with him and she says, "I just remember him leaving all the time and how hard that was because you stayed awake thinking about him."

"That was you, Mom. We were cold because there wasn't any firewood. I had to get up early to change the water in the frozen rabbit cages."

Her eyes wander away somewhere and when they return, she squints and lowers her brow like she's overwhelmed, rubbing her temples, confused as if staring into a mirror, surprised to find something other than her own reflection.

"No. You weren't cold. Were you? Stop exaggerating. What are you saying, sweetie?" She tilts her head as if searching for a word, scanning her mind for it. Then a calmness settles over her again. "No. It's better now. He was too sick and you're happier now that he's gone. This has been hard. This has been so hard on me. I need to lie down."

When I sit down to watch TV, she sits next to me and puts her hand out like I'm supposed to hold it. I don't know what to say so I hold her hand for a minute then try to make up some excuse to leave the room. I don't know how to tell her I don't want to sit on a couch with our fingers interlocked like those couples on TV and I know that if I did, it would hurt her feelings and I'm not allowed to do that.

She tells me a man approached her at the conference. "A nice man," she says. They talked for a long time. His name is Doug. He asked her to dinner. He's the vice president of sales for a local company that sells jams. He's "a normal guy. For once." He has a job and isn't a functional drunk or even a recovering drunk, a drunk that tries to be something else before doing the things drunks do again. "He's not an alcoholic. So that'll be new." He went through a divorce from a "very religious" wife. They have two kids.

"But why was he at a program conference?"

"What do you mean?"

"I mean if he's not using drugs or whatever, why was he even there?"

"Oh. Well, he's, um, dealt with some addiction issues."

"What does that mean?"

"There are different types of addiction and they all follow similar patterns and alcohol is just one of them but families can get sick from them anyway." I know she doesn't want me to ask what his addiction is.

He pulls up to the house on Breys Avenue on a Saturday morning in a blue Pontiac sedan and walks across the street holding a bouquet of flowers. I see him from the front window. He looks so formal, so out of place on this street of gravel driveways and broken-down cars where we live. He's wearing a brown tweed jacket with patches at the elbows and baggy jeans. His brown hair is parted neatly on the side above a face that seems to have no defining characteristics, like it isn't so much a face as an average of other faces blended together to create a person. He looks like one of those 1950s dads on *Leave It to Beaver,* swimming in his blazer as he peers around nervously walking up the front steps to knock on our door.

He's what Dad would call "a white dude."

"You can't trust 'em," Dad always says. "Those guys got secrets. Always. How can you trust someone who can't dance?"

"Hello, I'm Doug Brennan," he says, extending a hand for me in the living room.

"Hi."

"Your mother and I thought it was time I met you since you are very important to her." I have no idea how to respond to a statement like that.

"Cool."

He takes us to lunch at a place called Chalet that is like a fancy Denny's. I order eggs and sausage and toast and get to work coloring a cartoon ski house with the crayons the waitress brings me. Doug Brennan orders black coffee and oatmeal with raisins and brown sugar. He sips slowly from the cup, saying, "Mmmm," or "Whoa" as if diner coffee is the most surprising thing in the world.

The rhythm of his speech is odd. There are long pauses between sentences, as if he's allowing room for us to catch up, endlessly asking us if we understand him, as if what he's said requires some time to sink in before he can proceed. "Do you get that? Are you following?" He wipes his mouth with his napkin and folds it gently on the table, saying, "Miss, miss," to the waitress on the other side of the room carrying a full tray of food, "I'd like a refill."

It's like the trips we take to the zoo with the Talented and Gifted Program, to learn about exotic animals and observe their behavior up close. The sign next to this cage would read, "*The North American White Guy.*"

"It's important to build trust with an employer," he says, telling us about his secret to success in the jam business, the advice he gives all of his minimum-wage employees just entering the job market. "Anyone can apply for a job from the phone book or an ad in the newspaper. Do you get that? Are you with me?" That pause. "But the thing people don't understand about seeking employment is that the most important thing is trust."

He takes a sip from the thick white mug, looking back and forth between Mom and me. "Whoa. Hmmmm. This is good.

"Anyway, I tell the people I interview, 'No one should ever ask for a job. Never look for work. Never . . .'"

"What should they do?" Mom asks finally, trying to fill the pause.

"Build trust with potential employers."

"But what if they have a job available? Should they not ask for it?"

"No. Trust is all that matters. You sit right down and you say, 'Can you introduce me to five or ten people in your field with the power to hire and fire?'"

"What if they say no?"

"You ask them questions about their business. What is the bottom line? What is the most important thing in the jam business? for example. Are you following? You just ask them these sorts of things and then shut up and let them talk."

"Why?"

"Because no one ever asks them about their business and that makes them feel important."

"So you're learning to kiss ass," I say.

He studies us a moment, looking back and forth between Mom and me. "No, do you see why it's important to feel important? Does that register? Plus maybe you'll learn about the difference between marionberries and wild blackberries or how much fruit pulp is necessary for a proper jam to distinguish itself from a jelly. Anyway, when you're done you can ask for introductions again. And this time they might say yes to hiring you because now they trust you. Make sense?"

"So it's a scam," I say.

"No."

"But you really are looking for work so to pretend you're not is dishonest."

"You sound like you're thirty, ha-ha. Anyway, all you do is convince yourself on that day that you are not looking for work."

"Isn't that lying?"

"No. It can be true that day."

In the four breakfasts we have before he moves in with us, the ones where he tells us endlessly about canning and marketing at local craft fairs, about his philosophy in which he tells people to lie without calling it lying and Mom tells him about how "mature" I am for my age and how I'm going to grow up to do "great things," how Synanon was going to change the world and it really is too bad for all of those who started it how it fell apart, it never occurs to me that I might share a roof with this man in tweed who pauses between sentences.

Occasionally, I say something like "Can you believe Thatasshole Reagan thinks mental patients should run through the streets without any help? What a fuckin' shithead, right?"

Doug Brennan says, "Stop interrupting the adults. And you should not swear like that." There's a firmness in his voice, something like a threat.

When he moves his things in all at once and the house is suddenly filled with White Guy pictures of ducks and old airplanes and a new clock, a toaster oven, a waffle maker, when he brings in box after box of plaid ties and faded tennis shoes, V-neck sweaters, and an entire stamp collection while Mom flutters around him asking where this should go or that, when at last he goes to the grocery store and buys whatever food White Guys buy, he puts the groceries on a single shelf and calls me into the kitchen. He stands on a step stool with a small pair of reading glasses on his nose as he leans into the cabinet over me. "This is my cabinet with my food. I'm going to be living here with you guys and I need my own food, so you're not to touch this food in this cabinet." He gets down off the step stool and opens the fridge while I nod and observe the feeding habits up close. "And the food on this shelf is mine, okay? You're not to eat it or touch anything. Do you follow?" He points at a bottle of orange juice (which Mom says is pure sugar), a quart of yogurt, English muffins, and some plums.

"Got it. Don't touch your food." There is a bike to be ridden and cigarettes to be smoked and I have a date with Jake and a deck of cards.

THERE IS A strange silence in the house when I'm home. A formality. It's as if Mom wants me to act out a part for him, one in which I am the future doctor or lawyer or head of state she is training to change the world and she is the hard-fought, long-suffering woman bravely raising me against the odds instead of two survivors of a kind of wreckage.

I don't mind it so much. It's fun to inhabit yet another character in yet another script, to say things like "Thank you. I'd love some tea," and "I did *not* know the state bird of Iowa was the American goldfinch." Doug lapses into long explanations of the Inverted Jenny or a certain stamp-size portrait of Abraham Lincoln that sold for millions of dollars.

Two months into the new arrangement, I come home from school to find Mom on the floor of the living room crying. The pictures, the clock, the toaster oven and the waffle maker are all gone. I'm impressed by the speed at which he moved all of his things out of the house, like a thief in the night. Paul never touched anything when he left. It was probably because he didn't have room in his truck. He needed the space to sleep. "When I got here, all his clothes were gone. He didn't say where he was going. He just left. What is it about me that makes men leave?" She lays her head on her hands.

"Aw shit, Mom, I'm sorry." She's put Bob Dylan on the stereo, so you know it's serious.

She looks precisely like a girl who's fallen off her bike. "Well, he's no damn good if he's leaving you, Mom. You don't deserve it. I didn't eat his food. I swear."

Where have you been, my blue-eyed son?

"I know, sweetie. It's not your fault. I guess I'm just going to have to figure how to stop making this same mistake. I thought we were finally gonna be a real family. That you were finally gonna have a real father figure."

Where have you been, my darling young one?

She gives me a hug and goes into the bedroom to lie down. I go to the fridge to drink orange juice and make myself an English muffin.

I don't understand it. The whole point of the North American White Guy is that he's supposed to stick around, that he won't end up drunk in some ditch, running around after some woman or blowing the mortgage on a tip about a horse. That's why you put up with the boredom. So his sudden disappearance violates the whole spirit of the arrangement. I didn't mind so much if that's what she wanted. But she doesn't deserve this. It feels like a dirty trick.

I can feel her pain. I don't want to. I want to sit and listen to the Cure tape Jake gave me because it made me feel cool to scream, "Boys don't cry!" Robert Smith with his wild hair and lipstick, his cooing and groaning and "ah ah ahhhhhhing . . ." all over the place making me feel like my weirdness is cool, like I share a joke with the other weird people of the world who meet in our Secret Places, us imaginary boys who say we don't cry when we know we do.

I want to ride my bike to the park and do jumps off curbs, to bunny hop over cracks and puff my dirty old Winstons, to make it romantic like a pirate at sea, my mother home crying, my dad somewhere on the other side of the world, Paul dead (or not dead, nobody knows), and this dumb shit my mom fell for off doing God knows what while I eat his food.

Cigarettes kill. *Everything kills.* You shouldn't leave your mom alone. She needs you. *Gotta smoke. Gotta bunny hop. I can't hang with that shit, man.*

But I can feel her pain. I can precisely feel her loss as if it's my own. How empty it makes her. How needy. Desperate. I know how much this hurts. I hardly even know Doug Brennan but he means something to her. His presence calms her in some way and his absence devastates her. It's an incredible power to give somebody, I take note as I smoke, a pirate alone at sea, my bike leaning against a tree in the park, thinking,

The men who leave.
The women who stay home and cry.
The men who leave.

ALATEEN IS THE Al-Anon for kids they hold at the club on Friday nights. I go to the meetings while Mom goes to hers. Most of the kids at Alateen are older than I am, but there's one boy named Billy who is the same age. He's got huge yellow teeth that take over his face when he smiles and long nearly white blond hair that hangs over his head in a shag like David Lee Roth. He lives with his mom in West Salem. When we say the Serenity Prayer, which everybody knows by heart, he looks at me and rolls his eyes and says the words with his hand like a puppet. Someone then reads the traditions (no politics, this is self-supporting, don't fuck this up for us) and somebody is the chairperson. The chair runs the meeting and calls on people to talk. I'm too young to be the chair, but the older kids listen when I share and sometimes they ask me dumb questions like I'm a dumb little kid. "Did your mommy ever tell you to hide his drinking? Did she ever blame you? You know it's not your fault. It's a disease." Yeah, I know that. Everyone knows that.

I mostly listen because what does a kid know? Besides they're the ones with real problems. I'm not drinking like they are or having sex or an abortion like Kelly J says she had one time after she got pregnant because she was "too young to have a kid" and "didn't want to make the same mistakes as Mom." We say the Lord's Prayer and then we chant, "Keep coming back, it works!" I'm not really sure what it means for it to work. *What am I working? What is broken? Is it me?* I just like the words of the prayer and the stories from the older kids and having somewhere to go when no one is home.

Steps four and five are all about admitting what is wrong with you. About giving these things to God like a tray of dirty dishes after a meal. Step four: "Made a searching and fearless moral inventory of ourselves." Step five: "Admitted to God, to ourselves, and to another human being the exact nature of our wrongs." The word "God" is short for "higher power," which we all know can mean lots of things like the overwhelming force of nature, not just a guy with a beard in a chair. But if you can talk to him, if you can ask him things, doesn't that mean he's listening? A big endless sky doesn't listen to you. It just sits there and reminds you how small you are. So really this God is a listener and that means he's like a person so we're back to the man with the beard in the chair.

Billy says, "So if I admit what's wrong with me, if I tell God about the times I was bad, like the time I poured hot candle wax into my brother's Millennium Falcon, that'll stop my dad from drinking?"

"No, no. That's not how it works," Kelly J tells him, with her curly brown bangs poofed out like Madonna. "The steps are for *you,* to make *you* feel better."

"But I only feel bad when my dad leaves."

"That's not true, Billy. You said you felt bad when you hurt your brother."

"Not really. He deserved it. He threw my Chewbacca out the window of the car last week when we were driving to my aunt's house."

"Well, it sounds like maybe he should make amends too. Has he worked the steps? Is he in the program?"

"He's seven."

Billy and I talk on the phone on nights when Mom is gone because she needs more meetings now that Doug has left to "try to get her head together." Billy says his mom has dried parsley in her cabinet and you can roll it up and smoke it and it'll get you high. When he comes over to spend the night, we roll a giant joint with the parsley he swiped inside a piece of notebook paper. We go into the barn and he hands me the joint which is eight inches long and as fat as a summer sausage. I light it. The notebook paper catches fire and the parsley begins to smoke. I try to take a puff but the three-inch flame is getting closer to my face so I panic and drop it on the ground and stomp it out with my feet. Billy shakes his head and says, "Damn. There goes some good weed."

We make a plan to run away. Between us we have tents, a hatchet, sleeping bags, boots, some rope, canteens and backpacks. We figure if we can just get a canoe, we can float away down the Willamette somewhere and fish for our dinner, cooking at night around a campfire. All we need is the right day, the right weather, because you wouldn't want to do that in the rain and it's always raining. Maybe in the spring. It never occurs to us that the trip would have an end, that it would take us somewhere, that we would have to figure something else out when we got there. In our plan, there is only the river and our fishing poles and smoking Winstons around a campfire as we fry our fish in the woods.

I write a story about this for Mrs. Wolfe's class. She says she liked the one I wrote about the bunnies who take over the barn and start a war against the man who comes to thump their babies on the head. Bonnie likes my stories too and sometimes she asks me to make one up when we're "having a convo" on the bed while Tony and Dad watch the Dodgers. She put one up on the fridge. Mom never says anything about the stories because she wants me to grow up to be like John Lennon or Martin Luther King. I say, "But they got shot."

Mrs. Wolfe doesn't like the story. She calls me up to the front of class and asks me if I'm planning on running away and don't I know that's dangerous and should she talk to my mother about it? Her eyes are cross.

She stares at me with that concerned look the adults get every time you let them know what you're really thinking. "It's just a dumb story."

"So you're not really planning on going?"

"No." Maybe I am and maybe I'm not. The point is to plan. For Billy and me to have a plan because rivers take you places and we want to be anywhere but this dumb town.

"Okay. As long as it isn't real. You scared me. I won't tell your mom if you promise not to run away."

"I promise."

One time when I talk to Billy on the phone, when we speak for hours like I do with Bonnie sometimes or Dad, at the end of the phone call he says, "Okay dude talk to you later."

And I say, "All right. I love you."

"What?"

I feel a hotness on my cheek as I realize I made a mistake. "Aw shit. I thought I was talking to my mom for a second."

"You love me?"

"No. I was just confused. Like how you say goodbye to your mom."

"Ha-ha. You love me. Fag."

"Shut up. I got to go."

"Later."

He lets it go and doesn't tease me about it because he's a good friend like that. We just want to get high together or run off somewhere where we don't have to deal with gutter drunks or teachers or dumb parents who never listen or mean what they say. "Friends 'til cigarette butts wear pants," we say, even though we drift apart when he starts smoking the real weed he buys from another kid at Alateen.

When Mom later tells me Billy shot himself, I never get any details about why, nothing about a funeral, no Big Talk. It's just something she mentions once in passing.

"Your friend Billy killed himself" is all she ever says about it.

"Isn't there something we should do? How could he do that?" I don't know how to feel, just that my friend is gone and I start to cry. I can't help but wonder if things would have been different for Billy, for me, if we had just left. I picture his smiling face with his fuzzy yellow teeth, the easy way he slapped me five like a brother, like a skin-on-skin pact to keep our secrets from the adults who prowled around our lives. He knew I loved him and he was cool with it. *Friends 'til cigarette butts wear pants.*

She puts a hand over her mouth, searching for something. "Why are you crying? He was a disturbed kid. Just be glad that you guys didn't know each other that well."

She doesn't know about our plan to run away or how nice he was to me, how I told him I loved him and he never even teased me about it. She doesn't know that Billy and I just wanted to be somewhere we didn't have to pretend anymore and how he's gone and he never got to go and I'm still here.

"Let go and let God," she says, as she gathers her things to leave for a meeting.

THE HOUSE IS a mausoleum. It's either too big or too small for only Mom and me and we are both aware of the people who were once with us and are now gone: Tony, Doug and especially Paul. We don't talk about it but I know she's lonely because she's always at meetings or reading books with titles like *Women Who Love Too Much* and *You Can Heal Your Life.* I don't like cleaning the house because when the house is clean it feels emptier, a place for ghosts to walk undisturbed by the clutter of people going about their lives. I'm allowed to use hot water now when I do the dishes because Mom got a raise and she's "able to support this family" on just her income. We don't use food stamps or eat the big blocks of government cheese anymore. She even buys me some new clothes. She sells the Vega and buys a red Honda Accord hatchback. We celebrate with salad bar at Chalet and I try not to bring up the breakfasts with Doug Brennan.

One day when I get home from school, he's in the living room, sitting on the couch with Mom on his lap blushing like a teenager. There are cardboard boxes all over the floor.

"Hey, pal. Your mom and I made up." As if they'd been in a fight. Maybe he thinks I don't know that he just split one day without a word. Maybe he thinks children are too dumb for the truth.

"Oh."

"Yeah, sweetie, Doug's gonna be back with us and we're gonna be a family again."

"Oh."

He says he wants me to meet his kids now that everything is out in the open. They can come over and stay with us sometimes.

"You hear that, Mick? You're gonna have a new brother and sister."

"Oh."

Instant family. Just add water.

I wonder what wasn't in the open before. I wonder what these kids are like. I wonder why I feel so strange, why Mom is so quiet, so clueless, why Doug thinks he can walk back into this house with this bullshit explanation.

She tosses that word around so casually. I wonder what she means by it. We have our roles. *Am I the son? Is he the father now?* Are we going to bury him someday and cry over his grave or are we going to pretend he didn't exist once the tears are dry and the waffle maker is out on the curb again?

He kisses her on the lips and they stay locked for a moment. Paul would kiss Mom too but it was always funny because he'd dip her or peck her on the cheek or twirl her around and make us all laugh. Doug says, "Hey, pal, I guess we're gonna be roommates again."

"I'm gonna go ride my bike."

DOUG DOESN'T LIKE that I swear at Mom. He doesn't like that I'm always gone on my bike after school. He doesn't understand where I get off speaking to an adult like that. He makes fun of the bandanna on my knee. "You get wounded in battle?" He makes fun of my Robert Smith poster. "What's with the lipstick? Is he supposed to be some kind of cross-dresser?" He tells me not to eat his food. I eat it anyway, swiping a muffin or a Fig Newton or a bite of raspberry yogurt when I think he won't notice.

When I make the Jaycee relay team, the track team for Englewood Elementary that competes in the citywide track meet every year at the stadium at Bush's Pasture Park, Mom says, "Just make sure it doesn't interfere with your chores." I tell her about the tryouts on the dirt trail behind the school, how twenty kids showed up for the mile relay team and I got second behind only Mark Johnson, who was faster than everybody.

I like to pant and sweat, like I did on the long days when Paul used to take me to Minto-Brown Park. He said, "You know, in a long enough race, a man can outrun a horse." Which doesn't sound true but it is. I understand running in a way I never understood football or baseball, the sense that you could just go on and on forever, just you and your two feet, this normal body of yours suddenly capable of something amazing.

"Don't they have a football team?" Doug says.

"Track is better than football. More natural. You use it in every sport. And anyway someone should be an athlete in this house."

"Oh, yeah? You're the athlete here?"

"Yes."

"You know I played football in high school."

"That's nice."

"We were pretty good."

"Cool."

"You don't think I can play football?"

"You? No. You're a pussy."

"Mick! Don't talk to your stepdad like that."

"He's not my stepdad. You guys aren't married."

"You know what I mean."

"You think you're faster than me?"

"Yes."

"You want to make a wager?"

"That I'm faster than you? Sure. I'll dust you."

"Okay, let's race. If you lose, you have to do the dishes for a week. If I lose, I'll get you whatever you want for dinner."

We shake on it and walk out to the street. "This is stupid," Mom says and rolls her eyes.

We line up in the middle of Breys Avenue, leaning forward with our arms down, shaking our fingers. He doesn't bother to put on shorts, just his baggy White Guy jeans. "To the sign for B Street," Doug says, pointing to the intersection fifteen houses down.

"Okay."

"On your mark. Get set." My legs feel like wound springs, like I could practically fly down the street.

"Go!"

I put my head down and pump hard toward B Street. When I look up, he's already ten feet in front of me and pulling away. I charge hard, trying to will myself down the street as fast as I can but as his baggy jeans and white T-shirt and old tennis shoes get farther and farther in front of me, I slow down to a walk. He crosses B Street with his arms up and circles back.

"You know who was the star wide receiver on that football team?" He points both thumbs at his chest. "Me." We walk back to the house.

"Congratulations," Mom says. "You're faster than a ten-year-old."

"He wanted to race. It was all for fun." We walk into the kitchen and he points at the dishes in the sink. "I guess you'll be getting to work on those." He takes a drink of water and places it on the counter. "Wash this one too."

When I'm finished with the dishes, I ride to the trail in the woods next to the school, drop my bike and run until my legs ache, my head is dizzy and my lungs burn. It's nearly spring and the Jaycee Relays are still two months away. I probably don't even need to train because it's just some dumb race. But here in the woods, in the crisp dusk air as the sky turns from dark blue to black and I see my breath come out in clouds in front of me, I don't even care about the race. It isn't the point. Here beneath the trees I can become a shadow and just run.

DOUG IS THREE times my size. I'm made aware of this by the way he stands over me to get his cereal off the top of the fridge. He crowds close and says, "You need anything?" looking down. It's less a threat than a reminder like the way he lifts my bike with one hand over his head from the back porch and puts it in the barn that still smells like rabbit shit even though the rabbits are gone. When Mork poops on the stairs because he has diarrhea and nobody let him out, he drags him by his collar, points his nose at the pile of shit and hits him across the snout, "Bad dog!"

I scream, "Don't you hit him! He didn't know!"

"He needs to learn. This is the only way dogs learn anything."

When I go to the woods next to the school to train on the dirt track with the Jaycee Relays team, I can feel my body getting stronger, the power in my lungs as I fly down the dirt trail. Mark Johnson is faster than I am, but I'm not far behind. We do wind sprints and long laps and practice handing off the baton without dropping it. There isn't much that feels better than knowing you can use your own two feet to go wherever you like. Running is simple. That's what I like about it. It's something a caveman could understand. Who's the fastest to that rock? Go.

There is a crowd in the stands at the cinder track at Bush's Pasture Park on the day of the Jaycee Relays. The bleachers are filled with parents, teachers, friends, little brothers and sisters, cousins, aunts and uncles, some with flags, some in T-shirts matching the ones worn by the teams of kids from every school for thirty miles. Orange slices are handed around and cups filled with water. At the end of each race there's a good-hearted cheer from the crowd as the first graders then second graders then third graders receive their medals. As I warm up with Mark Johnson and the other kids on my team, I think this really is a great little town sometimes.

Rounding the final turn of my leadoff leg, I hear that crowd of mothers and fathers and aunts and uncles yell and clap for me and I feel my heart leap up into my throat as I become the shadow, the breath, the weightless messenger and I hand off the baton in third place. I grab my knees and feel the red blood in my face, the comfort of the grass. I am awake. I am alive. I stand and scream for Mark Johnson as he crosses the finish line second, running his anchor lap in sixty-three seconds, nearly catching the sixth grader from Four Corners Elementary who out-leans him.

I get a red ribbon with a medal and a small trophy to carry home. After the race, when everyone is leaving with their moms and dads, some on shoulders, some carried into station wagons and pickup trucks, Mark Johnson says, "Hey, Jollett, good race!"

"Thanks, man! You too!"

His dad says, "You need a ride? Where are your folks?"

I feel a flush, a warmth on my neck, a wrongness spreading to my knees like I missed something critical. "Oh, they're still in the stands."

"Well, we're going for pizza if you want to come."

I didn't think this far ahead and I know the lie sounds clumsy. I just forgot. There was the race and the crowd. The cinder track is so much faster than the dirt trail in the woods behind the school.

"Okay. I'll tell them. I'm not sure if we're busy because they said they were going to take me to Sizzler."

His dad looks at me. He's wearing a thin nylon blue jacket and jeans, the door to his station wagon open, his dark skin bunching around his eyes beneath a handsome shaved brown dome. I can feel them on me. "You sure you don't need a ride, son?"

"Oh, no no no no no. No. My parents are just over there. Good race, Mark!" I turn away. I can feel his eyes on me as I jog back toward the track, toward my bike which I locked to a pole beneath the stands. I ride my Huffy two miles home to the house on Breys Avenue, holding a grip in one hand and the trophy in the other. The house is empty so I put the trophy on the bookshelf next to my bed and make myself some scrambled eggs with sliced hot dogs. I put on my headphones and my copy of *Pornography* by the Cure.

"How was your running thing?" Mom asks when they get home from their Al-Anon meeting.

"We got second."

"Who got first?" Doug asks.

"Four Corners. But they were all sixth graders. Mark and I think we can take 'em next year."

"Better hope you grow."

"I will." I shoot him a look. "Even if I don't, I'll get faster. It's just training."

"Boys and sports," Mom says, beating on her chest.

"Sports are cool, Mom. And girls play sports too, you know."

"It's all just testosterone and proving who's the biggest, baddest alpha male."

"Running? No it isn't. It's raw speed and seeing who worked the hardest. That's fucking stupid."

"Don't talk to your mother that way."

"She's my mom. I can talk to her however the fuck I want."

"Mick, go to your room," Mom says.

"Fine by me."

Doug stands between me and the stairs to the basement. He stares down at me and says, "Apologize to your mother."

"For what?"

"For calling her stupid."

"I didn't call her stupid. I said what she said was stupid."

"Doug, let him go. It's fine."

"I don't understand why you let him talk to you that way, Gerry." I brush past him and go downstairs to look at my trophy, to feel the smooth red ribbon with my fingers, to put headphones on and hear Robert Smith scream, "It doesn't matter if we all die!" while I punch the mattress with my fist.

On Sunday, which is chore day, I procrastinate all morning, finding little things to do instead of dishes and mopping and vacuuming while Mom says, "Time to get to work. You can't put this off forever. How about you start now. Then you'll have your whole day to loaf off?" She reads a book in the bedroom. When I finally finish the dishes and the bathrooms and mopping and vacuuming, it's nearly dusk and I decide to go for a bike ride to Bush Park to run a few laps around the cinder track. As I'm leaving, Mom says, "You forgot to vacuum behind the couch in the living room. You have to move the couch to make sure you get the space beneath the window."

"I already vacuumed. I'm leaving now."

"Not until you vacuum the floor by the couch."

"Jesus fucking Christ, Mom, you're always complaining. I'm leaving now." Doug walks into the kitchen from the back porch to wash the small hand shovel he used to spread the compost over the vegetable gardens on the side of the house.

"I don't want to. I already did my chores."

Mom looks at Doug. "I'm not letting you leave, Mick. It's your responsibility to clean the living room and it's not done and if you want to test me, I'll take away your bike."

"It's my bike. I bought it with my own money. You can't take it away."

"I can and I will. Now go vacuum by the couch."

"God, Mom, you're such a fucking bitch."

I start for the vacuum in the hall closet. I hear something drop, a loud clang from the kitchen of metal on metal. I turn to see Doug walking toward me, his lips tight and his right hand raised. "You can't talk to your mother that way."

He pushes me hard in the chest and I fall on the ground. He jumps on top of me and pins me by my shoulders under his knees. He's heavy, way heavier than Tony and I feel a pinch in my back. It's hard to breathe. My fingers are trapped beneath his knees, bent at a strange angle. It feels like they're going to break. "Get the fuck off me!" I scream.

He rears his fist back and I feel a crack across my skull. My eyes go watery and a lightness fills my head. Through the liquid haze I see him above me, inching his face ever larger into my field of vision until I can't see anything but his angry mouth, the line of white spit forming between his teeth. He points a finger into my face and says, "Don't you ever talk to your mother like that again! You hear me?!"

Mom screams, "What are you doing?! Get off him!"

"Do you understand?" He turns to Mom and says, "He needs to learn! How else is he going to learn?"

She pushes him. "What are you thinking?!"

"What?! He called you a bitch!"

"I don't care! You can't do that!" All I can see is the mop of her permed brown hair, her fingers pulling on the collar of his blue T-shirt.

He stands up and looks down at me, turning his head slowly to look at my mother.

I feel a wetness dripping from my nose as I try to flex my sprained fingers. I wipe my eyes. My nose and mouth throb in unison like they're being pumped with air. I feel a slippery warmth over my tongue and teeth.

I know the script of this movie. I know what I'm supposed to say. He looks at me like he's asserted something. Like I've crossed a line and he's shown me where the line is and now that I know it, it is my job to acknowledge the line. To cower or whimper or ask for forgiveness, as if I'm supposed to thank him for pointing out where the line is. But all I can think about is Dad. How much tougher Dad is than he is, how Dad would beat the crap out of him if he were here.

I don't know what he would've done if Mom hadn't intervened. I can feel his hatred, but it doesn't really feel like I'm the thing he hates. I'm just the thing he can hit, the thing he can pin to the ground and whale on.

"You need to learn you can't talk to your mother that way. You owe her an apology. Well?" He stares at me with his arms crossed.

I stand up from the floor, squaring my legs beneath me as I spit and wipe my face.

"My dad is going to beat the fucking shit out of you!" I clench my fists with my head down and walk toward him. I don't have a plan or a thought in my head. "He's gonna fucking kill you! You hear me! He'll kill you!"

"Your dad isn't here."

Mom stands between us. "Stop, Mick. Calm down. It's okay."

"Fuck him! Fuck you! Fuck this!"

"Honey, stop."

"He can't hit me, Mom! He can't fucking hit me!"

"I know, sweetie. You're right. Let me talk to him." I move toward him with my fists up.

"Fuck you, you fucking loser!"

"He's lost control, Gerry. You can't let him act like this."

"This is my house! I can act how I want! Big man! Big fucking man you are!"

"Stay here," Mom says to me. She grabs Doug's hand and leads him to the backyard for a Big Talk.

I run out the front door. My bike is leaning against the porch. I turn right and pedal up the hill on Breys Avenue.

The cars on D Street have turned on their headlights and the sky is a midnight blue. It's a hot night for Oregon in late spring. It's almost summer and all I can think is I need to run away. How dumb I was to stay when I should've just run away a long time ago. *Pedal hard. Watch the cars.* I drift into lanes aiming at the headlights down the block, swerving left and right when they honk their horns. I head toward downtown, past the high school and the train tracks, past the cars whisking families, quiet families, happy families home on a Sunday night. The mall downtown is closed and the streets are abandoned except for the lights coming from the Y and the gold man standing with his ax on top of the marble dome of the state capitol. *When was it that we first met? When I saw you standing guard over us with your golden ax?* I cross the bridge to West Salem and skip a few rocks on the shores of the Willamette where Paul and I used to fish. I wonder where he is. I want to talk to him, to just sit quietly next to him while he drinks. That doesn't sound so bad. *I can live here. Right here at this spot.* I could camp in the woods, sleep beneath a pile of leaves in the forest. I've got twenty bucks and a stash of cigarettes in my pocket. That's at least enough for a few days. I walk back up to the bridge and light a cigarette, watching the tip turn red as I take a drag. I lean against the edge. *What would break my fall? Could I flap my ears and fly? When did I stop believing that?* I can almost hear Mom calling from the front porch of the house the way she used to when Tony was here and Paul was still alive.

The mall downtown is closed and he is lying in a riverbed somewhere. I know it. The later it gets, the more I wonder if I should go find him. *Is he even dead? Are you here somewhere?* I see the faces of the women and men in their cars, staring at the boy smoking a cigarette alone on the West Salem bridge on a Sunday night. I know there is nowhere to run and no place to sleep. I think the house is an illusion. Under it is frozen ground, beneath that a lake of black water. I can disappear into the current like a rock falling off a bridge. The boys in those cars on their way to Sunday dinner, to mashed potatoes and pot roast, rolls with butter. I feel sorry for them. *I am a shadow. I am the shadow of a shadow.* It feels good to let the nothingness fill me. *What breaks your fall?* I toss a rock and watch it arc over the river and disappear. I know how the conversation will go if I go home. *Where have you been? What have you been doing? Come on, out with it.* You don't deserve to know. *You smell like cigarettes. Did you steal them? Are you drinking? You know you're at risk for becoming an alcoholic. It's a family disease.* Yes, I know that. *Tell me the truth. Don't you lie to me, mister. The truth, the truth, the truth. Come on, out with it!* I don't have an answer. No words make sense. Paul is dead. Doug is a monster. The house is an illusion. There is only this frozen ground, this river of black water, this empty well, this blankness, these ghosts, nothing to do but forget about shelter and become the storm.

CALIFORNIA

*To care only for well-being seems to me positively
ill-bred. Whether it's good or bad, it is sometimes
very pleasant, too, to smash things.*

—FYODOR DOSTOEVSKY,
NOTES FROM THE UNDERGROUND

CHAPTER 23

THIS LAND IS YOUR LAND

I remember the first litter of tiny pink bunnies born naked and blind. How they crawled out from under their mother on the cold steel cage. It was my job to make sure there was a little cotton bed for them. Each day I came in to check on them, to give them new food and water, to make sure the ones that crawled out of the nest were put back safely.

One morning I came outside to the barn to find a baby bunny dead in the cage, his paw sticking out from the steel wire, a bloody gash along his neck. I picked him up, folding him into a brown leaf, and took him outside. I made a small hole in the ground next to a thicket of blackberry bushes in the alley, digging it out with the edge of Paul's blue hatchet. I would've said a prayer but I didn't know a prayer so I said, "You were a bunny that should've got to live free," and placed two sticks in the dirt to mark the grave.

When I asked Paul about it, he said, "Oh yeah, the mothers do that sometimes."

"Why?"

"It's nothing they do on purpose. They just can't help it."

AFTER MOM CALLED my father to explain and I heard her say, "They usually get along great. He was out of control," which Dad knew was a lie but no bones were broken so he wasn't going to fly all-the-way-the-hell up to Oregon and "end up back in jail," after Doug offered a weak apology, "Your mother says it's, uh, hard for you to understand but I just come from a different set of rules where boys are not allowed to call their mothers names but I do understand that those aren't the rules you're used to," after Mom cried on the way to the airport saying, "It breaks my heart for you to leave for the summer like this," I am in Los Angeles sitting in the living room of Dad and Bonnie's new house in Westchester, a mile from the westbound runway of Los Angeles International Airport.

Tony seems different. He's got long feathered hair, parted in the middle now. He's wearing new clothes that look store bought. I'm still wearing my five-year-old Salvation Army shoes and a stained *Star Wars* T-shirt that used to be his. He's fatter. He's lost the gaunt, hollow-eyed look we get in Oregon. At the airport when they came to pick me up, he looked at me with a smile and said, "Heeeeeeyy, little bro." He even gave me a half-shoulder hug. I flinched when he leaned in because I thought he was going to sock me one in the stomach.

None of it seems real. The new house is a low cream-and-yellow stucco building with a sloping front lawn of crabgrass, two bedrooms, and a living room. It's what they call a California bungalow. Bonnie says it's no bigger than a postage stamp but it's all they need. It sits along a row of other bungalows in a sleepy neighborhood. I wonder what Jake is doing back in Salem. After what happened with Doug, he told me he would run away with me if I wanted him to but we couldn't figure out anywhere to go so instead we just snuck out at night for a few weeks. I know Mom is sad and I wonder if Doug is being mean to her and if anyone is taking care of Mork.

You can hear the jets from the front porch. And if you stand on the corner at the end of the block, you can even see the massive 747s as they taxi down the runway. The windows and walls shake whenever one of the big planes passes by. There's the ocean to the west, the wetlands to the north, and the airport to the south. Inglewood is to the east. There are miles and miles of concrete strip malls, body shops, grocery stores, and fast-food chains between the quiet salt wind and the city of Inglewood. If you go up to the abandoned neighborhood by the beach, to the top of Sandpiper Road, where the high school kids go to make out, you can watch those big jets gather speed and practically knock you over as they soar into the sky and disappear in the clouds over the ocean. Living so close to the airport gives you a constant sense of movement, of people leaving and coming home, old lives ending and new ones beginning.

Tony suggests that we go hang out at the Bowl, which is what everyone calls El Dorado Bowling Alley. He says there's no adults around. "None that'll say shit, at least," so that means, "*Heads* can *kick it* and smoke and fuck around. You'll see. It's *sick*." I don't understand his slang. Who is this guy?

The Bowl sits at the edge of civilization in a strip mall with a grocery store, a park, a bank—before the empty land around the airport. Dad gives us ten bucks each. As we walk down the block, I expect at any moment Tony is going to trip me and take my ten dollars. Instead he says, "Keep an eye out," as he reaches into the bushes in front of the house two doors down and pulls out a pack of cigarettes. The pack is long and green with fancy lettering: Benson & Hedges Menthol 100's. When we get around the corner, he hands me one. I wonder when he gave up on Marlboro Reds.

"Marlboro Reds are for hicks and rednecks. These are better. Try it." I take a drag and feel the cool menthol fill my mouth and nose. It's like brushing your teeth with a campfire.

"You play Super Mario Bros.? They got one at the Bowl. It's *sick*." He keeps using that word. His new Vision skateboard is *sick,* the waves at El Porto in Manhattan Beach are gonna be *sick* this summer and he's bummed he's going to miss them but then he's going to football camp in Salem in a few days and that's going to be *sick* too.

I wonder when he forgot we are mortal enemies.

He tells me we can wash our hands at the Bowl to get the smoky smell off them and Dad and Bonnie will never know. "How's Mom? What's that new guy like? I heard he beat you up."

"He's a dick. Mom is Mom."

"Yeah, I hear you, bro."

I tell him that Doug's the whitest guy you'll ever meet. "Like, he collects stamps and shit. He's got all this food in the house that you're not allowed to eat. He puts it on shelves and you can't even touch it."

"Even Mom?"

"She's cool with it for some reason." I ask him if he heard about Paul. He nods.

"Mom says he drank himself to death."

Tony takes a long drag on the white-filtered cigarette hanging out of his mouth. He inhales deeply. I still don't inhale. I just puff, letting the smoke linger in my mouth and around my eyes. The trick is to hold it in your mouth awhile before blowing it out through puckered lips so it looks like you actually breathed it in.

"He was a good dude." We talk about the cartoons and the fishing trips and Mork, the coast, the rabbits. "He's really dead?"

"I think so. Mom says someone told her he had a really bad binge and died."

"Wait, so she doesn't know for sure?"

"Nobody does. It's either that or maybe he's a bum somewhere. She was very Mom about it." I know Tony misses Paul too but because his public stance is that all adults are full of shit, he doesn't say anything, just tosses his cigarette on the asphalt and steps on it with his foot.

"So we don't even know if he's alive or dead? Damn, bro. That's *sick.*"

At the Bowl he introduces me to the guys he hangs out with. It's a ragtag gang of white surfer-type guys in tapered pants and karate shoes, smoking cigarettes while they take turns playing Super Mario Bros. They nod at me, lifting their chins, and say, "Sup." No one seems to care that they are smoking, even though they're only teenagers. I light a Benson & Hedges Menthol 100 and smoke it right there next to the video games. I can feel the eyes on me, the disapproving looks from the adults as they walk by us juvenile delinquents. It feels good to feel bad.

Every family has a script. That's something I learned in Alateen, along with how to blow smoke rings and make a weed pipe from an apple. In our family script Dad is the big, tough, masculine father and Tony is *his* son. I am the sensitive one who belongs to Mom and Bonnie. Tony draws pictures like Dad does and people say they are "exactly alike." I like books, like Mom. At least that's what people say.

Once Tony leaves for Oregon for the summer to stay with Mom because she still technically has "legal custody" and insisted on it, it's just Bonnie and Dad and me in the house in Westchester, it doesn't seem like Dad cares about the script. I am surprised when he says, "Hey, come give me a hand," and I go outside to the garage to watch him stack boxes or organize his tools in the giant red Craftsman toolbox or to help him pack sunroofs into the orange industrial van he bought for his new business installing sunroofs. Mom says he's nine-fingered, which is what they called Dope Fiends in Synanon, meaning they have something like a disability.

But I count his fingers and there are always ten. Clasped around a jigsaw, messing up my hair, rubbing sunscreen on my back in the sand, tossing me in the waves at Toes Beach at sunset after we pack the van.

AT THE END of the summer Tony calls to say that he's decided to stay in Oregon for the school year. He made friends at the football camp and wants to play for the North Salem High Vikings football team in the fall. He says this casually, like it's his decision to make. At times like this he seems like a hero to me, the way he can ignore the rules the adults have made for us and do whatever he wants.

When we hang up, Bonnie says, "Well, what do you think?"

"About what?"

"About Tony staying in Oregon."

I say it makes sense because he's good at football. But all I can think about are the Indian burns and headlocks, the screaming matches, the weight of Doug's knees on my shoulders, my fingers twisted back and sprained, the bruises, the spit in his teeth, the hazy outline of a fist. There is an anger that is new. The well. The blackness. The storm.

I blurt out, "I don't want to go back to Salem."

The words fall out of my mouth before I have the chance to think about them. She turns her head and calls my dad into the bedroom. "Tell your father what you just told me."

I take a breath, unsure of myself, and tell him that I want to live in Los Angeles with them. Dad sits on the edge of the bed with his hands in his lap.

"Have you told your mother this?"

"No."

"Well, it's a big decision. And you'd have to talk to her. But of course you can come live here with us. You're my son."

It's strange to be referred to as his son, because everybody knows I am Mom's son, I am Bonnie's son, and Tony is *his* son.

"She's gonna be upset," Bonnie says. "I feel for her. Are you sure you want to do this?"

After a Big Talk, we call her from the kitchen and I tell her I have something important to tell her. I feel my throat go dry and struggle to find my voice. My hands are clammy as I wrap the white phone cord in circles around my fingers. There's a long pause on the other end of the line. "Okay?"

"Bonnie and Dad and I have been talking and since Tony is staying there to live with you and he and I don't really get along so well . . ." I know I can't mention Doug. I know I can't mention the wolf den or Paul or the 5:00 A.M. rabbit feedings, the slaughtering alone in the backyard with the ten-inch hunting knife that cuts my hand, the nights without food, her depressions that come like the rain, the feeling like my job is only to take care of her. There is a script, there were words I rehearsed not ten minutes ago with Bonnie and Dad, but I can't find them. *Tell her it's about Dad. She'll understand that. A boy needs a father figure. Isn't that what she's always saying?*

But there is only an empty place where the words should be. I simply can't make my voice do something she doesn't approve of.

I close my eyes, trying to find the words. "And, well, since I'm, uh, gonna be a teenager soon and I don't really know my dad that well and, um, a teenage boy needs his dad, like how you said with Tony . . ."

The words are drowned out by the songs I hear in my head, the lectures and talks and instructions on who I am supposed to be, what I am supposed to be in the world, the boy she is raising who is so special he can change it. The music. The old protest songs and folk tunes sung on those long car trips up to the woods:

> *This land is your land, this land is my land*
> *From California to the New York island*

We would sing along from the backseat. Sometimes we'd ask her to sing a song in Dutch or French and we'd go quiet as the strange words filled the car, wondering where she'd lived and who she was and how she'd learned to speak whole other languages in another world, in another life sometime long ago before the changes, the crash, the wreckage, the terrible choices they were given between changing the world and turning their children into orphans.

"I think I should come live here with Dad and Bonnie for a year."

I hear her take a long breath. I have a sinking feeling, exactly the way it felt to hit a baby bunny across the head, the presence of something dark inside me, something awful and cruel. And like the bunnies, I know she is stunned that for the first time in my life I am disagreeing with the World According to Mom.

"Is this because of Doug?"

"No."

"Because I told him if it didn't stop, I'd leave him and I meant it."

"I know. It's not Doug. I just think it's time I get to know my dad. It's only for a year."

"Your dad was the love of my life."

"Yes. You've told me that."

"He and Bonnie have more money. I can't compete."

"It has nothing to do with that. This house is smaller than yours."

"What did they say?"

"They said it was okay with them if it was okay with you."

"Well, if it's okay with them then I guess there's nothing I can do. Only for one year, okay?"

"Okay."

I hear her sigh heavily. There's a kind of calm as I hang up the phone. I know I've caught her off guard. I didn't think she would say yes. I know I've defied a rule, one made at a time before words, before I can remember, an ancient feeling that a promise has been broken.

These things are never said out loud. It's just something I know.

CHAPTER 24
"NORMAL"

On the way into school on the first day at Orville Wright Junior High in Westchester, as a real-live student at a Los Angeles city public school, I walk past a wall with the word "CSR" written in big bubbly cartoon letters. Beneath the letters is a drawing of a rat on a skateboard drinking a bottle of malt liquor. On an opposing wall in much sloppier black spray paint are the words "w/s ROLLING 60's 13." The letters seem to run together. They remind me of the hieroglyphics I saw on a trip to the public library in Salem, Oregon, with the Talented and Gifted Program. I have no idea what it means but I know it means something important. Why else would someone bother to write it on a wall?

The hallways are noisy. I'm surrounded by older, louder, bigger kids, some with Jheri curls, some with short waves, some tall and foreboding in blue-and-black flannel shirts buttoned up to their necks and hair that looks like it's been crimped at a salon. Some are dancing, spinning on backs or knees. They don't look at me. I am invisible to them. They walk with heads held high, some fists locked at the waist. The girls look like women to me, with makeup and nails and big voices screaming down the hallway while I stand beneath them: "Hey, Tamika! Tamika! Girl, you know I need my notebook!" They have breasts. Real breasts. And butts in tight jeans with hips and heels and a sway that pings back and forth while they walk chewing gum with teeth covered in braces.

As I walk down the hall, everyone says, "Surf's up, dude. Hey, dude, surf's up" because of my long blond hair, even though I've never been on a surfboard. There's music everywhere from radios carried around inside backpacks casually slung off one shoulder.

Even the handful of white faces seem different from the ones I knew in Oregon. Cleaner. Brighter somehow. Their clothes are new. They wear T-shirts with cartoons on them from T&C Surf Designs or Quiksilver. They use the word "radical" or the word "gnarly" or the word "awesome." Everyone seems rich.

Chris Faraday is a tall redheaded boy with freckles in a white T-shirt with a picture of an ape on a skateboard. He's got sleepy eyes and skin that looks like it's been tanned from days in the sun. He sits next to me in social studies. He's got a pair of thick British Knights sneakers on and a pack of purple Now and Laters open behind his book so our teacher, Mr. Schneider, can't see it. He leans into me and says, "Hey, dude, where you from?"

"Oregon."

"Oh shit, really? Damn. What's it like?"

I picture rain falling on the rabbit barn, the muddy shore of the Willamette River under the West Salem bridge, the red rabbit blood splattered on the gravel path next to the shed, the campsite next to the big rocks on the Oregon coast, the snow in the sand, Billy and I planning our trip, Billy as a ghost, Paul lying still in a creek bed, the spit in Doug's teeth, Mom crying on the floor of the wolf den next to the wood-burning stove.

"It's cool."

"Do you guys skate?"

"A little."

"Can you ollie?"

"Almost."

"What kind of board you got?"

"Nash."

"That's a little kid's board."

"Oh yeah, I know. My dad's going to get me a new one. We just haven't gone to get it yet."

In front of me is a girl named Tanisha Campbell who smiles with a mouthful of braces. "Hi!" Her hair is pulled tight on her head in a bun with little pink flower clips and golden hoop earrings that look like two dolphins jumping together to kiss beneath her earlobe. "What's your name?"

"Mike." I've decided that I'm tired of being teased for being named

Mikel, which sounds like a girl's name, and if I'm at a new school nobody knows me anyway so I may as well go by Mike. Everybody knows at least five Mikes.

"Hi, Mike. You need a pen? Mr. Schneider gets mad if you don't take notes while he talking."

Tanisha likes Blow Pops covered in red Jolly Ranchers. She keeps a couple in the zip-up plastic pen case snapped into her three-hole binder notebook. At the start of class every day she lends me a blue Bic ballpoint pen for notes, saying, "When you gonna start bringing your own pen?"

"They weigh me down." I blush because I have three in the small pocket on the front of my backpack. I just like the chance to talk to Tanisha. Sometimes she passes me notes over her shoulder that say, "If you could live anywhere you want, where would you live?" or "Look at that man stomach. Mr. Schneider need to eat more vegetables!" or "Daaaaamn a quiz! I didn't study. Did you?"

As I walk into class one day, Donte Parker, who is nearly as tall as Jake, though still only a seventh grader, runs up behind me and pushes me into the door frame as he leans into the room to yell, "The big one coming, y'all! Watch out!" Everyone is scared of the Big One, the earthquake that will destroy Southern California. It lurks at the edges of our minds like the Night Stalker, the serial killer who was in the news for all those murders and rapes and something called sodomy. My aunt Jeannie discovered a victim one night. It was one of her first calls as a rookie cop. The father was killed, the children raped. She said it was "horrific." Something about this place, despite the palm trees and warm weather, suggests there is a terrible, invisible rot that threatens the Good Life promised to the rows and rows of perfect houses with their perfect green lawns.

Tanisha yells at him, "You play too much! That's my friend."

At the end of the period, when the bell rings for lunch, Tanisha is standing outside the doorway waiting for me. "You got my pen?" I give it to her and she leans in to give me a hug. She puts her arm around my back, pulling me toward her, smelling of cinnamon and cocoa butter. I feel a warmth spread through my chest and radiate over my body, a feeling that marks her at that instant, like I could find her in my mind from then on as if on a map of the world. My first hug. "Bye," she says as I watch her walk away, a blur of acid-wash jeans. Somewhere beneath the sky-blue cotton of her thin sweatshirt dances the white line of an actual bra.

At lunch I sit at a table with some of the other boys from pre-algebra: Stephen Perkins, who is tall, kind and studious, quietly observing us all. Ryan Church, also tall with glasses and brown hair, sarcastic and good at basketball. And my favorite: Drew. He's blond and thin, smart like Jake and awkwardly dressed like me. He doesn't seem to understand the rules against knee-high socks or Reebok knockoffs from Payless ShoeSource either. Like me, he doesn't quite get the fashion code. He's the only other kid at Orville Wright Junior High School who knows about the Cure. His brother, who is a college DJ, makes him mix tapes filled with the Cure and the Smiths, Sigue Sigue Sputnik, and Siouxsie and the Banshees. We decide to stick together, sensing a strength in numbers, trading tapes. I give him *The Head on the Door*. He gives me *Some Great Reward* by Depeche Mode. It feels like we're the only two members of a club. Misfits Without Jackets.

It's an unspoken pact we've made, for mutual protection from the humiliation of junior high life: me the white trash latchkey son of an ex-con, he the do-gooder son of the PTA president. There's a balance struck. He makes me look more respectable. I make him look more reckless.

Chris Faraday comes and goes, floating between us and other groups, the kind of mouthy kid that no one likes but everyone tolerates for some reason. When he's out of earshot, Ryan always says, "That kid's an asshole." Ryan seems to have the school down. He hangs out with us misfits but he seems to understand how to fake fitting in better than we do. Maybe it's because he's good at basketball.

The kids from class talk about trips to Palm Springs or Hawaii, their dads who work as engineers or lawyers at the big Hughes Aircraft building on the side of the hill next to the enormous white letters spelling out "LMU" for Loyola Marymount University.

When I mention my hug with Tanisha, Chris Faraday says, "Oh yeah, I hugged Tanisha tons of times. That's my girl." I don't believe him. Tanisha has better taste than that.

"My dad says you got to be careful with black girls, though." He tears a piece of cherry Fruit Roll-Up from wax paper.

"What do you mean?"

"You know. Because they're a pain in the ass. He told me everything changed when the busing started."

"The busing?"

"Yeah, haven't you asked yourself why this school is like 80 percent black even though Westchester is 90 percent white?"

I never thought about it because everyone was white in Oregon and I just figured L.A. was the opposite. Anyway he sounds angry about it which doesn't make sense because that's the whole thing that makes this school good. All the mama jokes and dance moves. The new music: Guy and LeVert and Troop and Salt-N-Pepa. Plus the kids here can really break-dance. We had a break-dancing crew in Oregon but nobody was very good at it. Anyway, Tanisha is nicer to me than anyone else.

"You know what they say," he says.

"No. I don't."

"About black people."

"What?" I have no idea what this has to do with Tanisha Campbell who is the only beautiful thing about this school.

"Black people are lazy."

"No they're not. That's stupid."

He explains it like it's my mistake, like it's something I need to know, like I am silly or naive for never having learned it. "Seriously, you don't know this shit?"

I shake my head. It doesn't feel true. "That doesn't sound right."

"Yeah, and they eat chicken and watermelon."

"What's wrong with that?" I'd take chicken and watermelon over rabbit stew any day.

"It's just that they're usually kind of dirty and poor. You know, on food stamps with single moms and a dad in prison or on drugs."

I remember that none of these kids know we were on food stamps in Oregon and my dad was in prison and before that he was on heroin. Anyway, Dad makes fun of white guys in suits too. He'll hitch his pants up high on his waist and pretend to push invisible glasses up his nose as he shakes a disapproving finger. I wonder what Chris Faraday would say if I told him those things. Would he look at black people differently, or me?

"I'm just joking." He claps me on the back. "That's just what people say. It's kinda true, though. Hahahaha." Maybe he doesn't know about Martin

Luther King or Malcolm X, about the tear gas in People's Park, the Black Panthers in Oakland or trying to stop Thatasshole Reagan.

"It's not just blacks, though. Mexicans steal shit. You gotta watch out. And Orientals can't drive."

"I think you're making all this up," I say. It sounds so foreign and stupid. "Why would they steal things?"

"Because they're poor." There it is again. *Poor.* I think about the Monopoly money and the hand-me-downs, the big blocks of government cheese we melted into noodles, the trips to Goodwill for the bubble gum shoes. I picture their big houses, their moms with bobbed haircuts and cheery makeup, their dads sitting quietly, one leg crossed over the other, reading a newspaper. I don't know these people.

"What's our thing?" I ask.

"What do you mean?"

"I mean white people. What's our bad thing?"

"Oh. We're just normal."

CHAPTER 25

GOTH

A few months after I start school, Mom calls and says Tony is be-coming a goth. The football team didn't "work out" for him so he found a new crowd and started wearing eyeliner and lacy gloves, bolo ties and weird pointy shoes with thick rubber soles. She's pretty sure they're all on drugs. It doesn't surprise her, she says. "He's always struggled with the early signs of an addictive personality." But he's looking weirder these days in the pictures she sent, with his hair blown out in all directions like he stuck his finger in a socket.

He had a party and destroyed the house. She left him in charge for the weekend and he invited "every burnout in the city of Salem." When she got home from her conference, the house was filled with trash, cigarette butts, empty beer cans on the floor. The fireplace banister was broken. There was a hole in the living room wall leading to the bathroom that someone made with the orange maul from the toolshed. The floor of the wolf den was covered in puke. The floor in Tony's room looked as if snow had fallen because the rug was dusted in a thick layer of white powder. At first Mom thought it was drugs but it turned out to be laundry detergent.

Doug had left again, so she came home alone. "Imagine, going some-where to seek clarity and coming home to *that*," she says.

When she walked in, Tony was standing in the kitchen washing a dish. He looked up and calmly said, "So . . . how was your weekend?"

She says she can't take it anymore and he has to move back to L.A. He's out of control and he needs his father.

"I knew I was in deep shit so I was like fuck it, you know? We were in trouble anyway," he tells me, smoking a cigarette behind the Bowl a few days after he gets to Los Angeles. The Bowl is our constant destination, the place we go to hang out and smoke and be good at being bad. He says he didn't even know what happened at that party. He was passed out in his room the whole time.

"I guess shit got out of hand. When I woke up and saw what happened, all I could think was, 'Damn that was one *sick party*.'" He has black eyeliner on and a pair of tapered Dickies. He's wearing leopard-print Creepers, which are shoes that look like big elevated triangles, and a white shirt with a big collar buttoned all the way up to his chin. His hair is sprayed in different directions in big swooping arcs like ocean waves crashing together on his head. His fingernails are painted black. "We had to drive some heads home and we thought we had time to clean the house or make up a story about how it was robbed, but out of nowhere we saw Mom in her Honda on D Street. We *boned out,* like we drove fifty miles an hour down the alley to beat her home but there was no time to do anything. It was just too *fucked-up,* bro. The worst part is all my friends hate me now because she called their parents.

"Still, it was fuckin' *legendary*." He takes a drag from a long white menthol. "People were tripping acid in the barn, breaking down the walls. There was a punch made from vodka and peach schnapps, the music was loud and everyone was just *dancing*. Nobody gave a fuck. It was the greatest thing."

I don't know this person. The last time I saw Tony he wanted to play football and learn to pitch an overhand curve. Who are these friends he's talking about? What is this hair? I tell him I don't even understand why he wanted to go back there in the first place.

"Oh man, she had no idea what I was doing. I spent the whole summer drinking. I snuck out every night. I cut the screen off the window to use in my one-hitter pipe. I smoked cigarettes in the fucking house, while she was *home*. She came in once and I had just spilled a full ashtray on the floor and she didn't even *notice*. It was like living alone."

It's ironic. After all those meetings about the negative consequences of drug use, all those books and pamphlets, all those AA sayings hanging from the walls, "Let go and let God," "One day at a time," all the campouts and Big Talks and Child Psychology books about "roles children take on in addictive families," and despite it all, the house on Breys Avenue was destroyed by a drug party.

THE TABLE IN the dining room at Grandpa Nat and Grandma Juliette's house is covered in a long white cloth. On top of it are big glass jars with orange labels that read, "Manischewitz." One says, "Borscht." It's filled with a red beet soup. Another jar reads, "Gefilte Fish." Inside it is a gray fish-shaped mass suspended in goo that looks like something from the movie *Alien*. There's lox, smoked white fish, pickled herring in white cream sauce, stacks of huge crackers called matzo and bottles of Manischewitz Cherry and Grape Concord wine, all set out for the Passover Seder.

Bonnie told us that the Passover Seder is a Jewish feast in which Jews tell the story of their escape from slavery, read Hebrew and drink wine, even though she doesn't drink or believe in God. She is adamant that it is not a religious ceremony because religion is the cause of more death in the world than anything. She says we're just doing the Passover Seder for "tradition" so we can be exposed to different ideas.

"Those people had it rough with all that walking around in that heat with no air-conditioning." Grandma Juliette sits next to me, her running commentary about the dinner filling my ear while she laughs. "Where do you pish in the desert? There are no trees."

Across from me is an empty place setting. "That's for Elijah," Grandma says. "In case he decides to show up."

"Who's Elijah?"

"Don't you worry about him. He's always late."

Because I am the youngest, it's my job in the ceremony to read the four questions in Hebrew. The sheet of paper is handed down to me. The words are spelled out phonetically on the page, so I lift my grape juice and read aloud. Everyone stops when I read the questions, which Grandpa answers from his sheet. It's a strange feeling, to feel so much like I belong, to be young means that I have something to add. In Oregon we're always told how much we have to learn, that Mom understands the world, our lives, our own feelings better than we do. There is no place for an opinion and our youth is just getting in the way. But here at this big table with my aunts Jeannie and Nancy looking at me and smiling, with Grandma

Juliette in my ear and Grandfather Nat waiting for me to read the strange ancient words, I feel something else. Like I have something to add. I can see the joy in their faces when we show up at a dinner or a birthday party: "Look at the little ones! Come here!" as if there is nothing better in the world than to be a grandson.

Matzos are broken, candles lit, hands dipped, wine drunk, bitter herbs eaten, the big plates of smoked fish and pickled herring passed around. Grandma keeps spilling wine on the table because of her essential tremor. She yells, "Save some for Elijah! He's hungry!" Then, under her breath, as an aside to me, "Can you believe these *schmendricks*?"

"What's a *schmendrick*?"

"An idiot."

She tosses Yiddish out in the middle of sentences like a spice as she gives a running play-by-play of the story of Passover. "Those poor people, schlepping all across the desert covered in schmutz . . . That *fakaktah* pharaoh, he finally learned his lesson . . . Listen to him reading. I'm *shpilkes*. Here in front of the whole *mishpucha*. I'm so proud."

"Why do all the words in Yiddish sound like the thing they are?"

She looks at me. "What else are words supposed to sound like?"

I remember the time when a group of us were buying candy at the liquor store and I had only fifty cents. Everyone else had a dollar to contribute and Chris Faraday looked at me and said, "Dude, don't be *Jewish*."

I was confused. "What do you mean?"

"Don't be *cheap*, homey," he said. "Jews are fucking *cheap*. Don't you know that?"

I thought of my little grandma Juliette smiling and saying, "Mikel, dahhling, how's my boy?" My grandpa Nat who likes to talk to me about his magazines *The Nation* and *The Progressive*. He'll clip out an article and hand it to me to read like he just wants so much for me. They always pay for dinner when we go for Chinese and seem to want nothing more than more family, more love, to enjoy each other while we can. I don't know if it's because of Hitler or Chuck Dederich or my aunt Joey, who I never knew, because she died when she was only nineteen. But even if they didn't give me a hundred dollars every year on my birthday, I would say they were the most generous people I've ever met.

"No they're not." I couldn't sock him one because he was twice my size.

"Just give me another fucking dollar." I should've known the freckles would be trouble.

"Jews aren't cheap. Just so you know."

I didn't understand the anger, the way the words were spat out like rotten food.

I remember standing on the blacktop at lunch on my first day looking around and realizing I was the only white boy in sight. But I didn't feel out of place. At least not any more than I did with the white kids with their surf T-shirts and new shoes who made fun of my old jeans and bubble gum sneakers until Bonnie took me to Mervyn's to buy some new clothes so they wouldn't tease me.

I knew it was racism, all these things Chris Faraday talked about. And I knew that racists were on one team and we were on the other. Dad said he never joined a gang in prison. That because he was so dark with his Italian skin people thought he was mixed or Middle Eastern and so he just never fell in with the white gangs. He even had an unsteady truce with the black Muslims since helping a man from the Nation of Islam who was pinned under a bench press working out in the prison weight room one day. "Everyone just left me alone. They didn't know what I was." He takes pride in this, this ambiguity. He doesn't trust rich white men either. And even though Tony and I are towheaded Dutch-looking white boys, we know he's talking about the men with the ties and suits, the ones with sedans and jobs in offices and power in the government, the ones who put him in prison.

Tony and I sneak off into the kitchen, where half-empty glasses of wine sit on the countertop. I grab one and take a sip. It tastes like grape Kool-Aid and gasoline. My chest goes warm and Tony lifts a half-full glass and gulps it down. He dares me to try the cherry wine straight from the un-corked bottle on the kitchen table. I take a big swig, laughing as I feel it flow down through my stomach over my legs, which go rubbery. There's a sudden sweet amnesia, a shortening of time like a warm bath where I can just float and forget. *So this is why they do it.* What a relief, to not only feel good but feel *nothing*. It's like the moment thirty seconds after you stub your toe when you suddenly feel better. That is what the cherry wine feels like: the moment when the pain disappears. I wonder if this is what Paul felt in his truck with his bottle, if this is why he couldn't stop and just drank until he died. Is this why Dad had his needle in his cell? Why Tony was passed out on the floor among the trash from the party?

Is this what it means to become a man? A Jollett man? Tony and I slap each other on the back and sneak into the backyard to hide with the bottle of cherry wine. We crouch on the side of the house, passing it back and forth like bums around a fire. "Go easy, little bro. It tastes like candy but it'll make you sick." I feel the pulsing in my head, my vision blurry as I walk back and forth along the concrete path on the side of the house, testing my balance, a warmth in my chest radiating outward.

"Is this what it's always like?" Tony smiles at me and I'm just so happy to be in the club, after all the years on the girls' team with Bonnie and Mom, to finally be among the men.

"It's just a little wine. You never drank before?"

I'm not even embarrassed. I'm only eleven years old. "No." I stare at my hands as they become unsteady blurs in front of me.

We walk back into the room of candles, food, people laughing. I am light-headed, warm, groggy, stealing glances at my brother who smirks back at me because we have a secret and nobody knows we stole the wine. There's nothing like getting away with it.

THE DARK ALLEY behind the church at the top of the block is the perfect place to smoke weed. All the lights are off and the parking lot is empty and it is just Tony and me and his red glass weed pipe as he packs it with small green nuggets and hands it to me with a lighter. "Happy birthday, little bro." I hold it to my lips and light the bowl as I've seen him do so many times. I've started inhaling my Benson & Hedges Menthol 100's now so I figure it can't be so different and what better way to spend my twelfth birthday than to just get on with it? To get high.

I cough and hand the pipe back to him. He takes a hit. I feel a weightlessness in my legs, a dizziness, my lungs congested and black as I look at the parking lot, the alley, the brick walls of the church, as if seeing them for the first time. *I never noticed how small these bricks are. Why are trash dumpsters green? I'm glad my brother doesn't hate me anymore.*

Tony socks me one in the shoulder and we walk down the hill giggling. The house is warm and there are plates of spaghetti and garlic bread that

Dad made for my birthday laid out on the table as we eat dinner and Tony and I laugh until we're red in the face.

"You guys are in quite a mood," Bonnie says. She doesn't know. How could she? I am the good son, the one who can be trusted. And instead of being the little snitch, the sniveling shithead, the sellout, the mama's boy, I am my brother's accomplice. Spaghetti never tasted so good.

When my report card comes back with straight Ds, I am grounded. "I don't understand this," Bonnie says. "You've always been good at school." I shrug my shoulders and tell her I'll try harder, that it's just an adjustment to my new environment. What I don't tell her is that we smoke weed in the alley before first period, me and the other kids from the Bowl, that we ditch school sometimes and go to someone's house to drink vodka or whiskey. I don't know these guys very well with their surf T-shirts and karate shoes, but they think it's funny to see me, all of five feet two and twelve years old with a lit cigarette in my teeth and a beer in my hand.

I like the dare of it. *I'll show you just how much I don't give a fuck about your meetings and pamphlets, your entire full-of-shit world.* I think of my uncles, my dad, the men, all the men I never knew all those years wondering where the cowboys were, how they rode their horses, how they left town, always leaving. This is what we do. And maybe we're destined for prison or juvie but at least we aren't alone, crying in the corner with the women.

CHAPTER 26
BIG TALK

Doug treats me like we're old friends. On the way back to Salem from the Portland airport at the start of the summer, he keeps calling me "pal," as in "Hey, pal, how was the flight? Your mom and I got a nice house. You're going to have your own room, pal." It's clear they've had a Big Talk. There's an unsteady truce. I know he's performing for Mom. She hugged me until I had to push her away in the terminal and she insisted I hold her hand all through the airport even though I'm nearly as tall as she is. I was uncomfortable but in the World According to Mom, I am her sweet boy returning to her because we are close and she is my guide for becoming Something Important, so there are just no words for my discomfort. I don't trust Doug but at least he's not trying to hold my hand.

After Tony's party, Mom decided she couldn't live in the Breys Avenue house anymore so she sold it. Doug came back (again) once Tony moved to Los Angeles and they bought a new house in a better neighborhood over by Market Street where the sidewalks aren't crumbling and the driveways are made of actual pavement instead of gravel and dirt.

Doug drives the old VW camper van Mom and Paul bought for our trips up to Detroit Lake. He has trouble with the clutch, yelling at it as he tries to jam the long gear lever from third to fourth in the slow lane of I-5. I sit on the floor. There's a hole in the metal between my legs the size of a dime through which I can see the pavement flying by beneath me at fifty miles an hour.

Mom is in the seat at the card table next to the little camper stove. She asks me about the flight and school and wonders if the public schools in

Los Angeles can compete with the ones in Salem that she scouted out for us when we first left California. She says it's good that I was so advanced or else I might've fallen behind the other kids here. She blurts out, "I'm just so excited you're back for good!" pumping a fist in the air. "I think you'll still go to Parrish Middle School but it might be a different district now. You'll like the new neighborhood. It's cleaner and there are lots of places to ride your bike."

I freeze. I forgot. I don't know how I let this pass. We just never talked about it. She thought I was only staying in Los Angeles for a year. I never told her otherwise. It didn't even cross my mind. I can feel the hot blood on my neck and a dread for what's coming, for the Big Talk I know we are about to have.

"What do you mean, back for good?"

"I mean, you wanted to live with your dad for a year and now that's over so you're gonna come home."

"I'm not coming back here." I hear the words fall from my mouth before I can even think. I have no plan.

She puts her hand over her face and turns toward the window. She stares at the snowy outline of Mount Hood in the distance and says slowly, "What do you mean? You're not coming home?"

"Los Angeles is my home."

"You're leaving me?" She puts a hand over her eyes and starts to cry. Soon she is sobbing, her long brown hair covering her face and shoulders. She climbs off the bench and settles on the floor of the VW van, pulling her knees up to her shoulders with her head in her hands. "We had a deal. You were going to go there for a year, then come back to me."

I can feel a tug, a pull like a weight dragging me underwater.

"I'm sorry, Mom."

"You're really gonna leave me? You're my son," she says into her knees, under her hair, her forehead resting on her elbow. She practically screams, "How can you leave me? How? You're supposed to stay here. You're supposed to be with me."

Doug is silent as he struggles with the gears. *Downshifting from fourth to third. Gotta go easy with that old gearbox, tough guy.*

Mom's whole body shakes in convulsions. It's hard to watch. I put a hand up like I'm trying to shield my face from it, the naked intensity of it all. I say, "It's okay, Mom. It's going to be okay."

She just keeps repeating, "You're gonna leave me? How can you leave me? You're my son. You're mine. *Mine.*" There's the familiar blankness, the numbness that washes over me like novocaine in my chest so that I feel nothing but an emptiness and I'm able to say whatever needs to be said. It's nothing like being high, that warm, forgetful numbness. I feel cold like there's a scream being stifled behind glass and I'm on the other side pretending I can't hear it.

"We can still have quality time. We'll just make it count more."

"How can you leave me? How?"

I turn away, listening to the VW engine as it struggles down the highway through the impenetrable wall of pine trees.

THE NEW HOUSE on Windsor Avenue is on a quiet cul-de-sac near Market Street where everything is cleaner. It's a low green structure, more modern than the old A-frame on Breys Avenue, sitting behind a perfectly cut lawn. There's a tree in the front covered in yellow flowers, a real garage, and a big backyard surrounded by a wooden fence. All the lawns on the street have been mowed. All the houses have real paint or clean red brick and aluminum siding instead of decaying porches and mold and black streaks from old fires. There's brand-new furniture inside this new house, a new blue sectional couch, bookcases, and a polished oak dining table with matching chairs. It looks like a set, like a stage for actors.

I call Jake the minute we get to the house and he shows up ten minutes later. He's taller than I remember, six feet six now with long blond hair shaved up on the sides and bangs that fall past his chin. My giant has gotten some style. He's wearing a green sweatshirt, Bermuda shorts, and leather Florsheim penny loafers with no socks. He's tan. I don't know how he pulled that off in Salem, Oregon. It's a relief to see him.

He's obsessed with the Smiths. When we get to his new house out by the fairgrounds behind the AME Zion Church where the streets have no sidewalks and the weeds prey upon collapsing fences, stray cats linger in alleyways and large dogs lurch at you from behind broken-down porches, he puts *The Queen Is Dead* by the Smiths on his stereo in the drafty garage he was given as a bedroom. I don't understand what it's about except it seems like the singer wants to kill the queen of England. Or at the very least, see her in her underwear. It's not clear which. Jake assures me the guy is cool. He's thin with a massive square jaw and an enormous pompadour atop his head. His name is Morrissey and he gets all the girls.

Jake's stepdad, Craig, is out of prison. He was arrested and went to San Quentin, which is even meaner than Chino prison where Dad went. Jake says Craig told him he once shared the yard with Richard Ramirez, the Night Stalker who terrorized Southern California all last year, keeping me awake at night while Dad guarded the house with a baseball bat.

Craig is stocky with thick shoulders, short black hair and a black goatee. He wears tight white tank tops and brown pants like a cholo. He moves like a gorilla, his head down, leading with his forehead, arms slung low in front of him. He'll pound on the door to Jake's room in the garage and stick his head in, a lit cigarette in his teeth. "Jake, get the fuck up and clean this kitchen." Jake doesn't argue. He's a scary man. Jake looks small next to him even though he's nearly a foot taller.

We feel safer at night, after his parents go to bed, sitting in the garage playing cards and listening to music. So much music is about winning. Who's the baddest or the meanest or the best? How deep is your love? How tough is your crew? How much do you party?

No one writes songs about losers like us. No one but Morrissey. It's a relief to feel seen, to sit on the floor of the garage eating bologna sandwiches while he sings:

> I know I'm unlovable, you don't have to tell me,
> I don't have much in my life, but take it, it's yours,

The music is a bubble, a protective shield that surrounds us everywhere we go all summer, to the mall, the train tracks behind the high school, sneaking out at night to smoke cigarettes and hide from the cops, stealing beers from the fridge, hoping like hell Craig doesn't figure it out and burst into the room knocking Jake one in the mouth.

We are inseparable. We barely spend ten minutes apart the entire summer. We don't want to be understood. We don't want to play our part. We don't want to find "the peace of the forest," we're not interested in "family time by the fire." We just want to be left alone with our music. Exactly misunderstood. Precisely unlovable.

CHAPTER 27

MOTORCYCLES
WILL KILL YOU

The motorcycle parked in the center of the garage on Christmas morning is a red Honda XR80 dirt bike with a blue seat, black engine, black pegs, red springs, shiny chrome forks and a yellow front plate. I can't believe it. Since seeing a dirt bike at the L.A. County Fair, where we went to sell sunroofs for Dad's business, seeing those beautiful machines in mid-flight on some dusty desert path, I've been begging for one. But I didn't think it would actually happen.

Everyone in Synanon rode motorcycles. Mostly they rode small Japanese bikes. Dad was the rebel with his Harley, his old stories about racing cops from the border to San Diego, riding through the desert, watching the world go by at 120 miles an hour drunk and stoned with his brother Pete. It feels like the bike is an initiation. I am a gambler, a risk taker, my father's son.

Tony gets a yellow Yamaha YZ125 two-stroke that spits black smoke into the street when we start it up. We can't believe our luck. Bonnie is certain we are going to die.

We pack the bikes into the orange delivery van and drive to the makeshift dirt motorcycle course off a construction site on Sepulveda Boulevard called Hamburger Hill, named for the enormous steep dirt incline that rises five stories above the course to the Bluffs, the empty lots where older kids from the Bowl go to drink at night. There are moguls and a banked turn and even a jump where a kid can catch air and fly, kicking his feet out, hoping to land without breaking his neck.

Dad gives us a talk about braking and balance, awareness and acceleration, how to turn, and how to *keep the damn thing from killing you.*

When I finally start the engine and ease out the clutch, when I'm suited up in my boots and helmet and goggles in the hot, sweaty, noisy space of my head, there is a thrill in my chest like a liquid heat that spreads out over my shoulders and knees to my elbows and toes as I shift the gears and lean into the turn, pulling open the throttle on the straightaway.

Dad stands patiently on the far side of the dirt lot in his blue sweatshirt and jeans, a toothpick in his mouth, barking instructions as we go by, "Okay, good, now this time try getting up on the pegs when you go over those bumps. Keep your knees bent and hold the gas steady. Let the bike come up to meet you until it feels like you're gliding." I drop my Honda a few times on the turns, unused to the weight and power as I lean too far. "That's okay. Just pick it up before you start leaking gasoline all over the damn place." I dust off my pant leg and jump back on. "Good, now kick it in the ass and see what kind of power you're dealing with."

When we're done, he takes us to a pizza joint near the beach. We order Italian subs that we eat at a table in the sun. "There's nothing like it," he says. "The wind and the ground, the engine beneath you." I nod and chew my food, thinking there is no feeling in the world, no moment I would ever trade for this one, eating in the sun with my father, dusty, dirty, my hands stained, reeking of oil and gas and smoke from the exhaust.

TONY FIGHTS WITH Dad at night. He sneaks out of his room and doesn't care if he gets caught. He comes home in the middle of the night drunk or high or both, sneaking in through the bathroom window. He screams at Dad, "You can't tell me what to do!"

Dad says, "Oh yes I can! This is my house, mothafucker!" Tony leaves and Dad tells Bonnie he's calling the cops because he doesn't know what else to do. He picks up the phone, calls the police station and screams, "My son is out of control!" then hangs up before saying his name or address.

Dad says he's just trying to keep him alive, just trying to get him to his next birthday before he kills himself. He says this like he's been there before. He kicked heroin himself. He dealt with endless Dope Fiends in

Synanon. "There's no easy fix here," he says. "Maybe he will die. I don't know. It's his choice."

He says this like he doesn't care, with a shrug of his shoulders, snarling his lips into a scowl, but afterward, as the words settle over the room, as they fill up a corner and grow monstrous in size, his face changes and he only looks scared. Tony will apologize and Dad will forgive him immediately. Bonnie wants to ground him but Dad says he doesn't want to be "too hard on him. That he needs to stay connected."

Bonnie calls him an enabler and Dad says, "What do you want me to do? Let him die?" She shakes her head and goes into the bedroom, and when he walks out in the morning to go to the track, she tells me that he just sees too much of himself in Tony.

One night there's a call at the house saying Tony's been arrested for possession of marijuana. He's in jail somewhere in the valley. "What did you say?" Bonnie asks Dad when he hangs up the phone.

"I said, 'Good.'"

"So we're not going to pick him up?"

"No. Let him figure out his own way home. He needs some tough love." At the Al-Anon meetings in Salem everyone said alcoholics need "tough love," which means you don't just "enable their addiction by bailing them out of all their bullshit." Dad is an expert on this. Until he isn't.

Tony arrives at the house five hours later. He walks in the door and screams, "You were just going to let me stay there?" Bonnie won't even look at him. She says she's glad he made it home and it was his father's decision and if he'd like to talk about it that's fine but she will not be yelled at.

Dad walks into the room and screams, "You need to change your tone, my friend!"

Tony gets up in his face and says, "Or else what? I had to beg people for money and take four buses to get here, so don't you fucking tell me sh——"

Dad yells, "You need a fucking attitude adjustment! You hear me?! A fucking attitude adjustment! You think you can just do anything you want! You're gonna fucking kill yourself!" Dad walks up to him.

Tony screams at the top of his lungs, "What, are you gonna fuckin' hit me?! You can't do anything to me, you burnout piece of shit! I don't need to be here if you don't want me here!"

Dad is standing right in front of him, face-to-face. His face looks sad, scared. Tony is breathing hard, tears falling down his cheeks. Just as I think maybe Dad is going to let loose or sock him one in the jaw, he puts his arms around Tony and hugs him. I see Tony resist for a second, his black karate shoes shuffling on the carpet. But then he gives in and lays his head on Dad's shoulder and starts sobbing.

Bonnie raises an eyebrow and looks at me. Soon they're talking in the bedroom, all three of them. I can hear Tony pleading something over and over again. "But they're my friends. They're my friends . . ." Eventually, he walks out of the room and straight out the front door.

He doesn't call or come back home that night.

The next night I leave the Bowl with some of the older kids and walk to the Bluffs. I've been hanging out with Tony's friends after school since the day Ryan Church's mom saw me smoking on a corner with my skateboard. Word got around to the other PTA moms and now none of the kids from my classes are allowed to hang out with me after school because I'm officially a bad "influence." So even though I hang out with Ryan and Drew at school every day, after school I'm always with Tony's friends.

I'm wearing my green basketball jersey because I have a game in the morning at the park league I joined with some of the kids from my classes. When we get to the top of the hill, we see a group of boys standing in a circle holding drinks in brown paper bags. I see Tony in the circle with them.

"Heeeeey, little bro," he says and punches me in the shoulder. "You want a sip?" He hands me his forty of Olde English. I take a drink. It tastes like kerosene mixed with beer. After a few minutes, I feel lighter, that warm embrace, that relief, like maybe all this fighting is just a joke and Tony doesn't need a home and neither do I. We are pirates at sea and besides we're on the same team, so I'm just glad I'm not the one he's mad at.

"Are they pissed?"

"I think so. Where have you been?"

"Just crashing with Duck and Flesh on their floor." Duck and Flesh are Donald and David Fleishman, two brothers who live in an apartment down by the gas company in Playa del Rey. Duck is thin with the face of a forty-year-old man, even though he's Tony's age. Flesh is his younger brother who is only a year older than I am. At fourteen, he's the only one close to my age. Because their mother is gone so much, their place is the go-to crash pad for Tony and his friends. They both have motorcycles, so some days they ride with us, with their full body gear, their matching shoulder pads and shin guards and kidney belts.

"Oh, cool."

"I never thought Dad would get in my face like that." Tony stares at the ground, kicking the dirt with his karate shoes. "Like maybe Paul or Doug or something but not Dad." He lights a Marlboro Menthol and takes a drag. I can't keep up with his brands anymore.

"Yeah, he was really pissed. I think he's worried about you, though. He keeps saying how he's just trying to keep you alive." Tony nods his head and spits with his eyes closed as if to say, *Well, yeah.*

To be a drunk is to be a hero in a sad story.

Someone gives me a can of beer. We drink a few and a neighborhood security car arrives. The lights go off and a young man with a goatee in a thick brown jacket gets out, opening a door that says "Security Patrol." They all yell, "Rent a cop!" as he walks down to the circle and bumps fists. Someone hands him a pipe packed with weed. The security patrolman takes a hit. Everyone laughs.

After a few beers, someone suggests maybe it's time for a little destruction. They throw their arms around each other's shoulders and form a circle around the pile of empty beer cans. Someone grabs me, pulling me into the circle as we sing:

> *This is a world destruction. Your life ain't nothing!*
> *The human race is becoming a disgrace!*

We hop into Duck's VW beast and head to the apartment by the gas company where we finish a case of beer then run out into the alley. "We're just gonna do a little minor damage," Duck says to me as we run out the door. I don't know what to expect. I've seen them write graffiti on walls with big industrial pens or cans of spray paint. But this is different. It's wild bodies fanning out into the street like those old zombie movies, mindless and aimless.

I see Duck knock over a mailbox with his skinny arms and kick some potted plants on a white corner house, getting potted soil on the beige bottom of his black karate shoes. Flesh pulls a stream of Christmas lights off a roof as we watch the red and green glass bulbs explode in the street. When they hear the noise, the popping from the lights, they scatter, laughing and running in all directions like a game. I catch up at the next block and see Tony stomping sprinkler heads so I grab a trash can and dump it out, watching the contents spill onto the pristine sidewalk, covering it with leftover bottles and boxes of cereal, envelopes, catalogs, rotting fruit, coffee grinds.

I don't know why we're doing it, only that it's exciting to be here, outside the polite rules of this polite neighborhood as if the order itself demands chaos, and tonight we are its messenger. It's a black eye to the beautiful face of this upright neighborhood near the airport.

Fuck you and your cars and houses and 2.2 kids. Fuck you and your job at Hughes Aircraft building bombs for the government. Fuck your tie. Fuck your condescending smile. Fuck your garden trolls, your birdhouses, your wind chimes, your seasonal decorations hung on the veranda of your perfectly landscaped front yard. We are proof of your mistakes.

I climb a concrete wall and sit on top to toss a brick into a backyard pool. Duck tips over a black crotch rocket. We scatter when it hits the pavement and the gasoline begins to spill onto the driveway. Flesh and I split off from the group, down an alley at the bottom of a hill next to the Bowl. He picks up a two-by-four leaning against a garbage can and knocks a rearview mirror off a blue Chrysler sedan. I spit on its rear window. He says, "That's some pussy shit," so I fish a beer bottle out of a trash can and hold it like a football, aiming it at a corner house with a large picture window. He looks at me, "Don't act like you would."

I throw the bottle as hard as I can and hear it break through the living room window with a crash. A dog barks and lights go on in the house and without a word Flesh and I turn and run up the block at a full sprint. There's a mist that hangs around the streetlights, a light fog from the ocean two miles away, so that each one glows for five or ten feet creating hazy orbs that float above our heads like alien spacecraft. Every few seconds I look back thinking, *We are getting away with it. How are we getting away with it?*

We run all the way back to the apartment, where the crew is sitting on couches, drinking and eating chips. I start with a beer, then another, then another. We are laughing, everyone bragging about the destruction they wrought. Someone has weed and someone else has some pills. I know they've been taking LSD and PCP because Tony once told me he discovered the secret to the universe while "tripping balls" at the top of the Hollywood Bowl. It was the middle of the night and they were all looking at the stars on acid when he realized it. "What was it?" I asked him.

He cocked his head sideways, thought for a second, and said, "I forgot."

I swallow something small and oval and white and when the little wooden pipe is passed around, I take a couple hits and lean back. Soon the world is pushed to the end of a long, dark tunnel. I hear voices like echoes off the walls and suddenly feel very sober in the middle of my head. I watch the room as if on a TV set a hundred feet away from me in my tunnel. The chip in Duck's front tooth when he laughs. The way he raises his eyebrows at attention when people speak. Flesh sitting across from me in the overstuffed chair in his green flannel shirt, a beer in his lap, trying to get along with the older kids, saying, "Yeah, man," "Holy shit," "Fuckin' cops, right?"

Someone says, "Your little brother is fuuuucked-up," and Tony lays me on my side because the world is spinning now.

"You look pretty wasted, brother."

"I think he's gonna puke. Dude, do *not* let your little brother OD on my couch." I feel hands on my shoulders pushing me down on my side. A warm sticky liquid comes out of my mouth. It drips down my neck, over my hands, under my jersey, onto my chest. Someone yells, "Fuck that's nasty! Get a towel."

I look down, trying to hold my head in place, to focus my eyes. The puke is a chunky yellow and green. It smells of stale beer, Cool Ranch Doritos and something like vinegar mixed with sourdough bread. I close my eyes. Just for a second. Just to stop the room from spinning. I'm standing in the tunnel in the darkness by myself and I feel an urge to scream but I can't make my voice work. Is this what happened to Dad when he OD'd? *Is this what it felt like to be Billy at the end? Is he here somewhere? Is someone gonna pick me up and take me somewhere?*

I wish the ground would stop moving and I don't care about the guys or how I look because there's a feeling like a light being extinguished, like

I'm reaching for it but it's getting dimmer and dimmer until there is only darkness and the room is still and I put my arms around myself and rock back and forth. I see Paul and I see Dad and I wonder if it's my turn now. I feel so sick, sleepy as I stand three inches tall in my head. *How could I forget? I'm so stupid. I'm so fucking stupid.*

When I wake up, the living room is empty. My head is heavy. My stomach queasy. The sunlight penetrates the vertical blinds that have been left open. It's silent except for the sound of bodies breathing on the floor and a noise like a dial tone that seems to get louder with each throb of my skull. My basketball jersey is wet with beer and covered in yellow puke. I go into the kitchen as quietly as possible and take it off to wash it, squeezing the water out, hitting it against the side of the sink to get all the bits of Dorito and vomit. When I put it on again, it's still clammy and smells of beer. It smells that way as I walk slowly in a haze to the gym at Westchester Park, where I see Ryan Church and my other teammates from school, the ones from the honors classes I'm failing, the ones who are not allowed to invite me to their birthday parties because everyone knows I am a burnout, a bad kid. They're running in their clean jerseys, practically leaping as they jog laps to warm up for the game.

It's strange to feel so lonely. The point was to not feel lonely, to be among the men. But I am queasy and tired with a headache, trapped in my mind, sad and apart from my smiling teammates with their clean uniforms, their morning-bright eyes, their futures.

CHAPTER 28
IS THERE
LIFE ON MARS?

Mom calls and says she has big news. She's nearly out of breath. "Are you ready? You ready?" Nothing good ever comes from these moods. "Hold on. I'll let Doug tell you."

"Hey, pal."

"Oh, hey."

"Well . . . um . . . so I've decided your mom is a real classy lady and I asked her to marry me."

"Oh."

I hear Mom hoot in the background then rush up to the phone and say, "Isn't that great?"

"Wow."

She grabs the phone. "We're just going to do it at the courthouse since we've both been married before. I'm so excited to have someone to grow old with! We're going to be a family. All of us. You and Doug and me and Tony and Doug's kids. They're going to be your brother and sister! Isn't that great?"

"What are their names again?"

"Matthew and Catherine."

Instant family. Just add water.

"Oh yeah. Well, that's, um, that's, that's, that's great, Mom."

The engagement doesn't feel real because Doug has already left her four times. Four different times he packed up his belongings and disappeared without a word. Four different times she took him back when he showed up again like a lost alley cat. Each time she explained why *this* time was different, why Doug was truly sorry and a changed man. After a while it seemed like a sketch traced on paper over and over again in which the outlines of the traced object become blurrier and blurrier until the final image is so disfigured, you don't even know what it is anymore.

I say, "I'm very happy for you."

Tony doesn't think they'll make it to the wedding day. "He's got to stick around for like three months straight which would be some kind of record."

In the pictures Mom sends us from the ceremony, she wears flowers in her hair and a simple dress. Doug doesn't even bother to wear a suit to the courthouse, just his same gray tweed jacket with the blue elbow patches. He has a blank expression, staring forward while she smiles, wide-eyed and hopeful, holding her bouquet.

JAKE IS OBSESSED with David Bowie. When I get to Oregon for the summer, Bowie is all he'll talk about. He shows me pictures in a magazine from the Glass Spider Tour, which, according to Jake, is the largest rock-and-roll production ever attempted. There's Bowie with his sprayed mullet blond hair standing on a platform in a glittering gold suit, electric-blue angel wings lit up behind him as he sings. He seems like the coolest man on earth, his voice crackling through the speakers in Jake's musty garage, where we sleep while the warm rain soaks the broken-down Salem streets.

And if you say run, I'll run with you.

There's a huge electric spider covering the stage onto which Bowie is lowered in a golden chair. Jake knows Bowie's story by heart, the hippie art student who became an androgynous bisexual space alien named Ziggy Stardust who eventually morphed into the full-grown adult man who travels the world in the belly of a spider the size of a building.

The tour is coming to Portland, Oregon, at the end of the summer. It doesn't occur to us that we could go, that we could save bottles or mow lawns and maybe get a ride from someone. It's more like we're honored he would grace the Pacific Northwest with his presence. We didn't know he knew we existed.

All summer we try to imagine what Bowie might think of us. He is the standard by which everything is measured. Jake gets a pair of thick sunglasses with red shades like the ones Bowie wears in a poster he sees at Rising Sun Records downtown, where we go to browse the vinyl. We both hitch our pants a little higher. We buy hair gel, slicking our blond locks back, wishing we had the money to buy everything in the store.

"I don't think Bowie would play cribbage. He's more of a gin rummy man."

"How could you know? He probably plays some kind of card game he invented."

"Okay, so who's cooler, James Bond or David Bowie?"

"Bowie, for sure."

"Bond has a gun and makes out with models."

"Bowie could get any model he wants."

Jake has completed his transformation into stylish mod giant, wearing clothes strictly from the mall, cardigans and collared shirts and the expensive shoes he buys with money from his paper route. We make a striking pair. Me, short, knobby kneed, a mouth full of the braces Dad and Bonnie paid for so I wouldn't be so weird looking anymore and a general style that can best be described as a walking disaster of halfhearted gestures: a vintage collared shirt with a stain worn with beach shorts and a pair of old man shoes, puffing on a cigarette I'm clearly too young to smoke. And Jake, like some kind of British Paul Bunyan, six feet six in a trench coat and red glasses, hair slicked back in high-water pants inquiring about the new Smiths compilation and an import copy of *Never Mind the Bollocks* by the Sex Pistols.

Mom and Doug wear their silver wedding rings proudly, holding hands in public like the couples walking down the hall at my school. She seems happy and I'm glad for her even if I don't trust Doug with his weird food and weird habits and weird way of talking with all the pauses in it. He's nicer to me than he used to be. I know Mom told him if he ever beat me up again, she'd leave him but I don't think that's it. It's more like he's softened, humbled somehow.

At the end of the summer, Mom takes me to the airport in Portland in the red Honda Accord she packed for the weekend because she has a conference for her job at the state mental hospital. She has promised to buy me some new school clothes before I go and instead of taking me to Goodwill, she takes me to J. C. Penney, where she tells me to choose a hundred dollars' worth of clothes. I try on some shirts and two pairs of pants and decide to blow the whole thing on a pair of expensive dress shoes like Jake, which Mom thinks is wasteful, but when we go to pay she realizes she's forgotten her wallet so we head back to the house on Windsor Avenue.

When we pull in the driveway, the blinds are drawn. We walk in the house to find all the lights off. It's dark like a crypt in the middle of the day. "Hello?!" she calls out. The door to the bedroom opens and out walks Doug in his boxer shorts and a brown T-shirt.

He walks up to Mom quickly and gives her a kiss. Taking her by the shoulders and pushing his face into hers. "Hi, sweetheart," he says. She pulls her head away and looks at him, studying his face, her mouth sideways, her eyes squinting.

"What have you been doing?"

"Just hanging out." He looks at her, searching her face. I know I'm not wanted. I know I'm seeing something not meant for my eyes. I know this has something to do with the "other addictions" people go to the program for, the one Doug has that they talk about sometimes when he says he's going to meetings at a place called SA. It's too much to take in at once because Doug is an adult and we're not really sure what sex even is and because of the pamphlets they leave around the house, practically the first thing we ever learn about sex is that there are sex addicts.

But he looks so much like a little kid now. And Mom looks so much older, giving him the look she used to give Tony and me when she busted us hiding candy.

"Did you decide not to go?" he asks.

"No, I just forgot my wallet. I think I left it in the bedroom."

"I'll get it," Doug says, turning quickly and nearly jumping down the hall. She pauses for a second then follows him. I go outside and lean against the Honda in the driveway, putting on headphones to listen to *Louder Than Bombs* one more time.

He was a sweet and tender hooligan, hooligan, and he swore that he'll never, never do it again.

She's silent for the drive up I-5 to the airport. She drives fast because we're late and she doesn't want me to miss my flight. She puts her hand to her temple, resting her forehead between her thumb and finger as she watches the road.

I wonder what was in the bedroom. I don't have any words for it. It has a shape and color I can't fathom.

When Paul would disappear to drink in his truck in the woods, she would cry and cry and we knew why she was sad. It was obvious. He was gone and sick and we needed him to chop wood and warm the house and tend to the rabbits and calm Mom down. But this is different. It's insidious, hidden as if behind a screen, unnameable and therefore difficult to understand, less like a train wreck and more like a vague sickness that saps your strength. She doesn't cry or explain. She doesn't say, "Let go and let God," or "One day at a time," or "It's you and me against the world, kid." She just stares at the trees and highway signs.

I feel a disorientation, a force pulling me in different directions. I wonder if Doug is the source of this feeling or if Mom is or if I am. Why was the house dark? What was it I saw? What is this black sick feeling I have now? *There are different kinds of addictions.*

I know she wants me to pretend that I didn't see what I saw, to simply exclude it from the world that we acknowledge exists, the one where she has finally found an "honest man" who's going to "take care of her" instead of another addict. Holding the two ideas in my head—the thing that happened and the fact that we are not to acknowledge it—has the strange effect of making me feel numb. This makes it easier to pretend. Anyway, I am the one who left for California, the one who hurt her by leaving, and the least I can do is bury my questions and suspicions of him, the gut feeling that he leads a double life. I owe her that. That's what it means to be a good son.

She tells me about the time-share property they're buying into and the great "family trips" we are going to have, all of us, Tony and me and Catherine and Matthew and Doug and her, one big family. I know she believes it, this perfectly adequate dream of a family. I know it's my job to pretend to believe it too.

The flight can't come soon enough and I feel a rush of relief when the jet engines shake the plane and I am pinned to the back of my window seat watching Oregon fall away beneath me, the Portland skyline, the mountains, the bridges, the endless silent pines. All those places to hide.

CHAPTER 29

THE PLACE WE MEET A THOUSAND FEET BENEATH THE RACETRACK

Everyone says Tony is going to die. Flesh tells me he saw him tripping acid at a party. While everyone was drinking and dancing in the living room, Tony was in the bedroom screaming because he thought there were bears on the wall that were going to kill him. Eventually, he just climbed out the window and left. I know he's been doing coke because Duck let it slip at the Bowl one night that he couldn't even hang out with him anymore. When I asked why, he covered one nostril and took a snort. Everyone's got something to say about him, like he's an action hero, a young Marlon Brando in tapered Dickies and karate shoes. "Your brother's got a death wish, man. But that dude can take more drugs than any three people I know."

They say it like they are impressed, like he's a legend, like they respect him for it.

He puts a finger to his lips one afternoon as he walks out the door with the keys to the black Lincoln Continental Dad borrowed from Uncle Wes. "Don't say shit. I'll be back." He gives me a sneaky smile. I look out the window and watch him drive off. He's only sixteen with no license. He's still gone when Bonnie gets home. She asks me where the Lincoln is. I tell her I don't know but she figures it out soon enough. When Dad gets home, there's a noise on the front porch so Dad goes outside. The keys are sitting on the doormat. There's no sign of Tony but the Lincoln is parked down the street with the doors open.

We don't see him for a couple days because he knows he's in trouble and when he finally comes home, Dad yells at him to "get his shit together." It's a familiar fight. Dad is angry with him but also defends him. Bonnie is furious that he would take advantage of this sympathy Dad shows him. We all know he defends him like a wound, the way a boxer guards a broken rib.

"I just want him to see his next birthday."

Bonnie has a long discussion in the living room with Tony about "his future." He's got that wild look as he sits on the couch, breathing hard, rocking back and forth, staring at something on the far side of the room. His hair is dyed black now, his tight surf T-shirts cling to his thin, muscled frame and broad shoulders, his jaw jutting out.

Bonnie lectures him for taking the Lincoln and tells him he's grounded. He's twitching, his head bouncing, his eyes going to all corners of the room. He jumps up and says, "Why do you care what I do?" She says she loves him and wants him to be safe and it's clear he has a problem.

He says, "I just want to be with my friends. Can't you understand that? I finally have people who *care* about me and you're trying to take them away."

Dad says, "Aren't you tired of this shit?"

"Tired of what? I just want to be happy. Nobody wants me to be happy."

Bonnie shows him the note from the guidance counselor at Westchester High that says Tony hasn't been to school in three months. "You should see this. They sent it to us. Are you really skipping school every day? Where do you go?"

He stares at the purple slip with his name typed in the corner. "Nowhere. I just need space to think. Can't anyone around here understand that?" He's on the brink of tears. "My friends care about me. It's not like how it is around here."

Bonnie studies him, tilting her head, and says, "I'm just trying to talk to you."

Tony has the crazy look and he stands up and screams, "No you're not! You're trying to control me!"

He stands over her, all six feet two of his skinny, teenage Dope Fiend frame attached to a handsome face and bloodshot eyes. Dad tells him to calm down but he just keeps shaking. "You don't understand! Nobody understands!" He tries to walk out the front door but Dad blocks him.

Bonnie calls the police because she thinks there's going to be a fight.

I hear her say, "I don't know what to do. I think my son is on drugs. Can you send somebody?"

Dad stands in the doorway and yells, "You have to go to school! What the fuck do you think life is?! What, are you going to hang out with your friends for a living?!"

"We're going to have a big house where everyone can live and we'll be fine! We don't need you!" He stomps his feet like the time he broke his leg playing baseball in Oregon. He and Mom got into a fight and he just kept slamming his broken leg into the ground, tearing at the cast, saying, "I hate it here! I hate it here!" like he was holding his own body hostage.

There's a loud knock when the cops come and as soon as Bonnie says, "The police are here," Tony runs out the back door and disappears. The cop enters the house, a mass of walkie-talkie, black gun, black baton, and handcuffs. Bonnie says, "Our son is on drugs. He's getting violent and we don't know what to do. He just ran out the back." The cop says he's not going to go chasing some teenager around the street.

He asks what kinds of drugs Tony's on, whether he has been violent before, whether he's ever been arrested, whether he has any weapons and if he's threatened to use them. He says Tony probably needs to go to drug rehab and there are some good ones around if they're interested and to call if he tries to steal the car again.

When Tony finally comes home two days later, when he's crying and says he's sorry and he looks like he's been dragged through a hundred miles of dirt and gravel with his hair messed up and his tapered Dickies torn at the knee, a stained Quiksilver T-shirt and a scrape on his forehead that he says is "nothing, don't worry about it," and they have a meeting with the guidance counselor at Westchester High who runs the Just Say No program started by the wife of Thatasshole Reagan to keep all us kids off drugs. In the meeting the counselor asked, "Straight up, do you have a drug problem?" Tony said yes.

The next day they pack up a suitcase for him and take him to Santa Monica to live in a drug rehab house called Clare where teen drug addicts live together to help each other get sober which Dad says is the only way to do it "if you're serious" and anyway it's a fortunate turn of events because finally Tony will be "somewhere exactly like Synanon."

* * *

I CAN'T GET the image of Tony's tear-soaked face out of my head. He looked scared. I was scared for him, to see just how out of control he could get, to watch as the beer became weed became coke became acid became three months straight of ditching school became red eyes and nervous fingers twitching and crying on the couch in the living room.

The guys have always brought flasks to the Bowl, to be sipped in the parking lot in the bushes beneath a car ramp. One night Flesh brings a pistol. It feels heavier than I thought it would be when he hands it to me. I try to play it cool, to point in a corner, squinting my left eye to aim. He drops it into the small of his back under his shirt and we walk back inside the Bowl with cigarettes in our teeth like badges that read, "No Future."

The parties are meaner and I feel defenseless without Tony. I found Flesh snorting coke in the back of a Honda outside his house. He offered me some and I declined and he said it was no big deal and to go back inside. Duck had a rusty machete and was watching a possum as it waddled down the gutter. He ran up behind it and chopped the machete down onto the possum's back with an awful crunch. He was bigger so I couldn't yell at him and tell him it's bad enough to kill an animal if you're going to eat it, but to kill it for no reason was just cruel.

"Fucking psycho," I said, under my breath.

Duck looked at me and said, "What?"

"Nothing."

I felt a blackness settle into my stomach and I turned to walk home, thinking of my brother's sad face, how I didn't want to end up like him, how we just slipped into this moment. I wonder about this path we're on. It doesn't feel like anything I've chosen, more like a ditch I've fallen into. But it's different for Tony. He just kept falling, like the ditch was bottomless and there was no way out. Is this how it was with Dad? With Uncle Pete and Uncle Donnie? Is this what's waiting for me?

Flesh and I decide to ditch school to go for a motorcycle ride. I've got my fake signature down pat for the note. I wait until Bonnie leaves for work and Dad is gone on a job and I sneak my bike out from the garage. I meet Flesh at the apartment. Duck is there with some older guys and a freshly packed bong that they pass around. When it gets to me, I decline, thinking about what Dad says about drunk drivers.

"Can't smoke and ride," I say.

"Pussy."

We start our bikes in the alley and we are off, riding through the streets of Westchester illegally, the way Dad told me I never could. I look out for cops, thinking we'll be busted at any moment, trying to play it cool as we hop over curbs and spin out on green lawns, letting out a yell of glee, the cry of rebels and outlaws, the black smoke from the bikes filling the quiet air. Flesh leads the pack on the loose sand trail around the Bluffs as we head toward Hamburger Hill, for the turns and the hills, the track and the jump.

When we get to the track, we ride faster, like a pack of jackals, like ditching school to ride has suspended the laws of physics, like we have no future anyway, no rules, nothing but this moment with our bikes like a challenge against God. I lean into a turn in the dirt and feel my tire slip as I ease off the throttle and manage to stay upright. Over the moguls and around the embankment toward the big jump. I crank and shift. Crouch. I gain speed, with my legs bent, leaning forward to prepare for flight.

As I approach the jump, I suddenly see Flesh's black helmet peak over the crest, his blue flannel flapping in the wind. He's gone the wrong way over it and is heading directly toward me. *He's high, goddamn it.* I swerve to miss him, to miss the jump entirely. There is a low dirt wall to the left and I panic as I reach for the brake. I pull the throttle instead. My feet fall off the pegs and I struggle to hang on at forty miles an hour. There isn't time to think as the low wall approaches. It's twenty feet away, then ten, then five, then all at once I slam into it and I am airborne.

There is a brief dream of flight, of weightlessness and escape. There's no time for a complete thought, just the sense, like in my dreams, that flying is simply a matter of remembering. It's silent in my helmet, nothing but a quiet whisper of wind as the ground approaches.

I land on the back of my head and double over onto the concrete with a thud.

I blink for a moment, staring at the sky. When I close my eyes and try to breathe, no air comes. I try to stand but fall over and stumble facedown, a sharp pain in my side. I can't inhale and I can't walk and I can't see because everything is rotating and blurry. I try to scream inside my helmet but nothing comes but a sickly wheezing sound.

Duck is a ghostlike figure walking toward me in his red shoulder pads and boots. "Damn, motherfucker. You flew thirty feet."

"I. Can't. Breathe." I mouth the words. He tries to lift me by my shoulders but a sharp pain makes me nauseated and I think I'm going to throw up so I undo the straps and pull my helmet off to lie down on the concrete.

I stare up at the sky, trying to take tiny breaths, blinking as faces form in a circle over me, framed by the empty blue against white clouds. Flesh looks scared. Someone says, "Holy shit. Go call an ambulance."

When the paramedics arrive, they cut my shirt off and clap their hands over my face. They ask me my name and what hurts. I let the other boys answer because I can't think. They've got dark blue shirts on and dark blue pants and they roll me on my side, placing a wooden board underneath me. I feel straps over my legs and waist then straps around my head so that I can't look left or right or sit up and I am frozen rigid to the board. They lift me and Flesh's face comes into view. His eyes are wide and he's breathing hard. "Get my bike," I say as they lift me into the back of the ambulance where it's quieter and no one watches me and I can close my eyes while the paramedic stands over me. I hear the engine and feel the bumps of the road, lurching left and right as we head to somewhere I can sleep and figure out what's happened, thinking questions I can't quite finish in my head. *Where did we? Why is it so? How come I can't?*

The paramedic holds my hand hard, squeezing and yelling every time I close my eyes. He puts something into my wrist, something sharp that stings. He keeps asking me questions. *What's my phone number? Who are my parents?*

"Jim."

"Dad."

"Mechanic."

"Thirteen."

"Can I sleep now? My head hurts so bad. I just want to sleep. Where's my bike? Did someone get my bike?"

I nod out and wake up to see bright lights over me, squinting as I'm rolled down a hallway. Someone shines a flashlight into my eyes and someone else puts a tube on my wrist and I see a clear plastic container fill with dark red blood and I try to lean over to throw up but I can't move my neck so instead I throw up into my mouth and feel it fall over my face as I try to spit it out to breathe. A nurse grabs my jaw and holds it open while another sticks her hand in my mouth to sweep out what liquid there is and I try to hold in the next heave because I don't want to throw up on the nurse's hand. There's some kind of suction bag making a wheezing sound as it pulls on my tongue and cheek so I try to just close my eyes and pretend I can't feel my stomach.

When I open them again, I'm in a new room and someone is sticking a needle in my arm. I feel the prick of the needle then fall asleep again with my head pounding. This happens six or eight times.

Am I a man yet?

At some point I see Dad's dark brown chestnut boots shining against the green linoleum on the floor. I smell Bonnie's perfume and hear them talking to the doctor. She kisses me. "Hi, Suuuuuun. You all right? We were worried."

Dad sits by the bed in a chair with his legs crossed at the knees. I feel his short beard scratch against my cheek when he kisses me. "You're okay. You're okay," he says, rubbing my face. I look at him but I'm confused. I can't think. I just don't want to be in trouble because we ditched school and snuck our bikes out and got high. *I think he was high, Dad. I don't know. I don't think I was high. I'm sorry. I was trying to go over the jump and he was in the way. I'm sorry. I'll be grounded. I'll just be grounded forever.*

On the second morning, after the second night when I was woken every hour and asked questions and had blood taken, when I think I could handle any needle because I've been poked a hundred times since getting to the hospital and I don't even care anymore, I say I want to go home but Dad says I can't, because the doctors have to watch me and run tests but it'll be fine, they promise me.

The doctor says I have a ruptured spleen and a concussion and three contused ribs and if I hadn't been wearing my helmet I would be dead. Dad says, "No shit," and whistles, looking at me sideways. "Maybe we should take it easy on the motorcycles for a while."

When we leave the hospital, I get to stay home from school for two weeks. Tony calls me from drug rehab and says, "Heard you got in an accident, little bro. I hope you're okay, dude."

"How's not doing drugs?"

"It's not so bad. The people here are pretty cool. We just go to a lot of meetings and sit around most of the time." He tells me about his new girlfriend, Tiffany. She's only fourteen. Tony says she is blond and pretty and "cool as fuck." He hangs out with her most afternoons. Bonnie says they made a home tattoo kit with a needle and some Indian ink. He tattooed a round yin-yang on his ankle. But then he got bored and tattooed a hat and feet on it. He also tattooed "AJJ" on his arm, which he arranged in an overlapping fashion so that the horizontal line of the *A* became the top of the *J* to stand for "Anthony Joseph Jollett." He didn't like the first one he drew so he crossed it out—also in tattoo—and tattooed another one next to it. Bonnie says he's doodling on himself and someone should get him some fucking markers.

It's good to be home. I like that everyone was worried about me, that they thought I was going to die.

Bonnie has to go to the hospital too, for some tests. When she comes home, she says she has a tumor. It's as big as a grapefruit on her fallopian tube and has to come out immediately so there's going to be an operation. "I named it Raul," she says, trying to laugh. "What can I say? I'm a grower." But I know she's scared because she tells me she always wishes she had kids "from her own body," but that she can't and she starts to cry, trying to get the words out. She says she loves me, that even if she had other kids I would still always be "Suuuuuun" like when I was little with the deep voice and the big belly and the teeth like *Planet of the Apes*. She says that made me special to her and she's felt that way since she met me when I was six months old in Synanon, when we were taken from our moms and dads to become children of the universe.

We stay up late in their bedroom talking on the bed with the lights out, staring at the ceiling. The more she tells me how special I am to her, the more I feel like I need to tell her about all the bad things I've done. I'm so tired of hiding it, of pretending I am the good son. All the smoking and stealing, the destruction, drinking and drugs.

And I'm scared she's going to die and I don't know what I'd do without her because she's not like a stepmom but more like a mom who adopted me, who took care of me when no one else would. I don't want her to die thinking I'm someone I'm not, that I didn't turn out to be special like they thought I was.

Tony is in rehab and I was scared in the ambulance and Bonnie is scared because of the tumor named Raul and finally I just say, "I'm sorry, I'm so sorry," and before I know it, I tell her everything because I can't have her turn into an angel and see my life for all the lies I've hidden. I want her to see the quiet place where I am alone. The Secret Place. I don't want to be there by myself anymore.

She says it's okay and she understands because she knows it's a confession and you can't be mad during a confession, even though she doesn't really believe me at first because Tony is the bad son and I am the good son. But I say I want to get good grades and have a future and I don't want to end up like Tony twitching and strung out and sad on the couch. I want her to live and I don't want to die on my motorcycle. She hugs me and says we'll get through this. That's what families do.

She calls Dad in and tells him about the confession. He listens quietly and I say I'm sorry and he says he loves me because he knows I'm scared and he leans in and puts his arms around me, hugs me close to him and says, "It's all right. I'm just glad you're being honest now. I'll help you. So will Bonnie. We're gonna be fine. We're gonna stick together. You'll see. No one is going to die. No one is going anywhere, I promise."

DAD TAKES ME to Hollywood Park. Tony is in rehab and Bonnie is resting from her surgery when they removed Raul the tumor from her insides that grow things like a garden, just not babies. We've been bringing her bagels and soup and snacks as she lies under a big white blanket on the couch. The tumor is gone and she is recovering and she isn't going to die after all and everyone is relieved. She and I talk about high school, about how I want to run track when I get there now that I decided to quit smoking and drinking, how I love to run and I'm going to start trying in school. She tells me she believes in me, she loves me, she's glad we're all here and it's my life to make into whatever I want.

It's a crowded day at the racetrack. The familiar excitement fills the air, the sense of possibility, the earthy smell of horse manure and cold beer. Dad is quiet as we walk down to the cashiers to lay our bets for the day. We go to the sandwich shop and order two corned beef sandwiches on rye, two Sprites and two Carnation chocolate malted ice creams. We take the food back to our box and sit down.

We eat our food and watch the races, screaming for our picks down the homestretch, standing up with the roar of the crowd to scream, "Go, baby!" After a few races, we're still alive on the Pick Six when out of no-where Dad says, "Hey, listen, I want to talk to you."

He isn't one for Big Talks. Bonnie says he's not good at talking about his feelings but that he feels so much and it's hard for him.

He stares out over the dirt oval and says, "You know, you don't have to be like me." I look up at him. I don't know what to say. Aren't we Jollett men? Pirates and thieves, one step in front of the law?

"You're a smart kid and you can do more in life than I ever did and that's what I want for you. I fucked around a lot when I was your age and it didn't do much for me. I never thought you'd go that way."

He looks over his racing form. "Your brother was dealt a different hand and he's dealing with it now and that's good. But you have a real chance to do something special." He puts his racing form down and looks at me very seriously.

"Don't fuck it up. Don't do what I did. Go do something better."

His fist is balled on his knee and he taps it gently, the black hair on his hands against the faded blue jeans, the tiny dot tattoo on the knuckle of his middle finger. Is this tough love?

I fight the urge to cry because we are at the racetrack with the men and boys don't cry. For so long, I just wanted to be near to him, to be like him. All those nights alone in Oregon wondering what it means to be a man trying to piece it together like re-creating an image from a dream.

"I love you. You're my son. You can do things I never did. You know, I never wanted to get locked up." I see the memory fill his eyes. "We tell funny stories and all, but it was terrible. Being in prison is terrible. Being an addict is no fun. It's just darkness and you're alone and you can talk a big game but you're really just some dumb-shit kid running scared. I wish somebody had told me that when I was your age. I would've never gone to prison. But there just wasn't anyone. I think I maybe would have been a scientist or maybe a musician. I was in the Synanon choir. I got a good voice, you know."

I try to imagine him holding a guitar or a saxophone, standing on a stage in sunglasses with the Allman Brothers or Jackson Browne. I want him to be proud of me, more than anything in the world.

"Anyway, let's lay an extra bet on this next race. This is our horse." He puts his arm around my shoulders and squeezes me, letting it hang there for a moment while the earth stands still.

I tell him about the nights we destroyed property in the neighborhood, about Flesh and Duck and the time I almost OD'd, when the world was spinning and I was three inches tall in my head. He nods and says, "Let's just say it's good you got it out of your system early."

There is no judgment, just a warm feeling like he is on my side.

I wonder if this is just another way Mom lied to me about the world. *Your father who left me for a tramp. Your father with nine fingers. Your father who only likes sports and cars.* I know the words by heart, the implication that our lives are a story of escape and he is the villain. But here he is next to me reasoning with me, trying to get me to go down a different path. He doesn't even want me to become a Jollett man. Or maybe he wants to change what that means.

Dad and I go to the track every weekend for a while, while Bonnie recovers from her surgery and Tony is in his drug rehab. I learn to box my exacta bets and to broaden the Pick Six field on a race when I'm less sure about the winner. I learn the names of the guys who, like my dad, go there to sit in the sun and take in the day, to let the future have some possibility. They even start to ask me about my bets. *Who ya got in the fifth, kid?*

Sometimes we don't talk much. We just sit there and eat and stare off into the distance. There's that old feeling of being connected as if by a string. He doesn't say it but I know he likes sitting there next to me too, to just be a father who has a son.

When Bonnie goes back to work, she gets a promotion. She's going to be the first woman to be a vice president in the history of the company where she works. She says she's honored and she knows lots of women could've gotten there first but there was something called the glass ceiling that men put in their way. She started as a telemarketer but she just worked her way up with that big warm personality of hers, making calls, then training salespeople, then managing them, then starting a whole division of the company and bursting right through that glass ceiling. Dad and I are so proud of her, even though she has to work a lot. She says it's all men in the meetings at her company and that women have to work harder to make the same amount of money and I just think, *Who wouldn't want Bonnie in charge?*

She says Dad doesn't mind staying home with me while she works. "Say what you will about your father, he's always been a huge supporter of me and my career. He always tells me I'm good at my job and he's thankful that I work to support us. That's hard for some men. Not Dad. I work sixty hours a week and he makes sure I never even have to wash a dish."

It's weird because I was always told by Mom what a Neanderthal Dad is because he likes sports and old cars and so it just seems like so many things she told me that weren't true about him. Bonnie tells me, "It's like how he never once missed a single child support payment. Never once in your entire lives. He sent a check every month and it arrived on time." It's strange that Mom never mentioned this when she talked about how Dad abandoned us and I'm starting to think maybe he never abandoned Tony and me. He just didn't want to be with Mom anymore.

The promotion means Bonnie is going to be gone more working late so one day they sit me down for a Big Talk and tell me Dad is going to stop doing his sunroof company and start another company selling "gift specialties" from home so Bonnie can work more and he'll be at the house when I'm done with school. He tells me someone needs to look out for me so it may as well be him.

"That woman could talk a dog off a meat truck," he says, cooking his favorite dinner, short ribs and fried potatoes. She went to Synanon when she was nineteen, when she was marching for civil rights and attending sit-ins, when she was still a teenager, a "blond bombshell" who wanted a better world. She never went to college. She joined the commune that became a cult instead.

Dad cooks and keeps the house clean and talks on the phone with different businesses trying to sell them pens or cups or hats with their company logo on them. He wakes me up early on Saturday mornings for my chores so the two of us can get them done while Bonnie sleeps, before we head off to the track. I can feel how much he's placed his hopes on me. It's weird, to have this new idea of the man I'm becoming, that I might become, that I don't have to be a Dope Fiend or a fuckup, that there might be something else waiting for me.

We finalize our Pick Six order and head to the ticket counter to place our bets. All around us are men yelling at TV screens and men discussing horses and men slumped over their racing forms as I follow him through the crowd. All these men with their dreams, their systems and schemes.

The crowd gets thicker so it feels like we're walking through a tunnel.

I keep my eyes on Dad's red shirt and blue jeans in front of me, trying to stay close.

He never knew his father, not really. It was just his three brothers running wild and his mother cleaning hotel rooms to make ends meet. I wonder if maybe sometime long ago in another life, in a hospital bed or a jail cell or a dirty couch in the Synanon lobby next to a bucket filled with puke, feverish and shaking, he hoped to have a son someday who could do the things he never could.

When I get home that night and the day's events flash through my mind, I see him walking in front of me through the crowd of men. They form a tunnel around us, all these angry men with their high hopes for something new. I can feel their breath on my neck, the smell of beer, the thick ankles and cigarette smoke as I follow my father down that path. The tunnel darkens as we walk deeper into it, the way it does in a dream, following the logic of dreams, like we are heading for the center of the earth, a sacred place I imagine on cold nights when I just want to hold everyone in my family close. We follow the path down as it turns from men to dirt and we hear the sound of the track echoing behind us until it is cold and there is the faint sound of water. It's quiet as we enter a bright room. There's a crowd of people there, Dad as a skinny young man with a smile on his face and a black spit curl leaning against the wall with a lit cigarette; Mom as a sad little girl with striking green eyes and big Dutch cheeks standing alone in a corner; a teenage boy with dyed black hair, angrily pounding a broken leg against the ground; a bearded man with thinning black hair lying on the ground taking swigs from a bottle in a brown bag. Bonnie as a teenage girl, hopeful and smiling as she stares down at a small blond boy with an enormous overbite and a potbelly running between the adults, looking into each of their faces, searching for something. There's my grandpa Nat and my grandma Juliette. My aunts and cousins. My grandpa Frank in his chair and grandma Frieda smiling in her robe. There is a small green urn with white marbling sitting on a shelf above them, above that is a floating blue image of a man with a thick mustache talking to the little boy with the overbite. He says, *We are here together and we will always be. Nothing can ever change that. Not even death can take it away. That's what it means to be an F-A-M-I-L-Y. No matter what happens, we can always meet here in this room a thousand feet beneath Hollywood Park.*

CHAPTER 30

CHILDREN OF THE UNIVERSE

I've decided to change my name again. Mike was fine for junior high but now that I'm in high school, it sounds childish and so I start telling my new teachers to call me by my given name, the one Mom gave me that would be uniquely my own, so I could be a child of the universe. Mikel. It's strange to hear the name coming from the mouths of my teachers and it feels like an affectation at first because all my junior high friends, Drew, Ryan, Stephen Perkins, insist on calling me Mike.

By the time I finish my first semester of ninth grade at Westchester High School, the report card that Bonnie puts on the fridge reads five As and one B. I don't know what I thought school would be. Boring, I suppose. I thought it would be something I did like the standards I had to write when I got busted ditching school in junior high, a kind of repetitive punishment that I accepted because it was either do that or become a Dope Fiend.

But it wasn't like that at all. There was a pretty girl named Laura Dorset who sat in the front of my honors English class. She had sandy blond hair and a tiny nose tilted up just like a little ski jump. She wore leg warmers and a big white belt that covered her impossibly small waist. Most days I sat in the back and watched her and when we got to the unit on *The Scarlet Letter* by Hawthorne and our teacher, Mrs. Chavez, asked the class about the *A* stitched across the chest of Hester Prynne, Laura Dorset raised her hand and said very seriously that she thought the *A* stood for "able" and not "adulteress, as was her punishment." Something turned in me, to see this pretty girl taking the book so seriously. She put her hand down and the discussion moved on and for the first time in my life I did homework that night.

One sentence stood out to me as I read on the edge of my bed. I marked the page: "No man, for any considerable period, can wear one face to himself, and another to the multitude, without finally getting bewildered as to which may be the true." It made me think of the Secret Place, the place I hide with Robert Smith. I know this face. I've learned not to tell anyone at school about Synanon or Dad in prison or Paul dying or Mom in the bed staring up at the ceiling.

It's a mask, this face you create for others, one you hide behind as you laugh at jokes you don't understand and skip uncomfortable details, entire years of your life, as if they simply didn't happen.

I brought up the quote in our next discussion, raising my hand in class for the first time in my life, my heart pounding trying to sound serious, keeping an eye on Laura Dorset. Mrs. Chavez said I hit the major theme on its head and she wrote it on the blackboard for the class.

Next was *Lord of the Flies*, then *Of Mice and Men*. I wondered how the authors dreamed these stories up. It seemed like writers have the most important job in the world, to make books, to create a connection, a kind of telepathy between two minds in which one can inhabit the other. It doesn't seem like a thing that exists in the real world, to be an artist. The only careers we ever hear about are doctor or teacher or lawyer or banker or engineer. What does a writer do all day? Where does he pick up his paycheck? How does he even start? There are no answers.

I was shocked, as surprised as I've ever been about anything in my life, to find I liked school. I liked the books and the discussions in English. I liked learning about ancient civilizations in history class. I liked science with our microscopes and cell diagrams, the mystery of life explained. I was fascinated. What started as a kind of future goal quickly became something I loved for its own sake.

I would find myself up at eleven or midnight reading on the bed or taking notes from a textbook. Dad would lean in with a glass of milk and some crackers, shaking his head. "How's it going in here? You going blind from all this reading yet?" I would point to the book and he would nod and leave me with my studies.

Some nights he seemed proud and others he seemed almost confused. I knew I couldn't ask him for help with geometry or an essay, the way the other kids from class could, the ones whose parents had college degrees. And very quickly, after my first few report cards, a new feeling began to emerge over this, a shame like Dad was something to be hidden, something I had to fight against if I wanted to go to college. Because that was all I cared about, getting out, getting into college, finding a way to do something new. And being a Jollett man, the very thing that made me feel dangerous and cool, like I could flout all rules and conventions, suddenly felt like a liability and college—for a Jollett man whose uncles, brother and father had all been addicts who'd gone to jail—was nothing but a pipe dream.

WHEN WE GET to *Black Boy,* I work up the nerve to ask Laura Dorset on a date. To my surprise, she says yes. The class discussions all week center on how Richard Wright's family treats his ambition like a dangerous thing, so he learns to hide it. In the rural South at the turn of the century that ambition could get him killed. Still, he's driven to move up, to find a better station in life. I can't help but be inspired, to think if he can face the horrors he had to face, I can at least stay up late studying. Tanisha Campbell says this is how it's always been and that white people don't understand struggle because they don't have to deal with being poor, with living on food stamps in a broken home or a father in prison.

When Wright's mother tells him she wants to die, his body goes blank, his feelings frozen inside him while she lies still in the bed. This teaches him to be suspicious of joy, a feeling like he had to keep moving in order to escape the nameless fate trying to overtake him. I am breathless because that is exactly how I felt in Oregon when Mom would go into her depressions. I want so badly to be on whatever team Richard Wright is on. I know he faced things I never will, that I have the advantage of this white face I can wear like a mask, that when teachers or cops or my peers look at me, they don't see the food stamps and heroin and lineage of men who've gone to prison, all they see is my blond hair and my green eyes, the picture of a suburban white boy. And that Tanisha Campbell and my black peers, no matter how focused on the future they are, no matter how safe, settled, upwardly mobile their home lives are, when authority figures see a black teenager, what they see is a million stereotypes. So I know Richard Wright and I are very different and I am lucky in this way. But still, the feeling I have when I read the book is one of being seen. I recognize something of myself in his private world and his private thoughts. I admire him and I wish so much we could be friends, that his locker was near mine and we could have lunch together.

Laura and I pass notes between classes all week and before long I ask her to be my girlfriend, leaning in to her locker, the air thick with the smell of her perfume, my heart pounding as I place my hand on that tiny waist and stare at that little ski jump nose.

She says yes and it feels like the crashing of a thunderhead, this new world I glimpse at the edge of her locker in the E Building of Westchester High School beneath the flight path of those rumbling jets. Within a couple weeks, we are spending every minute together, holding hands in the hallways, staying up late to talk on the phone while I read her the lyrics to "Just Like Heaven" by the Cure. We eat lunch alone on the edge of campus, away from prying eyes, a great romance taking place beneath the eaves of the school library. A universe in a raindrop.

Some days I go to her house after school to study. Laura is a straight-A student and she explains to me how to take notes, how to keep track of assignments in a weekly calendar, how to budget time and plan assignments. I feel like a caveman learning about tools for the first time. When she gets stuck, she asks her father for help. He is an engineer at the Hughes Aircraft facility on the edge of the hill that leads up to Westchester. I think of Dad in his garage, surrounded by the engine parts and dirty rags, his red Craftsman toolbox and blue shop towels.

Her mother is a housewife with cropped black hair and a kind of birdlike anxiety. She follows us from room to room asking if we need food or water or help studying. It's an odd feeling, to be tended in this way. I feel like an amoeba in the presence of gazelles. Like these graceful, organized people are better than I am. Like they know something I don't. Like there is a code here and if I can just crack it, if I can learn to have a conversation with her, then I can gain an advantage.

Her mother interrogates me and I try to hold that face, the one I know

I have to show the world, the one that quickly crumbles under her questioning.

"So what does your father do, Mikel?"

"He managed a tire shop for a while."

"That's a good blue-collar job you can do with just a high school education. Good for him."

"He didn't go to high school."

"He didn't?"

"He dropped out in eighth grade."

"What did he do all day?"

"At first he just got in trouble, I guess, but then he ran drugs to Mexico and stole cars and credit card numbers. But he's clean now. Has been for years."

"What do you mean, *clean*?"

"It's kind of a long story." There is no way out of this. I am a circus freak. *Step right up and see the child raised without parents in a cult. He will never be anything but precisely this.*

"Um, well, when he got out of prison, he wanted to get clean from heroin, so he went to Synanon, which was this commune where he met my mom."

"Oh. Well, she seemed very nice when I met her the other night."

"That was Bonnie. But I call her my mom too."

"What does that mean? Where was your real mom?"

"Bonnie *is* my real mom. They both are, for different reasons."

"Okay, where was the woman who gave birth to you?"

"She was in Santa Monica, in the main Synanon facility there. It was an armory on the beach."

"Where were you?"

"Tomales Bay. That's in Marin County. North of San Francisco. In a different Synanon facility."

"And your mom was okay with this?"

"She was very sad. That's what she says."

"That doesn't sound like a school. That sounds like an orphanage. How old were you?"

"Six months."

"Six months! And this *school* . . . who ran it?"

"Other people in the commune."

"You mean other drug addicts?"

"I guess so. Not everybody was a drug addict. Some of them wanted to change the world. A lot of those drug addicts were great people."

"Did they go through a background screening to make sure they weren't criminals or abusers? Were they monitored? Were they finger-printed? Was there a training? Educational requirements? Certifications? Oversight? Anything like that?"

I feel a hot shame on my neck and I want to run away. I don't know how to explain to this woman that these people are people I love and they're not weird in the way she imagines them, that she is the weird one with her coupons and life out of *Leave It to Beaver*.

"I don't know. It wasn't like that. They were nice. Bonnie was there."

"What about when Bonnie wasn't there?"

"What do you mean?"

"I mean if Bonnie worked there, then she had to go home sometimes, so who was with you then? How do you know it was safe? How did your mom know to trust these people who ran this orphanage with her six-month-old baby? Where was your dad?"

"It, well, I, uh, I don't know. We were children of the universe."

It's strange to hear the stories we've been told about Synanon decon-structed in this way, to see them through the eyes of someone else, how quickly they fall apart under scrutiny. We've been told so many times that we were raised "in a school" and that it was a "a great school." No one ever stopped to think that maybe the kids were hurt by that school which wasn't a school but a group home or an orphanage. I can't help but think how much worse it would sound if she knew more.

I know she likes me. I even know that she approves of me in her way. I can smile a perfectly white smile now that my braces are off and my teeth are clean and I have a jaw instead of a mouth like an ape. I have a haircut and new clothes instead of hand-me-downs. I'm getting an A in honors English. I can repeat the words I know I'm supposed to say, the ones I learned from Drew. He's on the baseball team now, a star pitcher, and he's taken to wearing Cure T-shirts to school. Now that I've stopped being such a "bad kid," we're able to go to his house after school, where we study or shoot hoops in his backyard. I hear him talk to his mother, who is the president of the PTA, and I've learned the words I'm supposed to recite, the ones that speak to my plans, my goals, my future, my worth: "Yes, I'd love some toast, thank you . . . We're gonna hit the books. No, I'm not sure if I want to go to a UC or a private school yet."

She doesn't know how we waited in our beds for someone to pick us up. She doesn't know the shame of it. She doesn't know about Phil in the driveway. She doesn't know we had to run and hide behind the mountains. She doesn't know about Paul or the rabbits or food stamps or Mom frozen in the bed, how she told us it was our job to take care of her and we felt ourselves go numb as we slipped into a stone tower in the sky. And I will never tell her. I want to bury it like a key you drop in a well. I want to hide it under a hundred feet of water and brick. And it seems I can. Because all she says is what my teachers say: How remarkable it is that *I'm choosing a different path for myself.* How exciting it is that I'm *pursuing a future.* She doesn't know that the past isn't over. She doesn't know that it's a mask, this face I hold to the world.

CHAPTER 31

MORE HORSE
THAN JOCKEY

There were moments running down a trail with Paul on a crisp fall day at Minto-Brown Park in Salem at eight years old when I felt like I could run forever. The smell of mud and dried leaves on the ground, the way the snot would trickle down my face and I could feel my heart pounding through my chest as if it was about to carry me up into the sky by the sheer force of its beating. I wondered where the red line was, when my stomach would cramp or my asthma would flare up and we had to walk or lie still on the trail. How hard could I push? When did the body take over and say no? More often than not the pain was part of it: the fire in my gut as I jumped over a log or cut between bushes and roots, the feeling so palpable, of being alive, as I turned a corner and disappeared into some forgotten corner of the forest.

Running on the beach the first week of track and field practice has a similar feel to it. There are so few distance runners on a team dominated by sprinters and jumpers and throwers, the leftover remnants of the standout football and basketball programs. We awkward distance-running few are misfits mostly, too thin, too short, too clumsy for other sports. The distance runners are mostly the immigrant kids, the misfits, the ones who could never make the basketball team. We are Guatemalan and Ethiopian, Mexican, Salvadoran, Korean, and Italian/Dutch/French/ Dope Fiend. Getahun is the only other serious runner on the team, the only other one who wants to win races and isn't just trying to get out of PE. He escaped the civil war in Ethiopia and moved to the United States where he lives now with an uncle in Inglewood, goes to school and works a job at a tuxedo shop in the Fox Hills Mall. We become fast friends. I stopped hanging around the kids from the Bowl after the motorcycle accident. They're not bad guys but I knew I wasn't going to make a change if I didn't change the company I kept.

Getahun and I climb over steep hills in the empty neighborhood cleared of houses beneath jumbo jets hanging in the sky above us heading out to sea like rumbling pterodactyls while we sweat and pant in the salt air heavy with the smell of decaying seaweed and the occasional rotting seal washed up in the sand. The runs are pleasant. The thirst, the ancient feeling of movement, the commitment to the Hard Task, the relief as I stretch in the grass after a six-mile run, exactly young, exactly a body in the sun.

Interval workouts are something else entirely. They are a brush with death, with failure, with the pain that keeps a body earthbound despite the heady plans of the mind. Halfway through the second interval of the eight-by-four-hundred-yard set we are given the first week of practice, as I begin to tie up, it hits me that there is going to be nothing fun about this. It's just going to hurt. It feels unfair because I've already joined the team. I've already told the family, Laura, Drew, everyone, that track is my sport and I can't very well quit because interval training is too hard. By the fourth interval, an ache begins to set in, a depression that there is no refuge. A sinking nausea. A weight in my legs as I feel the burn of lactic acid like I'm fighting against taut cords, fluttery and rigid, pulling me backward. By the eighth interval, the physical pain turns to confusion, a tendency to lose track of time. I look around for a soft place for my thoughts and there is none.

It's here in this place, in this quiet frenzy at the edge of my body's limit, that I find something surprising. Anger.

A recurring image comes to mind. There is an empty room with three wooden chairs in it. My father is sitting in one, my brother is in the next, and there is a third chair, which is empty, reserved for me. They look up at me as if to say, "You're next." There is a blue floor and a shaft of light falling from a high window and I realize the room is a jail cell. I pump my arms and grit my teeth, feeling the spit fall from my mouth, and think, *I. Will. Not. Become. You.* I round the turn, dizzy and out of breath, focusing on the empty room and their faces, sad, expectant, like a prophecy I can't avoid.

This becomes my ritual on the track after school on interval workout days. A light fog falls over my brain, a quiet storm in the distance as Getahun and I warm up. There is a sphere in my chest, a small defined space that floats quietly, containing something. I think about remaining small forever. That I will never grow. That I will never be taller. That I will be here, stuck forever. There is no future for me. No options. No choices. I consider the dream of faraway people and places, the chance to walk among them, a chance I will miss because I am destined for mediocrity, for prison, for rehab, for jail and a squandered life. I squeeze my eyes hard and put it all in the sphere. And then, with sweat falling in my face, when the burn in my lungs sets in and I see the final straightaway, the white wooden stands to the right, our coach standing at the finish line with his stopwatch while my legs tie up and my lungs burn, I let it out. I empty the sphere. And there on the track, I feel the anger consume me, the helplessness. The desire to break free becomes like a scream turned to movement. I pump my arms, I feel something electric in my legs and I lean forward and picture the room, the chairs, the place waiting for me, the place I am destined to end up no matter what I do, a feeling that makes me able to run until I fall over.

I DON'T KNOW if this place is one my brother is going to leave behind since he was kicked out of rehab after nine months for having a girlfriend. They moved to Oregon, he and Tiffany, where the rent was cheaper and they could get a place together. They stayed with Mom awhile then found an apartment on the edge of town between the fairgrounds and the railroad tracks. He got a job working at a mobile home plant that he says isn't so bad except that it's cold when it rains because the plant is outside and he accidently drove a nail through his hand one day.

"Man, I don't know if this is what I want, little bro," he tells me over the phone. "I mean, school sucks but this sucks more." He tells me he's still sober, which is good because we were all scared he was going to die and now he merely seems miserable.

I met Tiffany once at a sober dance in the Clare courtyard. "Sober dances" were what they called the parties they had without drugs or alcohol. There was a DJ setting up lights when I got there, people putting out sodas and pretzels when Tony emerged from a hallway screaming, "Little bro!" He ran to me and hugged me hard like I was his best friend on earth. "The man has arrived! Let's get you some punch! You ready to rock this town?"

I could feel how much he loved me, how much he felt like we were two survivors of something. "I hear you're kicking ass in school, man. That's so great! I'm so proud of you." I don't have the heart to be mad at him anymore and something about being out of the house in Oregon makes it easier to see him this way: as a kindred spirit, a person who understands something no one else in the world could.

He looked handsome with his black hair and tan face, less gaunt without the drugs in his system. Behind him was a short blond girl with a mod haircut shaved up on the back of her scalp, huge swooping bangs falling across her face. She had five earrings in her left ear and countless necklaces and bracelets. "So you're the one I hear all about? Give me a hug, little brother." She seemed to think of me as family from the beginning, like a sister I never met.

We danced the wop to Cameo and did the running man to Bobby Brown, swirling around with the other teenage Dope Fiends lost in the music. I liked her. They slow danced and she stared up at him with dreamy eyes, whispering something in his ear that made them both laugh. It was obvious they were in love. When they were kicked out, they were given a choice to end it or leave. They chose to leave.

Dad says he's playing with fire leaving rehab like that. It may be true, but I understand it. If someone told me I had to choose between school and Laura, I would choose Laura. I don't think they remember how big it feels, to be seen by another for the first time, to look into the face of someone who sees not some snot-nosed punk with a funny haircut but a man, full of promise and power and tragedy.

When Tiffany got pregnant a few months later, she called Bonnie because she didn't have a mother to call. She was abandoned as a child and hadn't seen her mother in a decade so she didn't know where else to turn. She said she was scared but excited by the idea of becoming a mother herself. Bonnie tried to reason with her, saying, "Are you sure you're ready for this kind of responsibility? Don't you want a life? You're only fifteen years old."

But there was no reaching her. She wanted the baby and what do you tell a teenage Dope Fiend who's made up her mind?

Mom said it would be good for them, that becoming a father would force Tony to grow up a little because "young men like him" have spent their lives "acting out addictive impulses." Bonnie thought she was nuts.

Dad said, "They're going to do what the fuck they're going to do no matter what anyone says," and it's been that way "since the beginning of time," so everybody had better get used to it.

When the child came, when we got the call that the birth was uncomplicated and the child was a healthy baby boy with blond hair and blue eyes just like his dad's, there was a moment of hope when anything seemed possible, when we said, "Hell, they might just make it and I hope they do!" because how could you fail to love something so beautiful? How could anyone turn away from this perfect child of the universe, to leave him to wonder if he is alone in the world?

I WAS ELIMINATED in the city quarterfinals on the pink tartan track at Birmingham High but mine was the fastest time on the team and the fastest mile time of any freshman in the city. I even broke five minutes. I spent the summer in Oregon running the country roads east of the freeway. Sometimes Jake would follow me on a bike, his sockless Florsheim shoes slipping off the pedals as he sang "Push" by the Cure or told me about his new girlfriend. Sometimes I ran alone at dawn before the sun came up. Sometimes I ran late at night, sneaking out of the house after Mom and Doug went to bed. There's a blackness out beyond I-5, beyond the edge of the city as I slip down the country roads, the kind of night for which God created darkness, as if only to give a canvas to the light.

By the end of the summer, I am more horse than rider. I know my body, when to push, when to conserve, how to build up the sphere, how to let it loose. I imagine the races at Hollywood Park. I don't want to be the jockey. I don't even want to be the man who wins the bet. I want to be the horse.

Dad comes to all my track meets, sitting alone in the empty stands to cheer for me before walking the three blocks home. It's a surprise to see him there, waving and cheering in the sun as I lean into the final straightaway. He seems warmer somehow sitting on his hands with a smile on his face. He has no idea about the room and the chair, the anger that propels my workouts. I wonder if I've missed something crucial. He seems to understand the feeling of fighting through darkness, of trying to find a way to deal with something difficult.

My report cards are all on the fridge now. Dad will point them out when people come to visit like trophies in a case. "That's an A in AP Chemistry, folks. No joke, that class." When I receive an academic achievement award and I stand in a line with forty other students, afterward he says, "The only line I ever stood in was in Chino! Ha-ha." But he studies the award, shaking his head, fingering the embossed letters that spell out our shared name. Under his breath he whispers, "Them sonsabitches ain't buried us yet."

"What?"

"I'm just proud of you."

At the end of track season I qualify for the L.A. City Finals for the class C mile. The race is on my sixteenth birthday. The whole family comes to the pink tartan track built for the 1984 Olympics at Birmingham High School. "The whole *mishpucha* is here," Bonnie says with a laugh. There's Grandma Juliette and Grandpa Nat and my aunts Jeannie with her new boyfriend, Marc, Nancy, Dad, Bonnie and Laura. I can feel their eyes on me as Getahun and I warm up and stretch quietly in the grass.

We stand tall for the starting gun. I feel a lightness, like my stomach is filled with dust, my legs bunched like loaded springs. I'm rested, hydrated. I flex my fingers, bouncing on toes, testing a body that still feels new to me. The crack of the pistol echoes out over the stands and we are off. I tuck in behind the lead pack, the boys from Belmont and Granada Hills with their big distance-running programs two hundred strong that dwarf our ragtag team copying workouts from odd books found in running stores.

By the middle of the second lap, I lose track of them. I can see their heartbreakingly perfect strides pulling away. *Maybe I will never leave. Maybe it is hopeless to imagine anything could ever change.* I lower my head, trying to control the sphere. *Not yet.* By the middle of the third lap, I am tucked in behind the lead pack again, staring at the green Granada Hills singlet in front of me. Passing the stands, I hear the family cheering. I wonder if I'm going to let them down, if they came all this way for nothing.

The thought disintegrates into a fever dream of images: Dad, Tony, the room, the chairs, Paul and Minto-Brown, running alone in the woods behind Englewood School after he disappeared.

At the start of the bell lap, I stumble. My foot catches tartan and for a second I think I'm going to fall straight onto my face. But I catch myself, running wide out into the middle lanes. My legs go rubbery and my stomach sinks as I try to keep my feet under me. I hear the bell and there it is: the empty chair. The blue light. *Breathe. Push.* Dad's face looking at me. Tony staring at the ground. The walls covered in shadows, the floor dirty and stained, the light falling on the empty wooden seat. I hold the sphere in my hands, feeling it shake as I draft down the far straightaway. *You will never leave. You have no future, no future, no future.* I look up and we are in the final turn, the three runners in front of me leaning into their closing kicks. The sphere bursts and there is that sudden anger, that abandon and fear and helplessness all turning into fury as I pull out into lane two, the lane of dreamers, the lane of high hopes.

I hear the scream from the stands, my aunt Jeannie loudest of all, "Go, Mick!" as the shards of glass fall around my feet, something like sticky hot tar in my mouth, my face pulled back into a grotesque grimace. *Faster, shithead. Fucking run.* I see the expression on my coach's face as I pass by the long-jump pit. He looks curious. Almost sad. Maybe I imagine that. Maybe I'm the one who feels the sadness.

I pull even with the lead pack, the green singlet from Granada Hills to my left. My stride has turned to shit, all jutting knees with my head moving wildly. I close my eyes and I am two inches tall in my head. *When did we imagine we were at the bottom of a well?* I fall forward and feel the light brush of the white tape across my chest and I tumble down into the soft tartan like a drunk.

I land on my back and grab my knees. *Please. I must breathe. Please.*

The first thing I see when I open my eyes is Getahun. He is standing over me, his big smile, his round head, his thin, unsteady English, yelling out, "Heeeeeey, boy! Look at that! Don't you know? You won it! Take a lap, boy!" He pulls me up and throws his arms around my shoulders and we jog down to the green of the infield.

There's a quick medal ceremony and a picture that runs on the front page of the *Los Angeles Times* sports section. I walk up to the stands to hug

Grandma and Grandpa and Bonnie and Jeannie and Nancy and Laura, who gives me a kiss. Dad puts his arm around me and all I can think is he doesn't know. He doesn't even know that I'm here because of the chairs and the room, because I don't want to be like him.

Afterward, we go for a Chinese food birthday dinner at Fu's Palace on Pico Boulevard. Grandma Juliette cracks jokes over egg rolls and sweet-and-sour pork. "Did you see him? That's my grandson! I never saw such a thing! Who knew our boy was so fast?" Grandpa Nat raises a toast and we all join in with our glasses held. I catch Dad's eye. He keeps looking at me, curious, as he drinks his tea and gives me a wink, gazing off into space with a faraway look, then studying the spotless blue ribbon hanging around my neck like he won it himself.

I wish I could tell him. But there's no way to give voice to this thing in me, this contradiction, the pride and the anger, the confusion and shame, the thing driving me forward that I love this man who I don't want to be and I feel trapped by his choices to either abandon him or abandon my future.

CHAPTER 32

CAN YOU HEAR ME, MAJOR TOM?

The first time I see Drew play his acoustic guitar, it looks to me like something a cowboy would own. Something about the polished wood and the hokey shape reminds me of campfire sing-alongs and country singers sitting on hay bales wailing on about girls named Daisy. It seems out of place among the Depeche Mode poster on his wall, the *Meat Is Murder* T-shirt he wears all the time.

I don't see anything broken in Drew, any reason why he would like all these sad songs. Maybe it's just very well hidden. His brother, the college radio DJ at the U.S. Naval Academy, makes mix tapes for him, for his education: the Cure, the Smiths, Depeche Mode, Red Flag, Jane's Addiction, the Sex Pistols, the Pixies and Sigue Sigue Sputnik. He tapes these for me like we have a club of two, the only two people who like this music at a school dominated by Tony! Toni! Toné!, Paula Abdul and the Beastie Boys. He's switched from baseball to volleyball now and looks the part. Six foot three, thin, with blond hair bleached by the sun, tan skin covered in freckles. Sometimes in the middle of basketball at the park, he'll casually dunk a basketball like it's the easiest thing in the world. He carries this insouciance with him, like he finds all the effort everybody else puts into difficult tasks charming as he masters them with ease.

Some people are likable simply because they give off the constant impression that they like you, and something about this trait is calming and easy to trust. That's Drew.

His sister is a straight-A student, his dad is a successful lawyer and sometimes I wonder if it all seems like a big joke to him, like being from this sleepy suburb and having such genteel, well-educated parents give him the confidence to question it, as if charmed by all that uptight, upright nature, willing to laugh at it as one laughs at a certain shape of nose, an inherited feature passed between generations. He could be an astronaut, a doctor, a lawyer, a diplomat, and instead he wants to sit around and listen to the Cure with his former burnout friend. I can't help but respect that.

We've formed a kind of club with other guys who like good music: Eddie, short, kind, who loves Jane's Addiction; Pete, sarcastic and fearless, who loves the Stone Roses; Tim, who is into student government and Depeche Mode; and Gabe, the catcher from the baseball team with the thick build of an athlete and the mind of an artist. Our pack of misfits has grown. We all know there's safety in numbers.

The big steel-string guitar looks awkwardly large in Drew's lap, like some kind of corny prop. But when he starts to play the chords for "Please, Please, Please, Let Me Get What I Want" by the Smiths, strumming in a choppy motion, crooning quietly, his nasal voice filling the little room, something amazing happens.

> Haven't had a dream in a long time
> See, the life I've had can make a good man bad

No matter how clumsy, how imperfect, it seems like a kind of magic to conjure a moment in this way, like the song was sitting in the ether somewhere just waiting for someone to bring it to life. It isn't an object and it isn't a person and it isn't an idea. It's something else. It contains something. Sadness. Nostalgia, maybe. The sense of a person's essence, not just lyrics and a melody, but a presence, a feeling like a spirit has joined you. The spirit has a story and that story lives in these words and notes. There is a time and a place, a fact of existence, and we are suddenly not just two awkward boys sitting in a suburb beneath the flight path of Los Angeles International Airport but two people who are part of this world with its morbid wit, its stylish boredom, the layers of irony, the pompadour.

I'm spellbound. Even though the song, as sung by Drew on his acoustic guitar in his bedroom next to his wall-mounted collection of *Star Wars* action figures, sounds nothing like the Smiths, there is a sorcery at work and I need to learn how to use it. It's like deciding to learn how to fly, the power to conjure, the ability to transform a space. I want it for myself so I too can carry around these bits of magic.

He hands me his guitar. He shows me how to make a C chord. How to press down hard on the strings until the tips of my fingers hurt, careful to keep them behind the frets so as not to block the other strings. It hurts a little.

"After a while you get calluses. Until then you just got to let it hurt."

I pluck out the chord, string by string. Then he shows me how to move my fingers to make an E-minor chord, bunching them up near the top of the fret board.

After half an hour I can move between the two chords, tentatively, like a child taking first steps.

"Okay, now strum." He taps his foot. "Try to switch chords on the beat." I'm too slow with my fingers to keep up but it's close. He sings, low, almost in a whisper, with that lazy California drawl of his.

Ground control to Major Tom.

I look up at him, amazed. Jake and I have listened to that song in the garage hundreds of times, wondering about this strange man named David Bowie with his spaceship, this world somewhere far away where people sing about floating away forever. It all seems like some perfect expression of some perfect idea by some perfect artist on a hill somewhere. It never once occurred to me that in our own imperfect way we could sing the song ourselves.

When I get home, Bonnie says Grandma Juliette has an old Spanish guitar in the game room of their house. She used to play it for them when they were kids. It's just an old ratty thing but when we next go to the house off Fairfax and Wilshire, Grandma Juliette says I can have it. It's smaller than Drew's acoustic, with nylon strings and a hole in the front that looks like it was punched by a baby's fist. It takes a while to tune with the old tuning harmonica I find in the case. I sit in my room for hours thinking about David Bowie. What was he thinking when he wrote this? Where is he now and what would he tell me if he could? About school? About Laura? About the face I hold like a mask and the river beneath where I swim through my life. I alternate between the two chords, until my wrist is sore, until my fingers feel like they are going to bleed.

Can you hear me, Major Tom?

I learn the chords to the "Untitled" song by the Cure and "Ask" by the Smiths, singing in my scratchy, off-key voice that can barely carry a tune.

Sometimes when I'm up late studying, I hear a voice in my head telling me I'm a failure if I don't ace a test, if I don't find a way to be better than whatever it is I am. It's cruel, heartless, mean. *You piece of shit. You fucking loser piece of shit. Why do you bother, you fucking loser?* I hear the words over and over again on an unending loop. I have nowhere to put them, no way to understand them, only that my world is transformed suddenly and all I feel is this cold, bleak drive to become something else. Or if not, to fail and be left alone.

When it feels like too much, when I can't quiet the voice, I sit on the edge of my bed and strum the chords to those sad songs.

To know this thing exists, to go somewhere else and hear these words, to conjure them, is a relief, like I can breathe and it quiets that other voice.

Laura and I fight sometimes. Or more accurately, I am cruel to her sometimes. I don't know why. I'll tell her I don't really love her and she isn't good enough for me. I'll try to think of the meanest thing I can say. "You're too dumb." "You're too simple." "You're too sheltered to understand me." "You're ugly and you have no taste." I tell her it's over between us and I need someone else. I see her tears and feel a blankness wash over me. I see the panic in her eyes. I feel the loss I can inflict on her. It's like holding my breath, like I don't know myself because there is no self to know.

I'll kiss another girl, Tanisha Campbell from English class, my junior high crush, or Erica Nelson, in the weeds behind the football stadium. Word gets back to Laura and she writes me long notes with poems in them, notes that make it clear how much it hurts her to think of me with someone else, and I think "good." It feels safe to have this power. I don't know why.

The poems are sad and beautiful, filled with fear and a desire for comfort, images of lost children, sacred ghosts. There's depth beneath all her earnest girlishness, her braces and self-deprecating jokes, a sense that something made her leave girlhood too soon, that the woman who rushed in to fill the void was assembled in haste, fragmentary, incomplete as if born of the imagination of a girl.

But the thought is abstract in my mind and when I look inside, I feel only numb, as if she never existed, as if we were never captured in that universe in a raindrop, two people who found each other in this lame-ass school beneath the outbound jets.

Then it comes rushing back all at once and presents itself whole: I need her. I can't live without her. And she suddenly means *too* much. The amnesia is lifted and I can't go another day without holding her hand. I have to see her face. She doesn't deserve this. *I am a shit. I am a shit.* But the minute I feel the love, I also feel the guilt for having hurt her, having been cruel for no other reason than I couldn't stand to need her so much.

In the midst of the confusion, I'll sit on my bed and strum a D chord, mumbling some words over some crappy melody, and before I know it, I've started a song. I know it's bad as I'm singing it. *D to G to A, like every song ever written.* But it feels good to sing, to be in the Secret Place where I can put the mask down and visit my romantic and stylish friends who feel just as fucked-up as I do.

I do this whenever I am sad or overwhelmed or angry or bored. The songs are not good. The melodies are simple and the lyrics strain, saying too much or too little. It's nothing I'd ever play for someone else. I'd rather play a Bowie song. The point isn't to be good at it. The point is the music makes me feel like I belong somewhere, that this person I don't know, the one who swims beneath his life in a dark, chaotic, unknowable place, this one has a voice too.

CHAPTER 33

THE BIGGEST LIE
EVER TOLD

The Snake River Correctional Institution is a new prison in the high desert of eastern Oregon, five miles from the Idaho border. In the summer after my sixteenth birthday, Mom tells me she has a meeting to attend there and I could attend it with her, not the meeting itself, but the car ride. She explains that the car ride with her to this prison in the high desert will be my sixteenth birthday present.

"We can talk about your future and have quality time," she says. "Just you and me. Isn't that what you wanted for your birthday?"

I don't know how to tell her that it isn't, particularly. Because it seems to mean so much to her. She still sits next to me on the couch and expects me at sixteen years old to hold her hand while we watch TV, our fingers interlaced. When I get up and try to make a joke because I feel uncomfortable, she'll say something like "I guess I'm just not important to you," and her face will fall into that hangdog expression of disapproval. "I mean I never get to see you, Mick. Since you moved away."

There seem to be no good answers. I can either do something that makes me uncomfortable or feel guilty about refusing it. I used to think these invasions were just a kind of cluelessness about people, about boundaries, but I'm starting to think it's something else.

On the way through the mountainous corridor of the Cascade Mountains created by the Columbia River, driving down I-84, I tell her I'm in love with Laura.

"That's all just hormones," she says. "It's what kids do. They fall in love.

If you would've stayed in Oregon, you would have met a girl here and fallen in love. Laura sounds like a nice girl but there's nothing particularly special about her and there are plenty of nice girls in Oregon. You could've met one without leaving me."

The mountains are dusty and brown, dotted with huge boulders on either side of us. It's so different from the lush green Willamette Valley with all its rain and trees. There's a kind of silence in the car because I don't know how to respond, only that she's wrong about Laura, even though I know I owe her this trip, I owe her my gratitude for my life and for her forgiveness for running out on my job, which was to take care of her.

When we stop for gas, she points at a woman in a tight shoulder-less elastic rainbow top and says, "That woman is too fat for that top."

"Maybe she's comfortable," I say.

"What do you know now that you're so skinny from all that running?" She pats my stomach, sitting next to me in the car. "That's probably why you do it."

"No. I do it because I like to compete and I've always loved running."

"Yeah, but I bet it's a nice side effect," she says, shaking her head.

I remember all the times she told me I was fat growing up. It's strange because one afternoon as we were scanning old pictures in a photo album, when I saw pictures of myself in second, third, and fourth grade, all I saw was a healthy kid with a big overbite. If anything, the child in those photographs looked a little skinny, perhaps malnourished. I wonder why I thought he was fat, why, as a seven-year-old boy, I walked around thinking I'd done something bad and needed to suck my stomach in.

She tells me it's good that I run because the University of Oregon has a legendary track program and she can't wait for me to go there so I can be close. "Eugene is a cool town. There are lots of hippies." I don't know why she assumes I like hippies. That's her thing. I don't know why she thinks I wouldn't want to consider any other school. "Promise me you'll go there, so we can be close."

"Okay, I promise," I say, to end the conversation.

When we get to the town of Ontario a few miles from the Idaho border, Mom checks us into a motel and leaves for her meeting at the prison. She's gone all day. I turn on the TV and watch reruns of *I Love Lucy* until three o'clock when I lace up my sneakers and head out to the highway for a run.

The prison is new and they've repaved this part of the highway. The new tar stings my nostrils as I plod along with the sound of my muffled steps, jumping sideways when an eighteen-wheeler rumbles past.

It occurs to me that this is an odd birthday present, to be here alone at a prison in eastern Oregon. I think of my tenth birthday, when Paul had just left and it was still just Mom and me in the house on Breys Avenue. We still had the rabbits and it was slaughtering time and because we didn't want to "let all that good meat go to waste," we agreed I would do the slaughtering myself. I got out the white bucket and powdered the tree with lye. I picked up the twelve-week-old bunnies from their cages one by one and hit them on the skull with the iron rod, hanging them on the tree to cut off their heads. The hunting knife that Paul left in the barn was too big for me to hold properly, which made me clumsy with it. As I sawed at a rabbit's neck, I gouged a thick piece of skin right off the middle finger of my left hand. I grabbed it and shook it and tried to suck the blood but figured it would stop soon enough. But then, while slicing the tissue between fur and hide on another rabbit, I cut right through the webbing of my thumb, nearly piercing it completely. I didn't understand why it was so hard to handle the knife. I thought it would be easy to slaughter these rabbits on my birthday because nothing ever got to me, because I was the one who could do the necessary thing that had to be done. I began to blindly lash and thrust at the carcass until I sliced the skin at the top of my hand and yanked it away and realized there were thick streams of blood running down my fingers and wrist, falling into the bucket where it mingled with the rabbit blood and severed heads.

When I came inside, Mom was sitting at the big table in the kitchen with a carrot cake she'd made. "I made it without any sugar," she said, because sugar is a drug. "Happy birthday." She didn't notice the blood falling off my hand, running down my pants, dripping on the floor as I walked across the linoleum. I put the hand under the sink and let the water run over it then wrapped it in a napkin and sat down. She extended a hand for me to hold as we ate in silence. I told her I couldn't eat and hold her hand at the same time because my hand was cut and bleeding. She straightened up and said, "Why do you always have to be so difficult?"

I stop on the side of the highway there in the Oregon desert and look down at my left hand, flexing it in the sun. I can still see the scars. There are ten or so that pockmark the skin from those slaughtering sessions. I'm still breathing hard from my run as I look out over the reddish-brown hills leading to the prison. It's quiet except for the sound of the wind and my quick breath.

I think of my classmates in Los Angeles with their sixteenth birthday parties at restaurants or amusement parks, Derek's tenth birthday when we rented a VCR and watched *Airplane!,* staying up late to play truth or dare. It's never occurred to me that my birthday was anything other than a time I owe to her and that all this pretending, this role I know I must continually play, is costing me something. It's as if she doesn't even see me, only a person who is an extension of herself, one who left, who betrayed her, to whom she gave life and therefore a person from whom a life is owed.

It never occurred to me that other mothers don't feel this way.

For the first time in my life, right on the side of the highway near the Idaho border, it crosses my mind that she might not be completely sane. I think about the endless excuses I've made to myself and others about the world she constructs, the visions, the stories, the events which happened that she denied happened if they did not fit the narrative she created around herself—that these things might not just be the hallmark of a person who had a "hard life" but signs of real mental illness.

I remember the times I would describe her to people who would say something like "Sounds like she's a little off her rocker." They'd laugh a little and I'd go quiet as the words hung in the air awkwardly, waiting for me to confront them, to explain them or confirm them. But I couldn't. I was frozen. Because I was caught up in maintaining those narratives. I was a necessary piece of them, maybe the most necessary piece.

Laura and I once had a long discussion while wrapping Christmas presents. She wondered why I had to spend Christmas in Oregon, because she would miss me. I told her that I had to go to Oregon because a boy's job is to take care of his mother. She looked at me strangely. "What do you mean?"

"I mean. I'm the kid. I'm supposed to take care of her."

"Are you serious? I can't tell if you're serious."

"What?" I looked at her. She stared hard.

"Sweetheart, it's the exact opposite. You know that, right?"

I buried the thought like I bury all such thoughts.

There are just so many stories my mother tells herself, illusions she believes, understandings that pad her life, for the same reason they pad the walls at the state hospital: to take away the sharp edges. There are too many to keep track of: illusions about who Doug is and where Paul went. Illusions about my father, who "left her," about Bonnie, who "stole us," the woman Tony and I trust as much as anyone in the world. Events like Phil's beating or Paul's disappearance, which were ignored, as if they didn't even happen, as if they wouldn't affect us, as if they affected only her. It was never mentioned that we watched and screamed, that we had nightmares and anxiety, that we cried alone in the dark wondering what to do.

It's an odd feeling because I'm aware that I've always known it. It's just never been said out loud, in plain words: she lives in a different world, a different reality, one she has altered to make life easier.

There's an unreality to the feeling, a suspicion in my mind that I may be wrong or crazy for even thinking it. She is the one who has read all the books, attended all those self-help meetings. She's the expert on psychology, on *parenting*, firing off terms and theories, phrases and slogans like defensive blasts of a cannon guarding a fortress. She has armed herself to the teeth with psychology. And she uses that armament, those terms, like weapons to enforce a code, a strict set of understandings that we are required to have about this endless hall of mirrors: the one she's created with all the distorted reflections of what it means to be a "son," a "mother," a "friend," a "F-A-M-I-L-Y."

Our car trips are usually filled with long, chatty, wandering conversations. But for the first time, heading home from that hot dusty highway, we drive all the way across the state in silence.

An uneasy feeling follows me around all summer—between my daily runs, long phone calls with Laura in L.A., wasting time with Jake, and my fast-food job at the Oregon State Fair—the sense that people can hide entire journeys, entire lives behind a lie. As if reality is just an argument you can have with the world. Is the truth up for discussion? And if it is, what else is a lie?

Over time it's impossible to face all those delusions. Once you become lost in them—after thousands of days of denial—you simply can't confront the truth anymore, because you no longer know it. So you become a victim of your own dishonesty. I wonder if that's how it went with Mom.

How do you face a lie that big?

I fall asleep in the restless late-summer heat, closing my eyes to see the highway stretched out in front of me, winding through pastures and empty fields as it disappears over the horizon to some nameless destination. I'm overcome by the feeling that this is where we belong, we weirdos and orphans: out on empty highways among the pines and weary travelers, the men in their lipstick keeping us company as they sing their sad songs on the radio.

CHAPTER 34

MY DAD,
THE EX-CON

There is a distance growing between Dad and me. I know he's proud but I can feel his concern about how important college has become. There is a road I've been walking down, but I'm not sure yet if this new road is the detour or the main path, like at any minute it might just turn and I'll be back in that pit, the one that ends in rehab or prison. And Dad, he never finished eighth grade. Tony never got past ninth grade. Uncle Pete and Uncle Donny both dropped out of high school and ended up doing time. It's hard not to feel like no matter what I do, this is where I will end up. So I'm vigilant. I study long hours. I keep track of deadlines. And I wonder if Dad is now worried that trying to be the exception to the rule established by the men in our family is a kind of defiance, a way of saying, *You and I are not alike and we never will be.* And maybe it is.

When he was my age, he was running wild through the streets of San Diego, already a thief, already married, already a father, already a step in front of the law with his stolen credit card numbers, cars, drugs. I know he doesn't want this life for me but I can tell he's worried he's going to lose me to something else, an institution, an education, an affectation that will cost him a son.

A twelfth-grade headbanger named Greg Bauer has decided he doesn't like my "faggy" hair or my "faggy" clothes. The hair is long in front now, hanging down past my chin and my clothes consist of a pair of black twelve-hole Doc Martens boots, a black bomber jacket, and a David Bowie T-shirt. Every day at lunch or while prowling the hallways between classes, he will yell something over his shoulder like "I'm gonna fuckin' kill that little faggot."

He is six feet one with long black hair, steel-toed boots and a series of heavy metal rings on his right hand, including an eagle with spiked claws and a piece of flat steel through which he has driven the sharpened point of a box nail.

Every morning for months I walk to school with dread, wondering when I am going to be plucked from anonymity and put on display in front of my girlfriend, in front of the whole school, as the "little bitch" that Greg Bauer insists I am.

I don't know what to do about it, so I tell Dad. At first I think maybe he'll react the way the staid suburban fathers of my peers might, the ones who help them with their homework and give them advice about college applications. Dad knows more about 1957 Chevys than the UC system and it sometimes feels like this puts me at a disadvantage. I know that if Dad was like these men, he would call the principal or maybe Greg Bauer's parents to discuss the matter.

Instead, he removes his reading glasses very seriously, looks up from his racing form and says, "Well, you know, you're gonna have to kick his ass."

The idea floats in the air between us for a moment, suspended by its absurdity. At five feet seven, all of 128 pounds of essay-writing cross-country runner, it is not the answer I was expecting.

He sees the doubt on my face. "You *can* kick his ass, you know. Just because you're smaller don't mean shit."

Ten minutes later I am standing in the driveway in front of the house while Dad holds a pillow for me to punch, offering me instructions on how to fight, like a heavyweight boxer. "Keep your elbows in. Stay balanced. You want to put your entire body weight into the two inches at the front of your fist. Block first. Always lead with your left so you can block, then come over with a big right hand." I hit the pillow. "All you need is a good right cross. Or a quick strike to the windpipe, or the knee, or the nuts."

Like the good student I am, I stop to take notes in the notebook I've brought outside: *Block first. Punch throat. Kick groin.*

"There's no such thing as a clean street fight. Once you're in a fight, win."

"But is that fair?"

"Fuck fair. Fair doesn't matter. It's already violent. Be the *most* violent."

There are tricks he learned in prison, distractions and deflections and quick ways of gaining an advantage. He explains these things the way an astronomer might explain the properties of gravity to his son: calmly, with a commitment to getting the details right.

"If he walks up to you, spit in his face. When he goes to wipe it off, punch him in the throat with the side of your fist." He shows me how to hold my hand to aim for the wind box.

"If you have a stack of books in your hands, just walk up to him and toss them in the air. He'll grab 'em. That's just instinct. And in that second when his guard is down, you can break his nose."

We grab a couple books and I practice aiming for Dad's big Italian schnoz.

"You're getting it. The other thing you want to do is get yourself a roll of pennies. Wrap some tape around it and hold it in your right hand. It'll make your punch heavier and keep you from breaking your knuckles." He winks at me.

"Whatever you do, don't get stuck talking shit in some kind of rooster fight. He's bigger, so that helps him. Just catch him off guard and knock him on his ass."

I find an old roll of nickels in my desk drawer and wrap them in masking tape. I stay up late listening to Jane's Addiction, picturing the fight, trying to contain my fear.

I can hardly feel my feet beneath me as I walk to school with headphones on. A thousand scenarios run through my head, most of which end with me in the hospital. The worst ones don't even involve physical pain. It's the idea of being humiliated that really scares me, that I will be exposed for being precisely the "pussy" he says I am. That I am not Dad. I am not the battle-hardened ex-con who spent years in prison. I am the sensitive one, the cross-country runner, the president of two clubs, the writer whose stories go on the fridge, the one with a "bright future" even if beneath that there is a sense that none of it can last, that I will be discovered for the fraud I am, for the scared-shitless ball of anxiety, shame, nightmares and confusion I hide with all my might.

When I finally see Greg Bauer, leaning against a table with his cronies in trench coats in the cafeteria, slouching carelessly with a cocky smile, he yells out, "I'm gonna fuckin' kick that dude's ass."

I'm scared but I have the roll of nickels in my pocket and Dad in my ear and those banging drums from "Three Days" by Jane's Addiction echoing through my head and without thinking, I hear myself scream, "You're not gonna do shit!"

He jumps up, walking toward me in rooster fashion, chin forward, chest puffed. There is a commotion, the kind of din that happens whenever there is a fight at school as people start to gather, and I hear someone yell, "Take it upstairs! Too many teachers down here!" Greg Bauer gives me a hateful look as he turns slowly to walk up the stairs with the crowd of students. I follow.

When I emerge from the top of the concrete stairs, I see a large crowd of perhaps a hundred people gathered on the Senior Lawn in a circle. Standing at the center of the circle with his fists up and his chin down, hunched over with the sharpened rings on his fingers and his steel-tipped motorcycle boots, is Greg Bauer.

I put my head down and move straight toward him, squeezing the roll of nickels in my fist. As I approach him, I hear him say, "What's up then—"

But before he can get the words out, before I can think and slink away like I've done a hundred times, before the fear can paralyze me and tell me what a pussy I know I am in my heart, I gather all the rage and fear and anxiety, every ounce of my skinny frame, rock forward on my heels, and punch him as hard as I can, flat-fuck in the jaw.

"Deeeeeeeeeaaaaaaaaaaaaamn!" I hear a chorus of voices around me.

I square up, raise my fists and scream, "Fuck you!" as loud as I can, just as Dad told me to.

Then something strange happens. Something unexpected. I stop thinking and feel myself transform, as if no other thing exists in the world, as if there are no consequences, no yesterday and no tomorrow, as if all the taunts and slights and months of fear have, like a ball of gasoline, suddenly ignited into screaming, blind, pure, unadulterated rage.

I hear the words falling out of my mouth: *fucking-loser-piece-of-shit-motherfucking-dickhead-asshole-bitch-you-want-to-fucking-go-let's-go-I-will-fucking-kill-you.* It feels like speaking in tongues, like my mouth is disconnected from my mind, which is floating above, watching.

He throws a halfhearted jab and I dodge left—it was in the notes, after all—then follow with a right cross to his nose. I hear a crunch. He looks stunned. I feel myself bouncing but I don't really know why. There's no plan. Only the fight, the fist, his face, my desire to inflict harm, to hurt him, to destroy him, to destroy something in myself.

I wonder if this is how Dad felt in jail. That all the tough-guy talk I grew up with, the volume of his voice, the stories of his fighting prowess and that big, masculine exterior were just a shield for a fear. I wonder if this makes us the same. If we could switch places and he could be the straight-A student and I could be the ex-con.

Greg Bauer kicks me in the leg and I feel the steel tip of the boot sink into my shin, which starts to bleed. He swings at me with the box nail ring and I know I must avoid it, to keep the point of that nail away from my face. I dodge and pounce and scream and hit him again and again in the eye, the nose, the jaw, the throat.

There's a calmness in the center of my head. Everything is moving in slow motion, like I'm watching it unfold on television, the camera panning through the faces of my classmates as they stare at me: Monica Zuniga, tall and pretty with her thick black hair. She looks at me like she is confused, a little disgusted. Charles King from the track team in his loose white T-shirt, holding his fists low in front of himself as he screams. Drew, puzzled and curious, like he's staring at someone he doesn't know.

By the time we are broken up by the girls' soccer coach, Greg Bauer's face is covered in blood. There are jagged red streams flowing from his left eye, his swollen nostrils, the cut at the corner of his mouth. He looks tired as he walks toward a bench to sit. The frenzy of onlookers has turned to wild abandon, a kind of David-beats-Goliath glee in the air as I hear guys from the track team running down the hallway, jumping and yelling, "White boy from the crew fucked shit up!"

I retreat to a corner, breathing hard as I sit down on the steps. I can't stop trembling. I put my head between my knees and soon feel Laura sit down quietly next to me, draping herself over my back. I start to cry. I don't want to. But there is no way to hide it. It's all living outside me now.

This face is a lie. This life is a lie. I want to go home. I want to talk to Dad, to tell him I understand. There is something terrible about all of this. A man who lives in us both, to compensate for the fear. He stands guard over a weakness, a scared naked child, telling him not to show himself, that he is too weak, too pathetic, too fragile.

Is this, when you get right down to it, what it means to be a man?

Laura keeps saying, "It's okay, babe. It's over. It's okay."

I hear voices: "Why's he crying? What's wrong with him? He *won*."

I can't move. I wish I could. I am empty and I don't know what is happening and I just think, *It's a hard thing to have to know.*

When I get home from track practice, Dad is home as he is every day since he quit his job so he could be home with me while Bonnie works. I tell him about the fear and the fight, how I blocked and counterpunched, how I followed his instructions and won.

He takes it all in with that tan, weathered face of his, a curious look in his eye, clarifying details, asking for specifics. I know he wanted to protect me. I know he's happy for me, but there is something else. I'm surprised to see it, the kind of thing you can only spot if you've spent thousands of hours together. It's in the pauses, the way I can see him searching me for something between sentences. Sadness. I realize I feel it too: this mixture of pride and sadness as we see each other as men for the first time and realize how alike we are.

There was a golden field of chaparral behind the School at the Tomales Bay compound in Synanon. When we were still very small, we would run through it with our shaved heads, unaware of the world beyond the big road, stopping to dig for worms or chase jackrabbits when they stuck their faces up from their burrows. We had these experiences alone or in small groups. We missed our parents, who came and went from our lives like a certain shape of the moon, familiar and faraway at once. Some days when Dad would come to see us, I could feel my heart pound at the sound of his Harley in the driveway. I'd run toward him, seeing the mustached smile as he got off the bike and lifted my brother and me to tickle our bellies and kiss our cheeks. He was not so many years out of prison then, not so many years from the needle and the couch and all that violence. But his future was in front of him and his boys were with him and I know it steadied him because it steadied me too, to be so close, to feel this connection like we are branches of the same tree joined at the trunk, to sense his warmth, an affection I interpreted as a promise: that he would give whatever he had to give to us, even if he didn't have much to give. I spent years judging him for that deficit: for his flaws and errors, his limitations, cataloging all the ways I vowed to never turn out like him.

But something changed. The resentment is gone and in its place is a simple understanding. I don't want him to be like my friends' fathers with their degrees, their clean records, their *pressure,* and I know—as much as I know anything in the world—that this flawed, angry, funny, wise and affectionate man is on my side no matter where I go or what I do.

It's the greatest gift anyone has ever given me.

CHAPTER 35
THE LUCKY ONE

Dad used to worry I would get stuck-up. It's nothing he wants to admit. If Bonnie holds up a report card and says, "Wow. Just, wow. Where did all these As come from?" Dad will smile too. He'll play along. But he didn't always feel this way. Before I started getting good grades, he used to say educated people were mostly full of shit. "Some guys think they know everything because they got some fucking degree. Meanwhile, they got their heads up their asses and they can't even change a flat." I used to hear this all the time. "Why do you want to go to college so badly? We didn't go and we turned out fine." I'd say, because I want to learn new ideas and meet new people even though secretly I knew it was because I wanted to be a thousand miles from a prison yard and an AA meeting.

But he doesn't say those things anymore. When I'm up late studying, he brings me a snack and says he's proud of the work I'm doing, that it takes "heart." He lingers a minute in the doorway while I flip through my calculus textbook.

He likes to look through the brochures I've collected for the colleges I've visited. UC Santa Barbara with its beautiful campus near the ocean. UC Berkeley with its history, its intensity. Stanford with its massive white satellite dish sitting on a hill above its Romanesque architecture housing endless Nobel laureates. "This don't look half-bad," he says, turning the pages of the brochure while we watch a game in the living room. "You really got a shot at this stuff, huh?"

"I think so. We'll see."

Maybe it's because he's sick. He was feeling tired and nauseated for months, so he went to the doctor for blood tests. When they came back, the doctor said he had hepatitis C. He isn't sure how he got it, whether from a blood transfusion or from sharing dirty needles in prison. He needs to take interferon, which causes severe flu symptoms. He's weak and he can't sleep. He has to shoot the stuff into his stomach with big needles wrapped in yellow plastic that he keeps in the fridge next to the eggs. It gives him diarrhea and he's never hungry, so he loses weight. When he takes a shot, he winces in pain and he looks at me with a dark laugh. "Fucked-up, right?" I laugh too because the man can find a joke in anything. *What is a son? What is a father? What are we to each other now?* He's grown weaker and I've grown stronger and we see each other and neither one of us is the person we thought we were.

Hepatitis C causes cirrhosis of the liver, which is the same thing Grandma Frieda has now. It eats the liver bit by bit until there is nothing left but a wad of scar tissue. Dad quit drinking immediately because the liver can no longer process alcohol and alcohol only makes it worse. But Grandma didn't quit. Mom says she just sits in her chair with her mountain of pills, the highball glass of scotch sweating beads of water on the tray next to her. Mom is worried because Grandpa's back cancer is much worse now and it seems like he can't take care of her much longer.

Dad is trying his best to take care of himself. Doing his exercise every morning, eating healthy food, wrapping himself in a blanket as he sits in the empty stands at my track meets to root for me when I run the mile.

"Not bad," he says, closing the college brochures, putting down his reading glasses as he lowers the volume on the game. "I mean, shit, if you became a lawyer, you could make your whole living just defending the family."

I know he's worried about Tony. We all are. He's drinking again. He and Tiffany split up and three months later he was told that she was back out on the street using drugs. When the baby wasn't with Tony, she would leave him with people for weeks at a time. Sometimes it would be a friendly couple with children but sometimes it was strangers she hardly knew. One of them fed him nothing but corn syrup from a bottle which ruined his little teeth, making them brown and yellow with rot.

One of the people called Child Protective Services and the baby became a ward of the state. Mom intervened so that he wouldn't end up in foster care. But that didn't last long and eventually the baby ended up back with Tony, in a tiny apartment at the edge of town. Jake and Tony have become friends and Jake says that when he visits him, there are beer cans everywhere and a small child in diapers walking around while his father drinks on the couch.

Tiffany has disappeared. Nobody knows where she is. Jake said he heard a rumor that she has a new man and all they do is "party." It's a strange word to describe something that causes so much sadness.

When I talk to Tony, he seems distant, broken. He says, "I'm proud of you, little bro. You go make a mark on the world. Tell 'em where you came from." I can hear the sadness in his voice, like he's given up or just doesn't know what to do. It seems like too much for one person, to have a child and an addiction and the memory of all that time alone. "I tell everyone about you. My little brother's gonna be a brain surgeon or an astronaut or some shit. I believe in you, Mick. Seriously, it's like the only thing I do believe in."

ON THE DAY I receive my acceptance letter to Stanford University, Dad is the only one home. He's waiting for me in the garage with the radio on, working on his truck. "A packet came for you," he says with a smile. "You might want to check it out." There is a big white envelope sitting on the shop table next to the jigsaw. I tear it open, letting the paper fall to the floor where Dad has his tools laid out—a socket set, some pliers, Allen wrenches, glass jars filled with bolts and nuts. The letter on top says, "Congratulations! It is with great pleasure that I offer you admission into Stanford University." Before I can read another word, before I review the glossy brochures with pictures of students sitting in those Romanesque archways, before I review the financial aid scholarship I am offered that covers my tuition and housing and books, before any of it, I throw my arms around Dad's neck and we both start to cry.

I'm not sure if it's joy or sadness. It feels like something achieved but also something survived. Something found, maybe, a strength together that we did not have apart. I smell the Old Spice on his neck, feel his thick gold necklace against my head. I know he quit his job for me after the motorcycle accident. For this. I know Bonnie has worked to support us, for this. So it feels like it's ours. I let out a scream and Dad pumps his fist and we're jumping up and down with our arms around each other's shoulders. "You did this," he says. I run into the house to call Mom but she's gone so I leave a message that I have big news and go out to the front lawn to yell for the whole neighborhood to hear.

When I return to the garage, Dad is sitting on the floor with his elbows on his knees, an arm on the front fender of the Chevy, his head down, a hand over his eyes. I ask him what's wrong. He shakes his head and waves me away, a painful smile on his face. It's just the two of us there among the oil-stained rags and balled-up shop towels, the neat drawers of his red Craftsman toolbox. I know what he's thinking because I'm thinking it too.

We're still alive, you and me. Them sonsabitches ain't buried us yet.

TWO HOURS LATER Mom calls to tell me Grandma Frieda is dead. I can hear the tears through the phone as she explains that her mother's liver finally gave out, that despite the advanced cirrhosis she never stopped drinking until four days ago, when she quit cold turkey and the shock killed her.

I tell her I'm sorry and I love her and it's going to be okay. I listen quietly while she sobs. "I couldn't be close to her," she says. "She was so hard on me. But it's still difficult to lose my mom."

I think about the Dutch family that moved to America, the father who fought in a war for two countries, the mother who sat and drank every day, the three children, the oldest of whom was raised by nannies and grew up playing alone in the bombed-out craters of a war.

"So what's your big news?"

"Oh, well. I don't know if now's the time."

"No, tell me. I could use some good news."

"Well, I got into Stanford, Mom. A scholarship and everything. I can't believe it."

The line goes quiet and I wonder briefly if we lost the connection. "You there? Did you hear what I said?"

"So you're not going to go to the University of Oregon? To Eugene, like we talked about?"

"Mom, I got a scholarship to Stanford."

"But you promised me. This is going to be a very hard year for me. I was really excited you were going to be close."

I tell her I'm sorry. I tell her we'll talk. I tell her I feel bad for Grandpa and sad about Grandma. I tell her I love her and I have to go.

We hang up and I go for a run along the bike path. The whitecaps dot the water beyond the break of Dockweiler State Beach with its raised sand dunes fifteen feet high. I can hear my footsteps on the smooth concrete, see my shadow on the dunes. The excitement I felt has died down and in its place is a new thought, a lonely one.

I am the lucky one. I always was. I know they're all proud of me but there's something else, a feeling like a prisoner who has escaped, who has left others behind.

I try to remember a time before all this crisis. But when was that? What was there before? Did we ever sit quietly, eyes closed in a warm field untroubled by all these ghosts?

I already know the answer. And yet.

You can pretend the ghosts don't haunt you. But they do.

So it's bittersweet, the feeling as I run alone on the path. Grandma is dead, Grandpa is dying, Paul is dead (or in a gutter somewhere), Mom is devastated, Dad is sick, Tiffany is on the street again, Tony is working construction in the rain in Salem to support a child he is too young and too drunk to care for . . .

And me, I get to go to college.

HOLLYWOOD
PARK

*And now that you don't have to be perfect, you
can be good.*

—JOHN STEINBECK, EAST OF EDEN

CHAPTER 36

THE DREAM

All these kids are running heedlessly across the grass in the brilliant California sunshine, oblivious to the cars and golf carts, to time itself, as if frozen in a romantic tableau of cardinal reds and verdant greens, the ageless marriage of new blood and old money. Some wear visors, some wear sunglasses, some with short-cropped hair, some with ponytails and tie-dyed shirts retrieving Frisbees or blankets with lanky, unhurried strides. They look healthy. Tan. Well insured. They're all smiling. This is why they're here, all of them. For the Dream.

The Dream of Stanford University, the image chiseled in stone across the marble-block minds of all incoming students and scholars, is the facade at the front of campus, the picturesque scene sitting at the end of Palm Drive: a Romanesque quad with big earth-orange bricks like a modern-day Arch of Titus, the hundred-foot mosaic atop the gable of Memorial Church welcoming the righteous into the kingdom of heaven, the silhouette of the massive white satellite dish pointed skyward on the hills in the background. The stunning effect upon observers of this tableau is that here is a place with one foot rooted in the past, an eye toward the possibility of the future, and—right smack in the center of it all—the enthusiastic endorsement of God himself.

This is the precise dream I have in mind as Dad, Bonnie and I cruise the mile-long drive beneath the hundred-foot palm trees that guard the Stanford campus. Bonnie keeps saying how excited she is for me to have this opportunity. We are impressed by the impact, the row of palms that lead to the grass oval at the threshold of the Dream.

Dad is more direct, staring out at all that perfect academic art direction. "Man, this place is *not* fucking around."

It's an easy dream to get lost in. This shining beacon on a sunny California hill overflowing with optimism, crushing all doubt with confidence of its own rightness. The physics tank, the football stadium, Hoover Tower, Lake Lagunita, the golf course, Maples Pavilion, the Rodin Sculpture Garden, the hospital, the linear accelerator, the mausoleum, the spectacle at the front of campus, the rolling hills behind it—it's impossible not to get caught up in the feeling that you have arrived at the fount of wisdom, the place where you will finally achieve the great thing for which you have spent your life preparing. What else could possibly lie behind that perfect facade?

THE FIRST LUNCH of freshman orientation is divided between the different advocacy groups on campus. It is a kind of introduction to the diversity of college life. There is the Black Student Union Lunch, the Asian/Pacific Islander Lunch, the MEChA (Movimiento Estudiantil Chicanx de Aztlán) Lunch, the Native American Cultural Center Lunch, and then there is lunch. It may as well be called White Lunch. That's where I go. White Lunch.

The cafeteria at Roble Hall, my perfectly art-directed dream of a dorm, covered in ivy and everything, is a smorgasbord of game hats, flannels fraying at the seams, hiking gear, Gap jeans, well-pressed khakis, golf shirts, Bermuda shorts, ponytails and mock turtlenecks. I feel out of place in my twelve-hole Docs and bomber jacket. I've never seen so many white people. Tall ones and short ones and fat ones and skinny ones, ones who think they're cool and ones who have clearly given up. I'm used to being an acceptably white misfit in an 80 percent black public school in Los Angeles. I loved it there. It felt like a privilege to go to school among people who took Black History Month seriously, to feel a part of the struggle, that kinship with Richard Wright, to receive the warmth of the upright black parents from the track team with their prayers for me and pride in their children's achievements. The fashion shows, the talent shows, the barbecues, the dances, the gospel, the R&B and hip-hop, the feeling that outside our walls was a mostly white, mostly hostile society against which we must arm ourselves with powerful ideas. I felt that way too. I liked the snaps on the bus on the way home from track meets when someone would suddenly stand and say, "Jermaine mama so old, she knew the Dead Sea when it was still sick." It made me less ashamed that my father had been in prison, that we'd been raised on food stamps, that few men in my family ever graduated from high school. That was a familiar story at Westchester High. I liked the feeling of traveling this road upward with friends named Jabari and Tremayne and Tamika. I wasn't a code switcher like some of the white kids who adopted all things black in order to fit in. But it never once crossed my mind to feel different because I'd been poor white trash. I felt protected, if not by black culture itself, then by those kind black parents and my serious black classmates who wanted the same things I did. To get out. To move up. Some of their dads were in prison too.

So I can't help but wonder what I have in common with these kids, these East Coast prep school kids at White Lunch with their inside jokes and Gamecock hats. What are we supposed to talk about? Mayonnaise? The Gap?

I feel sized up. Measured. And I quickly learn, to my surprise and embarrassment, that in the eyes of my mostly white, mostly upper-class peers something in me is *lacking*. I just don't get the jokes. I just don't know what to say. Their questions are a kind of quiz I fail over and over again. In the lunches, the get-to-know-you dorm meetings, the late-night rap sessions, when people ask, "Where are you from?" or "Where were you born?" or "What do your parents do?" If I say "my dad managed a mechanic shop" or "well, I was born in a commune that became a cult called Synanon," I receive a patronizing, sympathetic look and the more I impugn myself for being different, for being weird, for having been brushed by negative forces outside my control—history or addiction or poverty—I see an expression form on their genteel faces, a kind of turned-up, barely hidden disgust, exactly as if I'd just cut a fart.

It's pity for the fact that I simply do not know the words I am supposed to say, the positive, humble, inspiring, outwardly self-effacing but lightly self-aggrandizing words about future plans and past achievements and guarded self-regard that shows how much I fit the mold of this shiny society on a hill, this Dream blessed by God himself with a foot in the past and an eye to the future.

I quickly learn to lie. I don't want their pity. I hear myself saying, "Shut the fuck up," in my own head as I mention Chino state prison or Tomales Bay or the food bank at the church.

It's not that I can't fit in. It's that I can fit in only by lying. By hiding. By pretending to be someone who knows how to answer each question correctly. During freshman orientation, as the dorm makes trips to football games or a Frisbee golf tournament or some ridiculous frat party at the edge of campus where the once-awkward upwardly mobile overachievers of America lean tenuously on walls nursing half-empty red Solo cups of stale beer from the keg, I learn to lean hard on AP test scores, the honors service club I was president of, the YMCA Youth and Government club in which I was Speaker of the Assembly, I learn to mention that my mother went to Berkeley (*don't mention tear gas or shaved heads or Thatasshole Reagan*), that my grandparents live nearby (*don't mention Grandma died of cirrhosis*), that I was L.A. city champion in the mile (*don't mention the long days running through the wooded park behind Englewood Elementary after my stepfather died, or didn't*). And definitely, do not mention, no matter what you do or how inviting the conversation seems to be for confession, the growing suspicion in the back of your mind that your mother may have a tenuous hold on reality.

I can make a new face to hold to the world, a new mask to hide behind.

The only place I feel comfortable is at the twice-a-day workouts with the track team. I spent the summer training among the oil derricks in the dusty hot hills just west of Inglewood. Ten miles every day. I was never recruited by the school, but I had a notion I could "walk on" to the team if I trained hard enough, which I did after meeting the coach and running a few workouts with the team on the golf course. It's a relief to be grounded in something so simple. Sweat and heavy breath, the ache in my belly and the burn in my lungs.

There is an easy camaraderie among people sharing such grueling daily toil—at this point it's twelve miles a day—and distance runners are an unassuming group. There are so many great athletes. I'm the only freshman who is not a state champion, the only one who runs in boxers and basketball shorts because I would've never dared to wear those tiny silk running shorts on the football field of Westchester High. They adopt me, like a mascot, affectionately referring to me as a "hack," as if taking pride in my awkward clothes and awkward stride, my homemade workouts pulled from old running books (or thin air) because we did not have a cross-country coach. It fades over time. Like a pack of horses, there's a bodily closeness that erases our differences as we focus on the Task at Hand. I tuck into the back of the pack and keep my head down, content to simply shut up and run.

A MONTH INTO freshman year, I get a call from Mom telling me that Grandpa Frank's back cancer has metastasized in his lungs and brain and there isn't much time left. She flies down and picks me up in front of my dorm in a rental car and we drive to a hospital in Los Gatos. I wonder why Doug didn't come.

There's a light dusting of white stubble on Grandpa Frank's sunken face as he lies in the hospital bed. He still looks somehow handsome, like a slightly deflated version of the proud and gentle man I've known since that day we left Synanon.

Mom and I sit next to him in chairs trying to tell him we're here as he nods in and out of consciousness, dizzy from the morphine. It's been six months since Grandma Frieda died. He's been fighting the cancer for ten years as it slowly reduced his once powerful back to the twisted, painful relic it has become. We thought he might beat it because he lived with it for so long. Like he was impervious to it. There was something miraculous about his battle. But it's as if Grandma's death was a mortal blow, like losing his reason for fighting.

We hold vigil for a week. In between classes and trips to the administrative office to get my work-study requirements for my financial aid scholarship, Mom arrives, tears in her eyes, a defeated expression on her face as we drive the twenty miles to the hospital in relative silence. Everyone in the family knows Grandpa is a good man with his short mustache and permanent smile, his easy jokes, his commitment to his family, to two countries, to his recently deceased wife, whom he tended the way a parent nurses a sick child.

I wear a medal he won in track and field in Holland in 1932 that he sent me when I got into Stanford. It hangs from a leather string tied around my neck. I feel it bounce against my chest when I run, reminding me of him. I feel a connection to him, hear his voice in my head sometimes when I think about the future. I've always felt such a pride to be his grandson. He's still got those strong hands. I can feel their strength as he grips mine in the bed. He's somewhat lucid when Mom leaves me with him before we go to dinner one night. His head is shaking and his mouth trembling and I can see him searching for words. I tell him I love him and I'm glad I knew him and I thank him for taking care of everyone. I want so badly to know what to do, how he made his way through this impossible, confusing world.

His lips quiver as he raises his head and stares at me, trying to form the words, his eyes glassy and blue. "Chin up," is all he says. I kiss his fist and he gives my hand a pump, like we've made a sacred agreement.

Two days later we arrive to find a kindly nurse who tells us he passed. Mom collapses on the chair in the visitors' lobby to cry and I put an arm around her shoulder to comfort her. It seems unfair to lose so much so quickly and I can't help but feel for her. He was a good man, a kind man, something like solid ground in a world of so much quicksand.

When she drops me off on campus, the Dream is still there, unaffected by sorrow. The church, the Roman arches, the satellite dish in the distance. I miss my grandfather already. The world seems emptier somehow and I have no place to find comfort. Laura and I broke up the day she left for UCSD, nearly four years to the day since I asked her to be my girlfriend standing next to her locker. It quickly felt like a mistake but when I called her three weeks later to win her back, she told me she had a new boyfriend and was in love. She said she got tired of all of my inconsistency, all the times I broke up with her then ran back to her. I felt my heart fall out of my chest and I carry with me an alarming desperation over it. I miss Dad and Bonnie with their jokes and easy love for me. I miss Drew and Jake and Morrissey and Bowie, the sense that it is enough to simply feel weird or fucked-up, to reject all this crushing optimism.

There's a party at Roble Hall, a din of cheesy pop music in the common area as I walk silently past to lace up my running shoes, put on my headphones—*Disintegration* by the Cure—and disappear into the dark, dark night.

THREE MONTHS LATER Mom calls to tell me Doug left her for another woman. She is sobbing. Inconsolable. It's been only three months since her second parent died, three months spent in grief and sorrow.

Even I am surprised at what a stunning betrayal it is. It was time for honesty, he told her. He just couldn't lie anymore. So he confessed to the mistress, the affair he had throughout their entire seven years of marriage.

There's a panic in her voice, a kind of hyperventilating staccato as she tries to process the thoughts in real time. I don't know what to tell her. It seems like a dirty trick, like all that doe-eyed talk of "someone to grow old with" was meant for precisely a time like this. And after years of holding that idea in front of her like a carrot, making her tolerate his inconsistency, his weird habits and weird rules about food, he simply left in the night when she needed him most. I think about his angry look when his knees pressed my arms into the ground, the disgust, the hatred in his eyes as he pulled his hand back and punched me in the face.

I don't know how to comfort her. I have the old feeling, the sense that I can feel her loss so perfectly, her pain and devastation. I croak out the words "It'll be okay," though I'm not really sure if that's true.

She tells me I drove him away by calling him a "pussy," by not accepting him as a father figure, that I never liked him and he knew it and that made him leave her.

I don't have the heart to fight her, to tell her that I moved out seven years ago, that he left her four different times before they ever even got married. There are sobs and gasps at the other end of the line and it seems cruel to deny her her reasoning. Not now. So I just listen and tell her I'm sorry and she can call me anytime, that it's not fair, that I will always be there for her, whatever that means.

SCHOOL IS A blur. On top of Organic Chemistry, Physics for Engineers, Integral Calculus, and all the Dante, Nietzsche, Plato, and other classics all Stanford freshmen must read to become educated people in the world, there is a three-mile morning run, weights, an eight- to ten-mile afternoon workout on the track, and an hour of rehab in the training center on the arthritic knee for which I take eighteen hundred milligrams of ibuprofen a day. There's no time to play guitar or sing songs, but I've managed through my daily workouts to become the fastest freshman in the Pac-10, the third fastest in the nation at the ten-thousand-meter run. I keep thinking I can just put it all into my running, that if I train hard enough, nothing will matter, if I can win a national title or make an Olympic team someday, all this will be but a minor hiccup on a road out, a road to Something Great.

I lie alone on the grass after long interval workouts, staring up at the sky wondering if I can just turn my body into stardust, grateful for the exhaustion, to turn the anxiety into motion, to have something to *do* with it.

On a quiet morning run, while preparing for Junior Nationals, a couple weeks after Pac-10 Championships, where I placed sixth, nestled in at the back of the pack, I feel a sudden sharp pain in my knee, as if someone fired a nail beneath my kneecap. I pull up short thinking it's a minor pain, the kind of thing that arrives suddenly and just as suddenly disappears. I try to walk it off. But each time I try to jog it out or ignore it, the pain returns, an electric shock going up my leg. I limp back to the field house.

The trainer advises me to take a week off, which I do, sweaty and anxious and roiling with nowhere to put it all. It feels like being trapped with all that energy, that fuel to run twelve to fifteen miles a day, a claustrophobic feeling, all fumes and nerves.

I try to run after a week off, but the pain is still there. After an X-ray and an MRI, the sports specialist at Stanford Medical Center tells me my season is done, that the cartilage in my knee is worn down from the awkward stride created by my flat left foot. There is a palpable resignation in his voice. "Surgery is rarely successful on distance runners. The slightest problem gets magnified by all the miles." He gives me a summer rehab schedule of physical therapy, weights, and swim workouts, but I know my running career is probably over.

I can't sleep. My appetite is gone. I have trouble focusing. It feels like my heart is going to leap out of my chest on each one of its thirty-eight beats per minute through a body whittled down to 4 percent body fat. I just want to run. I would trade twenty years of life for another year of training. That is my bargain. My way out. To become more horse than rider.

So I'm not prepared when I get the call. I'm not ready for it. I'm stretching in my dorm room when the phone rings and a polite woman asks me my name and explains she's calling to tell me my mother has checked herself into their facility. I'm not prepared for the polite voice, the instructions, the details about the treatment facility where she will be staying for the foreseeable future.

She is safe and unable to harm herself. She is in excellent care. She is going to undergo treatment and it's important that my brother and I visit her soon because she will need our support. There are so many questions: Is this some kind of nervous breakdown? Is she in a loony bin? Has she finally just *lost* it?

I'm simply not prepared.

There is a particular week for family visits, the voice tells me, and we should mark the week on our calendars because it's "an important part of her recovery." She needs to know that we support her, that her needs are important, that her feelings are real, that her struggles, her pain, her life are important to us, that we are thinking about her and ready to take care of her in whatever way she needs, because she's been through so much.

I hang up the phone and try to feel bad. I know I'm supposed to. I know she's severely depressed and in need of more from me. I know I'm supposed to take care of her, that this is what is required of the son she raised. But I don't know why she's going somewhere so far away. I don't know what led up to it. I only know that every time I think of the trip I'm supposed to take to the treatment facility in Arizona, or of the abusive man she married, or of the million ways in which I must pretend to be the person she wants me to be, I don't feel anything but the sense of an on-coming storm. I can't sleep. I can't study. I can hardly focus my eyes from the exhaustion most days. And I'm suddenly so angry I could scream.

THE MAN HAD on a blue shirt. He had a black beard. He wore small wire-frame glasses. He had a soft face, a kind face. He was sitting in the circle of family members who'd come to watch the "family share." His job, like everyone else's in the group, was to reflect upon what he'd heard when the two people had finished speaking to each other while sitting in the two wooden chairs placed three feet apart in the center of the circle. Our turn came and I spoke to Mom for about ten minutes. I don't remember exactly what I said. I tried to be honest, truly honest about how inconse-quential I felt as a child, how she did not show interest in my well-being, that my life was not my own, that my body was not my own, that I was made to do things I did not want to do, to play a role I did not want to play, that it was always clear to me that my needs weren't important, whether those needs were for sympathy or love or food or basic safety, I always felt like my only job was to take care of her and beyond that to go on and do something in the world that would reflect well on her. It was time now to listen to people "say what they heard" in my statement. An old man said, "It's time to cut the apron strings, lady." A woman said, "It sounds like your son feels overwhelmed by your inappropriate demands." One of the teenagers said, "I think he's a little mad because he had to take care of you for so long and so he never got to be a kid." Then the man in the blue shirt spoke. He had a black beard. He wore small wire-frame glasses. He spoke kindly.

"You're gonna have to accept that your trauma caused him trauma. It's hard for kids to deal with emotional abuse. You crossed all boundaries. You neglected his needs. You made him your caretaker. I don't know what to tell you. That's abuse."

He spoke quietly, staring at his hands, fumbling with his fingers with his head down. Mom said nothing. She only looked at me with her sad puppy-dog eyes, as if searching for something. I felt the breath leave my body as the words hung in the air.

Somebody said something else. Each in turn, one after the other, but I couldn't hear it, only the words spoken by the man in the blue shirt, until it got to Tony, who had just finished his own "family share" with her. He shook his head and lifted his hands as if to say, *I don't know what else there is to add.*

I looked around the room because I wondered why I couldn't breathe.

Am I supposed to say something? Am I supposed to answer? The group moved on and it was time for the next share. We all stayed in the circle and I caught Mom looking at me several times as if desperate to communicate something. I looked away. I looked down. I closed my eyes.

Emotional abuse. What does that even mean? We read *Oedipus Rex* in my classics course at Stanford. The man who wanders the earth blind after gouging his eyes out when he realizes he has married his own mother. I get that. I get that you would need to do something drastic, that the situation would mark you, curse you even. I feel a curse falling over me. *Children of neglect. Orphans. Inappropriate demands. Physical boundaries.* There is the sense that something is off, something indelible. That I missed it. I missed something essential, something everyone else can see.

I think maybe I can pretend the words weren't said or I didn't comprehend them. So many things were said by so many people. Maybe these particular ones can be avoided, just swept up with the detritus of dust from the desert coming in from the open windows.

Tony and I eat quietly in the lunchroom, staring down at our food, surrounded by the low beige walls as if they are closing in on us. "That was pretty fucked-up," Tony says. I nod and chew, looking down. "Why are we even here?" There's a tightness in my chest and I don't have a good answer, just a sense the room is spinning.

The man stared at his hands. He didn't look at either of us. She had on a thin green shawl and she was leaning forward in her chair. Her face was sad but searching as she looked at me with, what was it? *Guilt?* Is that what I saw?

Each morning we take a city bus from our motel at the edge of the desert to the treatment facility. It is a series of low southwestern-style buildings, decorated with Native American art, framed by cacti and the mountains in the distance. We walk in silence, Tony and I. I can feel the hot shame like the dry heat on my face. I don't know why we feel so bad. The stillness is oppressive.

It was almost a relief when she had checked herself into this place, a relief to just be out with it, to give the nameless thing a shape, like a fog that reveals the outline of a previously invisible object. *Oh, so that's the problem. She's mentally ill.* At first, I thought it was a mental institution, but it turns out it's more of a "recovery facility," a place for people to get clean off drugs or deal with major depression, schizophrenia, addiction, trauma. I don't know where she fits into this, other than the major depression, the long days staring at the ceiling or crying, but the outline has taken on a new shape, a larger one. I noticed in the group that she calls herself a "cult survivor" now. And I know she became too depressed to work, too depressed to leave her house, her bed. It seems like coming here was raising a white flag of surrender.

The man seemed like a nice person. Maybe late forties. Maybe he worked in some kind of mental health field, which is why he knew so much. Maybe he had a family of his own. It was a kind face. An unassuming voice. He meant well. He said the words matter-of-factly, like he was trying to deal with a problem, like how to fix broken shingles on a roof in the rain. He was trying to be helpful.

I can still hear his voice, the precise cadence. It was soft, what Bonnie would call "nebbishy." He was right. I knew he was right the minute the words left his mouth and filled the space between us.

THE OCEAN IS vast on the other side of the windshield of the white rental car parked on top of Sandpiper Hill under the westbound flight path of LAX. There is a black oil tanker parked to the south and tiny sailboats dotting the blue expanse to the north. "There it is. My ocean," Mom says, smiling and taking in the view. It's been three weeks since she left the facility in Arizona. "*My* ocean." That's what she always called it on trips to the Oregon coast or down the Pacific Coast Highway in California. We'd emerge from the mountains and see the Pacific appear in front of us and she'd yell out, "There's my ocean!" I often wondered if one person could own a whole ocean. If there was room for me to love the ocean too, to bodysurf with my dad or run down the sand on long afternoons before my knee injury. Is this hers too? The whole fucking ocean?

She tells me she wants to talk about the family share, that a man had mentioned a term and it was maybe something I didn't understand because I don't really know psychology very well and she does. The term was "emotional abuse." She says these things get thrown around and you can't pay attention to them because people don't really know what they mean.

I think, so she *knows*.

I've been swimming two miles a day trying to maintain my exercise habit that Tony says is just like being a dry drunk, the thing I do to "deal." My arms are tired and I'm glad for the exhaustion.

"So just don't put too much stock in it, Mick. It's good that you came to see me. I really needed your help." She says she's feeling better, that she's going to go to graduate school in Portland and get another master's degree, this one in religion. "I just want to shepherd others, to teach them the wisdom I have," she says.

I try to block out the feeling I have like anger turned inward. This hazy, blank white nothingness. I nod and mutter something about people oversharing, overanalyzing, as if I don't remember his face, the shirt, the beard, the voice, the precise sense I've had since that day that I am frozen in place.

I can feel her studying me. I'm surprised by how suddenly aggressive it is. How quickly she turns from victim to prosecutor. I want out of the car. I feel such an intense discomfort, like my body is not my own, like it is being invaded by her stare, by the intensity of her probing questions.

"So you understand that you were not abused?"

"Yes, Mom."

"You and your brother were lucky. You had a mother who loved you and took care of you. I did my best, you know. It wasn't easy to deal with all that and still have two kids to raise."

"Yes. I'm very grateful." I just want out. I just want to be anywhere else in the world. I want to run screaming from the car, but I don't have the words. I can't form them, not in her presence. It's been too long. The words just won't come.

She drops me off at the house in Westchester where I've been living all summer. Drew and I and the rest of our misfit music crew from high school worked as camp counselors at the YMCA and I've grown a beard, having developed a sudden urge to hide my face. I wear vintage flannels torn at the shoulder and Dickies cut at the knees. My favorite shirt is a blue short-sleeved collared uniform that reads "LA County Jail" across the back. I wear it open, with a white tank top underneath. I like the idea of people being scared of me. I've gotten a few more piercings into which I put safety pins and I've grown my hair out. Our group went to a music festival and I'd gone into the big pit near the front of the stage with Eddie. It felt good to be tossed among the bodies, to writhe and sway with the crowd, to throw elbows and high knees in the circle pit, to emerge muddy and bleeding and spent.

I've decided to bring my skateboard and guitar back to Stanford. I've been sitting alone and playing songs again, just staring at the wall and strumming chords, hoping words will come. I'm trying to prepare for the school year, for the training room and the pool, the infamous BioCore for biology majors known to separate the "lambs from the sheep," the challenging string of classes that awaits me back at Stanford. But it all seems overwhelming and there is an intense sense that I should not look inside myself, that I must keep busy. Keep running or, because I can't do that anymore, keep swimming, keep kicking—whatever thing a person does to keep from drowning.

THE DREAM AT the front of campus looks different from behind my dark sunglasses as I skate by and try to ollie off a curb. The facade and the dish and God are all still there. I know this idea exists for most of my peers. I don't mind them. They are mostly hardworking, cheerful people. I don't begrudge them their square clothes and pop music. The khakis and cardinal-red Stanford Ts. I don't mind their stares, the ever-present assumption that I am on drugs. I must seem spacey, riding my skate-board around campus at midnight, trying to study in the gutter outside my dorm. I just want to be outside, to be distracted.

I fail my first midterm in biochemistry. I studied twenty-four hours straight for it, but I skipped most of the lectures and, as it turns out, stud-ied the wrong things. My knee hasn't gotten any better. Five months of rest and it still hurts to jog. I blew my shoulder out from all the swimming and I can't even do that anymore so I find myself walking five miles a day, doing laps around Campus Drive in headphones, trying to quiet my anxiety, listening to Nirvana and Bowie and the Stone Roses, hoping to get enough exercise to sleep.

I have the recurring image of simply walking into the sea and disappear-ing. It's a comforting thought, this idea of escape. But what am I escaping from? What did I mess up so badly about this life of mine? Why do I sud-denly feel so worthless? Over and over again I think of drinking a mess of pills or jumping off the top of Hoover Tower. I don't know why I feel so marked, so alone, like nothing I'm ever going to be or do could change the simple fact that I am a broken human being and I do not deserve any good things.

After my third MRI, the Stanford doctors schedule me for knee surgery. They are planning to cut my lateral meniscus to change the way my patella tracks across the cartilage of my knee in hopes they can stop the progress of the arthritis. They're not sure it will work but nobody knows what to do and I'm just so desperate to run I'll try anything. I'm so tired of the ice and the physical therapy and the stretching, the electro-stim, the ultrasound therapy, the feeling that I am cursed to move lamely through the world.

It's a strange surgery, to simply cut a muscle and hope that the mechanics of my stride will work themselves out. I feel uneasy as I attend the pre-op exam the night before, as the kindly doctor pulls on my heel and asks me about my level of pain. He tells me to skip dinner and try to get some sleep. I toss around on my bed in my dorm room at Toyon Hall, my roommates from the track team sleeping in the next room. I'm beset by the feeling that something is very wrong, that I need to stop running, that there is something else I must face and the surgery suddenly seems desperate and strange.

My mind races through a wilderness.

What do you do when you're a scared-shitless kid that's been faking it for so long? You bury it. You polish your smile and study until you can't even focus your eyes. You buy yourself a big red sweater with an *S* across the chest, just like the Superchild you once were. You try to prove them all wrong. But you laugh at the wrong part of the joke and they see you trying too hard. You attempt to outrun it. But then you get injured and your mom goes insane and a kind man in a blue shirt with a trim black beard uses the words. *Emotional abuse. Crossing physical boundaries. Trauma. Neglect.*

I feel like a blank space covered in skin. There is no place for this walking blank thing among the warm beings, the ones with something inside, the people who can have a drink and laugh at a joke and look into their futures and see something other than the wretchedness I see in mine, the day that immeasurably thin skin falls away and I simply disappear. Into the ocean. My ocean. The one that will swallow me whole if I let it.

I sit up straight at 5:00 A.M. and call the Stanford Medical Center to cancel the surgery. The attending nurse sounds surprised. "So you want to reschedule?"

"No."

I hang up the phone and turn on a desk lamp, grabbing a pen and a notebook to write out a letter. "Dear Mom, I can't talk to you anymore . . . I need space to live my own life. There are too many things I am angry about, too many things to name . . . Do not contact me. Do not write me or call me. I don't know when I'll be in touch again, if ever. Your son, Mikel."

I put the letter into a white envelope and place a stamp in the upper-right-hand corner. I grab my skateboard and head downstairs, emerging from the dorm just as the sun is coming up. I skate to the center of campus, feeling the wind in my hair, the possibility of morning, the freedom of being alive as I make my way to the post office. I drop the envelope into the slot and turn to face campus.

It looks different. Brighter. Bigger. Cleaner. I can feel the sun on my face. The warm orange light is rising over the quad, reflecting the morning over all that wonderful architecture as I see my whole life in front of me like that road in eastern Oregon disappearing into the horizon.

I look around, stunned at how free I suddenly feel. *I can take any of these roads wherever they lead.* I take a deep breath of the crisp air, holding my skateboard against my knee as students shuffle to class around me.

Fuck it. Maybe I'll just drop out.

I SHAVE MY head with a pair of clippers and dye the buzz cut purple. I drop two classes and get put on academic probation. I meet some kids from Foothill College at an Adult Children of Alcoholics meeting I attend off campus in a desperate move to seek answers. One of them is a drummer. I buy a used amp and an electric guitar and we start to jam in a garage in Menlo Park. I change my major from biology to history and psychology. My history studies focus on Jewish history, the history of the Holocaust and anti-Semitism. I can't explain my interest in Jewish history except to say I think it makes me feel closer to Bonnie, closer to the Posners, my adopted Jewish family who treat me as their own. The big joke among the Jewish studies majors is that I am the "Tarzan of the Jews. He was raised by Jews and he walks among us, though he is a goy."

I enroll in Psych One, then Social Psychology, then the Psychology of Addiction, then the Psychology of Mind Control. We study cults. We read about Jonestown and the Peoples Temple and Vietnamese prison camps. It all feels familiar, like reading your own family history. I write my term paper on Synanon, reading *Escape from Utopia* and *Synanon,* the two dusty volumes everyone says are the definitive books on Synanon. I find myself scrolling through endless microfiche at Meyer Library, reading old copies of the *Point Reyes Light,* the newspaper that won a Pulitzer Prize reporting on Synanon.

I'm surprised by how popular Synanon was in American pop culture. I didn't realize there was a Hollywood movie made about it, starring Chuck Connors and Eartha Kitt. The Oscar-winning actor Edmond O'Brien played Chuck Dederich.

I didn't know Bob Dylan referenced Synanon in his song "Lenny Bruce," from his 1981 record, *Shot of Love.* The first two lines are

> *Lenny Bruce is dead but his ghost lived on and on*
> *Never did get any Golden Globe award, never made it to Synanon.*

All of it paints a picture in my mind of an experimental living community known for getting drug addicts clean that became a quest for something more: the dizzy, utopian dream of the 1960s come to life. At the time, before it went bad, it was *cool*. Actors and directors and artists hung out there, some of them playing the Game, like the comedian Steve Allen and the psychologist Abraham Maslow. The jazz musician Art Pepper went to Synanon to get clean, so did Frank Rehak from Miles Davis's band. Joe Pass even put out an album called *Sounds of Synanon*.

The story had changed by the mid-1970s, by the time it had become a multimillion-dollar nonprofit, steeped in a battle with the IRS over its nonprofit status because of rumors of violence. There was an *NBC Nightly News* exposé in 1978 saying as much, which caused a stir in the community and led to threats made against NBC executives.

In the midst of the IRS investigation, the LAPD raided Chuck's compound and that's when the tapes came out. The Old Man, who had once forbade violence, who had made nonviolence a pillar of the community, could be heard saying his infamous words: "We're not going to mess with the old-time, turn-the-other-cheek religious postures. Our religious posture is: Don't mess with us. You can get killed dead, literally dead. I am quite willing to break some lawyer's legs, and next break his wife's legs, and threaten to cut their child's arm off. That is the end of that lawyer. I really do want an ear in a glass of alcohol on my desk."

It's strange to see these things in print because they were always legends, a type of folklore we heard through the years in bits and pieces: the Tomales Bay compound, Chuck Dederich, the violence, the Imperial Marines, the thousand rifles, the Game, the shaved heads, the forced divorces and forced vasectomies. I come upon a story about a man beaten nearly to death in his driveway by men from Synanon while a little boy watched from the porch, my hands shaking, tears in my eyes, thinking about Phil, his face, the dark figures, the body lying limp in the driveway. That little boy.

I'm surprised by how violent it all is. Not just the violence against Phil and the other splittees, not just Chuck's paranoid words, but the violence of dropping out of society completely, the violence of cutting off contact with family members outside, of taking children from parents, husbands from wives. This is what it means to join a cult.

The Game is affectionately known in this literature as "attack therapy."

But I've never heard it described that way. Dad always said it was just a way to get through the hardened defenses of drug addicts because it was like AA in that there was a share, but unlike AA the rest of the group then picked the share apart, pointed out the lies, criticized, screamed and yelled, and made accusations—all to get the addict to admit to his problem. Except over many years, the Game transformed and became a form of brainwashing. Games lasted days, sometimes entire weekends. And eventually even the Old Man admitted it was a tool used to enforce the will of the leadership: for people to get forced vasectomies, to give up their kids, to split up marriages, abort babies and commit violence.

The School is hardly mentioned and when it is, it's glossed over, as if the children are accessories, as if the story of the commune that went rotten like bad milk did not affect them at all, as if it only happened to their parents, as if they were secure, safe from it within the walls of the orphanage where they were placed. I scour the articles and books for pictures of them, those skinny kids in thrift-store clothes, straining with toothy grins and shaved heads. I wonder about them. I wonder where they are and what they're doing and if they're having the same problems as I am, if they feel just as bewildered about their place in the world, their loneliness, their desire to flee.

The articles reference a "school" in which children are raised "communally," like a kibbutz. It doesn't mention that unlike on a kibbutz the children don't live with their parents; they don't even have interaction with their parents. They aren't even allowed to call them their parents. "Every adult in Synanon is your parent," is what they used to say. There's something powerful about the Orwellian turn of phrase in which everyone calls it a "school," as if with the use of this word the separation, the isolation, the abuse, the loneliness and the neglect of orphans can simply be swept under the rug like it never happened.

SINCE THE LETTER, Mom has left me alone but on my twenty-first birthday I receive a ten-page single-spaced letter explaining to me the circumstances around my birth: that she lost friends, lost prestige, that she was ostracized from her social circles, all because the Old Man had decided that there would be no more children born into Synanon and any new pregnancies must be aborted, and she refused to abort me.

She said she was "gamed" about it, which means she withstood all that "attack therapy," people screaming at her, calling her disloyal and ungrateful and arrogant, all because she wouldn't abort me. She says she felt that she was guarding a special life and it was her job to bring it into the world. It's a difficult thing to understand because I'm grateful she did this for me; I even admire her grit in the face of all that pressure. But it also feels like an incredible weight, like she is trying to explain, in exacting detail, why I owe her so much.

By the time we escaped, they were kidnapping children of splittees, bringing them back against their will. They were beating the Punk Squad kids, the court-appointed juvenile delinquents sent to Synanon to straighten out. Strangest of all, Chuck was drinking again. When he was arrested in 1978 for assault and conspiracy to commit murder, he was hammered-out-of-his-mind drunk.

The letter is her birthday present to me. I have a sickening feeling in my stomach and I wish she could be like other parents, simply glad for my existence without placing so much of a feeling like a balance is owed. So it seems like one of those protective illusions she carries, a story she tells that absolves her from being a parent. I never respond to the letter.

When I write a term paper on Synanon, trying to weave together the psychology of mind control and my family history with it, my TA, a kindly woman named Anne, tells me she wants to submit my paper to a psychology publication. I'm flattered but I tell her that I don't feel comfortable. I don't want everyone knowing my secrets. She has straight black hair and creamy white skin. We are sitting in her tiny office in the psych department at the front of the Romanesque quad.

"You know this stuff isn't your fault, right? Mikel, these aren't *your* secrets." I don't know how to tell her about the shame I feel, the sense of being marked and cursed.

Anne is gentle, her voice soft and warm. "It's nothing you could control. It was a cult. And where you lived was not good for children. Are you familiar with the theory of attachment? The idea that we base all of our relationships on the attachments we form with our parents early in life, especially in the first three years? I wouldn't be surprised if every child of Synanon has an attachment disorder. Do you know what that is?"

She shows me an article she's clipped for me. The risk of developing attachment disorders is higher in children who live in orphanages, or have been separated from their parents for long periods of time, or have a mother with depression. The fear of abandonment causes them to feel isolated, to create private worlds where they live alone. Some choose anger and become sullen and withdrawn in the presence of adults. Others are extremely outgoing, unable to distinguish between adults whom they are supposed to trust and those they cannot. For them, their lives are a performance, a kind of frenzied dance in which they feel like they must impress, as if that impression is the only way they can receive love. Children with attachment disorders grow up to have difficulty in relationships, which they seek out of need and then destroy out of fear, resulting in a lack of self-worth and a sense of isolation.

It's too much. I feel a sense like a dam about to break. She puts a hand on my shoulder. I keep thinking, *Is this me? Me and Tony?* I hardly know this woman but maybe that makes it easier and I start to cry right there in that tiny office in the psychology department in the Romanesque quad at the precipice of the Dream. I hide my face and wipe my eyes. I feel so embarrassed, so weak, so fragile. *Goddamn it, this is not supposed to be me.* I was supposed to get out. The castle, the high walls, the quiet room with all those ghosts. I never imagined it would lead me here.

"Children experience loneliness like shame." I repeat the line I've read under my breath. I write it in my notebook.

Children experience loneliness like shame. They imagine the reason they are alone is that there is something wrong with them, that they have done something bad, something that makes them too gross to touch.

I think back to the School, to all my questions about who raised us, who was with us, who picked us up when we cried, when we were sick, when we were upset. My brother sitting alone on that playground until he was nearly seven. The shaved heads, the toothy grins. Those boys and girls. What becomes of us? What role do we play in our fate? Are we just destined to be ashamed and alone? Marked for failure or insanity or, more prosaically, to feel imprisoned in our minds, longing for the very connections we are too broken to make?

I'm grateful for the information but I don't know what I'm supposed to do with it. I'm not given a counselor to call, nor does the paper on Synanon or any of the psychology projects lead me to any kind of lasting change. It's only a description. It's like a disembodied voice telling you in great detail that you are currently falling off a cliff: "You seem to be falling. You will soon hit the ground at approximately one hundred miles per hour. Your brain will splatter on the rocks below. This is because of the force of gravity from the mass of the earth acting upon your body at the rate of 9.8 meters per second per second. You were abandoned and abused and you have an attachment disorder."

Okay.

THE JAM SESSIONS with the Foothill kids become more serious. We bring in guitar pedals and crank the amps. I speed up a few of the countless bad folk songs I've written to rock-and-roll tempo. Eric, the tall blond-haired drummer from the Adult Children of Alcoholics meeting, keeps pace as I pound on my guitar and scream off-key into an old mike we've duct taped to a broken lamp. Nothing about it sounds good. But there are occasional moments when the loud guitar and the booming drum fuse together with a certain impromptu lyric and there is a brief feeling of transcendence, as if witnessing an apparition, a parting of the clouds to reveal a blinding beam of light and I feel like I'm floating weightless.

The moment passes and the guitar sounds thin, the drum is off tempo, and my low, raspy voice resembles a chain saw that has hit a knot and stalled.

Dad calls me once a week and we talk about classes and sports. I tell him about Saint Augustine, Maimonides, or cognitive dissonance and he tells me about the offensive schemes of the San Diego Chargers. It seems like a bargain we've made, to inhabit each other's world like this, to have this closeness with another grown man. He doesn't mind the purple hair and rock and roll. All he says about it is, "Things are starting to get *interesting*."

A group of us find ourselves at the Fillmore in San Francisco one night to see the band Weezer. The place has the contradictory air of faded glory: the smell of stale beer and old tile juxtaposed with a huge crystal chandelier and a raised stage suited for tragedy.

The opening act shuffles onto the stage. The lead singer is a tall, skinny, balding young man in thick glasses who proceeds to plug in his guitar, look to his bandmates and start a riff. It's like nothing I've ever heard before. He growls into the mike while his guitar player screeches something off-key and atonal, a mix of sweet melody and frustration. The lanky singer screams, "You've got it all wrong! You can't get it right!" and I can't help but bob my head.

I ask Eric their name and he tells me they are called Archers of Loaf.

"What the fuck does that mean?"

He shrugs.

By the fifth or sixth song the singer is growling, "The people gathered all around the radio to hear the transmission from the devil's soul, locked and stunned and sick and cold, toasting their dead hero." The drums are pounding, as loud and overwhelming as any hard rock show, but nothing about it carries the whiff of preening falsehood. It's all frustration and anger, a chaos among the blur of bad haircuts.

I think, *Why is this not the biggest band in the world?*

I don't care that it's devolved into discord and noise. I want the chaos. I want the noise. I feel relieved to be at the show, to be anonymous in the heat of bodies. There's no way this band knows about the cacophony of shame and anger swirling around my head, but it's as if they're playing the soundtrack to it. To be precisely broken. To just embrace it. To lose yourself in the crowd, find yourself in the dark.

We begin to go to shows as often as possible. To see Radiohead or Pavement, local punk bands or touring folksingers, artists who perform their pain onstage, who turn it into something beautiful or angry or cathartic or strange. I'm reminded of the long days listening to the Cure, the Secret Place where it was just Robert Smith and me, pounding fists into the bed at eleven years old wishing I was someone else, somewhere else. Did I realize I was wishing I was here? Right here with the energy from the crowd, the clapping, the feeling of buzz in my teeth like there might just be a riot tonight after all? Because I want it. I want the fucking riot. I want us to throw the chairs in the middle of the floor and light them on fire, to dance around them while we scream. And to know it might happen—that we might end up in the parking lot, torches in hand as we turn over a car, shirts off, fists raised, a primal bellow echoing up from our chests—that's the whole reason we're here.

Maybe it's the beer. Maybe it's a desire to not go home, to not really know what that is. Maybe like my parents, like all the people who joined the cult, it's a desire to just reject it all, the whole damn society, and start over. Maybe I'm lonely. Maybe I'm scared. Maybe I'm drunk, for the first time in my life, truly drunk and not caring about it, not thinking endlessly about the "addiction that runs in families" and just pounding vodka instead. Maybe I'm tired, from all the meetings, books and pamphlets, of being excluded from the basic desire to Just Not Give a Fuck. I'm a little scared because I know "alcoholism is a family disease" and I am thus playing with fire, but I guess that's the point: the fire. I want to do whatever it takes to burn it all down. Maybe I'm lonely because there is no place for me at school, among all that crushing optimism. But there's a place for me here in the darkness, here with the crowd where I can scream and wail and feel precisely weird. A place where you can take a kind of pride in pain. You wear it like a badge of honor the way a soldier wears medals on a uniform, symbols of battles fought long ago. *Yes, that's right, I'm not from the fucking suburbs. No, my dad was not a fucking lawyer. No, we were not tucked in and read a story at bedtime. We had nightmares and demons and it taught us to run. These are scars. All of them. Scars. And they are not going away. No, I don't feel okay about it.*

Take your pain and make it *useful*. That's what it means to be an artist. I never want to go home anyway.

BY THE TIME graduation arrives, we've been to at least a hundred shows. I know the rules by heart, the disinterested attitude, the ratty thrift-store clothes, a certain bob of the head that becomes a sway, the mosh, a frenzied jump around the circle pit, if there is one. It becomes second nature. Eric and the other kids from Foothill College are all planning to play music with their lives. I don't know what I'm planning to do with mine yet. It feels like my scholarship was a gift and with it came an obligation to give back, like a debt is owed to my community for the gift of an education. It occurs to me that teaching at a lower-income school might be a way to begin to repay this debt, so that's my plan for the fall.

I decide to invite Mom to graduation. We have not spoken since the letter. There's a kind of quiet acknowledgment when she arrives, a formality we fake for appearances after not speaking for so long, as if the previous three years were simply a hiccup. It's like putting a Band-Aid on a broken leg. She arrives, along with Dad and Bonnie and Grandma and .

Grandpa Posner, Tony and his son. Everyone tells me how proud they are. Dad most of all. He's gone from being suspicious of higher education to being one of those parents who walks around in a Stanford sweatshirt chatting up anyone who will listen about the rigors of his son's academic life. I don't mind. It feels like a concession, like we've acknowledged our differences and decided to tell each other about our individual worlds. He's still my favorite person to watch a Laker game with.

In the morning, a few of the guys from the track team I stayed friends with and I decide to wear track spikes and T-shirts that say "Stanford Track" beneath our robes, which we plan to unzip as we run ahead of the crowd of incoming graduates at Stanford Stadium before the commencement address. We smile as we do this, our hands raised in triumph, sprinting in front of the procession.

It's the first time I've worn track spikes since Pac-10 Championships, since before my injury and the trip to the treatment facility in Arizona, since the man in the blue shirt, the ocean, the letter.

Something is off. I feel it as I run around the pink oval in the bright sun, in front of the line of black-robed students, beneath the crowd of family and well-wishers. I feel hollow. Empty. Like I've buried something. Like that's what I was supposed to learn: take all that shame and lock it away in a room. Track it down and remove any remnants of it from my speech, from any accounting of my life to others. Curate it like the scene at the front of campus.

There is a mask to wear, the all-American white smile and all-American white face in the Stanford track T-shirt sprinting to accept his honors degree. And the plan is to just hold that mask in place for as long as possible.

Sometimes on quiet evenings I am stalked by the feeling that I can never be whole. I can never be honest about myself. I'm preyed upon by the sense that what is real about me is wretched or broken. So I try not to invite the quiet in. I try to keep things loud, to fake it: the smile, the mask, the facade, my own version of the Dream that brought me here, an eye on the past and an eye on the future—smiling, healthy, radiating confidence, baffled and running scared.

CHAPTER 37

THE FIRST DAY OF THE REST OF YOUR LIFE

Four years later I am driving up a dusty dirt road in an old white sedan packed with my few possessions, clothing, a wrought-iron desk lamp, my college diploma, an old hard drive covered in stickers, a photo album and twenty-five books from the Santa Monica Public Library. Buzzing electric towers stand guard over the valley around me like steel giants guarding a secret. They look down on the fields and ranches in the high desert fifty miles north of Los Angeles. All around me is scrub brush and dust, long chain-link fences and horse barns, abandoned cars sitting in fields of tall grass, rolling brown hills that demarcate a jagged horizon beyond which sits the largest desert in the Western Hemisphere. It's a good place to hide.

My new home is a double-wide trailer on the edge of a horse pasture at the back of my aunt Jeannie's ranch. There is an ever-present howl of wind, the occasional yip of a coyote, the rattle of snakes, the buzzing of wasps, fire ants, tarantulas, scorpions, the din of a place empty and wild.

I've come here because I didn't know where else to go, because working square jobs first as a teacher and then as a director of nonprofit programs had become unbearable, because I hated it and found that the mask I had so meticulously crafted in college was not enough, was nowhere near enough. In short, my plan didn't work.

Aunt Jeannie walks up the hill to greet me, a smile on her rosy cheeks as she throws her arms around me in her plush fleece jacket. "Mickey!

I'm so glad you made it." We've agreed that for room and board I will shovel horse manure and feed the horses twice a day. She's shrunk since she got sick from the diet pills she took. She'd put on weight after getting injured in the line of duty and in order to lose the weight, she tried pills which gave her pulmonary hypertension. It's eaten away at her energy, at her body, leaving her thin and frail. But there is still a toughness about her, a rugged warmth as she hugs me close, fiercely protective, fiercely committed to beating her illness at all costs. She surveys the valley and the tiny trailer. "It's not much, but it's cozy. There's a heater and a swamp cooler and plenty of water from the well. Are you sure you don't want to borrow a TV or something? Aren't you going to get lonely?" She opens the rickety wooden add-on porch door and we walk into a small anteroom in which heavy jackets hang on hooks over mud-caked boots. We kick the mud off our shoes and walk into a room with a kitchenette and a couch, faux-wood paneling and a small bedroom beyond the paper-thin walls. "Welcome to your new home." She beams at me. "We're so glad to have you here, but are you sure this is what you want?"

"I think so."

"Well, okay then. You can always come visit us down at the house if you get lonely sitting up here with all these books." She nods at the sedan packed to the roof outside the front window.

I'm here to write a novel. At least that's what I told everyone, that I'm sick of working, sick of trying to make myself capable of being a cog in a machine, so I'm going to the wilderness to write a science fiction novel about a world in which human beings can buy and sell sleep. The economy that results has people losing years of their lives (by sleeping for money). It feels like an appropriate metaphor for the dread I felt working every day, like I was watching my life slip away silently.

But there's something else. A fear. A new and alarming sense that after a string of failed relationships I may be different somehow, that I can't do something those around me can, and I know, though I don't say it, coming to this trailer is a kind of retreat.

I checked the books out in a flurry one afternoon, searching for the titles and authors that I had always wanted to read: Philip Roth, Nabokov, Alice Munro, Kafka and Tolstoy, F. Scott Fitzgerald and Camus. In college, I never read these books, even though I always knew I wanted to become a writer. Somehow reading these books felt like cheating, like I needed to see the world through my own eyes first.

But now, after trying to work, first as a high school English teacher, then as a program director at a YMCA near South Central L.A., after all the restlessness I felt having to go to one place every day, the sense that my time was taken from me, I just want to live in these books like paper houses and learn whatever it is they have to teach me.

There were two girlfriends. Both named Naomi. I dated one right after the other with a three-week gap in between. Despite sharing a name, they couldn't have been more different. One was a gawky, intellectual, possessive only child with a razor wit, the other a small, artistic, warm, silly, sweet, compassionate younger sister of five older brothers. One was two years older than me, the other three years younger. One was determined to make something of her career and her Columbia education; the other was content to dance around her tiny apartment listening to Modest Mouse while she painted. They became known by Drew and other friends as "the Naomis." Or sometimes as Naomi 1.0 and Naomi 2.0.

Naomi 1.0 and I had a conversation that began one night at a conference for nonprofit professionals and lasted a year and a half.

Naomi 2.0 and I went camping and hiking, dancing and drinking instead. We stayed up late watching bad reality television. Despite their differences, both relationships ended the same way, with tears and frustration as I left them, then returned, left, then returned, again and again and again, terrified of commitment but afraid of being alone.

In both relationships, every time things seemed to be getting serious, if there was a particularly good trip or a weekend visit with friends, I would find myself scheming to find a way out, worried that the relationship would trap me. There was a sudden palpable sense that I needed to break free, to end things. And so I did. I cataloged reasons and made accusations and found a way out. I would then stay in that state of free fall, feeling numb, for weeks, until suddenly, just as I did with Laura in high school, the truth of her—the tenderness, the shared experiences, the warmth of our friendship—would suddenly come rushing back to me like a wave that toppled me over and I'd crawl back begging for forgiveness.

I knew it was what Anne, my Stanford TA, called an attachment disorder, that my early experience as a kind of orphan kept me in a perpetual state of unease about becoming close to someone. I knew I seemed crazy to them at times. Flighty. Confusing. Dramatic. I seemed that way to myself. It was more like a reflex than a decision, a strange one for someone so constantly accused of being a "serial monogamist."

The fear filled my senses, replaced my entire emotional world with a new one in which all I could feel was a suffocation, a feeling like being trapped under glass. The minute I was free, a new kind of panic would set in, the age-old fear of abandonment. Except it wasn't the fear of being a single adult man in a dating world. It was the fear of a child left alone. Even then I knew it was out of place, inappropriate, amplified to an extreme that didn't match the ending of an adult relationship.

So it was confusing to live between these two extremes: fearing closeness, then obsessively needing the comfort it provided, to be forever like a Ping-Pong ball going back and forth between the two.

It's an odd feeling to be so bewildered by one's own actions, to look in the mirror and see the face of a stranger.

I watched with increasing alarm as friends got engaged, some married, others comfortably coupled off without going through the wild histrionics I put my relationships through. I didn't know exactly what was happening. Only that I was different, that I couldn't do something others could. Something vital.

It was an unsettling thought, that sense that here was something else wrong with me. And so it became important to hide it, which I was used to doing anyway. To wave a white flag and retreat. To come to a place where less was expected of me. To come here to this trailer at the edge of civilization. To simply give up on the whole thing.

There will be no white wedding. There will be no "nice girl but we're taking it slow, you'll like her when you meet her." No picket fence and kids and shared jokes under covers on quiet Sunday mornings. It's just not for me. I'll become something else instead. Something daring and romantic. Someone who takes all this pain and anguish and tries to create something useful with it, something beautiful if I can. An artist.

I had some short stories I'd started that were more like a series of half-hearted gestures, sketches of scenes or characters that began and went nowhere. I had hundreds of songs no one had ever heard and a lump in my throat when I thought about how badly I wanted to sing them for someone, to just be out at night with a microphone and an audience. If only I had a voice. If only I knew how. How does one even begin to imagine such a thing? Do these people even exist in the real world? It's like deciding to become a mermaid.

Chuck Dederich, the Old Man, the founder of Synanon, once famously said, "Today is the first day of the rest of your life." That might have been the one thing he got right. The future is a blank canvas if you just decide to let it be one.

Dad was more blunt about it when I told him about my decision. "Makes sense to me," he said. "Situations get too difficult sometimes and so it's better to just move on down the road. See what's down there, because whatever it is, it's got to be better than what you're living with."

That was my reasoning. Life isn't working out? Okay. Pack the car with as many books as you can carry, bring a guitar and an old keyboard, fill your empty pages with lyrics and stories. Read the books, the ones you always wondered about. Swallow your pride and because you can't do anything else, hold a job or maintain a relationship with another human being, move to a tiny trailer at the edge of the world and just get on with it. Write.

IT'S LONELY AT night in a trailer on the edge of a canyon listening to a pack of coyotes howl and yip at the moon. I have no cell reception, no phone, no television, nothing but the books and my empty screen, the cursor blinking at me like some kind of challenge. There's nothing to do but read and smoke, anxiously pluck out some writing five hours a day, then sing songs to the nervous horses in the pasture next to the trailer. To shovel horse shit twice a day, five hours a day, four hours a night.

In between writing binges and songwriting sessions, when I'm driven mad by the loneliness and isolation, when I need to hear a voice or do something besides stare at a computer screen or scribble lyrics in some dog-eared notebook, I go down to the city to visit my brother. He lives alone now in a small apartment near the beach in Playa del Rey. After Tiffany left, he and his son moved from Salem back to Los Angeles to be closer to Dad and Bonnie. Fatherhood turned out to be too much for him to take: he was just too young, too wild, too much the Dope Fiend he was born to be. Mom offered to take his son for a few months, just to let Tony "catch his breath." It was supposed to be a short visit. But a few months became a year, a year became a few years, and eventually it became a permanent living arrangement.

Mom has a new husband now; though they aren't married yet, that's how I always think of him. He's a tall, bald, goofy black man named Darwin whom she met through her new church in Tucson. He has deep-set eyes and a slight slouch to his walk. I like him. It's hard not to like him when I go to visit them so I can take Tony's son camping. Darwin is odd but kind, singing to himself as he slowly cooks dinner, tending to various home-improvement tasks around the house in the warm, slow, steady way of his. He tells old stories about his time as a civil rights activist and he seems like a gentle soul. He makes corny dad jokes with his son, who also lives with them, a sweet kid in rainbow Converse who likes Weird Al and taking apart old radios. He's the same age as Tony's son, which makes them something like brothers. They don't get along, except when they do, also like brothers.

It's easy to be an uncle, to show up with a baseball glove or a mix CD, to unpack it and ask Tony's son about fourth grade. I visit three or four times a year and we hike the local trails or sit and plan for a camping trip, going over lists of gear and cold-weather clothing, keeping things simple, instructional, tactile. He needs so many things I have, has so many questions I can answer. I don't try to be his dad. I can't be his dad. I know that. I just want to take him fishing or hiking, to ride roller coasters with him, to let him know I love him but also that I *like* him. I don't know why that seems so important.

He reminds me so much of Tony, the same guarded blue eyes, the same blond hair, the same attachment to his possessions, his pocketknife and compass, his markers and paper, as if they are guardians or friends, companions in a life spent in between so many different worlds.

He asks me about his dad sometimes, on long car trips to the Grand Canyon or Yosemite. He never speaks to him anymore, so I can feel him searching my face for answers I don't have as I try to concentrate on the highway. He wants to know little things, like did he play baseball or does he like the same music as me? Does he have big feet? Is he left-handed? What is his favorite food? He doesn't know his mother, who disappeared years ago, and I know the questions are all really one question: Why? Why did they let me go? Why am I alone here? Did I do something wrong?

I know this question well.

I don't know how to answer him. I feel protective of Tony and protective of his son. How do I tell him that his father is a good person but he's sick? It's a family disease, after all.

So instead we hike and cook and pitch tents and listen to the Cure and Modest Mouse on long car trips through the mountains. We walk through the rain in the White Mountains in northern Arizona and camp in the red dirt in Bryce Canyon, throwing a rope over a branch to make a bear hang above our makeshift campsite. We stand in line for the roller coasters at Magic Mountain or Disneyland, we toast our slushees and devour junk food at lunch. We run through the waves on the shore during long beach days, letting the cold salt water soak our shoes, and when it's time to leave, when I give him a hug to say goodbye, I feel the sense like a string being pulled to a breaking point. I see the sad, quizzical expression on his face as I pack my things to head back to my trailer at the edge of the world. I know we are supposed to stick together, we children of the universe.

It breaks my heart to see Tony's son being treated the way we were treated as kids, like his feelings don't matter. He seems ignored, almost captive. At one point, after listening to Mom berate him coldly for wanting a snack, I call Bonnie in a panic: "He's living there like some kind of stranger. There's no love in this house. I'm so sad for him." It seems like he isn't really part of a family so much as a person who is merely tolerated, like there is no affection for him, no joy taken in him.

I hardly spoke to Mom in the years between the college letter and the trips to see Tony's son. It was easier that way. Words are not easy. I'm still uncomfortable in her presence. I still have the ever-present feeling that my space is being invaded, my person discounted. Like at my college graduation, we make small talk and I try to keep the conversation light. But it inevitably turns serious in the desert home she built with the money Grandma and Grandpa left her when they died. We discuss trips to the beach in Oregon and AA campouts. It's easier to pretend that's all it was. She has an explanation for everything, what couldn't be helped, what unfairness befell her, a way of bringing the conversation back to all the ways she is a victim, always a victim.

When the subject turns to Doug, she tells me it's my fault he left. I remind her he had a mistress and I was eleven when I moved, that he hit me and left her four times before they got married. This registers momentarily. I can see it like a puzzle on her face, like she's trying to solve a complex math problem in her head. But she soon forgets and returns to her talking points. It's like running through cobwebs, this endless web of illusions and half-truths. She still thinks I owe her something for leaving. It feels crazy and I am angry with myself for trying to explain madness to madness.

I brought my guitar for the camping trip and decide to play her a song to lighten the mood. I sing a song I wrote based on a short story by Irwin Shaw called "The Girls in Their Summer Dresses." She listens politely and when it's over tells me, "Hmm. Well. That is one way to play music. It's not exactly folk music. It doesn't really have a message. Someday you might learn to write songs with a message." I tell her it's not really supposed to have one, at least not in any moralizing way. It's based on a piece of literature, so writing it felt like writing a short story, like I'm trying to capture the contradictions in the story. "Maybe you should just stick to writing!" She laughs in that mocking way of hers, full throated, her head tilted back to reveal her yellowing teeth and metal crowns.

At his apartment in Playa del Rey, Tony will come to the small screen door and greet me with a beer. We'll sit down in front of the TV on his black leather couch to play *Madden NFL* on his Xbox, chain-smoking like the delinquent teens we once were. Me with my Parliament Lights, he with his Marlboro Lights. I watch as Tony gets up again and again to refill his glass. He says he's just having a "few drinks," but each "drink" consists of an entire water glass filled to the rim with whiskey and ice cubes.

For the first couple of drinks, he's funny, charming, full of confidence and plans, telling me about his job doing sales for a large-scale printing company, the big clients he's landed, how he wants to start his own company someday. He makes jokes and claps me on the back. "That's a touchdown, little bro. Ayy-ohhhh! Hey, man, we should all take a trip to Mexico or something. Maybe cause some trouble." There is that old kindred feeling, like we are survivors of something, a plane crash maybe. Like we walked out of the wreckage and found ourselves surprised to be alive. But by the third or fourth glass, his eyes gloss over, his speech begins to slur, and he becomes erratic and emotional. Angry. At the government.

At Mom. At Doug. Even at Dad and Bonnie. It's everyone's fault. For every problem, every challenge, every issue he's ever faced, our parents and Synanon and the entire full-of-shit world are to blame.

I can sense his defensiveness about his son, so I don't bring it up, all the ways in which his son is facing challenges exactly like the ones he resents so much. I think that's what they mean when they say addiction runs in families.

One night we go to a party down in the Jungle, the row of low apartment buildings along the strand of beach in Playa del Rey between the marina and Dockweiler State Beach. It's a rooftop Halloween party. There is the visage of lights behind us, the endless black ocean to the west. Tony and I don't have costumes, but no one seems to mind. There's a keg in the corner, red Solo cups in the hands of half-dressed zombie surfers, Reagan, Nixon, JFK in rubber masks, a Beetlejuice, a Freddy Krueger, a St. Pauli girl, a few scary clowns. They all know Tony and they all slap me on the back like a lost cousin at a family reunion: "Oh, so you're Tony's brother! How does it feel to be related to a legend?"

We smoke and chat and dance and it all seems like a relief, the din of the party a welcome break from the isolation of my trailer in the wilderness. She approaches me in a giant brown cat suit, a few wisps of messy blond hair tumbling onto her forehead that she wipes away with a giant felt paw. "Hey, wanna thumb wrestle?" She has flirty brown eyes and there is something familiar about her, something that takes me off guard in the private room of my mind from which I've been watching the party. It's as if she simply opened the door and let herself in.

"I mean I was a thumb-wrestling champion back in the day." She unzips one of her paws to reveal a sturdy, wiry hand. "I don't want you to be intimidated. I'm obviously out of practice, so you may have a shot."

She places her hand in mine and cocks her thumb back. "Ready? Set. Go!" It's strange how a sudden intimate gesture can remove the space between people, the simple fact of our hands touching. I feel pulled from my private room, pulled inevitably into the present. I introduce myself, tell her I'm actually the state hot-hands champion but I've dabbled in thumb wrestling from time to time, though you have to be careful about injury when you're a two-sport athlete.

There is a look on her face, a willingness, as if we are two specimens of the same species, surrounded by so much alien fauna that quickly retreat into the background as we recognize a familiar dance in the other.

As we talk, I can see her checking my expression from the corner of her eye, feel the warmth of her hand. Her name is Amber. She is from Iowa. She's been here two months. She was raised on a dairy farm. She has my attention. I can't help but be charmed by this skinny woman in the ridiculous cat suit, so quick, so forthright. I decide to take a chance. "So do you have a boyfriend or what?"

"Sort of. He's over there in the zombie costume." She points toward the keg.

"How's it going?"

"What do you mean?"

"I mean is it better than this? Because this is pretty good." I point back and forth between us.

"Actually, no."

"Great."

Tony comes over and we start a thumb-wrestling tournament that is embraced wholeheartedly by the party at large. Amber and I split up, but I catch her looking at me as she glances up from her thumb-wrestling matches. When I walk off to use the restroom, she is waiting for me in the hallway.

"So you live up in the sticks?"

"Yep. Got my own double-wide and everything. The real exciting days are the ones when you catch the horses doing it."

"Awww." She smiles at me and slips a piece of paper into my pocket. "It's actually not serious with the zombie. I'm not really into zombies. Call me." She disappears around a corner, a fuzzy brown tail trailing behind her.

By the time we get back to his apartment, Tony is stumbling drunk on the brink of tears. Some time after the fourth or fifth drink, a transformation took place and all that good-natured warmth turned to self-pity. He tells me that I'm on his life insurance policy, that I am the only one who is, that he has put me as the sole beneficiary of every life insurance policy he's ever had. It seems to have some kind of special meaning to him, this gift he could give me by dying, as if the sum of his life could become a gift if it only ended in tragedy. I take it to mean he sees me as his family, the one he trusts, the one who knows something nobody else does, and I feel guilty for the ways I've privately judged him.

I tell him I want to start a band. That I moved to the trailer to write a novel but I've been writing songs and making demos instead. I don't really know where to begin. I know it sounds crazy because I've never really sung in front of anyone. But it feels real to me, like there's something there I should follow. "Anyway, they're all sad songs for some reason."

"Of course they're sad! What else would *we* write?" He stares down at the ground, swaying softly. "You and me are the only ones who know. Nobody else understands what happened."

He passes out on the couch, leaving me in the quiet living room with the leather couches, a glass of scotch sweating beads of water on the coffee table.

TWO DAYS LATER, Amber the farm girl from the Halloween party meets me at the Mexican restaurant at the bottom of the hill beneath the trailer where I live, in a town called Acton. She's smaller without the cat suit, but the quick wit, the sudden familiarity and the warmth are the same. After dinner, we go back up to the ranch and I kiss her next to a pile of horse manure, under a bluish moon, the coyotes yipping through the canyons in the background.

"I could get used to this," she says.

"I should've known the manure would do it for you."

"What can I say?" She looks at me. "I like big piles of shit."

By the end of the week, she is driving up to the trailer every day after work to cook dinner with me and go for long walks up to the buzzing towers at the top of the hill overlooking the Mojave Desert. There is a sudden relief, as if all the isolation and loneliness I felt have been replaced by something exciting, something new that makes me wonder if my decision to swear off relationships was a mistake, if the wreckage of the Naomis was a fluke and I am meant for something better now. It's a type of amnesia, this feeling. The best kind.

We make plans. We tell our stories. I sing her my sad songs. She cries on the couch, nestled in a corner, her small legs tucked under her, her brown eyes wet, black streaks of eyeliner falling over the constellation of blameless moles on her cheek. We are swept up, our minds racing through the fantasy of who we could become like two people running through the hallways of a new house, imagining the life they could live in it.

This lasts three weeks. Out of nowhere one day, the fear comes. It first creeps in when she suggests we go to Iowa so I can meet her family on the farm. I know, logically, that it's a perfectly normal suggestion given how much time we've been spending together. But instinctually, immediately, I feel a tightening in my chest that quickly winds itself up into a full-blown panic. It's bodily. My legs feel weighted. My hands tied. My breath shallow. I try my best to hide the feeling from her, to nod in assent or say something like "We'll see," as we discuss the possibility over several days and nights. But I can't shake the feeling that I have overcommitted, that she is not the person she pretends to be, that she is lying about her feelings for me, which are only like those one has for a ghost, the fake person I've conjured for her, that I have only been acting and she has been naive enough to have believed the act and that somehow implicates both of us.

The strange thing about the feeling is that it's not preceded by any concrete action. It's more like a suspicion: a creeping sense that there is something rotten at the heart of her, or rotten at the heart of me, because what else could explain the fear, the dread, the panic, I feel?

When I break it off with her a few days later, when I tell her I am "not ready for all this," she holds her small head against my chest, those familiar tears in her brown eyes, and says it can't be true, that there's nothing to be afraid of, that this sudden turn of feeling isn't real. I've told her about what my Stanford TA called my attachment disorder, the thing I inherited from living as an orphan in Synanon, from all those years in Oregon. She tells me it's just my fear talking and that everything is fine, that she is the same person I met at that Halloween party in a giant brown cat suit.

"Don't psychoanalyze me!" I yell. I can see the confusion on her face. "I'm not your fucking pet project, okay? It's over! Accept it! Just fucking leave!" I see her swallow hard and gather herself. I'm not even sure if I mean the words I'm saying. The weight they carry surprises me. I haven't thought any of this through. The words are a reflex, the way a child pulls his hand from a hot stove. I can feel the rift inside me, something warm being suffocated by something cold, a part of me that is in charge of another part of me.

She gathers the few things she's left in the trailer—her handbag, some clothes from the bedroom, a toothbrush on the sink in the tiny bathroom—and leaves.

I hear her car start on the gravel path next to the horse pasture. Her headlights illuminate the dull, dusty, vacant hills behind my trailer and she is gone.

My sleep is fitful and I wake up to an empty feeling, a guilt like the guilt I felt for the bunnies we killed on the gravel path outside the barn. I don't know who the bunny is, whether it's Amber—the light in her eyes extinguished by cruelty and sadness—or the relationship itself, this harmless, joyous thing I've stepped on and destroyed. Or if it's me, if I am the bunny, the part of me that hoped things could be different, that believed in her, that felt calm and safe.

The hollowness in my chest expands until there is a black hole of nothingness too big to contain. The clock ticks. My keyboard goes untouched. My guitar sits in a corner gathering dust. I go for a run. I feed the horses. I find a white wool sweatshirt she left behind balled up in a pile beside the bed. It smells like her.

Two days pass; then all at once a new feeling comes. A blinding white fear of being alone. It's less like the boredom, the fatalism of adult single life, and more like I am a baby lying beside a stream in a dark forest. Unprotected. I am afraid. The words flash across my mind: *You. Will. Always. Be. Alone.* Something bad is coming and there is nothing I can do to stop it. Why did I push her away? She was so soft and warm and kind and good and funny and I am now here standing alone at the precipice of this vast darkness.

I drive down to the city to her new apartment in Los Feliz on the Eastside of Los Angeles and call her from the alley beneath her bedroom. She answers and I tell her to go to her window. I wave. She comes down to let me in. I tell her I'm sorry. I tell her I'm crazy. I tell her I was an idiot and I didn't mean it. I just get confused sometimes. We reconcile, but I can feel her resistance, less like I'm a repentant drunk and more like she knows she can't say no—she's been hurting too, after all—but she dreads whatever is coming next. Or possibly I imagine that. Maybe she's simply glad to see me. I don't really know. I never know which of these feelings to believe, because they all coexist inside me: the simple one attracting me to her for all the reasons that are abundantly clear, the dark one telling me I am suffocated and trapped, the panic like that of a child terrified of being left alone.

WHEN I GET bored of trying to write the novel, which has mostly gone untouched while I write songs, when I long for new experiences, I find myself pitching an editor at a music magazine to assign me features about musicians. I just want to be close, to be out at night with the sweat of the crowd and the boom of the speakers. After twenty blind pitches, I'm finally given a few freelance assignments to write about live music. The editor likes my pieces, and when a vacancy comes up, he offers me a job as the new managing editor. The magazine is called *Filter*. I've been going to shows for so long it seems like a natural step. Watching the crowd in the back, jumping through the pit in the front, trying to understand why everyone is here. The recurring thought I have is that every show is a celebration of something. An idea. Sometimes that idea is as simple as sadness, or anger, or, for particularly bad shows, love. So the game I like to play is piecing together what idea we are celebrating tonight. The more specific the idea, the better the show.

Tonight we celebrate the shared sense that our ironic detachment from the world is both our greatest amusement and the feature most destructive to our lives. The thing we are celebrating is the fact that we know it and have the gall not to care.

Tonight we celebrate the wonder we had at sadness as children. Like finding a dead bird in the grass after a heavy rain and trying to imagine what came before and what comes after.

Tonight we celebrate mirrors, the harsh well-lit ones, the bent and twisty ones, the fabulous vanity we feel as the light reflects off our clothing and cheekbones while we strut between them.

Tonight we celebrate fucking. The mystery, the possibility our bodies offer us for transformation, the sense that our bodies know our selves better than we do.

It's a great job. I get to hear records before they come out. I get to fly to faraway music festivals in places like France and Iceland. I get to sit across from Tom Waits in a roadhouse in Marin County where I tell him about songwriting and my book and the trailer on the edge of the world and he tells me, in that broken chain-saw voice of his, "That's how you do it, man. After a while, it's like Emerson said, the universe conspires." I get to sit in the basement of a tiny bar in Alphabet City with Lou Reed, to be the erstwhile mop-topped journalist whom he tells, "Rock and roll can go, 'Ba, ba, baaah,' my friend. It cannot go, 'La, la, laaaah.'"

I love the seedy clubs, the pretentious, lively conversations with rock stars and writers casually sipping red wine in the back room with their legs crossed. The magazine staff is so small the editor in chief and I end up writing most of every issue, filing seven or eight feature stories per issue under different pen names, which we decide should sound like French Canadian hockey players, for some reason. We stay up all night on deadline at our office on Miracle Mile, copyediting, playing *Galaga,* and drinking beer. When morning comes, we crawl over to the print shop with our hard drive, making the 7:00 A.M. print deadline by maybe eight minutes.

With the money from the new job, I move out of the ranch and back to the city. I get a place on the Eastside in Los Feliz, one neighborhood away from the rock clubs in Silver Lake. It's a tiny upstairs studio apartment with espresso wood floors, a shade tree and a brick facade outside the unscreened window like something from the Latin Quarter in Paris. There's a kitchenette and a closet where I tape entire books to the wall with duct tape, *Notes from the Underground* and *The Trial,* right over my writing desk. I like the idea of Dostoevsky and Kafka looking down at me, fellow travelers in the 3:00 A.M. task of confession and poetry.

When I'm not writing stories on rock and roll, I'm still writing songs, fiddling with guitar effects, scribbling pages of lyrics in notebooks. Amber and I have settled into a perpetual state of not-quite-togetherness but not-quite-not-togetherness, which means we spend most of our time either breaking up or getting back together. I know she finds it exhausting. I know it's unfair to her. It's just like the feeling I got in college that my knowledge could not save me, that despite my earnest desire to be a better man, a better boyfriend, a better friend, I am caught between two emotional poles: one constantly running away, the other constantly running back.

Sometimes I think I'm like what I once imagined Dad to be, before I really knew him, when he was just an idea in my head. I pictured him as swashbuckling and charming, one foot in front of the law, living life by his wits, longed for and sought after as he moved from place to fascinating place. Other times, I wonder if I'm like Paul: a basically good man with a crippling disorder, trapped by impulses he can neither understand nor control. The worst of it is when I wonder if I'm like Doug. I read somewhere that victims of abuse identify not only with the victims but with the abusers as well, taking note of the power the abuse gives them. I wonder if I am this, that I've learned that the threat of leaving has given me a power, over Amber, over the women I met whenever we broke up, to be both present and absent, forever a captain setting sail on the horizon, always one foot on his vessel, so present and earnest about his desire to stay, so enraptured with the promise of the sea.

Something about rock and roll makes all of this bearable, like I am among fellow travelers in drink and an idea of love that is shared like a dark joke. So it feels like a secret life, to be interviewing rock stars by day and trying to write songs about my confusion by night. The interviews are a farce, this role play of musician and erstwhile journalist is only an act I put on for appearances because all I really want to know, as I swim in this black river beneath my life, is this: *How? How do you do this thing I want so desperately to do? How do you write a song?*

CHAPTER 38
WE CAN BE
HEROES

The long blond bangs fall over his mismatching blue and black eyes exactly the way they did in the posters. The posture is the same, a kind of excitable swishiness with feminine limbs and long fingers, his sharp chin and perfect Nordic nose. I'm a little surprised by the outcropping of gray stubble on his face, the odd effect of age and agelessness it creates, like talking to an oracle in some hidden cavern in the sky. But then it would be different than it was when I was thirteen. I'm a grown man now. I can't just blurt out all the ways I wanted to be him, how much he represented an unattainable ideal for Jake and me. He's an idea, not a person. So I can't just hug him and hold on tight, tell him I'm trying to understand something and I need his help. It's like speaking to the Wind. What do you ask the Wind?

I am nervous and jumpy. Palms sweaty. Heart pounding. Throat dry. An unsettled lightness in my stomach, a dizziness that has been with me since my editor told me that I would be here, sitting in a studio in Soho three feet away from David Bowie.

It's like floating.

There is a beam of light washing over his face from the high windows of the studio. It engulfs him, like stage lighting in a high school play set in heaven. He is wearing blue jeans and a woven blue-and-white cardigan, his long blond bangs falling into his eyes as he raises an oracular hand over his head and proclaims, "There is no God and man is a fool and that has always been the creed I stand by."

We've been talking about Andy Warhol and Nietzsche and he just blurted it out. I smile uncomfortably, surprised by how quickly he got to the point. We are a long way from the higher power at an AA campout.

I know my job is to play the role of journalist, to fire off questions about the guitar on song three and the "process in the studio." But nobody really cares about these things. They can make up their own minds. All people want to know is, *What is he like? Like, is he cool or a bit of a dick? And if so, is he cool about being a dick? Do you think he would like me?*

And all I want to know is the Secret. I know it's not that simple, but there is a sense I carry that he guards it like a treasure, that he knows something magical and I have this one heartbreakingly brief moment to ask him. So I immediately decide to ignore my proper role as journalist, my fear that he might be offended if I do, and just ask him about that Secret, how he writes songs.

I blurt out a short speech about 2:00 A.M. songwriting sessions and my now abandoned book and my deepest wish, which is to sing for an audience, and just ask him how he turns words into music, how he distinguishes between songwriting and prose.

He nods, a wry, flat smile forming on his British mouth as he stands in that perfect light (*How did he know where to stand? Is there a mark on the floor or something?*), as if he's heard this speech before.

"I think a prose writer can articulate ideas in a more straightforward way," he says. "But with a musician, the words are like a plaster that I lay on this armature of music. I don't see the words as carrying thoughts particularly. It's more like an array of feathers which produce a pattern. And the totality of that pattern set against this armature of music is enough to express what I'm feeling."

It sounds so simple when he says it. The music is a framework, the words are a pattern, together their purpose is to express the precise thing the songwriter feels.

"Do you ever feel alone in the world?" I ask him, because I feel like I can since we are floating through space together somewhere near Mars in this studio in New York City.

He cocks his head sideways and gives me a look. Or at least that's how I imagine it, that I am speaking to the Wind and the Wind is telling me its secrets, or isn't, or might.

"I think now we don't have a God. We are completely and totally at sea. So I think we feel a lot more content to accept that life is chaos. There is no structure to it. There is no plan."

I write that down: *Chaos is good. Structure is bad.* "My generation doesn't even see that. The absence of a plan. Because it's all we've ever known. This absence. This chaos." I try not to stare at him.

"I don't know what that must be like."

"It's like dancing at ground zero."

He stands up to pace in front of me, turning quietly in my direction. I sense this oddly paternal feeling from him as he looks at me bent over my notebook.

"I remember when I was sixteen years old," he says. "I was such an idealist about what could happen in the future. I can't read whether you younger people can feel the idealism we felt back in the '60s."

I think of Chuck, the Old Man, the Imperial Marines with their guns, the School, the violence, the shame we carry from living without parents, the broken marriages and broken families and broken hearts, the failed attempts at changing the world, all the ways that dizzy optimism turned to dread, to disappointment, the feeling we had like we were growing up in the bombed-out craters of the 1960s.

He says, "So I wonder if it is harder for you to feel that there definitely are things we should all abide by."

"I think I did when I was sixteen. But I spent the last few years feeling pretty fucked-up. So many things I thought were good, including parts of myself, turned out to be more complicated, more *broken*. And I can barely remember having a thought where love is just love, where there is peace and I feel like I deserve it, before all this contradiction in me came about."

"Yeah, that contradiction really fucks you all up, doesn't it?" He stares at me, his fingers clasped in front of his mouth.

"Yes."

The beam of light from the window has completely surrounded his face so that I'm seeing double, the polite Englishman in front of me and the oracle who answers the riddle, the sky man fallen to earth. He looks at me very seriously.

"Well, write about the contradiction then."

He goes to the wall-to-wall glass that separates the control room from a microphone in a sound booth and the conversation falls back into the familiar territory of record making, processes, influences. Soon a publicist leans in and points at her watch, which is my cue to leave. We shake hands and he pats me on the back kindly. He tells me it was lovely meeting me. He wishes me luck. If there was a ring, I would kiss it. An altar, and I would kneel.

I walk out to the elevator, down to the street in a daze. It's dusk. The taxicabs are turning on their headlights, the fluorescent twinkling of a thousand skyscraper windows illuminating the sky above me. A wind blows through my thrift-store scarf and moppish hair as I turn down Canal Street thinking about the moment alone with him. *Write about the contradiction.*

There was nothing about bridges, pre-choruses, hooks, or repetition, nothing about vocal range or guitar effects, all the mundane things I usually think about. The basic insight was to just ignore those things and write a song that expresses exactly how I feel, no matter how contradictory. It was both simpler and infinitely harder than what I imagined he would say.

SIX MONTHS OF writing and rewriting, scribbling, and struggling later, I am sitting in a tiny hotel room across from Central Park having a drunken conversation with a polite, middle-aged man in eyeliner and smeared lipstick named Robert Smith.

He still has the look, the one from my Cure posters. That's the first thing I thought when he walked into the room at a quarter to midnight. The stubble and makeup, the rat nest of hair, like a butterfly drunk on absinthe.

There is a bucket of beer cooling in the corner and after introductions and small talk, after the perfunctory discussion of who played what and where on the new record, after three or four beers from that cooler, after a publicist walked in and he waved her away saying, "We're extending, we're extending," after we are pacing the room like two insomniacs—he letting me smoke, me pretending not to notice his constant rambling, stream-of-consciousness sentences, the endless questions he utters aloud, asking himself about the nature of his career, his life, the private moments

I know so well (or imagine to) that brought me here—he stops squarely in the middle of the room, looks over at the tape recorder I've placed on the counter and says, "You people always wonder what I think about. But I think it's dead obvious. So I always think, *Well, how far can I go?*"

I don't know how to tell him as he stands there staring at me, peeling the wet label from the bottle in his hand, that it is impossible to me to be here in this room having this conversation with him at 2:00 A.M., when he's someone I grew up talking to, how he explained the world to me as I cried and longed for escape, to bridge the unimaginable gap between those two points on a map: a dingy room in Salem, Oregon, lost and sad and confused and alone, lips still swollen, head still spinning, stomach empty, mind reeling, and this one, here with him, in a rarefied space of earth across from him in New York City. And I think, *Well, how far can I go?*

I am dizzy from the late hours, trying not to stare too hard at him. It's strange, this distance his presence in my mind has created. Fame does that to people: gives birth to butterflies, then wraps them in cocoons. *Nobody loves a genius child. Kill him—and let his soul run wild!* That's how Langston Hughes put it.

"That was absolute shit anyway." He cocks a thumb toward the conference room where a group of suits had gathered earlier as we listened to his new record.

"No, I thought it was fine. Though maybe kinda weird to be just standing there like that as people talked over the album you just made."

"Someone told me I didn't have to stand there like that. There were certain parts, songs when I thought, oh, yeah, I'd be talking now too, and other times I thought, *Why the fuck is everyone talking?*"

"I was feeling that way the whole time. It was rude, for sure. Anyway, fuck 'em, man." The line is a bit of a pose, but hey. He laughs. I lift a beer. We toast.

When I tell him about the abandoned book, the quest for the Secret that has taken over my life, the late-night sessions where I scribble and play, scribble and play, what David Bowie told me, the oracle and the Wind, about embracing contradiction, he tilts his head, gives me a look that says something like "you poor dumb bastard."

Show me how you do that trick.

"Of course," he says slowly. "It's always been cathartic for me. I am by nature obsessive about everything, so I'd say that makes sense, to just beat it down, man. For some songs the only reason they exist is because I'm screaming at the world."

"That's all I want to do sometimes. Scream at the world. But it kind of feels like screaming at myself, you know?"

"Well, good. Because then people will respond to it saying, 'God, that's just *exactly* how I feel.'"

I don't know if it matters that his songs were about people in a different country at a different time and not specifically about orphans or cults or the men who drink themselves to death, the imaginary boys pleading and running. But it's strange how aware he is, how much he knows the effect he had, how I listened to those sad happy songs of his and thought, *This is just how I feel. I had no idea anyone else did too.*

Soon the conversation devolves into stories about touring and I sense his impatience because he has to go to the studio in a few minutes for remixing at 3:00 A.M. He goes on and on about "fucked-up situations," "fucked-up feelings," how life goes on anyway, that you find people who understand this and you tell them about it. Then you both can wake in the morning and feel better because the thing is named. *That's why you write the song. That right there. Write that down, you drunken ape.*

As we stumble toward the door to leave, he places his hand on my shoulder and turns me around gingerly. I brace myself, feeling his hot breath on my neck as he leans into my ear: "I fucking hate the idea of normal. Normal is all that's bad about living. All that's boring about life. Why be normal?"

I stare at him, wondering how to retrace the lines between reality and projection, the idea-come-to-life in my head and the dizzy, querulous, drunk middle-aged man in front of me with a ten o'clock shadow and a smudge of red lipstick across his mouth.

"To be honest," he whispers fiercely, "I have no idea what normal is."

Then he is gone and I am alone with my thoughts and the empty bottles of beer.

Why be normal? Destroy yourself and dance in the embers. Embrace the catharsis. Use it. The words resonate in my head as I cradle the tape recorder in my hands. Show them. Show them how weird you are; show them the person beneath the mask.

That's the whole magic trick of an essence brought to life by a song, to become an artist when you feel broken and you've decided to turn it into beauty. To make the pain *useful*. The longing, the fear, the heartache and dread, the ability to see these broken pieces of yourself like cracks in an armor through which you are better able to see the world: too broken to be normal, just broken enough to see beauty.

My God, Robert, what an idea.

CHAPTER 39
WISHING WELL

Back in my tiny Parisian apartment on the Eastside of Los Angeles, beneath the steady stare of Franz and Fyodor, I hunch over my synthesizer playing piano chords, pounding the keys, the same three chords over and over again. When I get claustrophobic, I walk through the neighborhood of sidewalk cafés and corner bars, taco stands and vintage clothing stores. I just want to feel the night air on my face. Some nights I see the line of people hiking up Vermont Avenue to the Greek Theatre at the top of the hill in Griffith Park. There's something magical about that place, the way the music floats over the canyon, the sound of an electric guitar as it reaches the ear of a coyote sniffing the wind.

When I get back to my flat and turn on the keyboard and stare out into the street, those simple chords sound to me how running feels at night, the way the images burst from the darkness, the echo of the electric piano overlapping with itself like feet on cool pavement, down back alleys, under lonely streetlights. Why am I running? What am I running from? Who? I write some lines down and sing them over and over again, until the sprinklers come on at 3:00 A.M. and I finally say goodnight to my friends Franz and Fyodor.

For eight months I return to the song to revise it, first on a piece of old cardboard that sits on top of the synthesizer where I scribble lyrics while I sing, then in a notebook with pages crossed out. The restlessness. The street. The gasp that echoes up as if from the bottom of the well. The fact that I don't understand myself, these impulses that shock and surprise and upend my world. These things I hide. *Find the contradiction. Write about that.*

There are twenty drafts, enough discarded lyrics to write ten songs, until finally one night, after eight months, I reach the end of the song, listen for the decay of the delay to die down into silence, and think, *There. That is exactly how I feel.*

I lean back from my desk and stare up at the ghosts staring back at me. The images dance around the room. I call the song "Wishing Well." It's the first thing I've ever written that feels like it's mine. I have a thousand other songs, but this one feels new, like it came from a different place.

The room is silent. It's 1:00 A.M. There's nothing but the whir of the ceiling fan and the sound of faraway traffic from the street outside the window. It occurs to me that I've been working on it for eight months straight and no one has ever heard this song.

ONCE I'VE WRITTEN five songs in this same exhausting way, once I've rewritten every lyric, planned every note, every guitar riff, every keyboard string section I've programmed into the cheap recording software I bought, I finally decide it's time to just get on with it, to find a way to stand on a stage and sing these songs of mine, to start a band.

I don't know where else to begin, so I place a pathetic ad in a local music magazine. In it, I mention Lou Reed, the Cure, and David Bowie, hoping that it will find its way to the right people.

There is a drummer with a goatee who answers it with whom I spend five dreary afternoons, after which he quits because, he says, "the songs just aren't there, man. Where are the hooks?" There is a young bass player in all black with five gold necklaces who gets excited by the influences I named but who disappears after three sessions into the rock-and-roll ether. There is another drummer who quits because he gets a paid gig with a folksinger, yet another bass player who has already toured the country with another band. He tells me the idea of putting out a record and going on tour is a pipe dream of mine, that I am delusional to think anyone would ever want to hear these "rambling nonsense songs."

So when a short, skinny, handsome drummer with long sideburns and a pair of washed-out old Converse drops by the apartment to discuss my demo, the whole idea seems like some quixotic fantasy, like tilting at windmills with electric guitars. His name is Daren Taylor. He is from Fresno. He seems different from the other semipro players and big-talk hustlers, the guys who discuss "gigging" and "studio session work." He's weirder. Quieter. Sarcastic. He makes a few jokes about Siouxsie and the Banshees, the tour Robert Smith did with them as a guitar player where they all called him "Fat Bob." He heard the demo, the one I made with Drew playing the guitar parts, because Drew was the best guitar player I knew.

Daren liked the songs, especially the one about the wishing well. He reminds me of Jake with his air of ironic humor, his deep knowledge of music, his sense we're all screwed anyway so we might as well have some fun while we can.

I tell him sheepishly that I've decided to name the project the Airborne Toxic Event, after a section of the book *White Noise* by Don DeLillo. I explain that Jack Gladney, the protagonist, is scared he's going to die because he's been exposed to an enormous toxic cloud that the media gives the Orwellian name "the Airborne Toxic Event." The cloud makes him realize his time is precious and short and he must make the most of it while he can.

A few people told me, "It's a weird name," and it's "kinda long," and "It sounds like some bad OC death metal thingy." I don't know if the point is for people to understand. Or if it's better for the name to be disorienting, a blank tableau upon which one can sketch whatever ideas one chooses. *Why be normal?*

Daren gets it.

"So what do you want to do with all this?"

"You know, play shows, make a record, see where it leads, the whole thing."

He nods his head slowly. "Okay, I'm in."

"What do you mean?"

"I mean, let's start a band."

I take a breath to hide my giddiness. "Cool."

We make a plan to meet for rehearsals at a friend's studio. He leaves me his phone number and an email address. I glance at it as he walks out the door. It reads, "*Daren:* One_imaginary_boy@yahoo.com."

Of course.

CHAPTER 40

BREAKING

Standing center stage in front of a five-piece rock band as the sound swells behind me feels exactly like being the captain of a spaceship I don't quite know how to fly. It isn't at all what I imagined it would be. It might be the way the subwoofers make the room shake when Daren hits his kick drum, a visceral *boom* right at the center of my chest, or the way the guitar lines seem to bounce around the room, over the stage, the exposed air-conditioning ducts, the bottles at the bar, the signs for the exit and bathroom. I hear my voice amplified to an inhuman volume, see the faces of the people holding drinks—friends and friends of friends mostly, who've come because we begged them to. They look up at me as I take a deep breath and begin. And here is this thing I've longed for for so long, the image come to life as I stood in the audience watching other bands, wondering what I would do if I was ever the one standing center stage at the microphone.

Okay, smart guy, now what?

I don't know how to hold my guitar or which foot to put my weight on. I don't know where to look. I don't know if I'm supposed to dance or stand still. I hope I'm singing in tune and I hope everyone remembers their parts. I look through the crowd from face to face but it's too much, too many people to take in, too many lives to consider. Some watch distractedly. Some talk. Some stare. I try to un-focus my eyes. I try not to see them, the people in their judgment, their detachment. I try to avoid the slick tight jeans and vintage jackets, the jagged bangs and elegant haircuts, the subtle tattoos, country hats, feather necklaces, heavy boots, rings, key chains, slouching expressions, narrow disinterested eyes, the signifiers worn like the bright plumage of exotic birds, and just focus on what they're hiding.

There is one thing I know, one thought that runs through my mind as I stand exposed and nervous under the cheap bright twirling lights: *You have to show them. You came all this way. Now just show them.*

Daren and I booked the show before we had any other bandmates. After months of rehearsal in a claustrophobic studio space, full of adrenaline, jumping around in our short shorts and tank tops, we felt we'd discovered something. Occasionally, we would stop after a particularly fraught section of music and I'd look up at him, a little embarrassed, wondering what to make of it, all this screaming and pouncing. He would just nod his head and say something like "Fuck yeah, man."

How could I not love him for that?

We tried auditioning more of those semipro "gigging" players, but they just kept flaking on us. *Fuck them,* we thought. *We'll do it as a two piece.* So we booked a show at the Echo on Sunset in Echo Park, a damp, beer-soaked room Drew and I had been to countless times to watch other bands. You can smell the fury in such places; it's in the peeling posters, the sting of the nostrils from the bleached tile floor.

Then, one day a few weeks before the gig, my friend Steven dropped by the apartment. A writer from *Filter,* he was a spindly, tall, stylish Taiwanese American man holding a white Fender Jaguar guitar, the perfect complement to the black one I owned. I played him the demos. He plugged in and played the riffs by ear. That's all it was. I asked him to play the show. He said yes.

Next came Anna, a *Filter* intern whom I ran into at a taco shop drunk at midnight. We toasted our tacos in a drunken gesture, and she mentioned she played violin. I had written some string parts on a few songs. She could come up to the stage for those songs, then leave again, like a guest attraction. So I asked her if she would play the show. She said yes.

Finally, there was my friend's neighbor, a double bass player named Noah who joined us for the one and only practice two days before the show, as a favor. If nothing else, I thought, the enormous upright bass, the size and shape of a lifeboat, would make for a great prop. When we finally gathered for that one and only practice, I was filled with such gratitude, such awe, feeling an incredible sense of privilege to have all these talented people playing these sad songs of mine.

We decided to wear only black and white. There was some talk about *White Noise* and the idea of TV static, of seeing ourselves as instruments of what Andy Warhol referred to as a "happening," how we could disappear into the "occurrence," become instruments "of the moment." But it was probably because that was the only way we would all match.

Daren and I salvaged the hood of a rusted-out yellow Alfa Romeo at a junkyard in Sun Valley, thinking if we put it on the stage and miked it as if it was a piece of his kit, the car hood would add to this sense of "happening," of racket come to life. Every few songs, it is Anna's job to run to the back of the stage and pound on the car hood with a mallet.

Something about it made sense: part revival, part confessional, part circus—that's rock and roll.

After a few songs, I stop thinking about my feet or my clothes, my bad hair, my inadequately low, scratchy voice, and I just think about the songs. Where I was when I wrote them, how it felt to be in those moments, to long to be here. The band plays their parts perfectly, every note. I am so grateful to them. Amber is in the crowd somewhere. The audience is fickle. Some clap. Some don't. Some pay attention and some talk the whole time. Some come up to me afterward with beaming faces and say something like "I had no idea! Wow!" Others seem unimpressed. I don't care. I'm just glad they're here in this room, drifting through space with me. I would take them all home if I could.

It's a gift to stand and sing, to jump and spit and sweat, to say the things I never thought I could say out loud, to be at the center of this precious moment, this stage, the only place I have nothing to hide.

It feels like flying.

WE BOOK ANOTHER show. Then another. Most are disappointing and there is a feeling like performing alone to an empty theater.

We are at a record store. *Should we set up beside the import rack or just stand next to the counter? Will that block the line? I mean, if anyone shows up.*

We are at a small stage in a room adjacent to a Mexican restaurant. *Why do they need these heavy plush red curtains? Are they worried people will see us eating chips back here? There's no one out there but the waitstaff anyway.*

We are at the Elks Lodge in Palm Springs. *I remember this. I used to sit and listen to speeches about the future in rooms just like this, in another lifetime, when I had a future.*

We are at a radio station in Seattle that has started playing one of our songs. *Who brought the set list? Are you sure your cousin doesn't mind if we crash on his floor? We have to leave by 5:00 A.M. so Daren can get back for work.*

We are trudging through alleyways, unloading cars, lifting amps, unwinding cords, tuning strings, twiddling reverb knobs, waiting impatiently at the bar for the other bands to finish for our heartbreakingly brief half an hour onstage, for this one moment to stand onstage for the scores of people, the handful of people, the one person who may look at us as if to say,

Tell me about when you were young and you stared at a violet sky wondering why it made your heart turn in your chest. Tell me of the private loves you had, when you thought you might live forever. Tell me how this thought came crashing down one day and destroyed you. Tell me how you rose from those ashes. Sing to me.

THERE'S SOMETHING ELSE. A feeling that follows me through those squalid rooms and half-empty halls: the ever-increasing sense that I will fail spectacularly. That in doing so, I will embarrass myself and reveal a naked ambition, an inadequate mind; to try so hard, to care so much, to be so serious about this bit of silliness, will only make me look silly too.

I tell Dad about this feeling one day at Hollywood Park, sitting in the box seats. He likes the box seats. He says it means you're serious. It's a little strange because I know he likes to sit on the benches in the sun like the other regulars on the days I don't come with him. But when I come with him once a month, to eat lunch and make our bets, always going in together on the Pick Six, he likes to get a box, like we are landed gentry from another time.

He doesn't know about the bright room I carry with me in my mind a thousand feet beneath the racetrack, the dreamscape I go to visit my F-A-M-I-L-Y, feeling like everyone is young again and we will never die. I never tell him about that. He's not one for metaphors. It's like we've divided the world between us and we come here to share it, to tell the other what we've seen. He gets V8 engines and classic cars, football, World War II, Mussolini, black-and-white movies, Old Spice, fistfights, Mexico, "calling people on their bullshit," George Carlin, Jackson Browne and the Allman Brothers. He seems content to leave metaphors to my world, along with "college," long-distance running, Russian literature and indie rock.

He loves that I started a band. When I sit next to him in the baby-blue 1959 Chevy Apache he restored with my uncle Donnie, he likes to put on *Eat a Peach* by the Allman Brothers and crank the stereo. It has to be loud for the sound to get over the purr of the five-hundred-horsepower engine that can be heard for blocks. He'll cock a thumb and rock his elbows, look at me and say, "Now, that's one smokin' guitar. You guys should do something like that."

He and Bonnie come to the shows and sit backstage smiling at everyone like it's the most natural thing in the world, to be sitting there, cowboy boots propped up on the table in the greenroom while the bands scurry around him drinking beer, going over set lists in their hoodies and tight jeans.

I tell him I feel ridiculous sometimes, that I have friends who think I'm kidding myself, that I'm squandering a writing career or something more responsible like law school in favor of something so impossible as rock and roll. He cocks an eyebrow at me and says, "Fuck 'em. What do they know?"

"I don't know, Dad. I'm just scared all the time. Maybe it won't work out and I'll look like an idiot for committing so much to this silly thing."

"Good!" He looks up from the program, leaning back in the metal folding chair in our box near the finish line, and smiles at me. "It's good to be scared! That's how you know you've risked something. That's the whole point of taking a gamble on something: you don't know how it's going to turn out. There's no payoff without risk."

"I just feel like people are laughing at me, Dad."

"Let them. Listen, being scared to fail, taking a big chance when you don't know how it's going to turn out, that's how every great story begins. If you already knew the ending, it wouldn't be very good, would it?"

"I guess not."

"Anyway, at least you're not bored out of your mind in some cubicle, or locked up in a jail cell." He stares down at the horses promenading onto the track, manes braided, hides oiled, all glistening muscles and bright colorful numbers. "Don't ever forget that I believe in you."

TONY COMES TO all the shows. I see him standing at the side of the room with his shirt rolled up at the sleeves, his strong tattooed arms crossed in front of him, a thick silver necklace joined by a small padlock around his neck as he bobs his head with the drumbeat. I know the necklace is supposed to be some kind of punk statement, a new look he's adopted since moving away from Playa del Rey to an übercool industrial loft building in downtown L.A., but the padlock seems more immediate than that, like he knows he's chained to something.

He's not one for the theater of competitive irony of the Silver Lake rock-and-roll scene. He just stands at the side of the room watching his brother.

The crowds grow. The rooms fill. Friends bring friends and we stop having to ask so much. I don't really know why. I know we take it all very seriously and I know that people seem to respond to that, to the seriousness of this ridiculous thing, the ridiculousness of being so serious about it.

On the night we sell out the club we started at in Echo Park, Tony is the first one to arrive, already at the door by the beginning of sound check. He's memorized every word to every song. He asks me for pages with the lyrics printed out. I see him singing when I scan the room from the stage. He sways, sipping his scotch and soda, raising it in the air to cheer at the end of each song. I can feel his pride in me. His glee. It's comforting to have him there, and even though I worry about his drinking, I think maybe he has it under control, at least for now.

So I am shocked when he calls me one afternoon to tell me he's addicted to heroin and he's scared he's going to jump off the roof of the ten-story building where he lives.

I don't know what I thought, but not this. His voice is creaky and desperate as he tells me he's been shooting heroin in the bathroom, just as Dad used to do. He's also smoking crack, taking a mountain of pills and drinking a fifth of whiskey every night. The words fail to register. I just thought he was a kind of dime-store drunk. Heroin? Fucking *crack*?

"I don't know what I might do, Mick. I'm scared I'm just going to kill myself. I need help. Can you help me? I don't know what to do."

He doesn't seem like the proud, strong, tattooed guy singing along at the side of the room, but more like the sad boy with the shaved head whom I remember from Synanon, the one who sat alone at the edge of the playground until he was nearly seven years old.

I tell him not to move. I drive my car across town, speeding the whole way, hoping he doesn't jump, thinking about my brother, the one who guards me, the one I must guard the way a boxer guards a broken rib. I keep him on the line the whole time. *I'm on Sunset. I'm passing the fire station, I'm going under the 101, I'm turning left on Second Street. Please don't do anything. Please. I'm almost there, I swear. I'm not leaving. I'll be right by you. We can go somewhere and talk about it. We can go somewhere and not talk about it. I'm here, I'm here, I'm here. Please don't die.*

I turn right on Wall and see him sitting on the concrete stoop of his apartment building, his hair big and wild, his neck thin, his eyes squinted, his shoulders slumped in his gray sweatshirt, the padlock hanging beneath his chin. I get out of the car and he gets up and I throw my arms around him. He feels heavy, empty, like I am holding a dead body.

"It's okay, big bro. We're going to get you sorted out."

"I don't know how I got here. I don't know what I'm going to do, Mick. I don't want to die. I can't do this anymore."

"It's okay. Let's just get in the car. We'll go talk it out. I'll sit with you while you kick if you want. Just like Dad always talked about. I'll sit right next to you. You're going to be okay. I'm not going anywhere."

"It was so stupid. I don't know what I was thinking fucking with that stuff. I can't be here. I just can't be here anymore."

"I know. I know." He buries his head in his big hands, his body shaking.

"I feel so sick."

"You don't need to do anything but get in the car."

"I don't want to die. I don't want to die," he keeps saying as he rocks back and forth.

He gets in the car and we call Dad and Bonnie and he tells them the whole story, how he smoked heroin on a whim at a party and then started buying needles and packets to heat and inject. He's been taking Vicodin and Percocet for years now, he says. It started with a back injury, but he just kept it up, taking more and more. He's up to forty-five Vicodin pills a day, along with the fifth of whiskey. The crack came last. He bought it to try speedballs, injecting the heroin first, then smoking the cocaine rocks with a glass pipe until he fell over on his kitchen floor.

"It wasn't even fun. It was just like trying to extinguish something by the end. Like trying to bury myself beneath the drugs."

For a brief moment, they think he's joking. Nobody knew how bad it was. They tell us to come over to the house in Westchester, that we need to figure it out as a family, that they're here. We're all here. "No one is going anywhere."

We drive to Westchester and by the time we arrive, Bonnie has called five drug rehab centers. She hugs Tony at the door. She tries to talk to him about the different options, but Dad is furious, already knee-deep in tough love with that gruff no-bullshit voice of his. "That's really fucking stupid, you know. What the fuck is wrong with you? Didn't you learn anything from me? Heroin? That shit will *kill* you."

Tony stares at the ground, too weak to respond. He's got huge black circles under his eyes and heavily chapped lips, that wild look as he shakes lightly and taps his foot. I sit next to him, an arm draped around his shoulders.

Two hours later we are standing in the parking lot at Brotman Medical Center, a twelve-step-based rehab facility on Venice Boulevard. It's dusk, a cold blue sky retreating to blackness over us as we stand in the wind. Tony throws up behind an ambulance. His body is already going through withdrawals. A paramedic asks if he needs help and I tell him we're on our way to the drug rehab. He nods like he's seen it before.

Upstairs, we check Tony in and they put him in an empty white room. His tremor has gotten worse. He has a terrified look in his eyes as we gather to leave. He shouts at Dad, "What the fuck did you ever do, old man?! Huh?! You think you're so much better than me?!"

I tell him to calm down. I know he's anxious and angry from the withdrawals. "Fuck off!" he yells at me and kicks a chair which bounces off the empty white wall.

"Have fun kicking heroin," I say, walking out, exhausted, annoyed, angry, worried.

We don't hear from him for a week. The doctor calls and says he couldn't go on methadone because his liver was too weak, so he just had to kick cold turkey. They could hear him screaming from the nursing center down the hall, pounding on the walls and retching into the bucket they left for him. It was hard to witness, but there was no other way because the mixture of opiates and alcohol over many years had destroyed his liver. The doctor tells us he had the worst liver enzymes they'd ever seen and if he would've waited one more month he would be dead.

I'm just glad he's there. It feels like he's safe, for now, like we are standing on the edge of a nightmare. We imagine these things romantically sometimes, the pirates on the run, the sanguine Dope Fiends one step in front of the law. But it's not like that. It's fear and worry. It's my father's desperate anger and tears, the truth we quietly acknowledge that if he died, if we lost a brother, a son, it wouldn't feel romantic or tragic or mysterious. We would only feel cursed.

WE ARE MAKING a record. We are debating reverb. We are editing guitar riffs. I am singing, listening to the songs come to life, trying to imagine if this particular version captures the feeling, the specific one, the one that is mine, the contradiction that I swore to uphold at the altars of David Bowie and Robert Smith. *Is the snare too loud to feel like loneliness? Does this keyboard effect really capture desperation? How much chorus pedal on this part makes it sound restless? The scream is too loud, the whisper is too quiet, the rack toms need to sound like trash cans in an alley, the voice should be in an empty field at midnight, not a church on a Sunday morning. I don't know. I don't know. Make it longer. Make it shorter. Make it meaner. Make it quiet. Make it loud.*

Amber and I are done. Amber and I are trying again. Amber and I are somewhere in between done and trying again. She is tired of it. I am tired of it. The break becomes more permanent. I see her out at a bar one night with another man. The band on the stage plays a sad song and I can't help but stare at her as she smiles coquettishly at him, the stranger with the long black hair in the blue flannel and baggy jeans. *Who is this guy? Why is this making me crazy?* She sips her vodka tonic; I pound beer after beer. She leaves and I feel like I'm about to burst. I run into Steven by the door. "You all right, man? You look like you've seen a ghost."

Fine. Fine. I'm fine. I'm fine. That little face, the big cat suit, the flirty eyes looking at him now, the quick smiles and prodding touches, the lightly suggestive jokes, all for the stranger in the flannel. I am stumbling out into the parking lot. I am walking into trash cans on Sunset. I am tripping under streetlights outside her apartment, knowing I can't call, I can't go home. Do I love her? Is this love? What is this thing I have created that I need so much but can't seem to keep?

There is no sidewalk, only dizziness, a blur of people staring as I fall into bushes, try to stand, tear my jeans and catch a glimpse of myself in the reflection of the window of the 7-Eleven on Vermont. I see a sad, rumpled shadow of a man. Swaying and drunk, I walk the five blocks home at 2:00 A.M. and pass out on my bed.

In the morning, I splash water on my face, sit down at my keyboard with my guitar and write a song about it. I don't leave my apartment for three days. I keep the blinds drawn and the door shut. I order in Chinese food and live off the week-old bread and cheese in the fridge. I just want to follow David Bowie's instruction: find the contradiction; write about it. I can hear Robert Smith's words echoing through my head: "Why be normal?"

THE DOCTOR SAYS Dad needs a heart operation or he will die. That's what Bonnie tells me when we finally finish the record. There's no time to celebrate finishing because my mind is suddenly hijacked by fear. My dad in a bed. My dad in a box. There are complications, risks. The doctor says the big problem is that his cardiomyopathy makes him a bad candidate for surgery, so the surgery itself might kill him. It's risky, but then so is doing nothing. There are no good answers. It all sounds like something Dad would say.

It's hard to hear words like that without the sudden feeling like I am pinned beneath them and can't breathe, as if the weight of the *S* for "surgery" has wrapped its curvy spine around my throat. In the weeks leading up to the operation, I am always a little out of breath, a shallow puddle of fear and anxiety in my chest. My mind is on a hospital bed where I picture a tan man with tubes in his nose, vulnerable, trapped.

Now that we've finished the record, we've booked a series of shows every Thursday for the month of January at a club in Silver Lake called Spaceland. The "residency," as it is called, is treated as a kind of coming-out party, the measure of a band in the Los Angeles music scene. Our third show of the month is scheduled for the same day as Dad's operation. In the week leading up to that show, two big local radio stations have taken an interest in the song I wrote about the night I ran into Amber with the stranger. The song is called "Sometime Around Midnight." It's not anything I ever thought would get played on the radio. There's no chorus or middle eight or what those gigging professional musicians called "hooks." It's just a short story set to music.

The day before the surgery, one of the big radio stations starts playing the song regularly, right in between the White Stripes, Nirvana, and the Red Hot Chili Peppers. When I hear it, my heart practically leaps from my chest. It's like standing at the fifty-yard line in front of a crowded football stadium naked, like everything I've tried to hide has suddenly become exposed to intense public scrutiny. It also sounds a little lo-fi next to those bands, like you can almost hear someone coughing in the background.

The station plays the song five times a day and I keep getting calls from people who say they heard it. When I check at night, there are scores of unread emails from various music industry professionals, agents, A&R reps. We don't even have a manager. They all want to come to the show at Spaceland the next night. It seems so strange to me, after years of being told how the internet was going to change music, that it's such a big deal for a song to be played on the radio.

When I wake up on the morning of the show, I've already got a voice mail from Bonnie that she left when they wheeled Dad in for surgery at 6:00 A.M. I can hear the nervousness in her voice, the fear of something black and nameless. "We're just gonna try and stay positive today because we don't have any choice."

I shower and drive to Cedars-Sinai, where Bonnie and I sit together in the fifth-floor lounge, waiting. I try to imagine where Dad is, sitting alone in some pre-op room, his face beneath an oxygen mask. I want to sit next to him, to stand over the shoulder of the surgeon to make sure he doesn't screw it up.

A nurse comes out. There is a delay. Something about a surgeon and a conflicting procedure. Bonnie is apoplectic. "But what about his blood sugars? Isn't there only a small window of time here? Don't you need to start soon? Is he just sitting back there alone?" The nurse tries to reassure her as she wipes her tears from her face, avoiding the looks from the other families in the waiting room.

By two o'clock I have to drive across town for a sound check at the club. It seems stupid to play a show on a day like this, but by the time I get to Spaceland, there is already a small crowd of people out front. We go through the sound check and I am frozen with the fear in my chest, the nameless lump that grows as I worry about what could happen. *What if he dies? Will we cancel the show? Will we play the show anyway? What a dumb selfish thing to worry about. Does any of this even matter? Why is everything such a performance?*

I walk out of sound check and the line out front has grown to maybe a hundred people, down to the auto shop at the corner. Nobody recognizes me. I don't know why they would.

I drive back to Cedars-Sinai, where Bonnie is still sitting in the fifth-floor lounge. She's got tears in her eyes when I get there, shaking her head, saying, "It's taking too long. They should've been done by now. It's too much. This is too much. I can't take it, Mick." I hug her tight and try to calm her, to calm myself, feeling the panic rising in my chest. *Can I help? What can I do? My dad. My dad. No.*

At six o'clock, a short, kindly doctor in a white lab coat walks up to us in our chairs. He's an Asian man with a tidy haircut sweeping his thick black hair across from his forehead. He has his hands folded in front of him.

"Are you Bonnie Lou Jollett?" Bonnie changed her name when they ran off to Vegas to finally get married five years ago because they needed to in order to keep their health insurance. I was the only witness. Tony and I have taken to simply calling her "Lou," since it makes our Jewish mother from L.A. sound like she's a Southern belle.

She looks up and croaks, "How's my guy?"

"Jim made it through the procedure and he's resting now. We were able to place the stent in his heart and we think he's going to feel much better from now on."

Bonnie lets out a gasp. She grabs the doctor's hands and puts them to her forehead. "Thank you. Thank you. I don't know what I would've done."

I feel a wave of relief wash over me. It's instant. Like a blast of hot air. Suddenly the world is warm again and light again and there is a future in front of us and the room has lost the nightmarish proportions. We are lucky.

An hour later we walk in to see Dad in the post-op area. He looks frail and thin in the small bed. It's hard to see him this way, the strong man who held us in the waves, tired and frail, covered in white wires running beneath his hospital gown, the steady beep of a heart monitor next to his bed. I grab his hand. He opens his eyes. "Heyyyyy, duuuude." He blinks. I kiss his cheek. I want so badly to protect him.

Bonnie keeps kissing his forehead, sobbing as she leans over him and says, "Oh, baby, I was so scared. I'm so glad you're all right." She cries onto his hospital gown.

Tony arrives. He's been living in a halfway house in Culver City. He goes to work every day and to an AA meeting every night. He looks better. Still haggard, tired, fuzzy and quiet. But there's a healthy glow to his cheek instead of the strung out, gaunt, exhausted, dehydrated look he had when we dropped him off at rehab. The light is returning to his big blue eyes.

He leans over the bed and Dad grabs his hand with one hand and my hand with the other, nodding, looking back and forth between us. "We're all right," he says. "Everyone's still here." We lean in and hug, our foreheads pressed together.

I grab on to Bonnie, who's sobbing. "It's okay, Lou. We're all okay."

Dad looks up at me and asks, "Don't you have a show to play?"

I'd nearly forgotten. I kiss Dad on the cheek and hug Bonnie and Tony. I run through the halls of the hospital, feeling like I'm practically floating, past the old men coughing in their beds, the women sleeping on their backs with their mouths open. The unlucky ones. *My father is alive! My father is alive!*

In the parking garage I nearly crash into another car. Turn right out of the driveway. Left on Third. Head east. The radio is on. I hear a DJ mention my show at Spaceland. It all seems so abstract, like something happening to other people in another part of the world.

When I get to the club in Silver Lake, there is a line around the block. It doesn't make sense. The club holds only about three hundred people, but there must be eight hundred snaking down the street, around the auto shop, up the next block. I don't know these faces. *Who are these people? Was there a fire?*

The band is waiting in the tiny greenroom behind the stage. Daren looks up at me when I walk in. "Is he okay?" I nod my head with a smile and Daren gives me a hug. "Fuck yeah." I feel at this moment so grateful to have a fellow traveler, a friend, another imaginary boy who knows how precious this imaginary world is.

CHAPTER 41

"GOOD EVENING. THIS IS ALL I HAVE"

By the time we play the Coachella Valley Music and Arts Festival, by the time we stand on that enormous main stage under those massive black speakers, looking out over an audience that stretches for five football fields in front of us, just two spots before Morrissey himself with his pompadour and lyrics written as if in blood across my heart, it feels like the idea of the band no longer belongs to me. It belongs to others.

It's strange when that happens, when something that was once in your mind becomes an object in the world with a size and a shape, a thing that can conjure ideas in the minds of others. The songs seem like children who left home and traveled the world. They had their own experiences in the minds of others. It's imperfect, this form of telepathy. And it's wonderful. It's also disappointing. To feel simultaneously seen and invisible.

I threw up backstage before our set, in the grass behind our trailer. I was certain nobody would come, that the crowd would disperse when we took the stage. Or they would jeer, maybe throw things. Or worst of all, they simply wouldn't pay attention.

Shyness is nice and shyness can stop you from doing all the things in life you'd like to.

After the record came out on a local indie label, we went on tour. We rented a black Sprinter van that looked like an airport shuttle and booked shows in every major city in the United States. The strangest thing at first was the simple fact that people kept showing up. It was one thing to play a show in Echo Park, quite another to arrive in Philadelphia or Austin or

Chicago and see two or three hundred people waiting in line outside the club. I didn't understand it. I got the logic that the record was being shared and a song was on the radio. We sat for interviews and people asked me questions just like the ones I used to ask other musicians, and I answered them. But there was an unreality to it all, like it was a dream from which I was about to awake. Each night, I left the stage with the feeling that I wanted to take the audience home. I'd meet them in a line after the show, shaking hands and taking pictures, and notice some people with actual tears in their eyes, looking at me as if to ask if I understood. *Yes, I do. I'm glad you're here. Why did you come? Is it because you have a Secret Place too? Did you invite me in for the same reasons I once invited others into mine?*

It felt sacred, this place, to stand on the other side of the bridge I imagined at twelve years old and know it was all real, these feelings that connect us like lost children.

I would lace up my big brown boots, put on my sweat-streaked jeans still wet from the night before and twiddle with the guitar pedals at the front of the stage, the distortion, reverb, delay. Microphones were plugged in, cords taped in arcs across the stage as I stand on an X during sound check while someone focused the spotlight. From the back of the room the tech would yell, "Let me hear the kick! Okay, now the floor tom! Vocal stage right!" Backstage in a tiny greenroom, there was always beer on ice, wine bottles open next to vodka, whiskey, mixers. The conversation is light before the show. *Did you see that scene by the lake when we drove in? I think there was an accident. There were three ambulances. I think a man was killed. No. Wait. Was I still asleep? Did I dream that? Did anyone else dream that?*

The taste of salt in my mouth as I swallow spit to sing, the sting of hair product in my eyes from the sweat beneath those hot lights, an electric shock from an ungrounded microphone when it zaps my lips and I jump back, the faces, all the different faces I don't want to let down as I un-focus my eyes and peer around the room. We begin. A blur of energy. Dizziness. Sweat. Stomping and clapping and screaming and singing. I wake up in a cheap motel next to Daren or Steven or Noah. We get some coffee from the breakfast bar. We drive to the next city. We set up our gear. We search for food, then go to sound check, then back to the motel to shower. We go over vocal warm-ups and set lists. Then the show, the dream come to life, the bursting lights and screaming and wailing, a place to find that connection, that thing I long for. Then it's quiet again as we watch the crowd file out from the rafters above the stage, hoping our colds don't get worse, drinking tea, or whiskey, or whiskey with tea for our stuffed noses and froggy throats. We go wilding through the streets to find a local bar at midnight, to savor this moment, this one precious moment: alive and awake in a rock-and-roll band in some dirty back alley on the moon. Sometimes we end up in a living room or a city park at 2:00 A.M. lighting fireworks, howling and jumping, then stumbling back to the motel to sleep before it is time to drive to the next town. And the next.

When we get to Portland, Jake is waiting at the back of the venue, his hands in his pockets, an enormous grin on his face as he watches me on the stage. The Wonder Ballroom is a big box with polished wooden floors that looks like the kind of place where they once held sock hops in the 1950s. The room has good energy. Jake is hard to miss, as always—my friend who looks like a six-foot-six, 260-pound Viking with a long blond beard smiling at me from the back of the room. He's married now with two daughters. Tony and I both attended his wedding, flying up to Oregon to watch Jake cry like a baby, red in the face and swaying for the entire ceremony while his bride looked on, mildly annoyed, mildly amused.

He greets me with a hug, practically lifting me off the ground, and says, "What is up, you big fucking rock star? How did you convince all these people you were important?"

"Oh, believe me, nobody thinks that."

"Yes they do, man. There was a line out front. I had to push my way to get in. People were *upset.*"

We settle in at the bar with a couple glasses of scotch on the rocks so

I can "ice" my voice, which has been failing me for a few shows now, all sung out, screamed out, talked out.

He puts an enormous hand on my shoulder and shakes me like a bear. "So what's it like, man? You got, like, groupies and shit?"

"No. It's hardly Led Zeppelin around here. Backstage is usually a plate of hummus and, like, someone's aunt." I tell Jake about the tour, how strange it is that though I'm so far away from home all the time, the band has become a kind of meeting point for the family.

My aunt Pam moved to Atlanta, and when she heard her nephew's band was coming to town, she was determined to watch me play, even though we were in a tiny beer-soaked club called the Drunken Unicorn in which my matronly, kind middle-aged aunt watched me play from the back of the room while the exposed pipes dripped condensation on her from the ceiling. She told me that after the show, as she was heading upstairs, some guy stopped her and said, "You know where you are, right?" Yes, she said. I'm here to watch my nephew.

My uncle Jon came to a show with my cousin Heidi. He still had that long beard, that soft, affable way of his. Both of his boys grew up to be gymnasts like their grandfather, learning their skills in a gym he owned. There's a new sadness around his eyes, a hint of tragedy since his wife, Andy, died. She was exercising in the front yard outside the third house they built by hand in Nevada City. She came inside with a terrible headache. Jon got her some water. When she threw up, Jon called an ambulance that arrived shortly. They joked around with her because she was the nurse who had conducted their training. They placed her on a gurney and loaded her into the ambulance. When my uncle got to the hospital, they told him she had a subdural hematoma and died before they even got to the highway. He asked me about the tour over dinner and seemed genuinely charmed by the fact that his nephew's life took the turn it did. He's a kind man. You can see the kindness in his eyes from behind his big bushy beard and I can't help but think of the life others are leading, filled with promise and tragedy, while I attend sound checks and sleep off hangovers in cheap motels.

"It must be weird to have all these people knowing your songs," Jake says. "I mentioned you to one of my co-workers the other day and she couldn't believe I knew you. I was like, *Know* him? I fucking *made* him."

He laughs, checking my gaze. "Well, not really, but you know what I mean."

"It is weird. I don't know how to explain it."

"I saw you guys on *Letterman*. It seems like he really liked you."

"It helped to have that string quartet playing with us." Anna's brother Andrew is also a classically trained violinist whose ensemble, the Calder Quartet, flew to New York to play *Late Night with David Letterman* with us. It did feel like a kind of arrival, like the joke was spiraling out of control: this song that was just a sad story about Amber that so many people knew by heart, this record about restlessness, about wanting to be anywhere but my own head, taken seriously by so many people.

There is a giddiness to it. We all feel it. We get compared to bands we love; we've made (a little) money, enough to buy an actual car and still pay rent. We're all aware of how rare a thing it is and the best nights are the ones when we play a show and we know the audience loved it and we're practically leaping arm in arm as we exit the stage. It's a wonderful feeling to be able to live a dream.

But the irony that keeps occurring to me as I sing these songs night after night, as they conjure the image of Naomi dancing sweetly around her place, her colorful acrylics scattered on the floor beneath her feet, or of Amber balled up in the corner of that dirty yellow couch in the trailer on the edge of the world, is that I couldn't actually *have* the relationships. I could only sing about them. I couldn't be in them, so I wrote these stories to try to make sense of them. It's so much easier to sing these sad songs than to live out the relationships they are about, easier to simply climb up the stone tower in the sky where I feel safe.

I smile at Jake. "Yeah, it felt like being launched into space. You know that scene in *The Right Stuff* when they're walking in slow motion and the rocket is warming up in the background? It was like that."

"That's so fucking cool, man. Goddamn." He shakes me again.

I want to laugh with him, to pretend all of this isn't overwhelming. It's just that it never occurred to me how I might appear to others in this hall of mirrors I'd constructed, that there would be these thoughts I would guard, private things I kept to myself. Performing on the stage on a good night leaves a buzz in my chest that I carry with me like a secret. I return to it again and again, the look on their faces, the roar of their voices as they meet mine, a place where I felt anxious, then bold, then elated, then floating as if lifted by the energy in the room. Walking down the street with headphones on some quiet afternoon in yet another faceless town, I think, *None of these people know and I'm not going to tell them.*

But when those moments end and the buzz is gone and the reality sets in that I know I am lost and that this facsimile, however splendid or romantic, cannot erase the basic feeling that I am alone and it is because I am damaged and it will always be that way, the whole thing seems less like a romantic story and more like an intoxication from which I awake to see the consequences, like those kids on LSD in the 1960s who died thinking they could fly.

And now we're at Coachella, the same Coachella I attended three times as a journalist. The same one where I flashed my backstage/VIP credentials as I followed rock stars around, secretly hoping somebody might mistake me for one, the same Coachella where I watched from the back as the tiny speck of rarefied artists took the stage, as the din came to a standstill, and the artist began to sing, my heart soaring. That Coachella.

It's different from up close. Nerve-racking. We mount the rickety steps at the back of the stage. Everything seems bigger than everything else. It's hard to hold one thought in mind, my chest all nerves, my head spinning. We swat each other and pat each other and hug each other, holding on for comfort, for strength, fellow travelers on this road we never really thought we would walk down. I can't feel my feet or the air on my face as we emerge from behind a side-stage curtain and see the people, some leaning on banisters at the front, some lying on blankets in the back smoking weed. I walk to the microphone at center stage, close my eyes and begin to play. Soon there is a drum behind me and I see the faces in the front row, some singing along, some beginning to clap. I start to feel like I can move, wandering over to Steven as he plays his perfect riffs on guitar and we exchange a smile. I sing until I lose my breath, I pant and run, thinking, *Show them, just fucking show them.* And when it's over, when we walk off that stage and hug in the field behind it, we are relieved, intoxicated from the moment, downright *high.* And this, too, becomes a feeling I guard like a jealous secret.

After *Letterman* and Coachella, we sign to a larger label and get word that the tour is going to be extended. We are going to have a bus now where we sleep at night, driving between venues. We're going to play *The Tonight Show*, Austin City Limits, Lollapalooza, *Late Night with Conan O'Brien* and *Jimmy Kimmel Live!* A few of the songs get placed in movies, in TV shows, one in a car commercial. It doesn't even make sense to keep an apartment anymore, because I'm never home. I have to move out the next time we're in L.A. We are booked in bigger and bigger rooms. The days run together now that we are on a bus, sleeping in small bursts in a kind of rumbling coffin, disoriented and far from home, never quite asleep, never quite awake. Life comes at us like a collage.

We are in Minneapolis. *Did I even sleep? I remember the shaking in the dark, twisting and turning through what I assume were hills, though it's hard to know in that dark little fever dream they call a sleep compartment.*

And then Chicago. *A friend! We ran together at the front of the pack on graduation day! Do you remember? We were younger and bursting with, what was it? Hope? No. Life? No. Pride? I'm not sure. I was hiding something and now it's plain. Or it isn't. I can't really tell. You've married. You've had a child. She is beautiful. I'm so sorry your wife has cancer. I'm so sorry you've been through so much. No, I don't have things I love more than anything else. I have this.*

And then Cleveland. *I'll be at the casino. I'll just sit at this table and think of Dad. I miss him. I'm worried about his heart. He's okay. He's okay. He's okay. He's proud of me. I am his son. What is a son? I miss being a son, sitting in the sun with a racing form making jokes, eating corned beef sandwiches and feeling calm.*

And then Seattle. *A phone call. Mikel, dahhling? How's the road? Don't you worry about your grandma Juliette, I'm fine. It's quiet since Grandpa died. He loved you, you know. He was so proud. No, I know you couldn't be here. I'm just sad. I miss my boy. I think I hear him sometimes. No, we all understand. You're in the world now. You're living your life.*

And then Portland again. *Jake! Jake! Look at this! Look what we did! Look at all the people! All those lives! Where are they now? They're at the bar! They're lined up at the front of the stage! We did this! You did! You don't know it, but you did! I remember the wedding. Of course I do. Tony spoke and your mother was drunk and your bride did that funny dance in her wedding dress. We laughed until we fell over and I tore my pants and you picked me up and carried me through the room with my boxers hanging* out. *Your girls are beautiful. You are a man. You have a family. No, I don't have that. I have this.*

Then we are in San Francisco. Then San Diego and finally Los Angeles. *I can't do it, Tony. I can't. You've got to help me. I can't move a thing. I have to have everything moved out in two hours. I'm supposed to be at sound check right now. There was a time when we were just going to move in together, but I fucked it all up. Of course I did. I let everyone down. I'm sorry. I'm so sorry. I don't know what to do. I have a flight to London at midnight. You will? You'll come over and do it for me? No, no, no, no. I couldn't ask that. Are you sure? Oh, thank you. Thank you. I can just get all my things from storage later. A brother. A brother. How much I need a brother. I'm so glad you didn't die.*

Lights down. A brief silence as the wind whistles through the hills. *They came after all. I can't believe it. I guess I can sing. I can always sing.* Good evening. Thank you for being here. This is all I have.

Then we're stomping. Then we're screaming. Then we're clapping. Then the keyboard swells and the violin floats in from the hills, a catch in my throat, a moment to look out and look up and wonder.

Maybe I'll just walk into the sea alone, carrying these broken pieces with me. That's how I always imagined it: I was alone as I walked into the waves to disappear. I can feel the water licking my toes, the soft sand beneath my feet. But then I lift my eyes and see there are others, women with lace dresses fanning behind them like wedding veils drenched in sea-foam, men losing their hats in the wind, their trousers stuck to their legs by the waves, hundreds of them, thousands (on a good night, if the promoter did his job), all of us disappearing into the ocean together.

The questions. *Why are we? How did this? What was the? When did we all?*

There is no one answer. There are as many answers as bodies in the room. There are ten times as many answers as bodies in the room, some terrifying, some charming, some cunning, some innocent, some a hundred feet tall, godlike and invincible, others tiny and frail, beseeching and ironic. Something occurs to me as I stand under that light where I wish to disappear, something I remember like a forgotten milk tooth from a time before shame. There was a book of matches, a river, a red dot of light, something was lost and then I too became lost and then, finally, I chose to lose myself on purpose, to become the ghost that haunts my castle in the sky.

CHAPTER 42
BROKEN

"Hi, I'm Tony, and I'm an alcoholic."

"Hi, Tony!"

He stands at a wooden lectern in a community center in Culver City on Washington Boulevard, near the freeway. Seventy-five metal folding chairs fan out in front of him. The smell of burned coffee and cigarette smoke fills the room. I'm in the front row because he asked me to come watch him tell his story. The room is silent. Everyone is watching my brother as he gathers himself. He's wearing glasses and a baseball hat, his strong, heavily tattooed arms grasping the edges of the wood for balance. He has broad shoulders and a handsome face, ruddy, rakish—a light in his sparkling blue eyes. *That's new. I don't think I've ever seen that. When did that happen? Where was I?*

He's been speaking at prisons, telling his story in hopes that it will help others. That's AA. Build a ladder to the sky. Climb it. Help others up.

"I don't know where to begin, so I guess I'll just begin by saying drinking was never fun for me." He takes a sip of coffee. "And you know, that's the whole thing with drinking. You say you're having fun. And I think I pretended it was fun because that's what we did. We partied. That's what we called it. So if you asked me, I'd say I was partying too. But the truth is I was sad and ashamed and I drank because I felt bad and I wanted to stop feeling bad."

The silence is heavy in the room. It's hard to ignore his voice, his words that carry such weight. The truth just sounds different.

There are old-timers with ten years of sobriety, hands on their laps, listening with quiet smiles, young Dope Fiends with messy hair and disheveled clothes, one week sober, having just detoxed at Brotman rehab center, leaning forward with wild eyes.

There's literature at the back table, like the pamphlets Mom used to leave around the house, the big book of AA with its twelve steps, the laminated sheets for the meeting chair with the steps and traditions.

"I can't tell you how many nights were spent like that. You lose track after a while. But I was always first to leave the party, because I wasn't really there to party. The truth is I felt very alone for most of my life and drinking was a relief. The first time I ever tried that bottle of Thunderbird wine at thirteen years old, the one I stole from the Plaid Pantry, I was *in*. That moment changed my life. I finally found my best friend. I was drinking every single night by the next week.

"You gotta understand, I've never been anywhere I felt comfortable. I was born in a place called Synanon and we didn't even know our parents and then we had to escape when I was almost seven. We moved constantly. Our mother was very depressed; our stepdad was a drunk and he disappeared, or died. We never even knew. So anyway, I always felt like an outsider, this strange kid from this strange place, angry at the world in hand-me-down clothes. And then I had that one drink, that Thunderbird wine, and for once I felt like I belonged. I felt comfortable in my own skin. Literally from that moment on nothing else mattered."

He tells the whole story, drinking in high school, the rebelliousness and anger, the sense like he was trying to extinguish something. He talks about the years of being a "functional" addict, of holding down a job and paying rent while getting drunk every night. Then came the pills. Percocet and Vicodin. Two became five became ten became forty-five a day.

He pauses when he mentions his son. A pain fills his blue eyes, a straining. He wipes a small tear from behind his glasses. He gathers himself, drumming his fingers on the wood. The room is silent. "I think about my son every day. I know I was not in a place to be a good father to him. I wish so much I could've been. That one's hard. You talk about regrets and I have some others but that's the hardest one." He clears his throat. "But all you can do is try to make amends. Try to deal with what's real today. The truth is the shame of it, of knowing I could've done better by him, it was really hard to live with." I can't believe these are my brother's words, this wisdom, this calm reflection, this strength.

"When I first tried heroin, it was the best thing I'd ever felt. I thought, *Holy shit, now we're talkin'*. I don't need to live and feel pain. I could just do *this*. But heroin will kill you quick. And it wasn't six months before I felt like I was gonna die. And like the drinking, by the end it wasn't even fun. You're just sitting alone in an apartment trying to blot everything out. I knew I needed help. That if I didn't get help, I would be dead. That's probably why I'm here, if I'm completely honest. That's probably the only reason I'm here. Because the only alternative was death. That's how much the drugs and alcohol had a hold on me. In a way it's easier this way, to know I have no choice.

"So I went to Brotman. I dried out in that room, just puking and shaking, feeling sicker than I've ever felt in my life. I couldn't take methadone because my liver enzymes were so bad the doctors said it would kill me. We had group meetings every day but it was hard to listen; I was itching so bad to go out again and use. But I just kept coming back to, *well, it's either this or death*. I chose to not be dead. But it was close." He laughs. The room laughs.

"I started working steps, going to meetings every day, finding myself in these rooms with people who'd walked down the same road as me, who knew every lie I could tell myself or others to hide my habit. It's tough, man. Especially in the beginning. You just kind of have to put your head down and do it. But after a few months I started sleeping again. I started feeling okay. Healthy, you know? And then a strange thing happened. I found I liked being with others, that it was so much better to be here with friends, with people who understand me than to be using alone in the dark. That's the thing I always wanted anyway. To just be around people who understand me."

All I can think as I watch him speak is how much I know about that dark place, how I've felt it and wished I had what he had. That there is so much in me that feels like it needs to be drowned out, so I keep the noise up.

"I don't have all the answers," he says. "Nobody does. All I can say is I'm here. I'm *trying*. I'm going to *keep* trying. And for those of you who are new, I can see you sitting there in the back, itching to get out and use again. I know you don't know what to make of all this shit, all these fuckin' weirdos talking about bullshit like serenity and acceptance and regret.

These strange steps. Kinda touchy-feely, right? I just want to say, that's where it's at. In your *feelings*. We've all had those thoughts, the ones that tell you to say fuck it and drink or fuck it and go get high because otherwise what's the point of just walking around feeling like you want to die? Listen, you have friends in this room. People who want to help. Everyone here knows what you're going through because we've been through it too. You don't have to be alone. You can come to a meeting. You can find a sponsor. I'll sponsor you if you want. That's why we're here. And I promise you, this life is so much better than the one spent using in the dark. It's good to be with people, among friends. My brother is here because I'm giving him my three-year chip."

He looks at me. I am shaking. It's all so familiar and real and I'm so glad he didn't die and I remember how angry he was when we were kids and how abandoned he was at the School in Synanon, sitting alone on the playground with no mom or dad, how Mom turned him into a mental patient when we left, blaming him for his anger instead of acknowledging he had every reason in the world to be angry. I feel so proud of him now, in awe of his journey, so lost in mine.

"Anyway, I'm grateful. Grateful for tonight. Grateful for this program. Grateful for all of you. Thank you." The room erupts in applause and the chair thanks him for speaking and someone brings a small chocolate cake from the back and gives it to me to give to him. I walk to the front and he blows out the candles and gives me a hug. He doesn't let go, just squeezes me tight and says, "I love you, little bro. I don't know where I'd be without you." I kiss his cheek and tell him I'm proud of him and the room forms a giant circle and we all hold hands and say the Lord's Prayer just like we did at the AA campouts when we were kids. When it's over, he is mobbed by the young Dope Fiends who surround him like nervous children. They ask him questions, with a look in their eyes like the world depends on what he says next, like he has something they need to breathe.

They go outside to smoke and I sit in the chair in the front row and think about what he said, how far my life is from anything like the serenity or acceptance or peace he described, how much I live in that darkness, dancing around it like a moth around a flame.

* * *

GRANDMA JULIETTE DIED the week the tour ended. They called me and I drove over to the house in Westchester in a panic to see her with the breathing machine still pushing air into her nose. I pulled the tubes out of her nostrils because everyone seemed stunned, motionless, as if it wasn't real as long as the machine did its work. I checked her pulse at her neck and told everyone she was gone and sat next to her in her little red sweatshirt, my arm around her shoulders as her spirit soared through the room while Aunt Nancy screamed and Bonnie cried in my father's arms.

I felt her spirit again when we played the homecoming show at Walt Disney Concert Hall in downtown Los Angeles five days later, her presence, the sense that she and my grandfather were dancing in the air above the audience, right next to that beautiful pipe organ shaped like an enormous haystack. I sang a song that reminded me of them, missing them, fully aware of how far I was from the thing they had, the thing I wish I could have: a partner, a friend, a great love to dance with in a beautiful place after I die.

There was a moment in Amsterdam, in a hotel room near the end of the European tour, after the flight to London, the day when my brother had to move all of my things from the apartment I never visited anymore. We spent weeks in the U.K., then Germany, drinking every night. I was taking Xanax and Ambien to sleep and a couple hundred milligrams of Sudafed every day just to function, a holdover from all those head colds we caught in the States. It was supposed to be for my sinuses, but the colds were long gone and I took it every morning with my coffee. It felt like a wall I could push my body through if I just tried hard enough, to be ever further from a normal day, a restful night, on edge and anxious, squeezed and vacant, filled as if with a nameless gas that kept me going for the shows.

We went to one of the many cafés along the canal at the center of the city and I ate a large chocolate pot muffin. It didn't seem to be doing much, so after a few minutes chatting with the band, I ate another. It was a rainy afternoon. I left the café to walk back to the hotel to sleep because we had the day off. The weed hit me about halfway there. The sidewalk began to sway and I felt an intense cold as I listened to the random Dutch phrases that reminded me of another time, a war, a wreckage.

When I got back to my hotel room, I sat on the edge of the bed, hungover and exhausted after months on the road, as high as I've ever been in my life, my arms clasped around my shoulders as I shook back and forth for six hours, my mind winding down a pathway thinking only that I had screwed it all up, the chance at love, the chance for something real, that I didn't deserve any of it, that I sang all these songs about love but it was all bullshit because what did I know? What *could* I know, when right at the center of my heart there was only an empty pit, that I had never cared enough about myself to put anything else there instead?

I remembered there was a decision at the center of it, one made long ago in a tiny trailer at the edge of the world, reeling and confused and angry and hopeless, to just reject these things: love and closeness and faith in another, in favor of a different life. To give up and try to make the pain *useful.*

The decision had produced wonderful gifts, but it didn't solve the problem at the center, the problem so crystal clear to me as I watch my brother smoke and laugh with the young Dope Fiends on the street outside, a problem that plagues me, following me through sleepless nights and quiet empty days at the end of the tour, slipping into the cracks of my thoughts, a notion that comes to me when I don't look too hard, the way an image comes in a dream.

What does it mean to be broken?

It means no one picked us up when we cried and we thought it was our fault and we carried the shame of that loneliness with us throughout our lives and we weren't able to give it a name because no one acknowledged it, including us.

We hid ourselves. We created masks. We built stone towers where we felt safe.

As we got older, the shame became anger at others for the loneliness we felt, for the confusion, eventually for things we'd done that we wished we hadn't, the people we hurt, the relationships destroyed because of that shame, wondering to ourselves, Are we monsters? Orphans? Are we insane? There was no one to tell.

I can see my brother's round cheeks and blond hair, his sad eyes as he leans against a stump in his corduroy jacket in the field behind the Tomales Bay compound. No wonder he smoked crack and shot heroin and drank himself blind.

When you peel away all the layers of masculinity—the cleverness, power, sarcasm, the strength we built (or faked), the toughness (which is really just quiet suffering), white knuckles, bodies covered in boots and beards, muscles, green ink skulls, arrows and ghosts, hearts surrounded as if by barbed wire—what you see is a sad boy in the dark afraid that he will always be alone because that is the first thing he ever learned about life.

We don't want to look at any of it, because there's just too much to look at, too many times we hurt others or ourselves, when we decided we didn't deserve tenderness or warmth, or that maybe these things didn't even exist.

It's so much work. To admit it and admit it and realize you can't change. To go to meetings and you still can't change, to whisper these things into a willing ear in some quiet room at dawn and still you can't change, to say it to the occasional friend who gives you advice, offering his phone number to call if you need a hand, and still you can't change, to write it in a song, in thorough detail, aware, awake, viewing it from up close and from far away, drenched in metaphor and irony, and still you can't change, to scream it into a microphone in front of a crowd of people who've felt it too, and despite the speakers, the stage, the lights, the sweat, the gritted teeth, you go home to a place you tried to bring the whole world into and realize you are there alone—and still you can't change.

"SO, WHY ARE you here?"

The room upstairs at the back of the house is small, wrapped with windows that let in the bright California sunshine. There are chairs and a desk and trees outside where the occasional squirrel scurries by. The faint sound of water echoes up from a fountain in the courtyard. A kindly, young British man named Misha sits across from me. He's got rosy cheeks and warm eyes. My mind races through all the confusing things I feel, wondering which pose to adopt, which mask to wear, how to take it off, if this will even do me any good.

"What do you mean?"

"I mean what prompted you to seek therapy?"

I hear the words fall out of my mouth before there is time to think: "I want to be able to fall in love and I don't understand why I can't, only that I know that I am the problem and I have to change."

Okay.

CHAPTER 43

A FOREST, A RIVER, A MOUNTAIN, A SWAMP

He stares at me and I stare back. The silence hangs over the room. What have I walked into here? It's strange to have so much space to fill, to be met with quiet. It's not really like having a conversation, more like being in an empty landscape with a very kind and quiet guide.

Misha is patient, prompting my words with grunts and nods, the occasional Britishism: "Well, yeah, but you can't control that one, mate." He never says much. There isn't much to look at. Just an emptiness to fill.

It takes a few weeks to get going, to start talking about anything of substance, but I soon find so many feelings I didn't realize I had: grief over Paul dying, confusion over him maybe not dying, shock and fear over Phil getting beaten in front of me, the blankness like negative space at the edge of a watercolor I feel when I try to contend with Mom's version of events, confusion over never having gotten a chance to deal with the pain of these moments, to think about them and see them in the light because they were never acknowledged. I find so much anger, over having been forced to be a caretaker of a severely depressed woman who did not consider my needs, who saw me solely through the lens of her own victimhood. I learn more about attachment disorders, the emotional world of orphans I inherited from living in the Synanon School, how being raised in a place without parents destroyed any chance we could've had to see our world as a stable place, leaving us afraid and ashamed, as if our loneliness was our own fault. The attachment disorder made us unable to trust close relationships because the first thing we ever learned is that people leave you. Then it also made us panic at the prospect of being alone.

It's slow, difficult, excruciating work.

Most of the features around Mom are like quicksand. Over time, Misha and I come to believe she has narcissistic personality disorder or the closely related borderline personality disorder, or elements of both. It's never anything we can verify, more a puzzle we reconstruct as we slowly review events.

She still has trouble with reality. It's not accurate to say she's crazy in any cartoonish way. She can navigate a supermarket and balance a checkbook. She is still astute about the political moment, still attending sit-ins and protests, marches. But there are odd moments when it seems reality is a puzzle to her.

When the tour went through Phoenix and she and her husband picked me up to take me to dinner, I was sitting in the backseat as we drove on the highway and she asked if I was wearing deodorant. It seemed like an odd question. I told her I was. "Well, can we pull over and can you wipe it off? I'm allergic to deodorants." When we got to the restaurant, I went into the bathroom and for the briefest moment considered wiping off the deodorant from under my arms. But then I caught myself, wondering which reality I was going to live in, hers or mine? How much of my life was spent inhabiting that strange reality of hers, the one adjacent to the real world, the one in which she is a perpetual victim, a long-suffering hero, and it is my job to confirm this, to explain it to the world, to explain the world to her?

I went back to the table and she asked me if I wiped it off. I told her I did. "Yes, I can tell." She sniffed the air. "That's much better. Thank you."

There are countless moments like this. Children of narcissists learn their feelings don't matter to the narcissistic parent. The child carries an ever-present sense that he must bury his own ideas about the world, his own self, and do the thing required of him to please the narcissist, to receive the impossible-to-reach love and approval he craves. In short he doesn't really know himself because he spends his life seeking to fulfill the fantasy world of the narcissistic parent.

Not all narcissists are brash, cocky, or even extroverted. Some get the constant attention they crave from the world by playing the victim.

Children of this type of narcissist tend to feel more like the parent's spouse than child, burdened with the responsibility for the parent's well-being. When I learned this one day, I shouted, "Bingo!" and laughed out loud. It wasn't funny; it was just such a relief to have a name for the thing I've lived with for so long: Mom and her demands, her life story full of holes and easily debunked lies, the panicking sense I always had that it was my job to take care of her.

Parents with narcissistic personality disorder or borderline personality disorder tend to cross physical boundaries. Without a feedback mechanism to understand which touch is appropriate, which body language is comfortable for others, which types of affection are welcome, they tend to invade the space of others, to leave others feeling physically uncomfortable in their presence. We are not taught our own right to determine which touches are welcome, which forms of affection are welcome. Our personal space is violated by such parents who do not recognize our need or desire for space, because they see us only as extensions of themselves.

The crossing of physical boundaries can lead to tremendous shame in adulthood and a tendency to put up with unwanted touching and sexual advances. We simply are left with the feeling that we are not allowed to say no, because we were taught that the narcissist's needs are more important than our own.

Parents with NPD tend to view their children in strict aesthetic terms, wanting them to be cute and berating any physical flaws because the parents believe these flaws reflect poorly on them. It's so strange to me how I spent years as a child believing I was fat because of this. When I look back at old photos, I see only a perfectly healthy little boy.

Narcissistic and BPD parents often pit their children against each other. One becomes the chosen child, the repository of all the parent's best qualities, receiving the most attention, praise and pressure to perform. Another becomes the scapegoat. He is often blamed as the reason for the narcissist's behavior and the reflection of all the parent's worst qualities. The scapegoated child resents the attention the chosen child receives. The chosen child resents the undeserved resentment and anger from the scapegoat. It is so strange to me, upon learning these things, to see how much my brother and my relationship as children hewed to these precise patterns.

It's all so familiar, so precise, the simple and terrifying moment when you see your life as if in the key to a map and say, *Yes, there. Exactly that.*

Narcissistic personality disorder is somewhat misnamed. It conjures an image of a person who is in love with himself, a person who regards himself above all others. That isn't accurate. The defining feature of the Narcissus myth is that when Narcissus looks into the water, he sees only his own reflection. That is how it is with people with NPD. They look into a world, into their relationships, and are so terrified, so misshapen they can only see self-protective images of themselves, who their kids will be, who their spouse is, what this or that idea represents to the world.

NPD and BPD are notoriously difficult to treat because narcissists are so deeply caught in the self-protective web they've created. Narcissists simply don't know they are narcissists and if told will reject the idea. Some say there is an element of autism or Asperger's syndrome at work, a sense that human emotion is somewhat baffling to them and so they tend to fake emotions and view them through a transactional lens. Will this situation benefit me? This tends to be a more common question in the mind of the narcissist than the kind of instinctual give-and-take of human relationships involving empathy, sympathy and love.

They are, of course, emotionally abusive parents. The child is unseen, unheard, which is all another way of saying unloved.

In retrospect, it all seems so obvious. And it takes a long, long time to sink in, for Misha and me to complete the full picture. It's difficult to admit when a parent does something bad because a piece of that parent is always in you. So a piece of you always feels like you did it too. There is a sense of feeling marked, cursed, destined to walk the earth like a fundamentally flawed object. It's not true. It only feels that way.

And anyway my life is my own responsibility now. Not Synanon's, not Mom's. Mine. And one of the hardest impediments to change is the sense of grievance, the feeling of defensiveness for these scars that I would never have chosen. But there's no salvation in defensiveness. It's a dead end, a bottomless pit in the landscape that goes nowhere but down. And no matter the origin, I have to slowly learn to be responsible for my own actions and emotional world.

Change is slow. Change is slow. Change is slow. And it takes a long time to feel like I know myself, to understand the landscape in my mind, to see the ways I acted out of fear, to understand the instinctual panics I felt and calm them.

Eventually, the landscape begins to make sense and I learn where the pitfalls are. Here is a mountain of fear. Over there is a river of regret. Down there is a swamp of shame. Next to it, a meadow of hope. Travel with care.

It takes time, but I learn to laugh at myself, to tolerate discomfort, to accept these things that were once so hard to accept.

It's not easy. I get depressed. I get anxious about it. I learn to just sit with it, that the thing Dad always told me about acceptance and heartache was true: "Sometimes you just have to sit on your hands and hurt."

What can I say? It was uncomfortable and it took years and it was the only way to change.

CHAPTER 44

GREEK

There years later, I am standing on the stage of the Greek Theatre, just up the hill from the tiny Parisian apartment in Los Feliz where I first wrote about the wishing well. Blocks of seats fan out in front of me like giant red bricks dug into the greenery of the hillside. I walked the aisles when I first arrived, after seeing the band name on the marquee, just to be sure it was the same place and not something from a dream. That happens sometimes. I have a dream in my sleep compartment of the tour bus. We're playing somewhere like the moon or a windswept glacier in the middle of the Atlantic, looking back across the empty space and thinking how far we've come, how impossibly far from home we are.

Daren is on the stage adjusting his kit, the steady thump of a kick drum echoes across the canyon as Bill, our beloved longtime tour manager, calls for more rack tom, now some hi-hat. Daren pounds out a disco beat as he whispers in rhythm into his mike, "Boots and pants and boots and pants," switching to the rack tom and floor tom, saying, "Pat Boone, Debby Boone, Pat Boone, Debby Boone." An old touring joke.

It's been a strange day.

After sound check, the family arrives. Tony comes first, as always. He brings his wife and their baby daughter, Juliette, a beautiful little girl with Shirley Temple curls and enormous blue eyes. He is seven years sober now. Tan and rested, he carries his baby girl through the cavernous hall-ways behind the stage, lifting her up as she screams in glee. He seems so much like all the promise of his life has been realized, that his sobriety hasn't so much fundamentally changed his essence as empowered every-thing good about him: his wit, his undying commitment to his daughter, whom he places right at the center of his life, walking her to school and taking her to dance classes, amusement parks, the beach, so he can be like an anchor for her in the waves. He's reached out to his son, making phone calls and inquiring about his life. His son isn't ready. He's still too angry. Tony doesn't press but lets him know he's here to talk whenever he's ready.

As I watch him swing his daughter in the hallway, I wonder if he knows what his addiction cost his son, how much he just wanted the same father his sister has. I know Tony has regrets because he's so honest about it in meetings, so it's strange to think how we can be all these things at once. Disappointing to some, cherished by others. Whenever I ask him about it, he tells me he's trying but that it's just too much to face at once and his first priority is staying sober, that the anxiety he feels quickly becomes overwhelming and he needs more time because he simply can't handle it. This makes sense to me.

Tony does triathlons for charity now and owns the successful large-scale printing company he always dreamed of owning. He bought the Posner house off Fairfax and Wilshire after Grandma and Grandpa died, the one Bonnie and her sisters grew up in. His big renovation was to add a pool so his daughter would have somewhere to swim.

I'm so proud of him I could burst.

Dad and Bonnie are next. Bonnie is a whirlwind of jokes and hugs, her voice, her presence like a song, sitting each of my bandmates down to ask them about their lives. "And your kitty, is he okay? Did he miss you on the tour? That happens, you know. They know." She's still sad since her sister Jeannie died of the pulmonary hypertension she lived with for fifteen years, despite being told she only had two years to live. She fought it the whole way. Her doctors called her "the warrior." Bonnie was there every step and carries with her the same feeling her father carried: that life is brief and we must hold on to one another and cherish the moments we have with the ones we love while we still can.

Dad is so thin. He almost didn't come, because he felt so poorly. His liver is nearly gone now, just a chewed-up wad of scar tissue, cirrhotic and ravaged. It has created a host of problems for him that have robbed him of muscle and energy. He just fights through it, determined to beat it. He's changed his diet, his workout routine. He's tried herbal remedies and countless treatments, drugs, procedures. He's still got that quick step, that wink as our eyes meet from across a room crowded with friends and family. There's champagne open because it's not every day you get to play the Greek Theatre, to see a dream realized in the flesh. Dad knows it. Like everything, we've talked about this day.

He says he wants to go on tour with us, that he has a great voice and could maybe join the band for the encore. He's never seen New York City, so he wants to join the East Coast leg of the tour. He'll even get on an airplane, which is something he generally refuses to do. But he's determined. "We'll watch the shows and maybe take in a Broadway play, eat one of those three-pound pastrami sandwiches I've heard about."

The last to arrive is Lizette, my new girlfriend. She walks into the room with a smile as she hugs Bonnie and my dad, does a little jig with Juliette. We've been dating for a few months now. That's the word we use. Dating. But it isn't like that. It's more like being recognized by another, like you could spot each other in a crowd. I carry this feeling with me as I see her cross the room to say hi to Daren, her long brown hair and light brown eyes, her raised eyebrows as she picks up the store-bought salsa from the table, laughs and says, "Guys, we could do better. This is *embarrassing*. We deserve some real sa-ul-sa in here." She pronounces the word in a native Spanish style, her Mexican and Salvadoran pride showing. She occasionally looks up at me and I look back and this is the thing we share: that we are watchers, both of us, and we recognize this trait in the other, someone else who is trying to make it up as they make their way through the world.

I don't know how to explain how I finally fell in love except to say that when it happened, the words practically flew out of my mouth. I didn't choose them. The feeling just filled me until words erupted into the space between us.

I don't know how to describe the feeling except that we began a conversation one night that went on for five hours. We talked the next night and that conversation lasted five hours too. Then the next. And the next. And then we decided to be together and we are still having that same conversation.

It's strange that after years of chasing noise and then trying to understand it, actually falling in love felt like waking up to all the quiet in the world. No wind, no rain, no far-off sirens, just the precise silence of my mind as I hold that thing that makes me calm. I guess you could say that after years with Misha, I was ready for love. But it still surprised me. She still surprised me.

She.

I still visit Misha every week and so walking through this new love has been like learning a new language. It's foreign to me, like Greek. I have to ignore so many of my old instincts: to trust when I am scared or angry or confused; to create a space for uncertainty, for doubt, even boredom; to see those things in myself that have kept me alone and simply make a different choice. What I did not expect is how calming it would be to open all the doorways of my heart and find there is no reason to keep them closed.

She hands my father a plate of tortilla chips as she disparages the salsa. He liked her from the minute he met her. "I get you and her," he said the day he met her. "You make sense. I can't explain it except some people just work together." That was how he put it as we walked out of the house the day I brought her to meet him and Bonnie. "You'd be crazy to let that girl out of your sight."

"I don't plan to."

She didn't mind the long ritual of pills Dad had to take before dinner, the endless pictures Bonnie was determined to show her of Grandma and Grandpa, Jeannie, Uncle Pete, or Grandma Mary. I mentioned she was a singer and they demanded she sing something on the spot, which she did. She filled the small house in Westchester with her big voice singing "O Holy Night," leaving them like it left me when I first heard it. Quieted. Calmed. When we left, she hugged them both for a long time and I was surprised at the comfort this was. I didn't expect it, this realization that fathers and sons and mothers and daughters are connected somehow to new love.

It's such a relief. No one tells you that about love. Or at least no one ever told me. That I don't have to work so hard to keep up appearances. I can put down the mask. Our conversation is easy and unending. We follow it across nervous mornings and tear-filled nights. There are confessions and jokes and silly evenings watching bad movies on the couch while we cuddle and talk and talk and talk. *What's wrong with that dude's hair? Ohhh damn, did she really just say that? This son of a bitch right here.* Little things, good things, sad things, quiet thoughts I've never told a soul, because I was too scared of what they might think. She just listens and nods her head. She'll say something like "Yeah, I get that." And for some reason those are the most comforting words I've ever heard.

I'm lost a lot of the time; I don't really know how to talk about it. *Yeah, I get that.* My mother was bad to us and I don't know how to be about it. *Yeah, I get that.* I put on an act most of the time. *Yeah, I get that.* I've found something in you and I don't think I can let go, which scares me a little. *Yeah, I get that.* My dad is sick and I don't know what I'm going to do if he dies. *Oh, babe. Babe, babe, babe, babe, babe, babe. Shhhhh. I'm right here. I get that. I love you.*

She tells me her secrets and it's my turn to listen and this is perhaps the most comforting thing of all, to be able to calm her anxiety, to see her doubts, and instead of running away as I've always done, to simply say, "Yeah, I get that," and for the first time in my life, stay.

TONY SITS WITH his elbow on my father's shoulder as he balances baby Juliette on his shin. Bonnie leans into my dad in her way, grabbing his hand to kiss it and hold him close. Dad chats with the band members, who are drinking champagne and going over the set list. Lizette is on my lap and I feel my heart bursting as I pull her to me.

Every show is a celebration of something. That's the thought I have as we take the stage later that night, as we see that beautiful hillside light up in front of us. *Why are we here? With these people who have a place in their hearts like the one we have in ours?* It's not so simple and it's fair to say that we're the types of people who wouldn't be interested if it was.

So what are *we* celebrating?

I think maybe we're celebrating something very basic: the fact that we *survived.* That the bad things that happened to us didn't break us. We're still here and there is still a chance—as we dance and stomp and jump and sway—for something new to happen, something wonderful. That feeling connects us. We are calmed by it. Soothed. Inspired. The speakers bellow and the drums echo off the hillside. The guitars roar and the violin traces a melody. We can hear our voices coming back to us in unison, all of us together, crying out to the night sky, *We're here! We're alive! And we know it because we're singing! Can you hear us? We're singing!*

CHAPTER 45

THE MEN AND
THEIR DREAMS

When the family arrives from San Diego, Lizette is there to greet them. She introduces herself in the lobby on the third floor, the hospice floor, where Dad has been moved after starting the morphine drip. She helps with getting coffee and water, reminding people where the bathrooms are. She remembers the stories and connects them to the faces in the room. "Oh, you're the one who has all the clocks! I've heard so much about you. I love your jacket." She holds court. She helps. "Well, he's been better, but I'm sure he'd love to see you." She's good at this. I don't understand it, how a woman so beautiful could be willing to spend her Friday night in a hospital waiting room.

My dad's brother Wes with his gentle, bearlike voice, his brother Donny, the loud, brash one, my aunt Linda, who was raised apart from them but has come into the family fold, kind and sarcastic, our cousins Cindy and David, my parents' neighbors and old friends, we all assemble at the way station of Cedars-Sinai as if standing on a platform waiting for a train to arrive. There are hugs and quiet words and one by one everyone goes in to talk to Dad.

Tony hugs me and leaves an arm on my shoulder as we stand together in the waiting room. There are things only a brother understands.

After everyone leaves, it is my turn and I go in to talk to him.

"Heyyy, Dad. Heyyy." It's nearly midnight. Bonnie and I trade off every day so he's never alone. She gets the days. I'm there nights.

"Hey, Mick," he whispers lightly, a slight smile across his lips.

I'm not sure if he can understand me because he's groggy from the morphine, coming in and out of consciousness. I just want to feel like his son for a few more minutes.

"How are you feeling?"

"Like shit."

"Oh, well, yeah. That happens." I run my hand over his short hair as if to wipe it from his eyebrows. I stroke his beard and stare into his glassy eyes. He looks so small beneath the thin white hospital blanket.

"I want you to know something."

"Oh, yeah, what's that?"

"I'm going to ask Lizette to marry me, Dad."

"Ohhhh," he says, smiling and nodding faintly. "That's good."

"You're the first person I told."

"She doesn't . . . know yet?"

"No, I'm working on a plan."

"You sure . . . you sure you're ready for all that?"

"I'm ready to try."

He smiles and closes his eyes. I want him to imagine the day, because I know he can't be there. The way the light will stream through the leaves of the trees swaying over a procession of friends and family, Lizette, glowing in her wedding dress at the top of a hill at sunset. Maybe he will see the child, imagine him with his eyes, his nose, his sense of humor. Maybe he will see me. I've been a son for so long and I want to become a father, to be what he was for me. I trust this love of his.

"Don't." He looks down as I stare at him, wondering what he means as he struggles with the words. He grabs my hand and smiles at me, his hazel-green eyes beaming,

"Don't fuck it up."

and then he is gone

and nothing in the world can ease the unimaginable pain

It's not that we didn't see it coming. We did. Bonnie and I. Tony and I. Lizette and I. There were long talks about it and endless surgeries, treatments, regimens, lunches at the cafeteria of the North Tower of Cedars-Sinai. We even had a favorite place to sit. We named it. "The Posner-Jollett Memorial Table. One thousand sandwiches eaten."

It's that the finality of death is so hard to face because it tears a hole in the universe. It's like looking up and seeing a nothingness where the sky used to be. Death is like a play on a stage suddenly interrupted by a hurricane. There you are, standing there reciting your lines, following your scene cues, when the building starts to shake and the roof comes flying off, somebody jumps up in the back and screams that the theater is on fire as you run for cover wondering why you didn't see it coming, why nothing prepared you for this moment—no book, no movie script, no breathless talk at midnight. It's confusing. It takes time for the reality to set in. It was all a play. There was a storm outside and it has removed the roof and now we must hide. You wake up feeling fine and then you remember again and begin to sob. The sky is gone. He is gone. The universe only appears permanent. And you know now that it isn't. And it never was. And neither was he. And neither are you. And for some reason this is the saddest thought in all the world.

I simply can't wrap my mind around the space left by his absence. The baffling enormity of it.

Bonnie, as always, is comforting. She hugs me and tells me she loves me and that he was proud of me and that she misses him too. When we go to the house in Westchester, we bring food because that's what people do. They eat. Neighbors bring brownies and casseroles. Cousins show up with chips and salsa. There is a table of hummus and chicken and meatballs and for some reason it feels good to eat. Like you have to fill this hole with something so it may as well be food. Lizette and I stay at the house, in my father's bed where he slept when he got really sick. I wear his shirts and pants. I walk around in his boots and put on his rings. I excuse myself from the people in the living room and find myself lying still on the bed grasping his pillow, sobbing. Lizette comes in and lies next to me. We don't move for hours.

Bonnie wakes up in the middle of the night. She's in the living room looking at pictures, of her father and mother, her sister, her husband, my father. I wonder how she handles it all, to have lost all the people she loved most. We tell old stories. The trips in summers when Tony and I would come to visit. All the dogs they loved, the little terrier named Guy who was so nervous he would scare himself when he farted, the small aboveground pool they bought when Tony and his son lived with them briefly that we named the "white trash" pool. The way Dad would dance into the room in his bikini underwear when we were kids, dragging his foot behind him and saying, "This is the move. You gotta drag your leg and say, 'Hey, Mama, you need a date tonight?'"

We laugh and we cry and agree the family is too small now. It's time we started growing again.

"Are you okay, sweetie?" Bonnie keeps asking me, rubbing the tears from my eyes.

"Not really, Lou," I say, shaking my head. "But what choice do I have?"

"I'm so sorry. I know how much you loved him. He was so proud of you. You and Tony were all he ever talked about. The men you are. You know he never cared if you were successful or anything. He just wanted you to be good people. Honest. Kind. There for your family. That was my guy."

There is nowhere to put the grief and no way to make sense of it and nothing to do but hold on to each other trying not to be alone with it.

After a week Lizette and I pack up our things to go home. We never discussed coming and never discuss leaving. It just felt like the right time. Bonnie squeezes each of us as we walk out the front door when something occurs to her. She gives me a look.

"What is it, Lou?"

"Holy shit. We sat shivah." We both laugh and I feel so proud to be her son, to be Jew-ish, to be part of this family of people who found each other after losing so much.

WAKING UP ON my birthday a few days after his funeral, I realize I have an appointment to retrieve his ashes. The funeral was a blur. I thought it would be hard but it wasn't. It was comforting. Jake flew in from Nebraska. Drew sat right next to me as we ate food and told stories about the ranch where my uncle still lives. All my old friends came: Eddie and Ryan, Stephen Perkins, Tim, Gabe and Pete. They just sat by me like old friends do and it occurred to me how much these friendships are a gift.

So many people talked about how warm my dad was. There were kids from the street in Westchester who'd grown up at the house after school while my dad helped them with their homework or brought them an ice cream drumstick from the fridge. They're teenagers now, weeping at losing a man they also thought of like a father. It surprised even me to see how beloved he was. It seemed like a fitting occasion for a man who was never honored at a luncheon, never received an award or commendation, never even had a proper wedding. I can't help but think that the people we celebrate publicly and the ones we secretly love the most are rarely the same.

I get dressed and drive to an anonymous storefront in Eagle Rock. There's a wall of urns, each with a yellow Post-it note on which is written a name and a number. I see the tall marbled green urn with the name "Jim Jollett" written beneath it. I walk out to the curb with the urn under my arm, open the door and strap him into the front seat of the black '66 Chevy Chevelle we restored together.

Okay, Dad, where do you want to go?

I turn on his favorite song. "The Pretender" by Jackson Browne.

I'm gonna rent myself a house in the shade of the freeway.

We get on the freeway. *You all right in there?* I can hear him in my head. I don't know how anybody handles anything. There's no container for the thing he was now that he's gone. It's an irrational number. Infinity divided by zero. That's probably why we put people in containers when they die: coffins, urns, mausoleums—to give a physical shape to the absence.

I stare out at the cars all around me trying to figure out where to go. I have no plan. *Maybe Vegas. He loved Vegas.* Will people stare as I walk from the casino to the sports book holding a marbled green urn under my arm? My dad died and it's my birthday and nobody can say anything because I'm allowed to lose my shit. Could we shoot craps together, the urn and I? Or play blackjack? Could we sit in a diner and order breakfast? *I'll have the waffles. The urn would like a pastrami sandwich and a chocolate malted milkshake. Could we trouble you for a long straw?*

The 210 is a bullshit freeway. There are so many of them in Los Angeles. In all the places beyond downtown and the beach, Hollywood, Disneyland, there are all these forgotten people who grew up and died fixing cars, cleaning motel rooms, bobbing in the waves in the water next to the factories with their sons on beaches where no tourists venture. You can see them there in the background. They make up the scenery, the negative space in a photograph snapped by some tourist and dropped in a drawer.

A sign ahead reads, "Santa Anita Park." *Of course. Why didn't I think of this before?* I follow the exit to Foothill Boulevard, down the winding road under the canopy of tall trees. I park the Chevelle in a faraway corner of the enormous concrete lot. I unstrap the urn from the passenger seat and open the lid. There is a heavy plastic bag inside that holds his ashes, a metal dog tag clipped to the top. *Hey, Dad.* I pull the bag out and hold it in my hand to feel the weight.

I cut it open with a pocketknife and pour the ashes into the urn, making sure to leave some in the plastic bag. The car fills with a cloud of dust. It gets in my eyes, my nose, my lungs, the upholstery. *Goddamn it, Dad!* I laugh as I wipe the ashes from my T-shirt and black jeans.

I get out of the car and put the plastic bag containing my father's ashes in the small of my back, exactly like the drug smuggler he once was. I hear the bugle playing in the distance, the familiar, earthy smell of manure and dirt, the hot concrete breathing beneath my feet. I put my sunglasses on and walk toward the gate.

Dad. Da. Pop. Poppy.

I buy a ticket and a racing form, making my way to a spot high in the stands. Palm trees dot the infield, an enormous jumbotron hangs over the finish line showing the results from Del Mar and Belmont, the odds for the lineup in the first race. I walk through the crowd and hear the voices: "Shit, man, everybody bettin' four. But I'm telling you he ain't got no legs for it. The whole field gonna run out fast and take away his legs." *The men and their dreams.*

I go to the concession and buy a corned beef sandwich, a large Sprite and a Carnation chocolate malted ice cream. *Our food.* I place a bet and head for the stands. *I got Papa Turf in the fifth for a hundred to win, Dad. I boxed the exacta with Surfing Angel because it sounds like something from a movie.*

I eat the food and study the races. The way the men watch the horses on the final straightaway, the moment of high hopes and broken dreams. I notice the four towers, one on each corner rising up a hundred feet above, where security watches the track. There are cameras and people who are paid to make sure nobody interferes with the race. *Am I willing to go to jail today? What would a gambling control commission say about bringing human remains to a racetrack?*

I go into the bathroom and empty the paper soda cup into a sink. I wash it clean and dry it with paper towels. I head into a stall and remove the plastic bag filled with ashes from the small of my back. I pour them into the cup and walk out, holding it like a soft drink I'm saving for later. There is something ancient about it, an element of sacrifice, a medieval sense of ritual: *I am Mikel of the House of Jollett, I hereby commit my father to this track in the city of Santa Anita, sanctified in warm horsey blood.*

I walk down to the track with my heart pounding, trying to look casual, aiming for a spot at the start of the final straightaway, a place behind a concrete archway, hidden from the view of the giant towers, a place no one will look after the race passes, after the howls, the rise of the crowd, and the pack galloping toward the finish line, after the green tractors that follow have dampened the dust behind them. I time my walk with the beginning of the race when I hear the starting bell.

"And away they go!"

Okay, Dad. It's just you and me. This is so fucked-up, right?

"And it's Crimson Giant starting off strong followed by Rocket Heat."

Fifty feet to the spot. Wait for them. Wait for them.

"And here comes Papa Turf making a move on the outside. They're heading into the turn."

Twenty feet. Breathe. Ten feet. You can do this. Five feet.

"Rocket Heat lunges ahead of the pack."

The horses pass right in front of me, all straining muscles and foaming mouths, the small men bent forward, whipping them faster into the Future. I hear the crowd come to life as the people get up to root them home.

I approach the white railing at the edge of the track and fling my father's ashes into the air.

I watch the cloud of dust form, suspended momentarily in a small burst before gently falling to the ground.

There are no witnesses, no brass army band, no twenty-one-gun salute, no headline, just me and Dad, some ash and a used-up old paper cup. It's better this way. Lose the pomp and circumstance and focus on what's real. Dad would appreciate that. Dirt. Ash. Sun. Wind. The soughing of the tractors and the ghosts rising in the stands.

CHAPTER 46
SALEM, OREGON

The house on Breys Avenue is smaller than I remember it. There is still the gravel driveway, the porch where we kept our bikes, the brick chimney where Paul practiced his sweeping. We flew up from Los Angeles to Portland and drove south down I-5 to stand in this spot. Tony's son lives here in Salem now, with his girlfriend and his daughter. Tony never said it, but I know we're here because he wants to make amends. Or start to. I know it's not easy for him, even though the trip was his idea, which is why he asked me to come along. *He's trying.* I love him for that.

We probably look strange. Two grown men leaning shoulder to shoulder against a small rental car staring at a house.

"Should we knock on the door or something?"

"I don't know. What do you think?"

"I'm not sure. Maybe we should just stand here a minute."

"Weird, right?"

"So weird. That's a nicer fence than the one we had, but it looks like they got rid of the vegetable gardens."

"Good move."

"Yeah, no shit."

There's a silence, the warm sun beating down on our faces, a light breeze shuddering the leaves through the trees.

"I keep going over it and over it," I say. "And I don't think I have a single good memory in that house. Like I know we must've had some good times but I can't think of any right now."

He shakes his head. "Me neither."

"It's worse than I thought it would be. I don't know what I expected."

"It was a hard place to live."

He pops a piece of gum in his mouth and checks his phone. "Like a desert." I know he's anxious to see his son, that this trip is difficult for him for other reasons. "I'll get the directions."

"Hold on. I just have to wrap my head around this."

"We got time."

A few days after Dad died, I had to go to Cedars-Sinai to complete the paperwork for his death certificate. It was Mother's Day and I decided to call Mom. I figured I could, for the first time since I was perhaps seventeen years old, reach out to her for comfort and allow her to be like a balm, that this might be a kind of olive branch, this easy bit of parenting, this basic soothing of a son grieving over the death of his father.

She answered and I could hardly get the words out. The hospital. The death certificate. My father gone. So much pain. I expected her to simply say those simple words, the ones I needed to hear: *You are my son and I love you. I'm so sorry this happened.*

She said, "It was always so painful to me that you left me to go live with him. I don't know how you could do that to me."

I was confused. These two conflicting realities: the mother in my mind, the one I was reaching out to, still hoping she could reach back, and the one on the other end of the line.

"It was always very hard for me that you became close with your father instead of me."

I felt the numbness wash over me, the blank white nothingness I carried for so long as if I could simply disappear, to evaporate into silent clouds.

I wiped my eyes. "You . . . what?"

"I know you're sad your father died, but think of how hard it has been for me to know you were closer with him."

I didn't know what to say, so I told her I had to go and hung up the phone.

I remembered Phil Ritter, our roommate from Synanon who was beaten in the driveway by the men from Synanon. He lives near Seattle now. He'd heard about the band and reached out to get in touch with me.

I called him one day to catch up. He's such a kind man, still trying to change the world, focused now on climate change. When we spoke, I asked him about that day in Berkeley and he told me the story from his perspective, how he didn't remember much except being hit on the head and looking up to see me watching from the porch, how our eyes met and he thought, *This is too much for a child Mikel's age to witness.* That's what he remembers most: the look on my face. I remember his expression among that terrible chaos. It stuck with me. I would see it in my dreams, in the moments after when I would wake up screaming. The screams, the blood, the clubs, and that kind face, full of sorrow.

I tried to work backward from that moment, from the story Mom told me about that day. How she corrected me and told me I wasn't there. How the reality of it was too much to bear so she simply invented a new one. I never saw a therapist or went to a child counselor. We never talked about it. She ignored the nightmares, my pleas to be acknowledged, as if they simply didn't exist. In the retelling I heard through the years of that day, she always described it as a terrible thing that happened not to Phil, or me, or Tony, who watched from across the street, but to *her*.

This happened when Paul died. Or didn't. It was a type of instruction, to forget, to pick and choose which elements of reality we acknowledged, as if she was trying to teach me her secret way of coping with life. And then on that day I drove down Third Street across Los Angeles to pick up my father's death certificate, when I was at my most vulnerable, her first thought, her only thought, was of herself.

I know there is a disorder at work. It took time to figure these things out because we simply don't have a language to talk about them. We talk about schizophrenics and depressives, alcoholics and autistics, but narcissistic personality disorder and the closely related borderline personality disorder—these mental illnesses that create relationships without empathy, without love, filled with delusion and manipulation—they are slippery and ghostlike. They take years to unravel, partly because the person who suffers from them simply doesn't know he has it.

I could, even at that moment, feel bad for her, for the bad things that happened to her, how scared she must have been, how utterly alone she must've been to require this way of coping with a world that was too painful for her to live in, to simply invent another one instead. The crippling depression, the divorces, the cult that left her penniless and without a friend, all of these things only added to the problem. And I can sympathize with her. Even now. That has never been the problem.

So standing there in front of the house in Salem, Oregon, trying to think of one good memory, I see this other moment so clearly instead: driving toward Cedars-Sinai hospital in Los Angeles three days after my father died, the light blue sky, the puffy clouds above the trees as I approach mid-city in the black '66 Chevelle Dad and I restored together, the smell of gasoline in the air from that big engine we dropped in it. Looking up, a hole of confusion and grief torn through my heart where my father was, my mind was racing through memories of Phil, Paul, Doug and Mom as I understood, finally, that she is never going to be the mother I have spent a lifetime hoping she would be and it's time I just accept it.

Okay.

From the distance that decision created, I've found it's easier to appreciate the things about her that make her unique, to hear an old folk song or some random Dutch phrase in Amsterdam, to find myself saying something about Thatasshole Reagan and remember that if nothing else I was given a thorough political education. I like these things about her. It's easier to appreciate them at a distance. You can never really hate someone whose pain you know so well.

THE GARDENS ON the side of the house are gone but the barn Paul built is still standing. I doubt there are any rabbits in it. Tony and I walk around to the alley in the back to check. The chain-link fence has been replaced by a wooden one. The dog run is gone but the tree where we slaughtered rabbits is still standing, naked and leafless in the sun.

I see Paul everywhere. His blue hatchet, the orange maul, the short bearded man in a flannel chopping wood or scooping feed from a bucket. An internet investigation by Lizette one day revealed that he might have only recently died. It's not clear. I don't know why it never occurred to me to find out for myself. Maybe because I figured the mystery had only two possible outcomes and both were terrible. Perhaps he spent all that time on the street, eventually reconnecting with a brother before his death. I hate to think of him being alone. I don't think he had any other kids and

I wish I could've told him what he meant to me. That I loved him, that he will always be my family, that his jokes and kindness and attention, the quiet days along the Willamette, how much that affection was like cool water in a dry, parched desert. That I didn't care that he was broken. Everyone I love is broken. Or was. That's how we recognize each other.

MY SON WAS born on a quiet February morning on the third floor of Cedars-Sinai hospital exactly one floor below the room my father died in. He came into the world purple and screaming, his arms small, his fingers tiny, his face swollen. They wiped him down and warmed him up and handed him to his mother, where he nursed, rooted his head into her shoulder and fell asleep.

That night I cradled him in my arms when he woke up while Lizette recovered in the bed thinking, *You've had the weirdest day, little man.* The world seems so impossibly dangerous, so many sharp corners and so many hard places, so many things I must protect him from. I put him down and lay awake listening to his breath, all the little gurgles and sneezes, the steady rhythm of his breathing. The sounds bring such a blinding joy to my chest. *What was in these barren corners before you arrived?* When we take him home, he fills the quiet hallways of our house with his cries. My eyes linger on those fingers and count his toes. All those years, all those times when I'd see a family at a park or a restaurant, their closeness, their physical proximity to each other, the comforting ease of it, I felt like a stranger looking in from a window. And I wondered if I would ever have these basic things that seem like magic to me now as we lie on the bed and play music, he kicks his feet to "Burning Down the House" by Talking Heads, and we laugh, our arms hanging over the side to scratch the ears of the black Labrador we rescued and named Bowie.

It feels magical to me, this gift I never thought I would have, a family. To simply be a husband to a wife, a father to a son.

Our wedding day was a beautiful promise but I think I became a husband not by wearing a tuxedo and reciting the breathless lines I recited that day but later, when I was able, finally, to add new features to the landscape: a quiet stream of patience and acceptance, a shady grove for tolerating the fear I felt that once prompted me to run, a big open valley of forgiveness, loyalty, belief in her, and above all else a warm field we try to visit every day, joy. I love my wife with a deep passion but even after a short time it's clear to me that the heart of marriage is an epic friendship.

When my son reached six months old, the age at which Synanon children were taken from their parents, the thought occurred to me how monstrous it would be to give him to strangers. How devastatingly hard on him, on us. It seems so much clearer to me as a father than it did as a child. This was abuse. It was wrong. It was violent and destructive. Crippling. It left every single child this happened to a lifetime of extreme emotional difficulty. Countless stories of abuse have emerged, told by the children of Synanon who've become adults: molestations and beatings, ritualistic shaming and endless neglect, children pinned down and shaved to the scalp for minor infractions, the teenagers constantly trying to run away, parents disappearing for years on end, leaving their kids in a dog-eat-dog world, competing with other children for basic needs of comfort, love, security, leaving a hole too big to fill and a lifetime of insecurity, a fear of closeness. These are the precise kinds of stories one hears about orphanages. I don't blame my mother or father and I know they did not realize what a grievous mistake it was to put us in that place. And I'm eternally grateful Bonnie was there because it made it easier, at least for me. But it was a cult. Cults make people do bad things. Chuck was the Leader and he decided one day that we wouldn't have parents. And we didn't. It was that simple. I think of my grandfather Nat, who lost a family in the Holocaust to that idea, who used to remind us all, "Power corrupts. Absolute power corrupts absolutely." Of all the stories Synanon tells about itself in those dusty books and online discussion boards for the people who left, there is a massive hole when it comes to the children, who were made to live like orphans. It's no one's fault. It's everyone's fault. It doesn't matter whose fault it is, only that we understand ourselves now, we orphaned children of the universe, so we can find a path back from all that pain.

I can hardly stand the thought of not seeing my son each morning. That little face, the way he looks at me from across the table and we both crack a smile like we share a joke, our silly games running breathless through the house, bath time, bedtime, the lazy mornings in bed with him and my wife, feeling quiet and whole. There is nothing more precious to me. None of it was what I imagined, which is that it would be like a feeling that always warmed me or made me aware of how much I am loved. But it is not like this. It's more a fierce sense that I am not important, that I would instantly give my life for theirs. My nightmares are no longer about things that might happen to me but about the horrible things that could happen to them. If I got sick, who would read to him before bedtime? And if I died, who would take care of him? Who would be his father? Her husband? So I must stay healthy because he deserves a father. I must stay humble and continue to add features to the landscape because she deserves a good husband. We are a family and that means we need each other. It's not that I've disappeared. It's that this simple and impossible thing has given my life a purpose.

WE DRIVE TO South Salem to pick up Tony's son. We have a day planned at a swimming hole on the Willamette, not far from where Paul used to take us fishing. I can feel Tony's anxiety as we drive through the streets of Salem. He keeps checking my face, then his phone, then the window, then my face again, bouncing his knee in anticipation. The city seems charming to me. Even though I can't think of any good memories in the house on Breys Avenue, I have countless good memories of the YMCA, the Boys Club, the Little League games at Parrish Field, the races at Bush Park.

His son meets us at the door of a small ground-floor apartment. He's got a little blond girl in his heavily tattooed arms. He gives us a toothy smile and puts his daughter down to hug his dad, then throws an arm around my neck. It's so good to see him, to feel that old sensation like we are connected as if by a string that can only stretch so far. We sit in the living room playing games with the little girl, talking about child care, weight lifting, his new job working construction. He says he's just trying to work now, to support his daughter and his girlfriend.

I wish I could tell him that I know how hard he's had it, that I can see how hard he's working now, that there are mysteries at work and I hope he will unravel them in his own time and his own way, that I love him and we are connected and we always will be.

We drive to the river and park the car, carrying our things down to the shore. Towels, a cooler with sandwiches and sodas, a deck of cards. We set up a picnic spot and take off our shoes to wade into the river. There is a soft babble of water over rocks, the white ripple of a current shaded by trees and moss-covered boulders. There's a warm sun on our faces, a bramble of blackberry bushes along the highway where we parked, a faraway wind whistling through the pines in the distance.

Tony lets out a whoop and jumps off a rock, pulling his knees to his chest to do a cannonball; the splash soaks us and we follow suit, wading out to the big rock and jumping into the swimming hole. We walk up the hill to pick sun-warmed blackberries to eat with our salami sandwiches.

Dad would've loved this. He always loved a day in the sun. The buzzing of the grass and the sound of the water, the break of waves against the shore, a sun-warmed peach and salty chips eaten in wet trunks in the sand. He was good with quiet.

I wish Dad could've known our son. He reminds me of him, the same eyes that look right at you to share a laugh, like that's the best thing there is in the world. I know I wouldn't have my own family now if it weren't for my father. I think of how much he was like a beacon in a fog, an unlikely source of light guiding me back to a place where I would find wholeness, family, acceptance, quiet.

I fall asleep in the sand and wake up to hear Tony and his son talking about fatherhood, something about changing diaper sizes too late. It occurs to me that we are all of us both fathers and sons now. I don't know if they had a Big Talk or if they just sat in the sand with their feet in the water. There is so much to unravel. But I can't ignore how good it feels to be here, skipping stones and splashing in the water, sharing a laugh with a brother who is a son who is also a father now, the sense of belonging we have when we are together, we three children of the universe.

CHAPTER 47

THE END OF
EVERYTHING

They tore down the grandstand at Hollywood Park three weeks after my father died. The land was purchased by a midwestern real estate baron who bought it to make room for a new NFL stadium, a mixed-use performance/retail space that will soon become the largest sports complex in the world. The explosions could be heard for miles, an awful creaking sound followed by a cloud of dust that rose hundreds of feet in the air like a tear in the sky. The rows of yellow excavators devoured the rest, their buckets digging through the rubble of metal railings and concrete stairs, clearing the way for the future on real estate deemed too valuable for the rusting dreams of dying men.

I know there's a profit motive at work but there's a simpler logic to me: that it just could not exist without him. That the track, the horses, the dirt oval and our seats in the stands where we ate and talked are inseparable from him in my mind, a place we dreamed up so we would have somewhere to go, somewhere I was safe, somewhere to be together, a place I could visit in my memory.

So many things seem that way to me now: intricate, wondrous structures that disappear and over time become intricate, wondrous memories. Like there are these waking dreams to visit when I need to hear a voice or ask advice; I can find it in a bright room crowded with people, all waiting for the chance to speak to me.

When I visit the room beneath the racetrack, when I stand in the confusion my father's death created looking for an answer, I wonder which moment this is, the future or the past, how I found the tunnel, that place burned into my imagination, and followed it a thousand feet down through the dirt and soil, rocks and bones and ash to that room. After a lifetime of searching for the fractured pieces, it's the only place my family feels whole.

The room is bright and clear and I can see everyone's face. The young man with the spit curl and the little girl with the Dutch cheeks. A handsome man with piercing blue eyes reading with a pretty young woman on his lap, telling an off-color joke in his ear, their four daughters around them. The kind Italian woman worried for the children, the svelte man doing tai chi, laughing with the boy with the spit curl in cowboy boots, the bright blond teenage girl singing a song. It's warm, the light like heat on my skin, a comforting stillness to be among my F-A-M-I-L-Y again.

A short man approaches me. He has strong hands and a little blond mustache, my grandpa Frank, who fought for two armies.

He asks me what I'm doing in this room a thousand feet beneath a racetrack that does not exist anymore.

Well, my father died and nothing made sense so I had to write it down so it could make sense again.

I see. Does it?

A little. More than it did, anyway. And now I have a place I can go to visit him and all of you.

But this place isn't real. It'll be gone when you are.

That's why I wrote it down.

He scratches his chin. *There's a lot of sadness in this story.*

I guess so. Happy things too and, yeah, sad.

None of us wanted that for you, not even her. He points to the little girl with Dutch cheeks standing in a crater.

Yes, I know that. Anyway, it was like a gift, or at least it's easier to think of it that way. You know, you make your pain useful. That's how you make art.

Like your story?

I guess so.

He stares at the blank white walls that rise up to the echo of imaginary hooves.

How about now? You're a father so that means someday you will live in another room in another mind just like this one.

That's true. It doesn't seem so bad. Is it?

Well, it's hard not having a future anymore, to just live here at the end of everything. But at least it's not the DMV!

He slaps me on the back. *Jokes! It's important to laugh. But tell me, is it still so painful? The place in your chest?*

No, not really. There's something new there instead. It took a long, long time, but I guess it's, it's, love? Right in the place where the pain used to be.

Wonderful. That's all we ever wanted for you.

He places a small, strong hand on my shoulder, squeezes me, whispers: *Now go make that useful too.*

ACKNOWLEDGMENTS

My deepest gratitude to our dear friends who helped with feedback on early drafts of the book: Lyle and Limor Zimskind, Andrew Spitser, Steven Chen, Steven Leckart, and Amy Westervelt. To my brilliant agent, Susan Golomb, who is a force of nature. To my wonderful publisher, Jamie Raab, who loves books and believes in them. To my peers from Synanon whose stories, insights, and friendship were invaluable: Guy Endore-Kaiser, Noah Kaiser, Dmitri Fagel. To Judy Muller and Phil Ritter, who always loved the children. To my uncle Wes, my uncle Donny, my aunt Pam, and my uncle Jon, who I thank for their knowledge and wisdom on the family and its stories. To my brother, Tony, who is as generous a soul as exists in the world. To my mother, Bonnie. Thank God for you. And to my best friend in the world, my wife, Lizette, without whom this book would not exist.

CELADON
BOOKS
NEW YORK

Founded in 2017, Celadon Books, a division of
Macmillan Publishers, publishes a highly curated list
of twenty to twenty-five new titles a year. The list of
both fiction and nonfiction is eclectic and focuses
on publishing commercial and literary books and
discovering and nurturing talent.